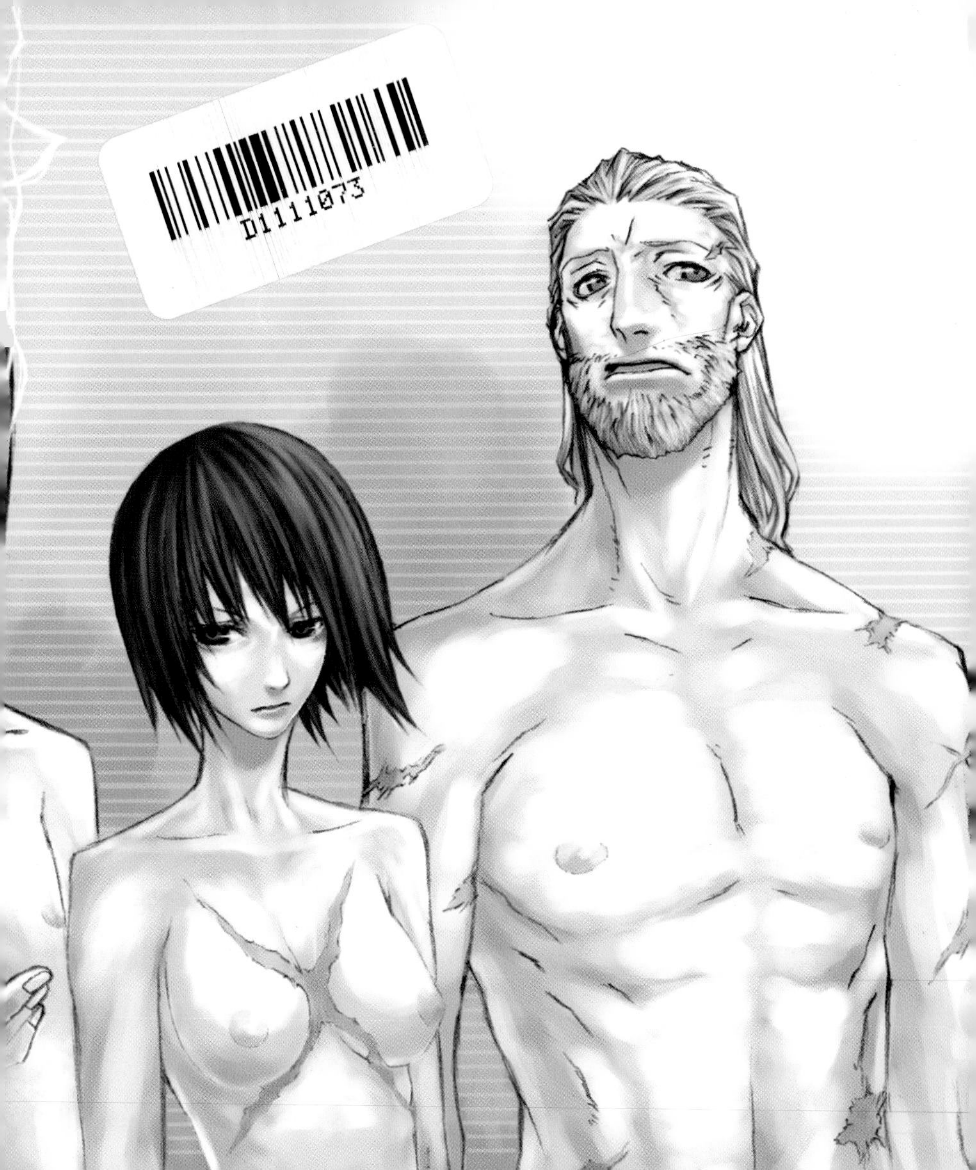

OGS
.001
OW MIWA

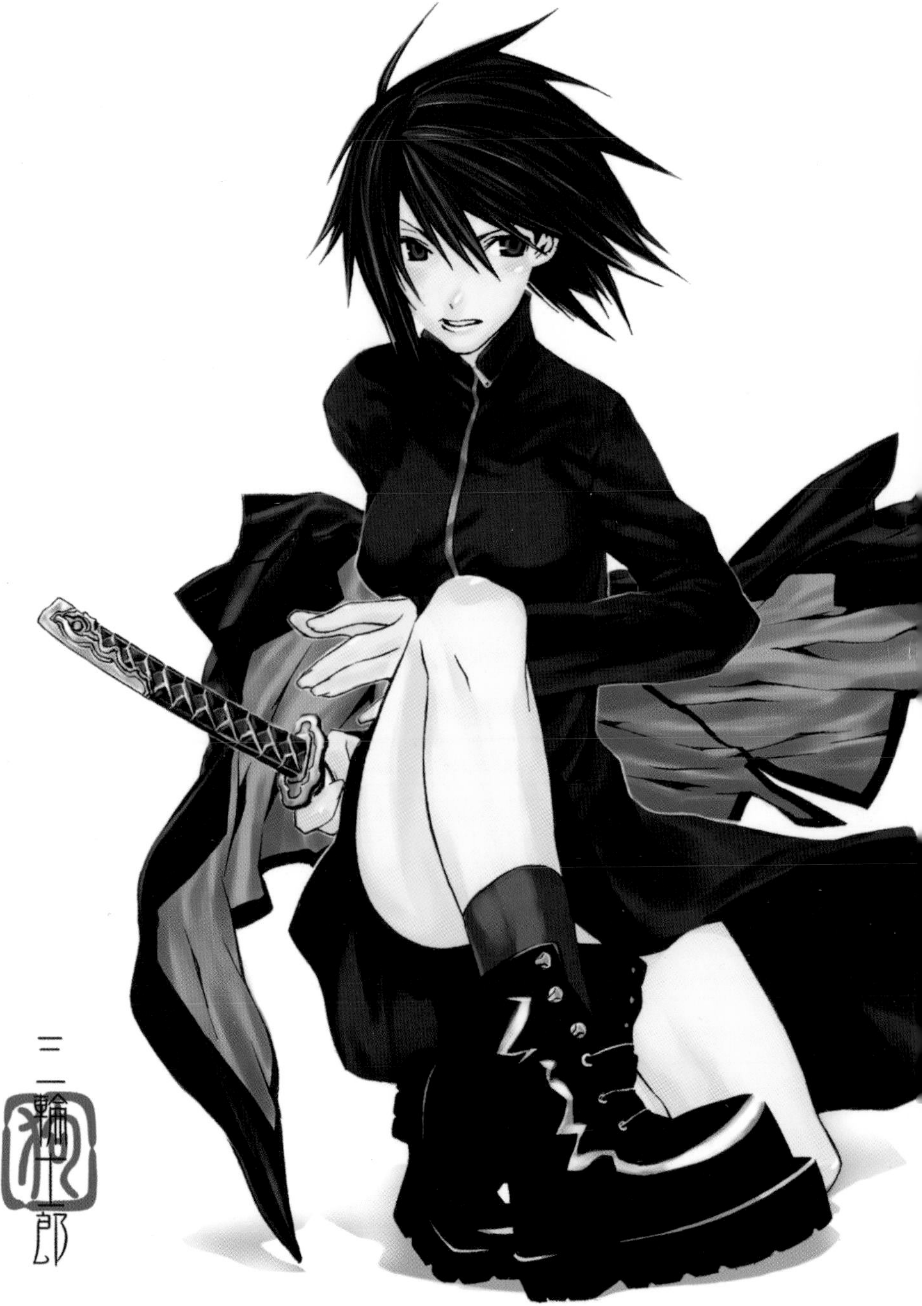

2001 Shirow Miwa

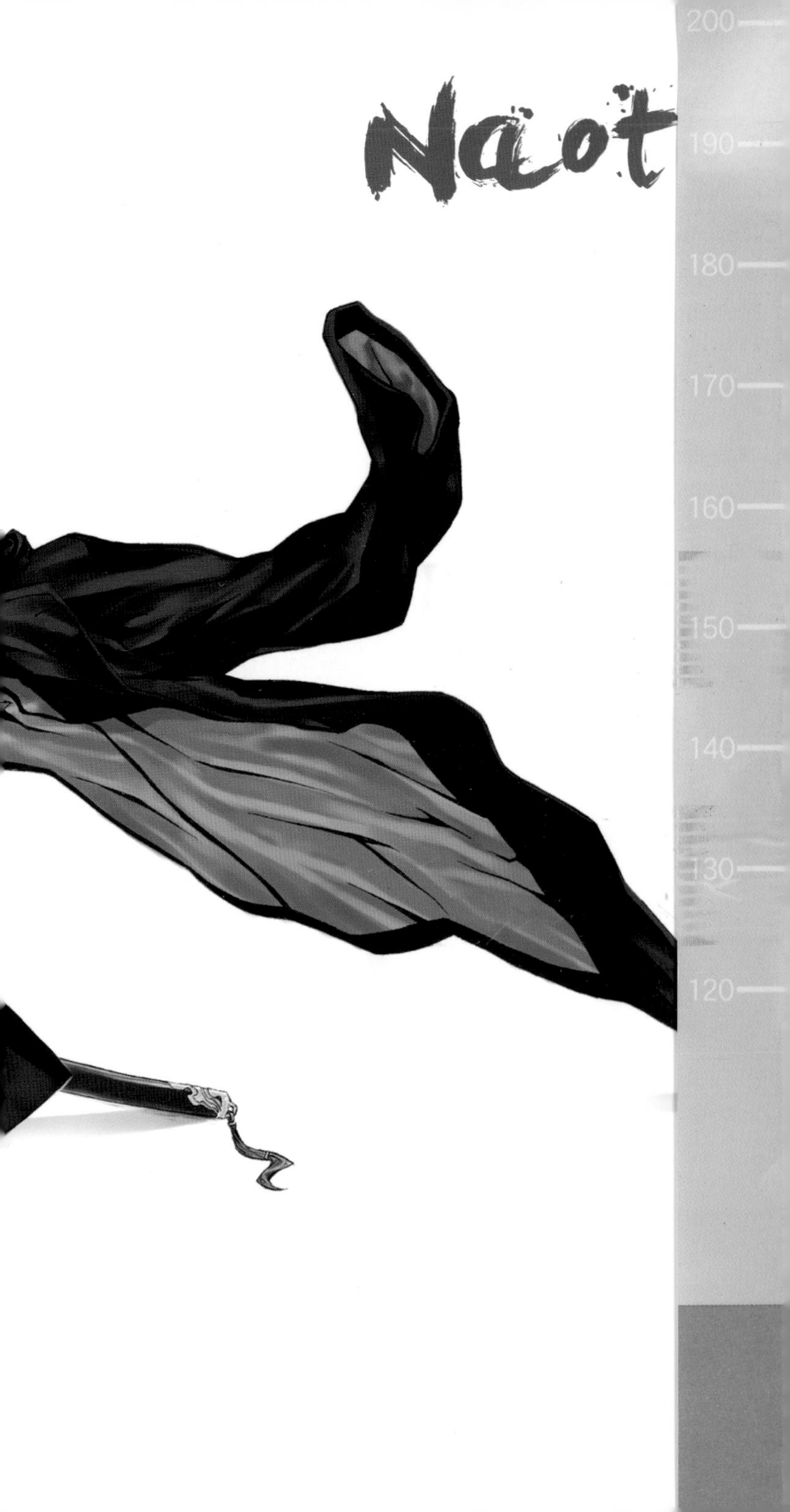
Naot
200
190
180
170
160
150
140
130
120

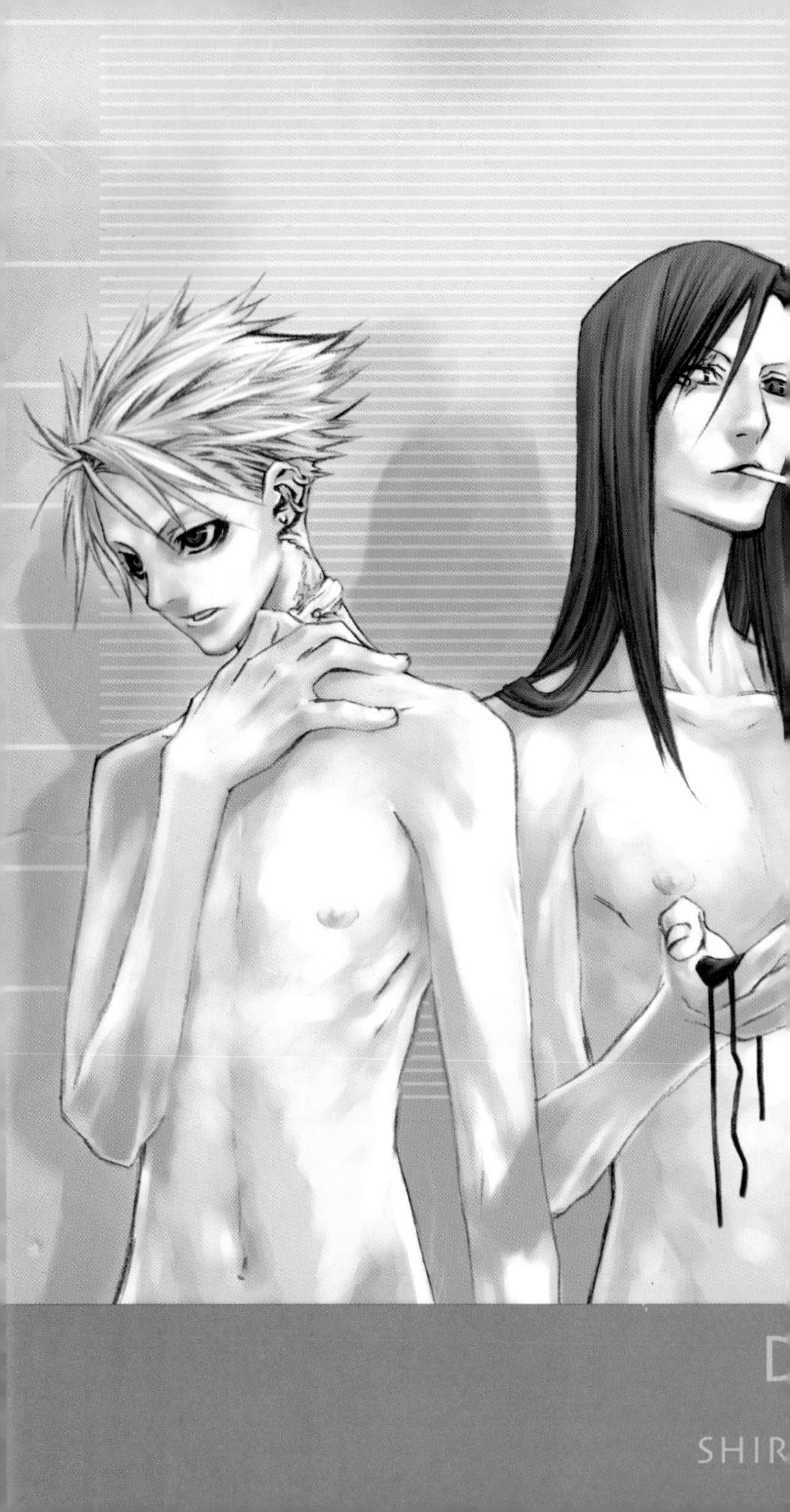

D

SHIR

"Ian killed the boss and is now the don."

That's all that was in the letter from Kiri.

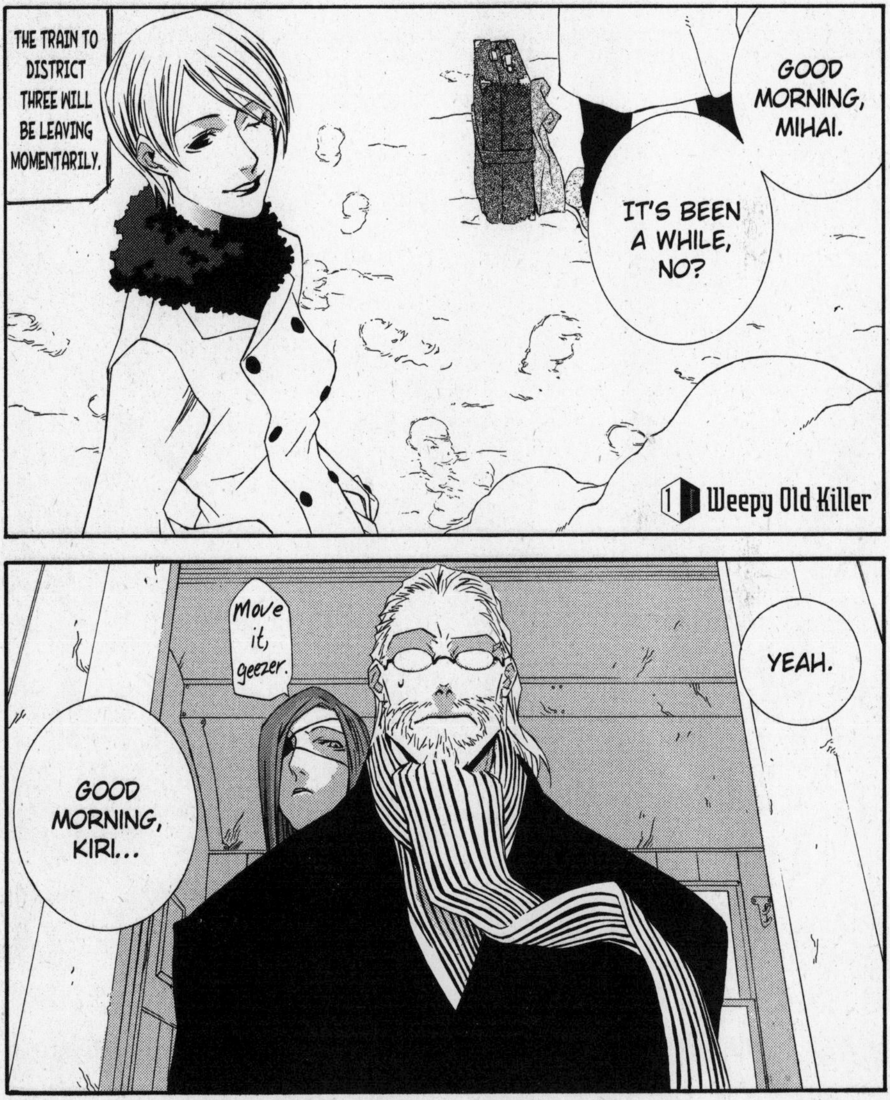

GOOD MORNING, MIHAI.
IT'S BEEN A WHILE, NO?
THE TRAIN TO DISTRICT THREE WILL BE LEAVING MOMENTARILY.
1 Weepy Old Killer
YEAH.
Move it, geezer.
GOOD MORNING, KIRI...

1 Weepy Old Killer

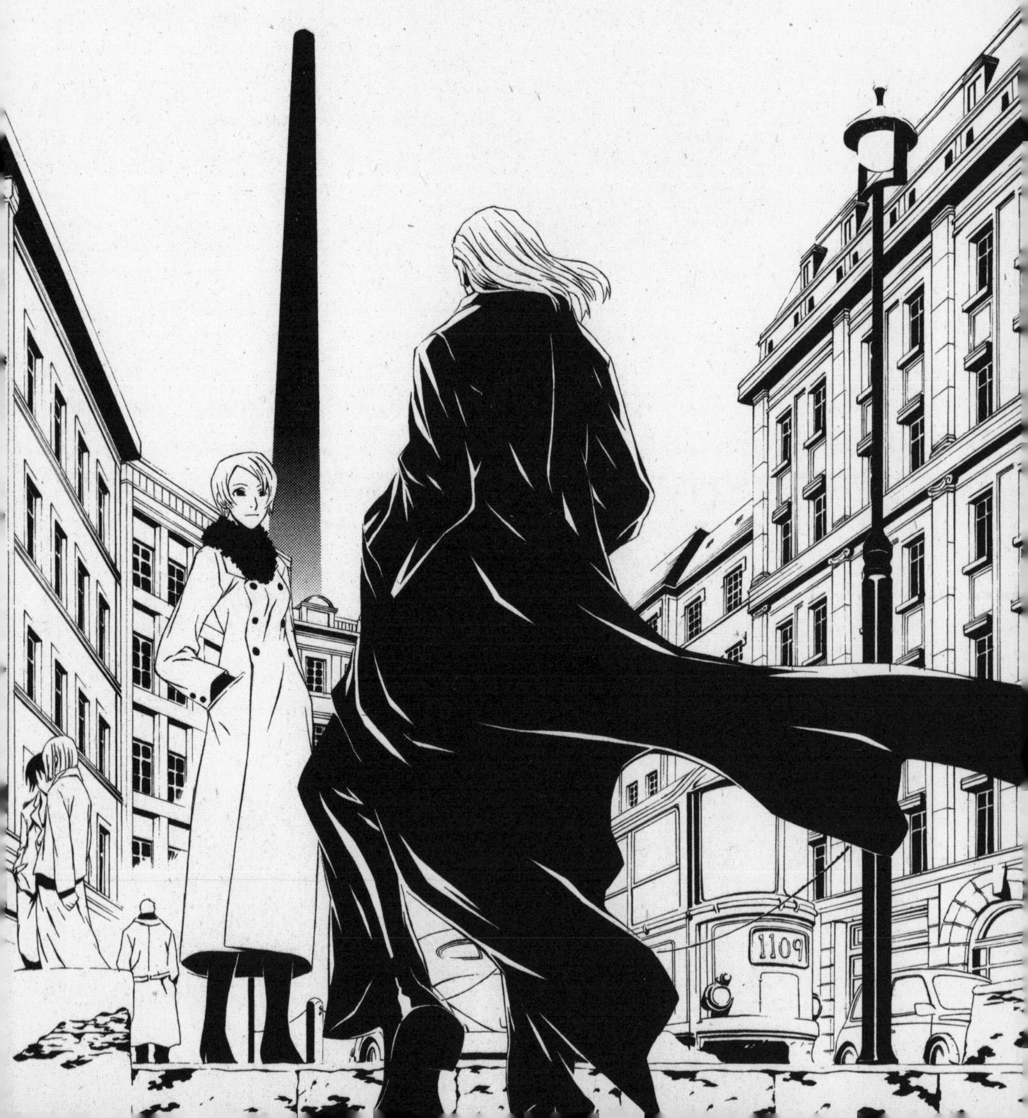
1109

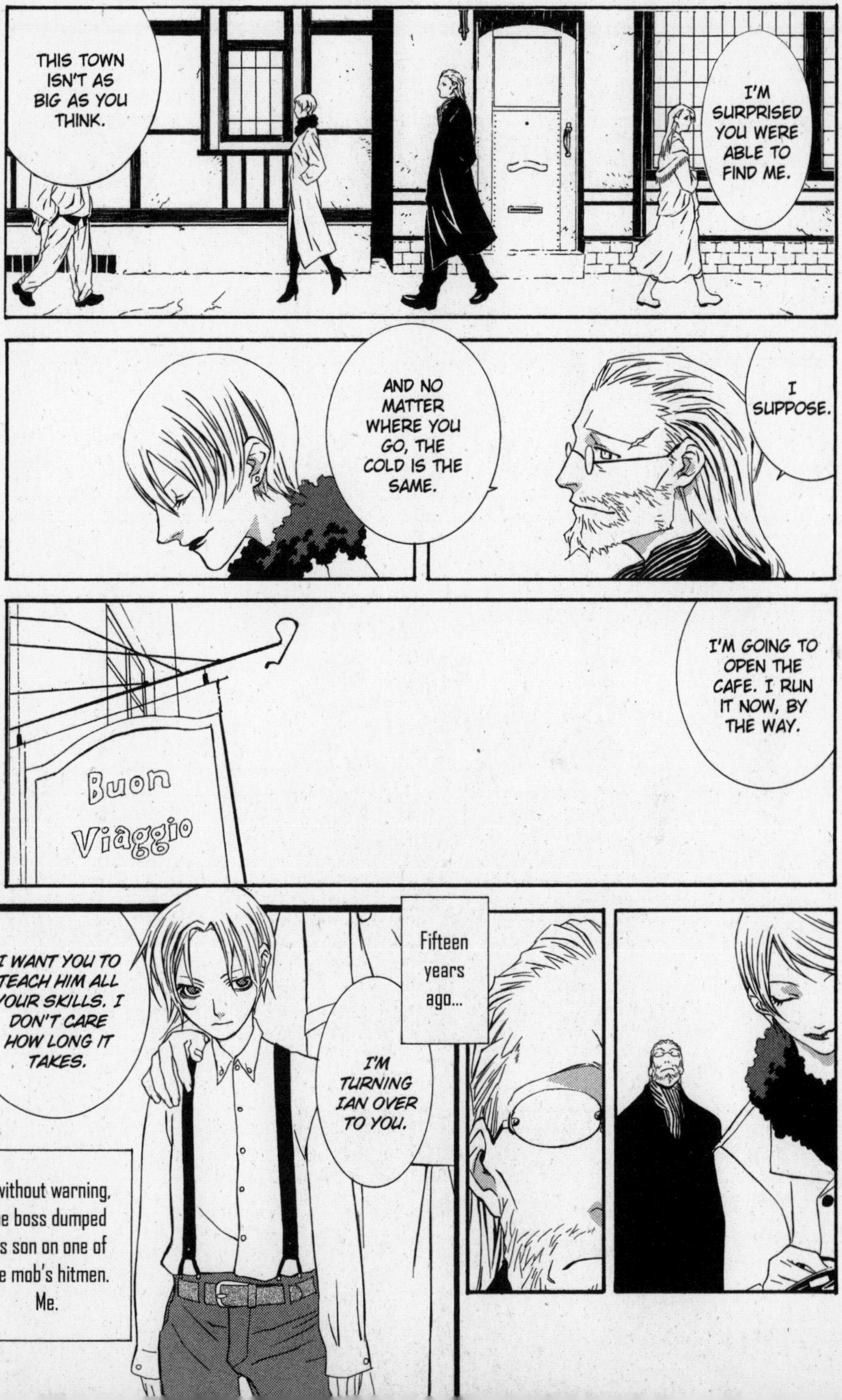
I'M SURPRISED YOU WERE ABLE TO FIND ME.
THIS TOWN ISN'T AS BIG AS YOU THINK.
I SUPPOSE.
AND NO MATTER WHERE YOU GO, THE COLD IS THE SAME.
I'M GOING TO OPEN THE CAFE. I RUN IT NOW, BY THE WAY.
Buon Viaggio
Fifteen years ago...
I'M TURNING IAN OVER TO YOU.
I WANT YOU TO TEACH HIM ALL YOUR SKILLS. I DON'T CARE HOW LONG IT TAKES.
...without warning, the boss dumped his son on one of the mob's hitmen. Me.

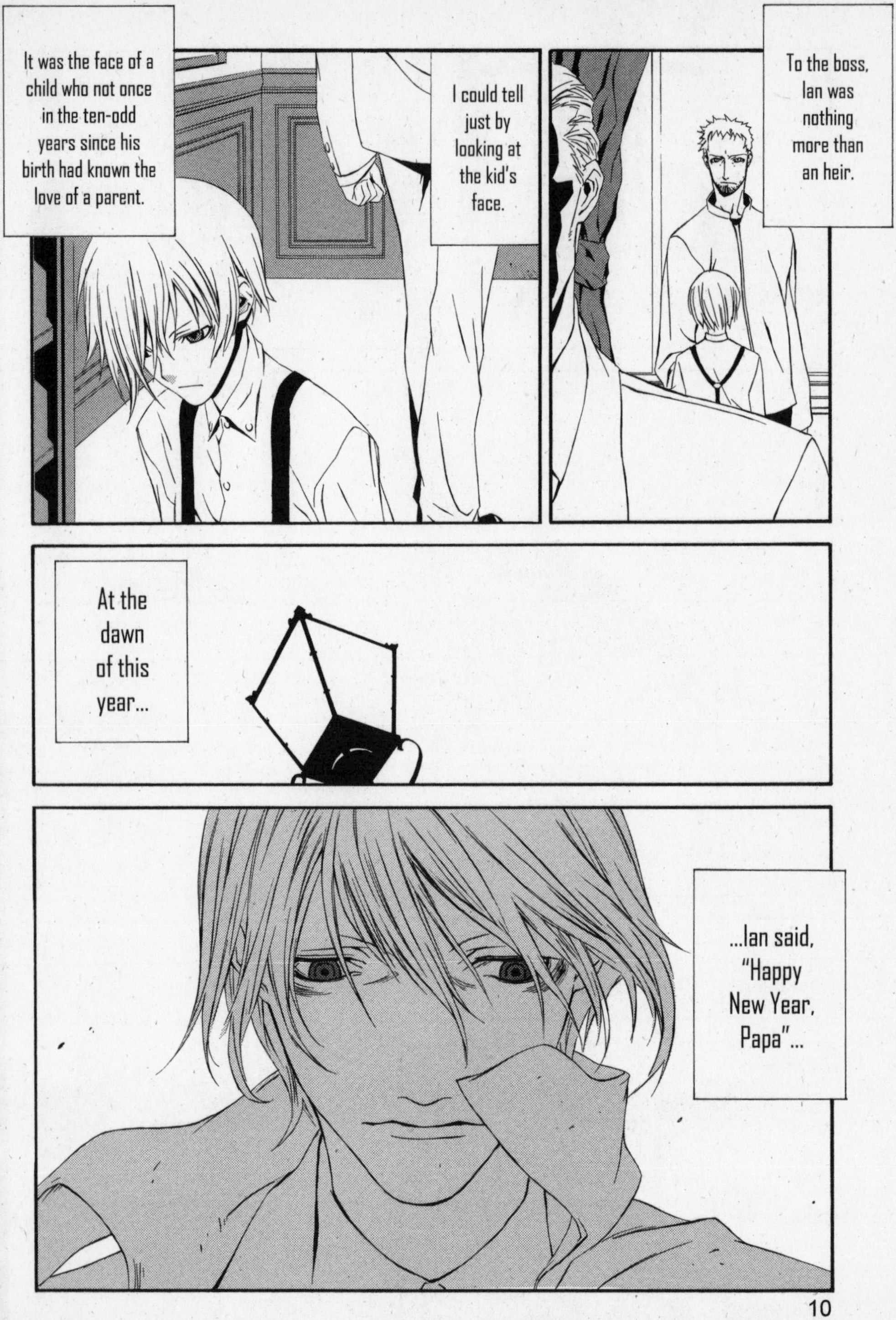
To the boss, Ian was nothing more than an heir.
I could tell just by looking at the kid's face.
It was the face of a child who not once in the ten-odd years since his birth had known the love of a parent.
At the dawn of this year...
...Ian said, "Happy New Year, Papa"...

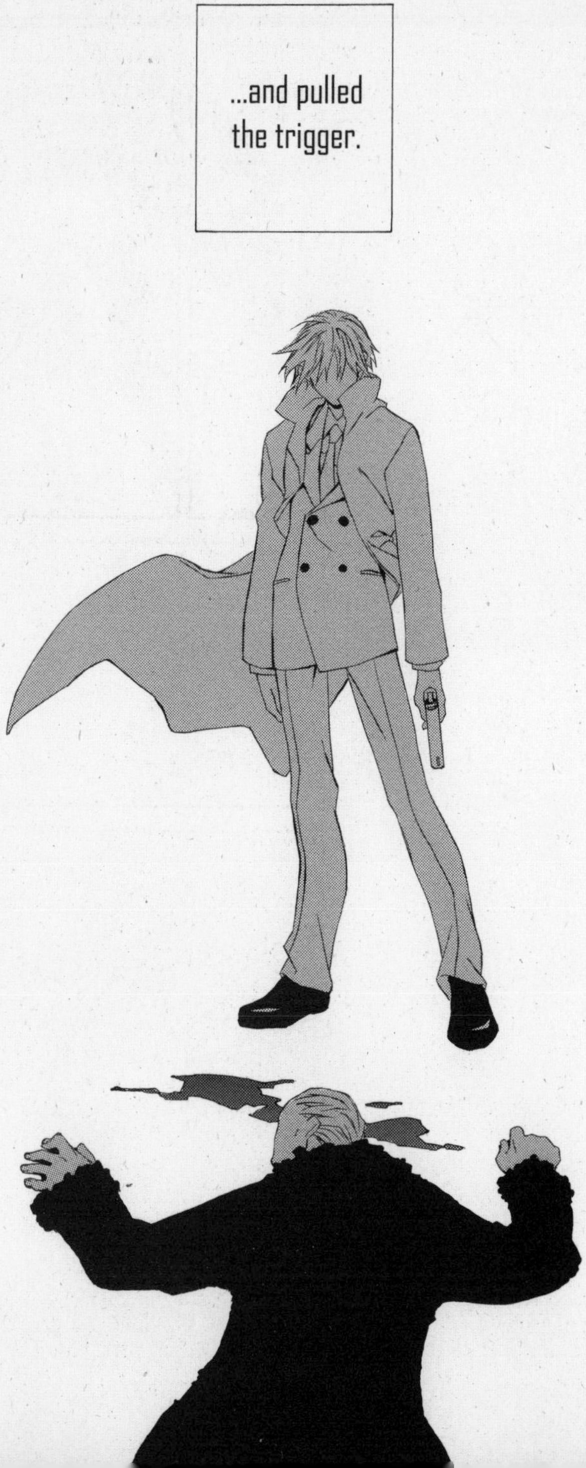
...and pulled
the trigger.

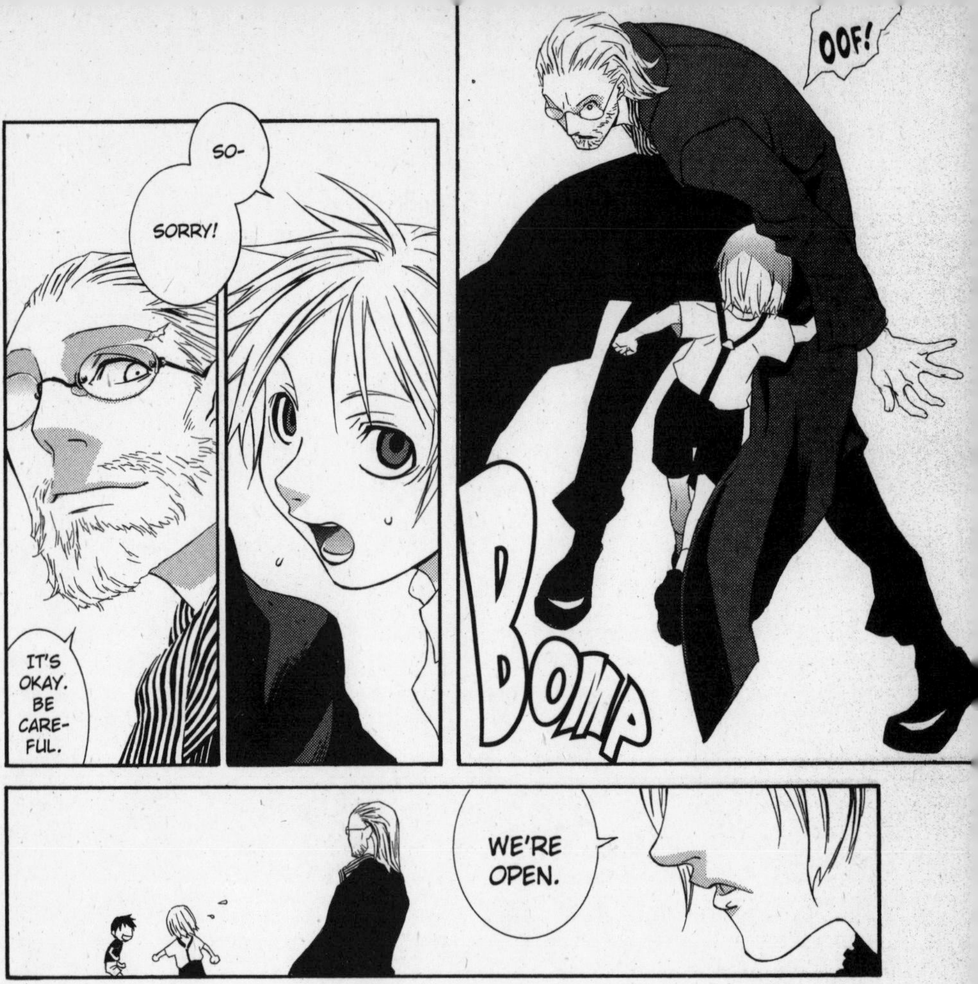
OOF!
BOMP
SO-
SORRY!
IT'S OKAY. BE CARE-FUL.
WE'RE OPEN.

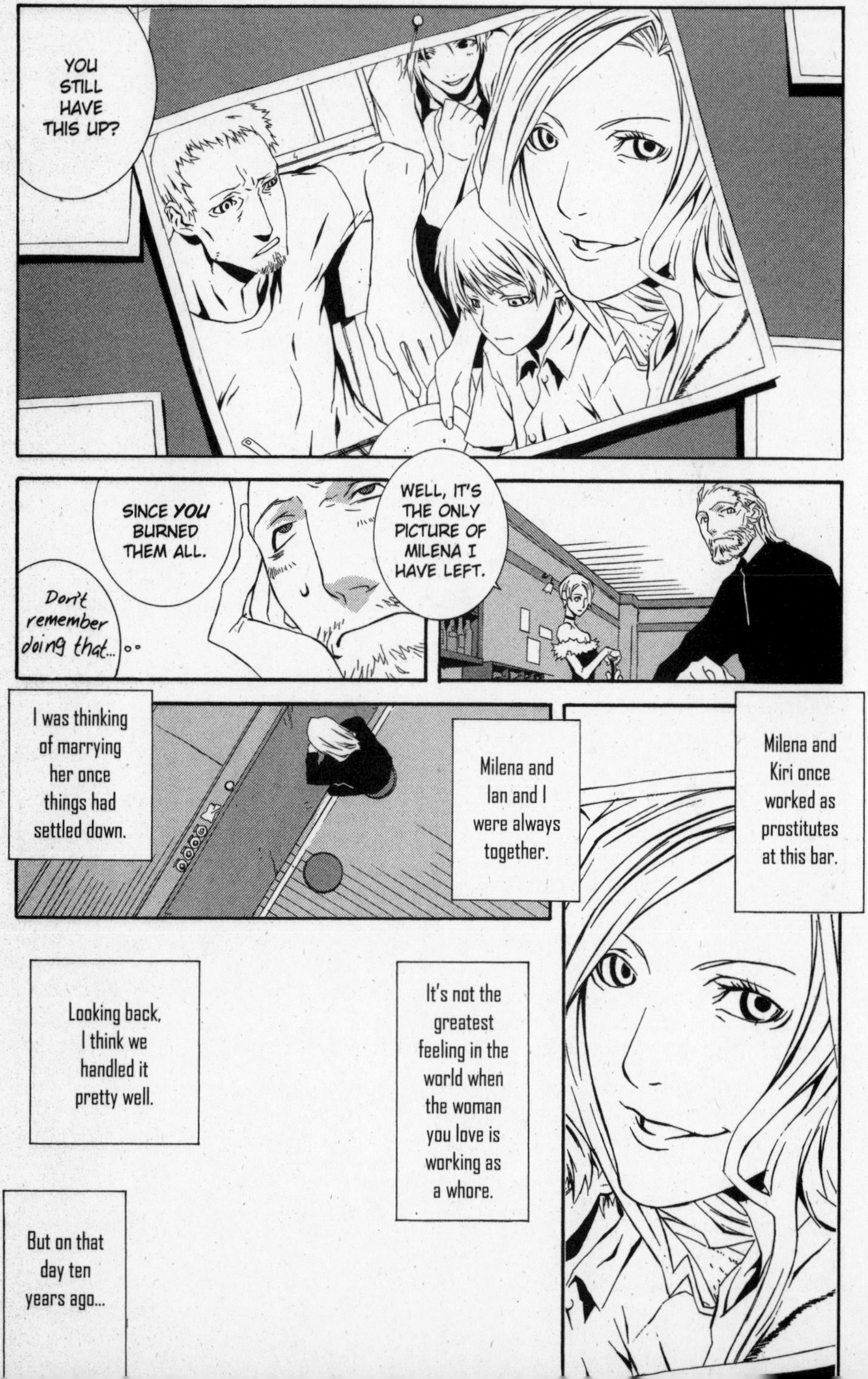
YOU STILL HAVE THIS UP?
WELL, IT'S THE ONLY PICTURE OF MILENA I HAVE LEFT.
SINCE *YOU* BURNED THEM ALL.
Don't remember doing that...
Milena and Kiri once worked as prostitutes at this bar.
Milena and Ian and I were always together.
I was thinking of marrying her once things had settled down.
It's not the greatest feeling in the world when the woman you love is working as a whore.
Looking back, I think we handled it pretty well.
But on that day ten years ago...

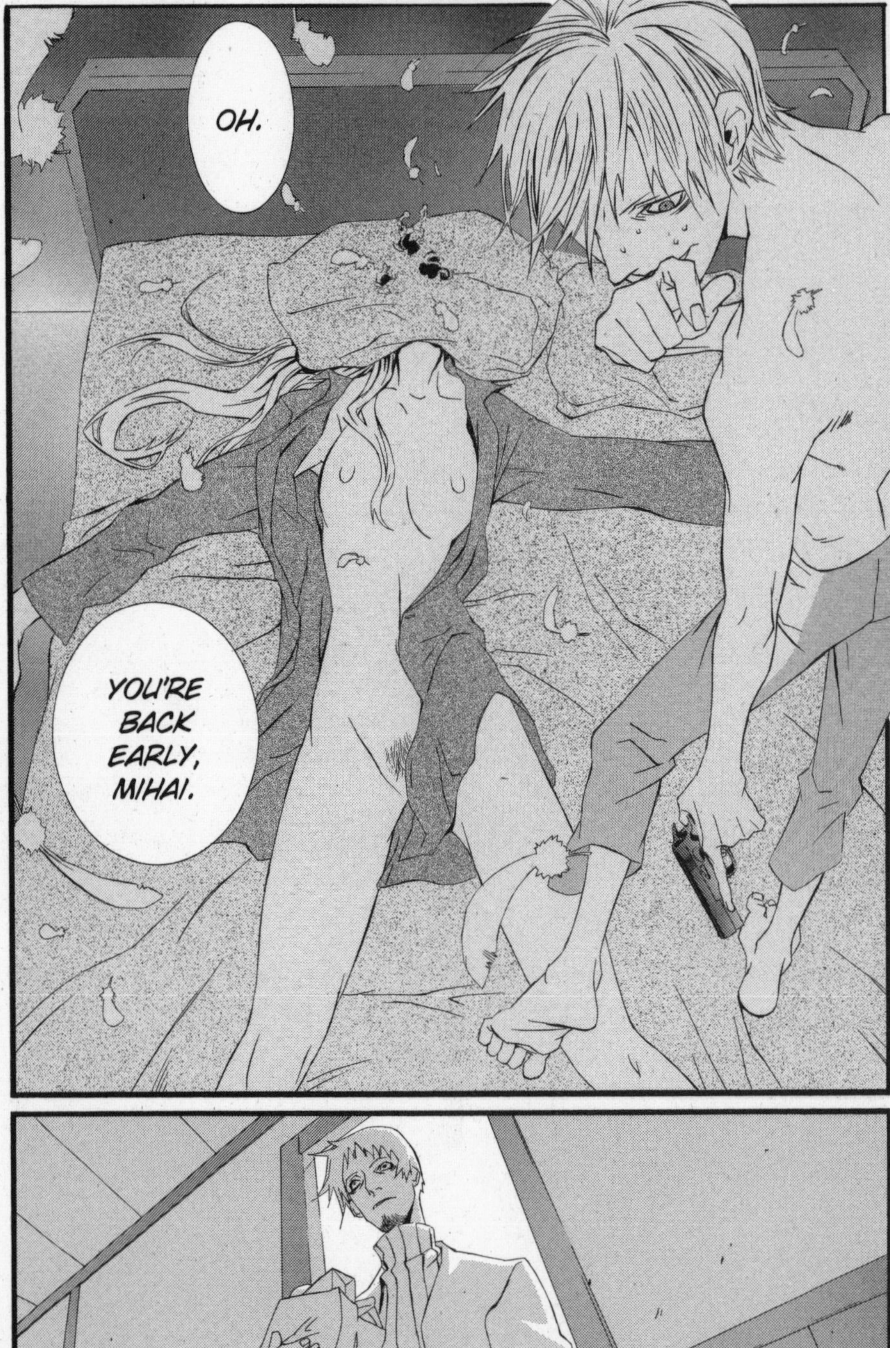
OH.
YOU'RE BACK EARLY, MIHAI.

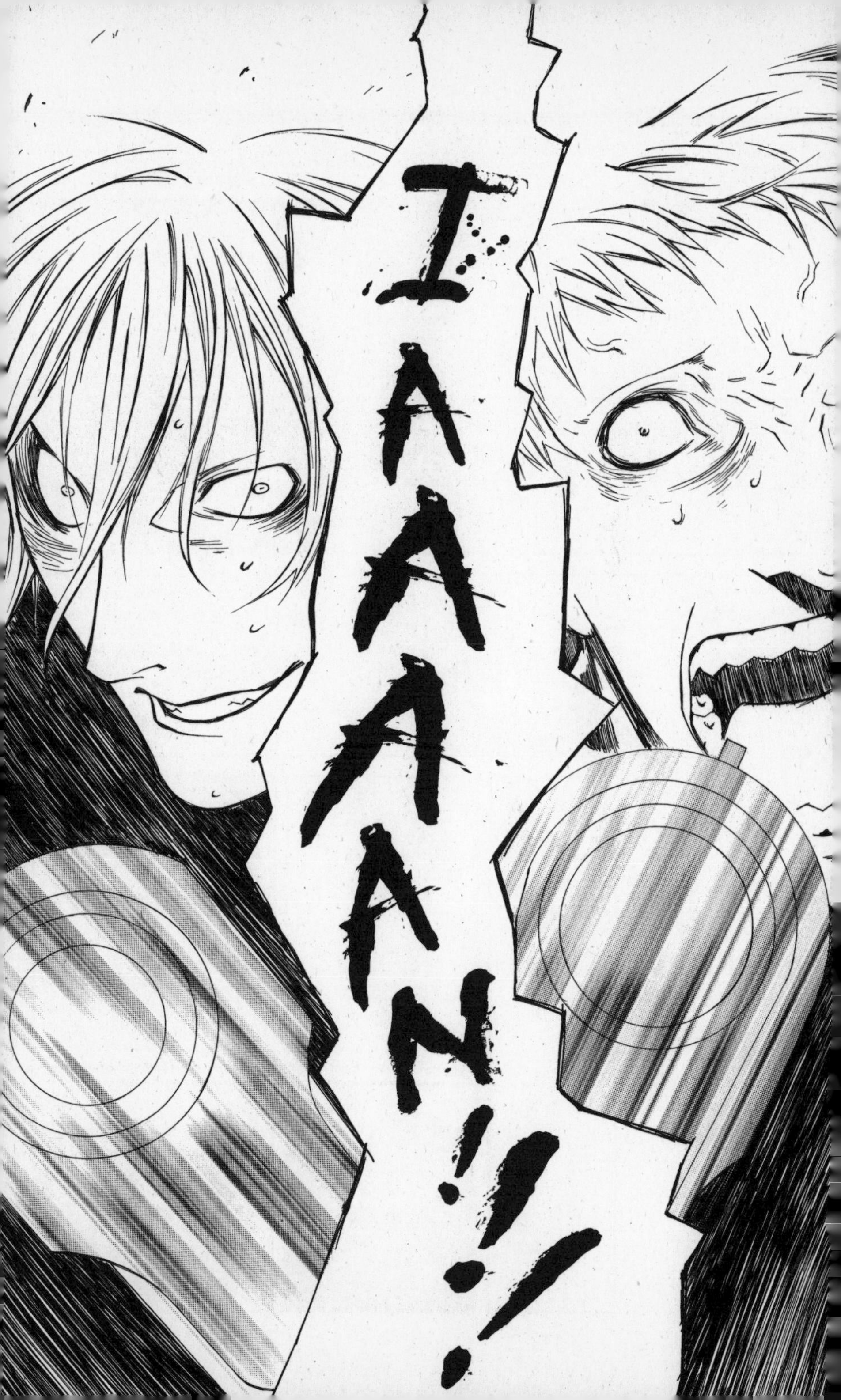
IAAAAN!!!

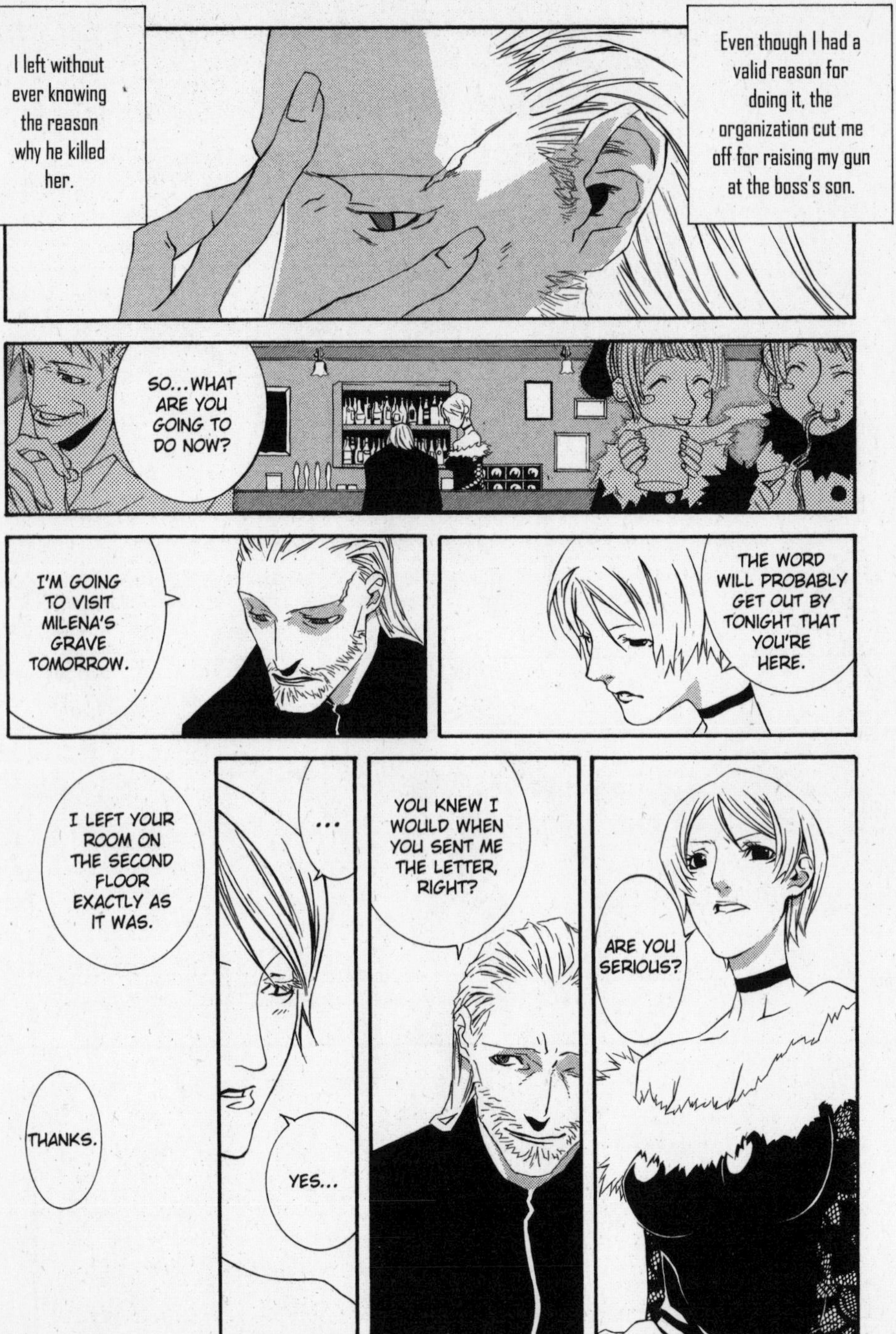
Even though I had a valid reason for doing it, the organization cut me off for raising my gun at the boss's son.
I left without ever knowing the reason why he killed her.
SO...WHAT ARE YOU GOING TO DO NOW?
THE WORD WILL PROBABLY GET OUT BY TONIGHT THAT YOU'RE HERE.
I'M GOING TO VISIT MILENA'S GRAVE TOMORROW.
ARE YOU SERIOUS?
YOU KNEW I WOULD WHEN YOU SENT ME THE LETTER, RIGHT?
...
I LEFT YOUR ROOM ON THE SECOND FLOOR EXACTLY AS IT WAS.
YES...
THANKS.

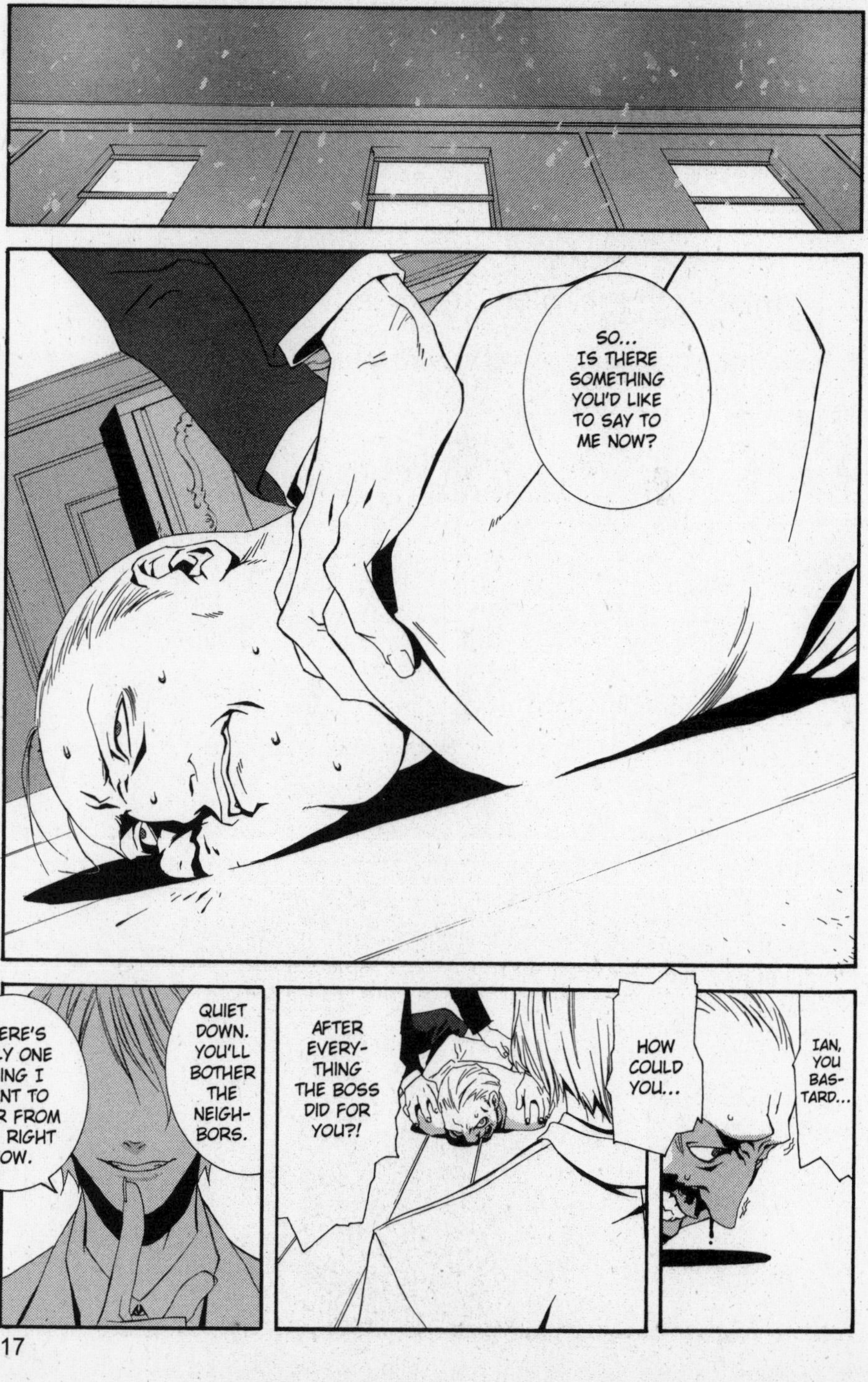
SO... IS THERE SOMETHING YOU'D LIKE TO SAY TO ME NOW?
IAN, YOU BASTARD...
HOW COULD YOU...
AFTER EVERYTHING THE BOSS DID FOR YOU?!
QUIET DOWN. YOU'LL BOTHER THE NEIGHBORS.
THERE'S ONLY ONE THING I WANT TO HEAR FROM YOU RIGHT NOW.

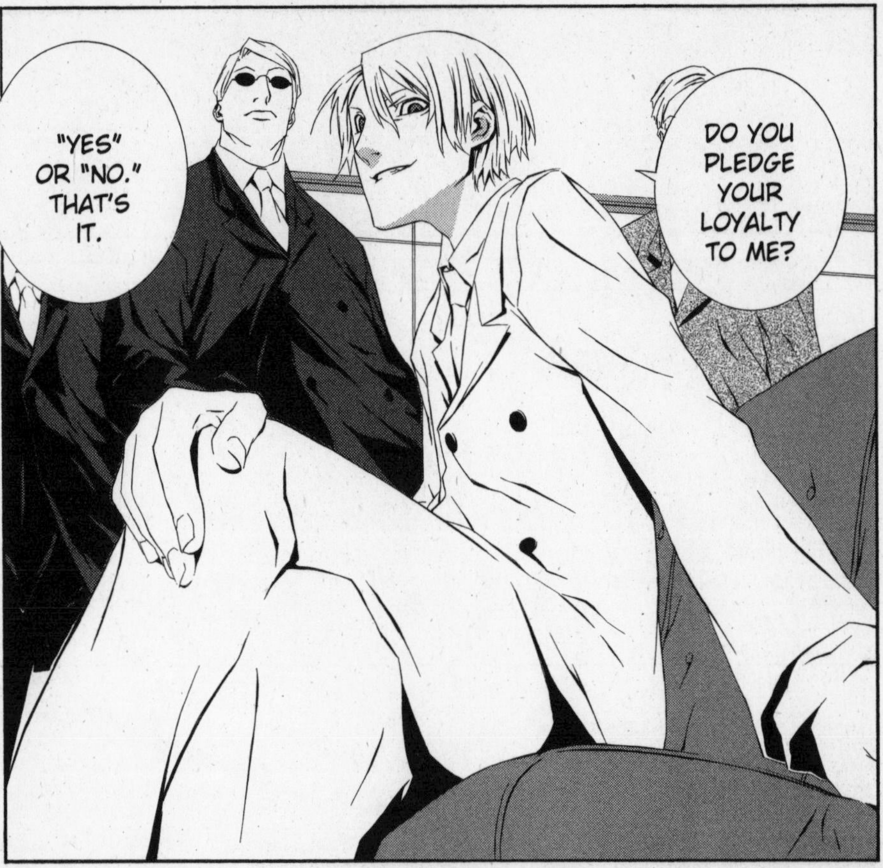
DO YOU PLEDGE YOUR LOYALTY TO ME?
"YES" OR "NO." THAT'S IT.

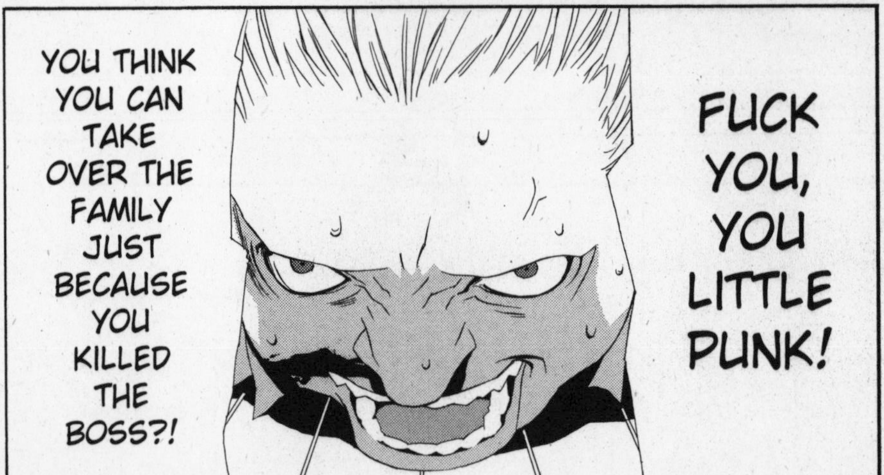
FUCK YOU, YOU LITTLE PUNK!
YOU THINK YOU CAN TAKE OVER THE FAMILY JUST BECAUSE YOU KILLED THE BOSS?!

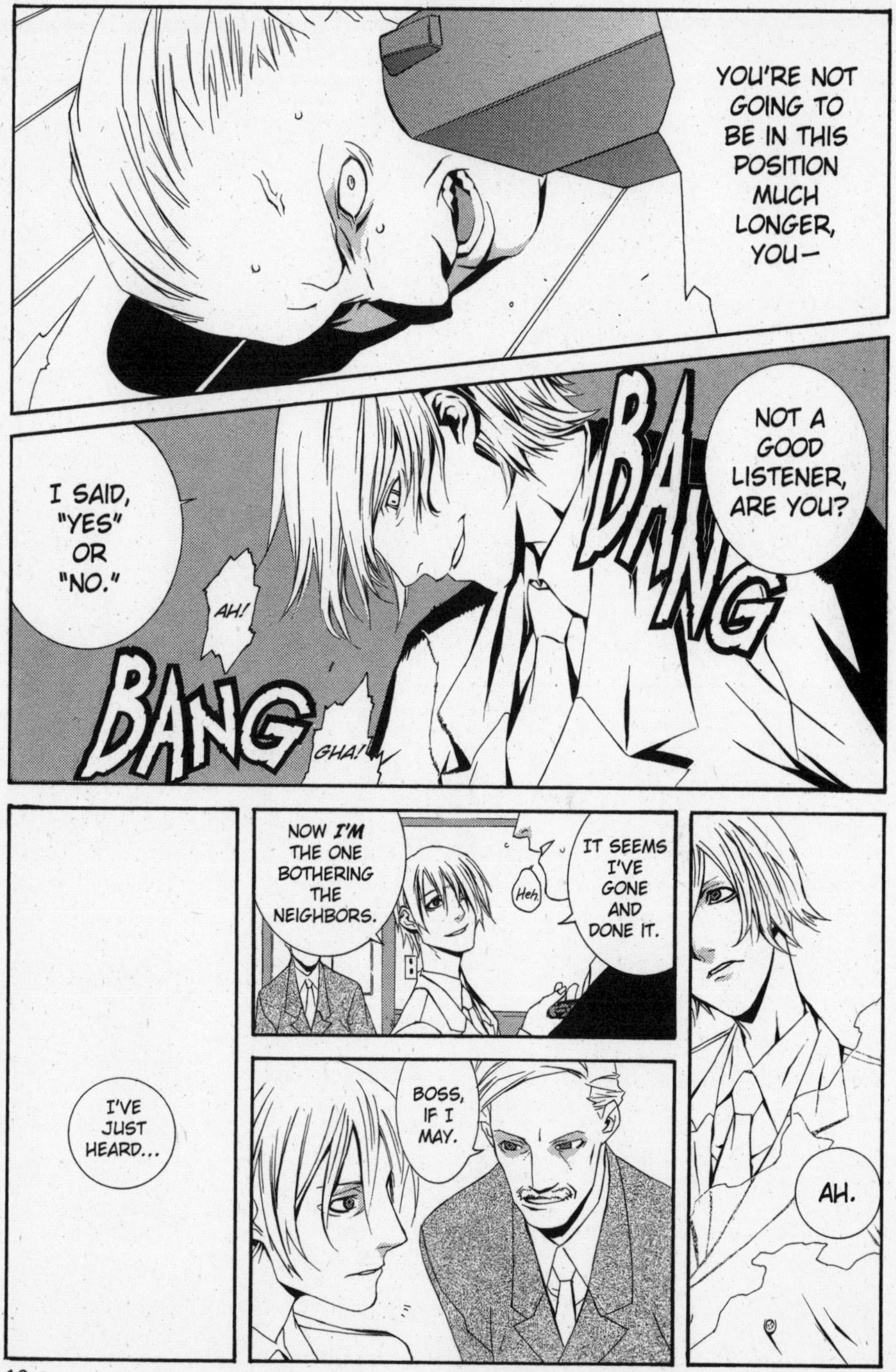
YOU'RE NOT GOING TO BE IN THIS POSITION MUCH LONGER, YOU—
NOT A GOOD LISTENER, ARE YOU?
BANG
I SAID, "YES" OR "NO."
AH!
BANG
GHA!
AH.
IT SEEMS I'VE GONE AND DONE IT.
Heh.
NOW *I'M* THE ONE BOTHERING THE NEIGHBORS.
BOSS, IF I MAY.
I'VE JUST HEARD...

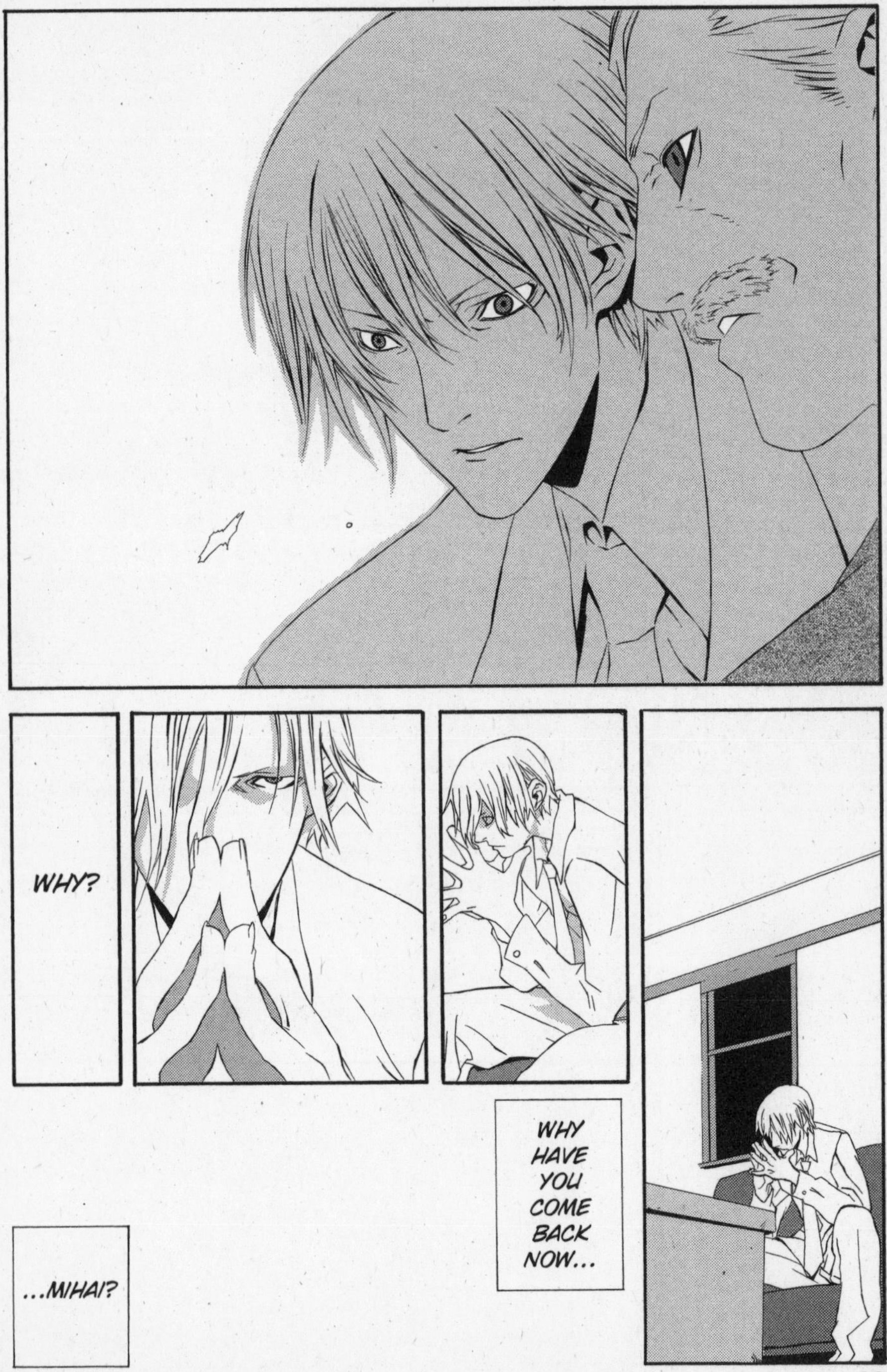
WHY?
WHY HAVE YOU COME BACK NOW...
...MIHAI?

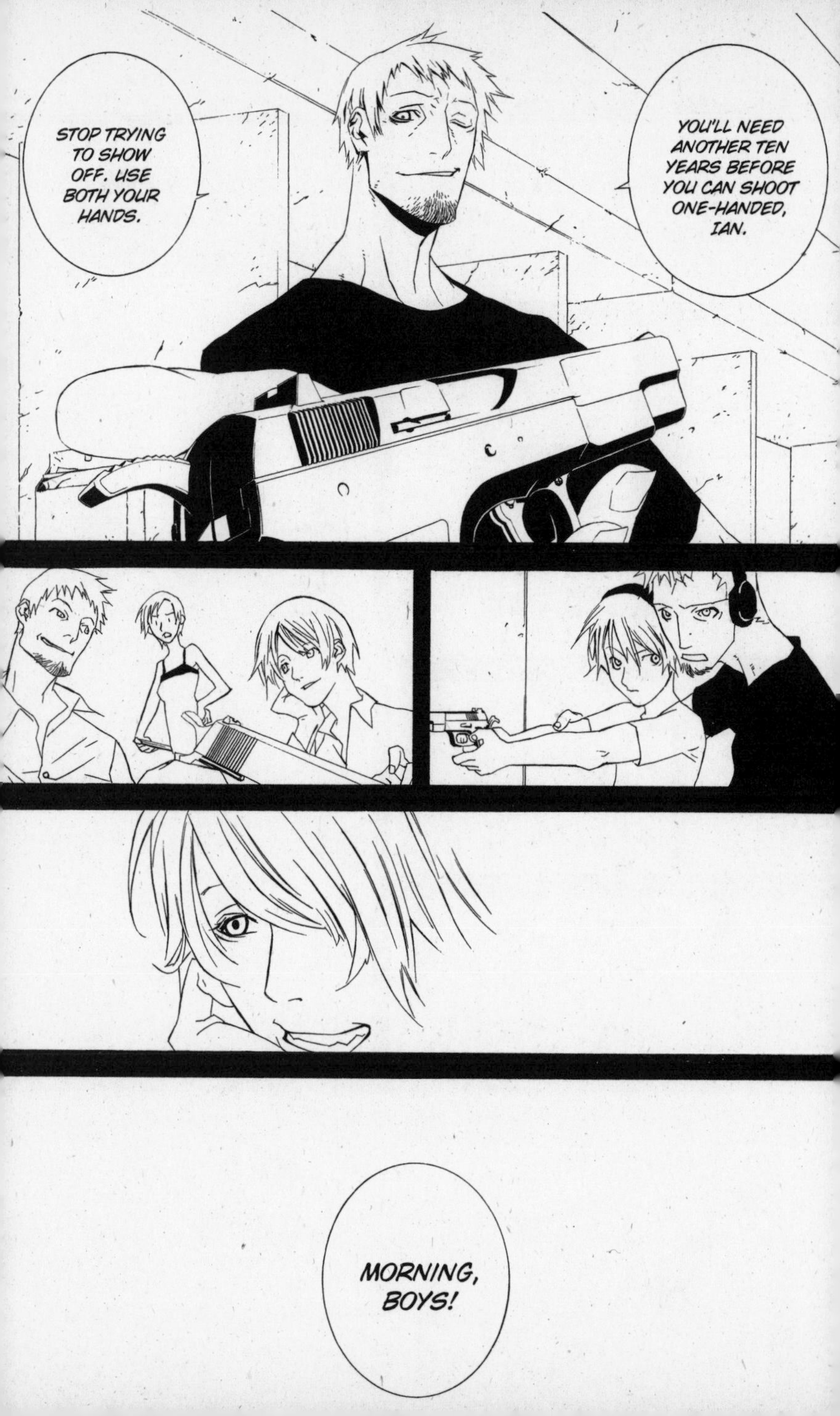
YOU'LL NEED ANOTHER TEN YEARS BEFORE YOU CAN SHOOT ONE-HANDED, IAN.
STOP TRYING TO SHOW OFF. USE BOTH YOUR HANDS.
MORNING, BOYS!

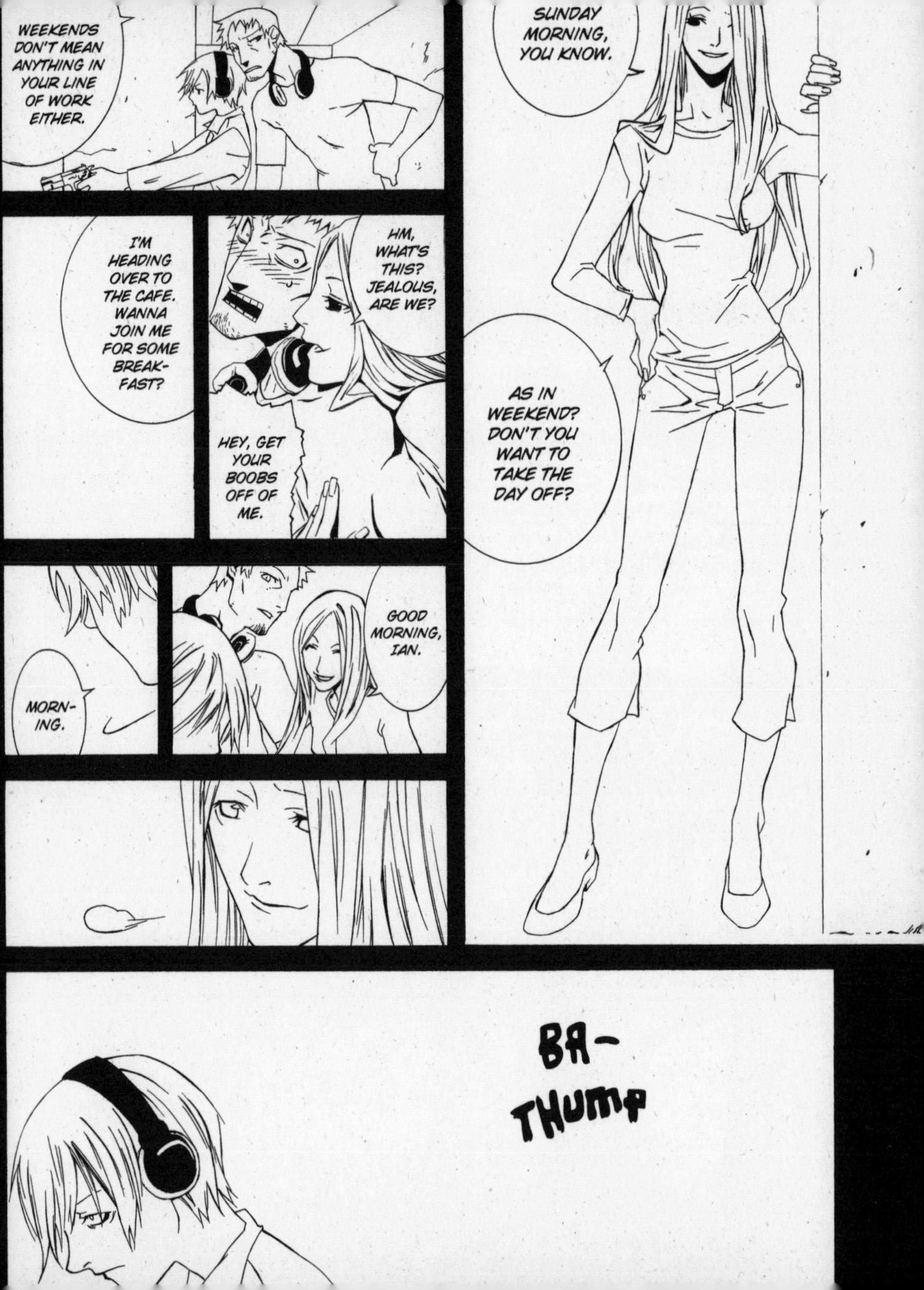
SUNDAY MORNING, YOU KNOW.
AS IN WEEKEND? DON'T YOU WANT TO TAKE THE DAY OFF?
WEEKENDS DON'T MEAN ANYTHING IN YOUR LINE OF WORK EITHER.
HM, WHAT'S THIS? JEALOUS, ARE WE?
HEY, GET YOUR BOOBS OFF OF ME.
I'M HEADING OVER TO THE CAFE. WANNA JOIN ME FOR SOME BREAK-FAST?
GOOD MORNING, IAN.
MORN-ING.
BA-THUMP

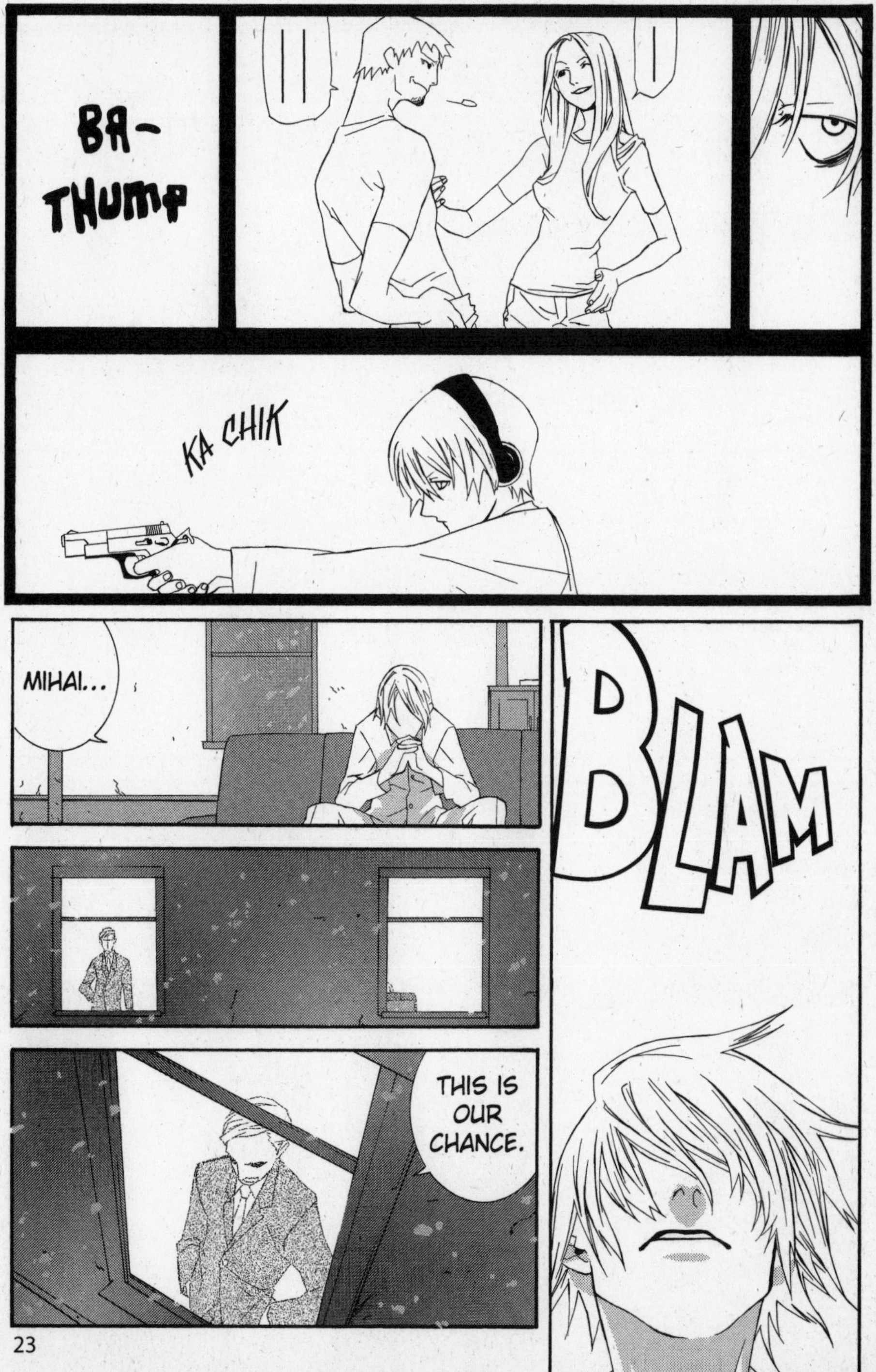
!
!!
BA-THUMP
KA CHIK
BLAM
MIHAI...
THIS IS OUR CHANCE.

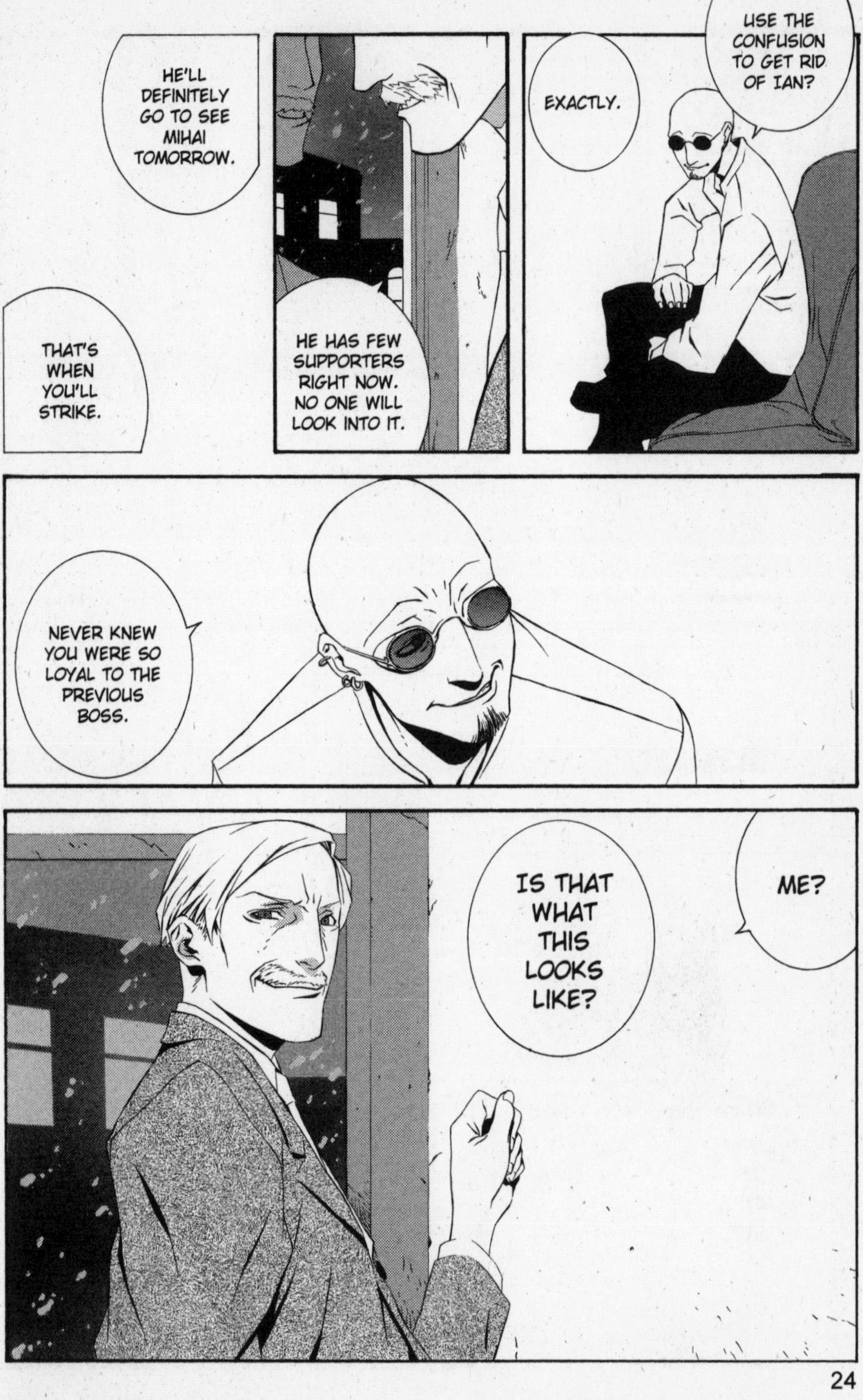
USE THE CONFUSION TO GET RID OF IAN?
EXACTLY.
HE'LL DEFINITELY GO TO SEE MIHAI TOMORROW.
HE HAS FEW SUPPORTERS RIGHT NOW. NO ONE WILL LOOK INTO IT.
THAT'S WHEN YOU'LL STRIKE.
NEVER KNEW YOU WERE SO LOYAL TO THE PREVIOUS BOSS.
ME?
IS THAT WHAT THIS LOOKS LIKE?

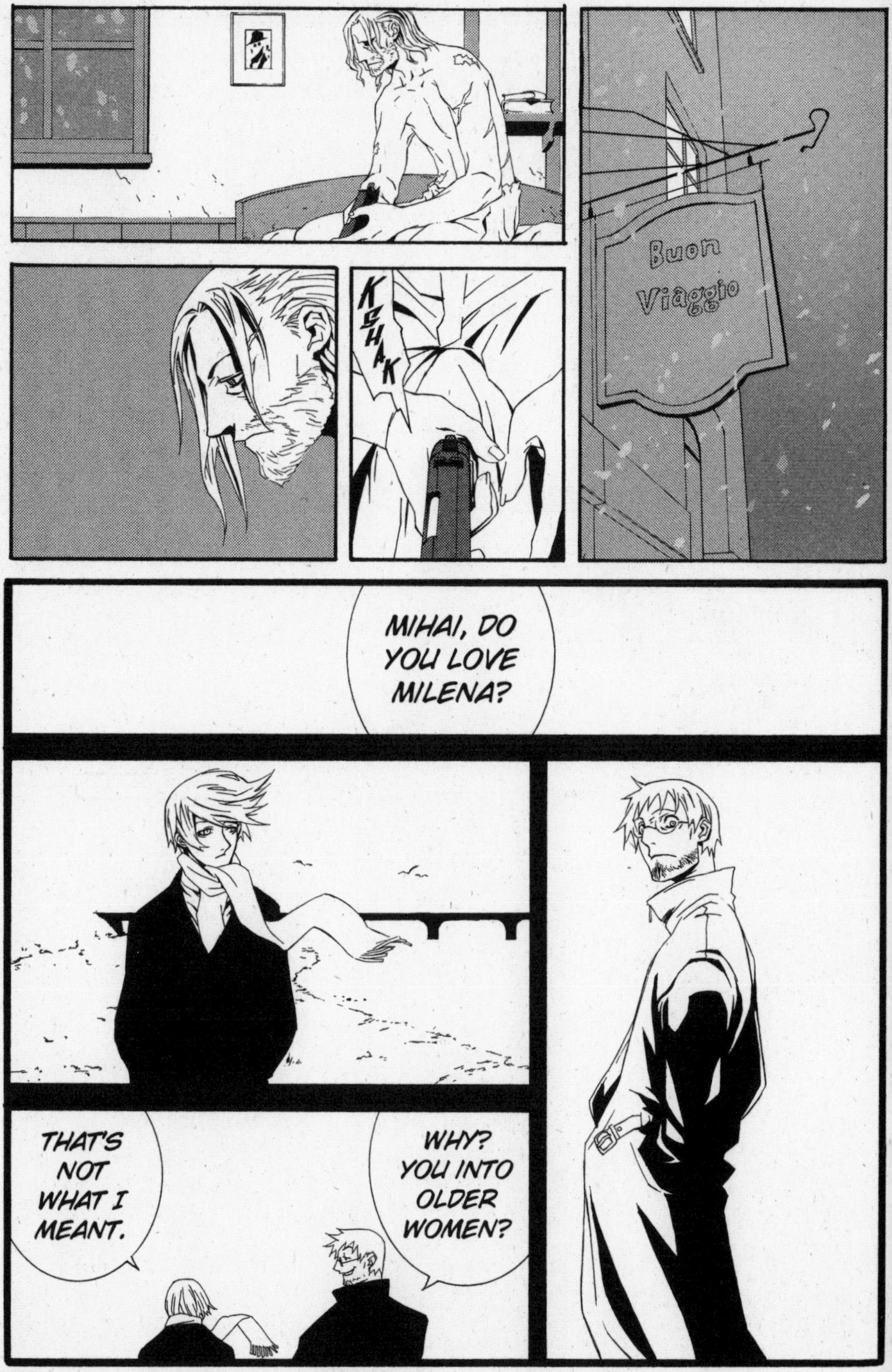
Buon Viaggio
KCHAK
MIHAI, DO YOU LOVE MILENA?
WHY? YOU INTO OLDER WOMEN?
THAT'S NOT WHAT I MEANT.

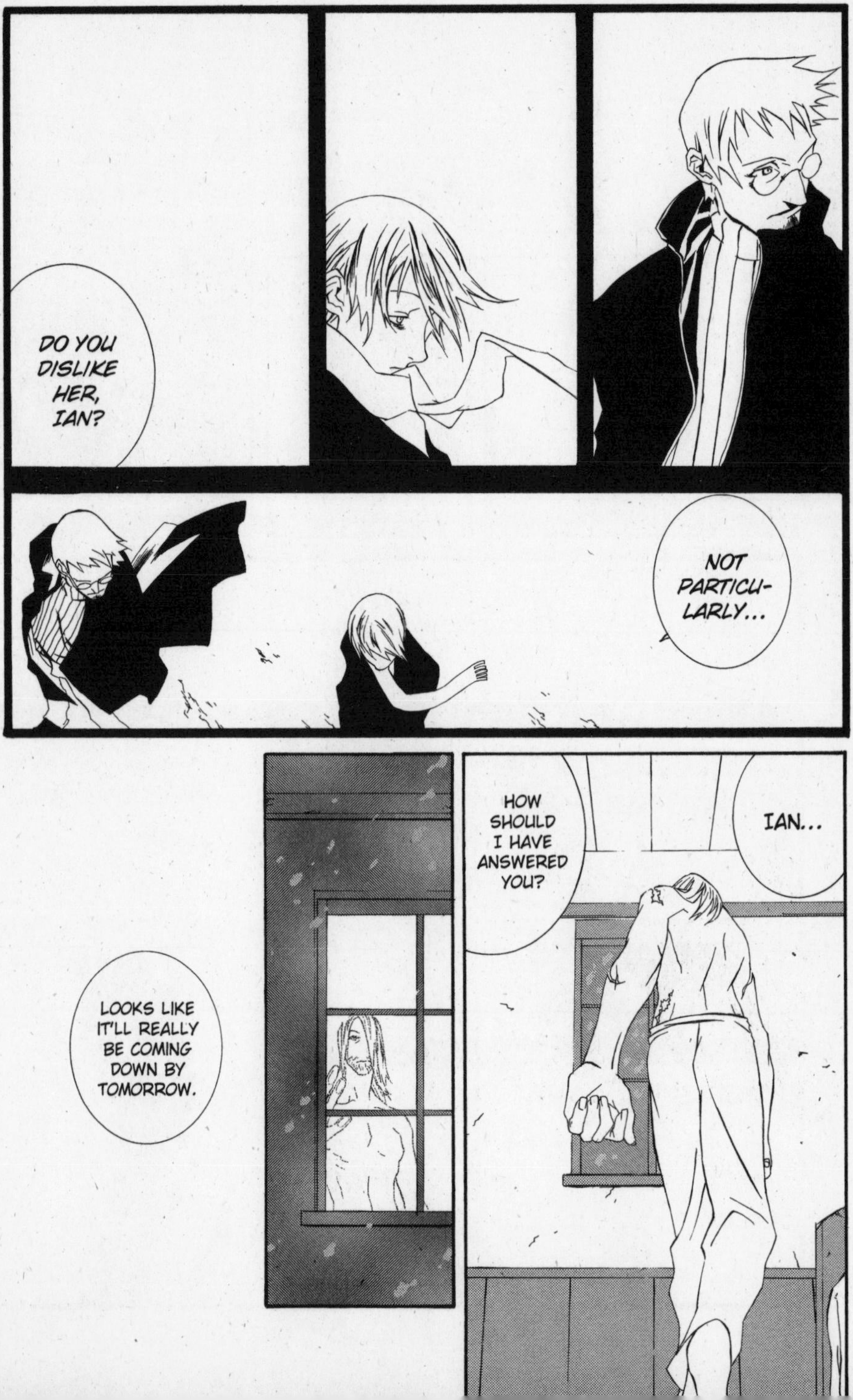
DO YOU DISLIKE HER, IAN?
NOT PARTICU-LARLY...
IAN...
HOW SHOULD I HAVE ANSWERED YOU?
LOOKS LIKE IT'LL REALLY BE COMING DOWN BY TOMORROW.

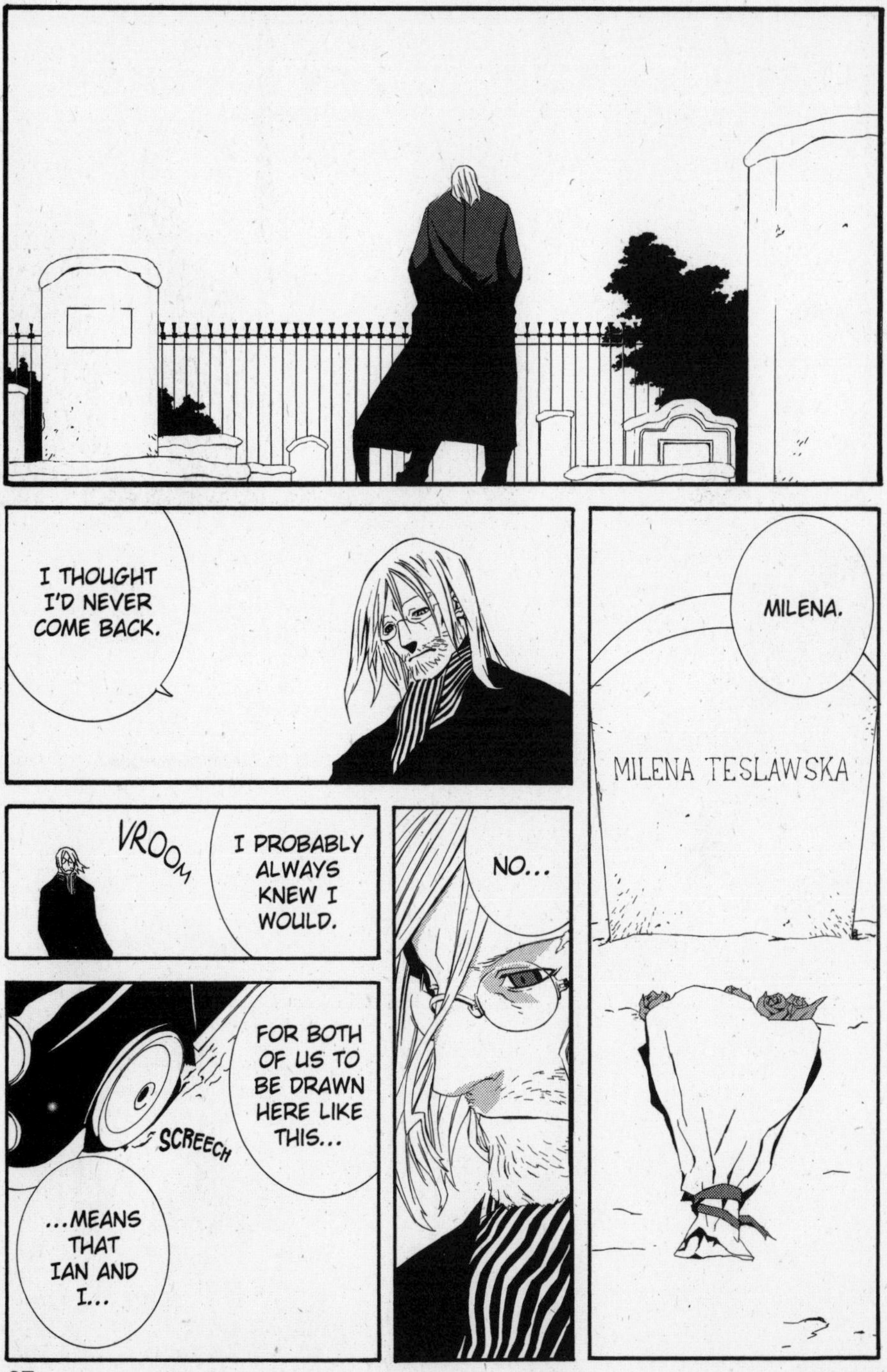
MILENA.
MILENA TESLAWSKA
I THOUGHT I'D NEVER COME BACK.
NO...
I PROBABLY ALWAYS KNEW I WOULD.
VROOM
FOR BOTH OF US TO BE DRAWN HERE LIKE THIS...
SCREECH
...MEANS THAT IAN AND I...

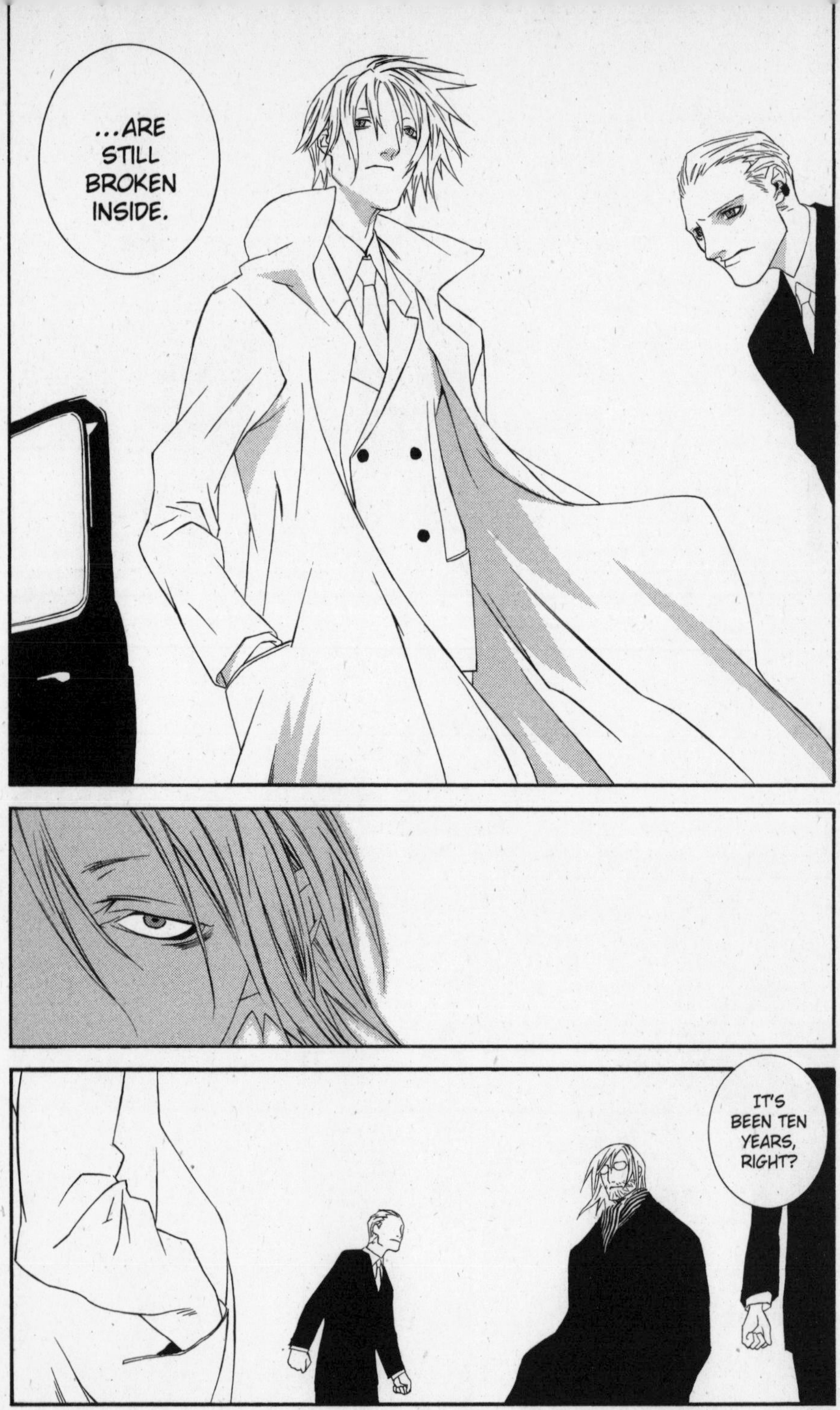
...ARE STILL BROKEN INSIDE.
IT'S BEEN TEN YEARS, RIGHT?

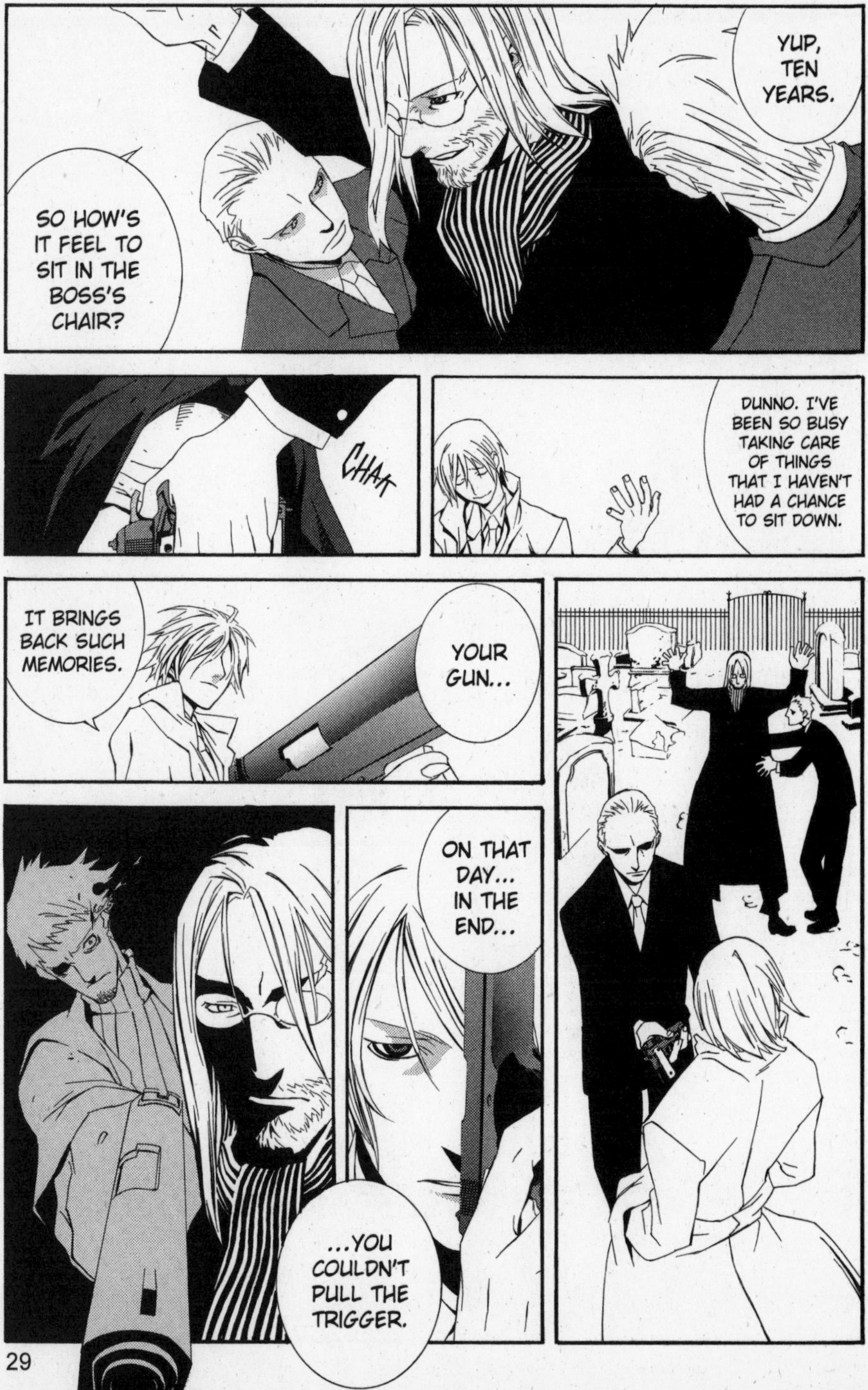
YUP, TEN YEARS.
SO HOW'S IT FEEL TO SIT IN THE BOSS'S CHAIR?
DUNNO. I'VE BEEN SO BUSY TAKING CARE OF THINGS THAT I HAVEN'T HAD A CHANCE TO SIT DOWN.
CHAK
YOUR GUN...
IT BRINGS BACK SUCH MEMORIES.
ON THAT DAY... IN THE END...
...YOU COULDN'T PULL THE TRIGGER.

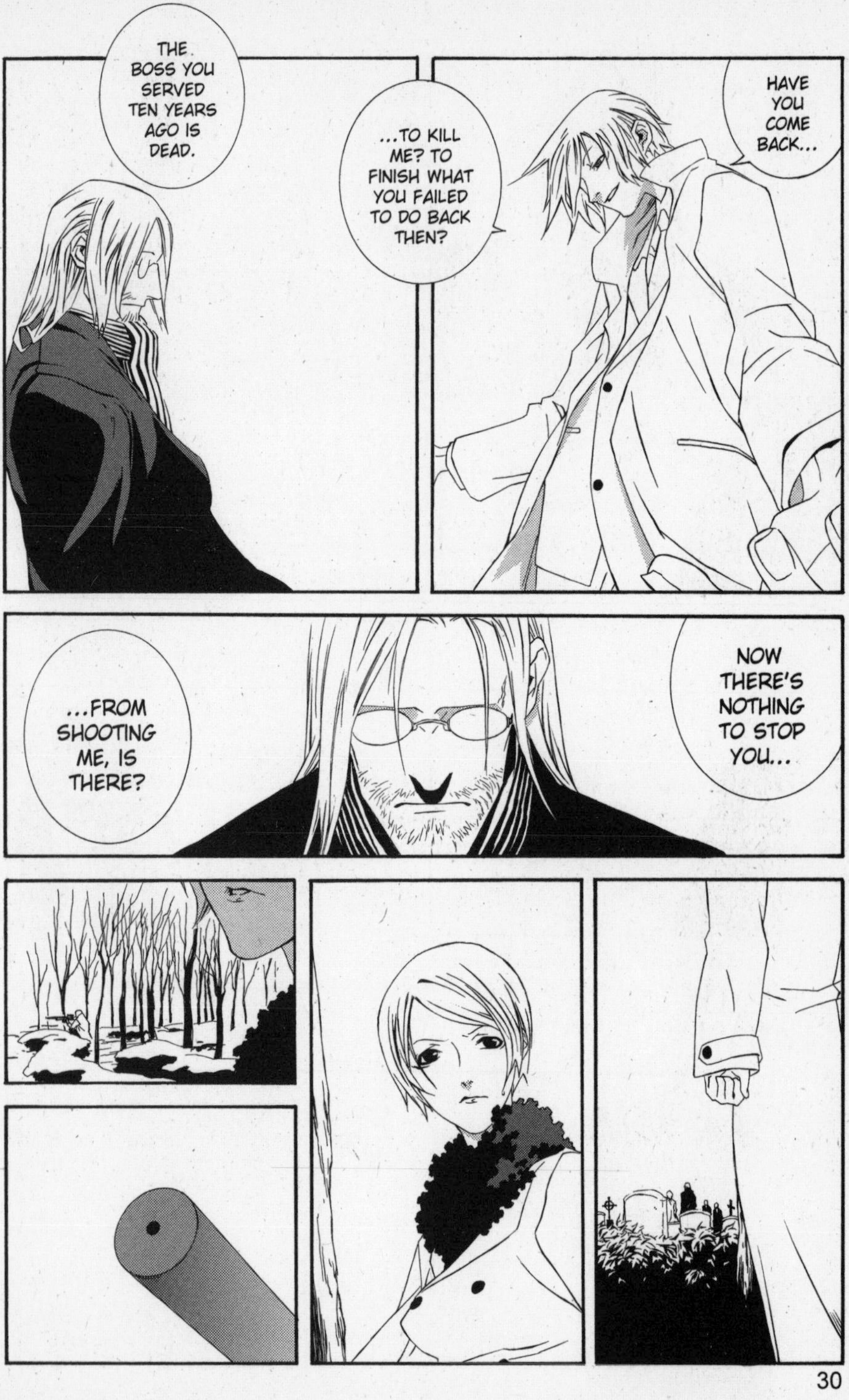
HAVE YOU COME BACK...
...TO KILL ME? TO FINISH WHAT YOU FAILED TO DO BACK THEN?
THE BOSS YOU SERVED TEN YEARS AGO IS DEAD.
NOW THERE'S NOTHING TO STOP YOU...
...FROM SHOOTING ME, IS THERE?

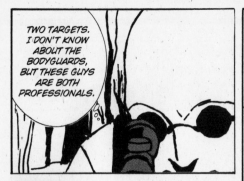

TWO TARGETS. I DON'T KNOW ABOUT THE BODYGUARDS, BUT THESE GUYS ARE BOTH PROFESSIONALS.

WHEN I HAVE A SINGLE LINE OF FIRE...

...I'LL TAKE BOTH OF THEM OUT AT ONCE.

WHY?

WHY DID YOU KILL MILENA?

IF YOU WERE GOING TO KILL ME, WHY HAVE YOU LET ME LIVE UNTIL NOW?

31

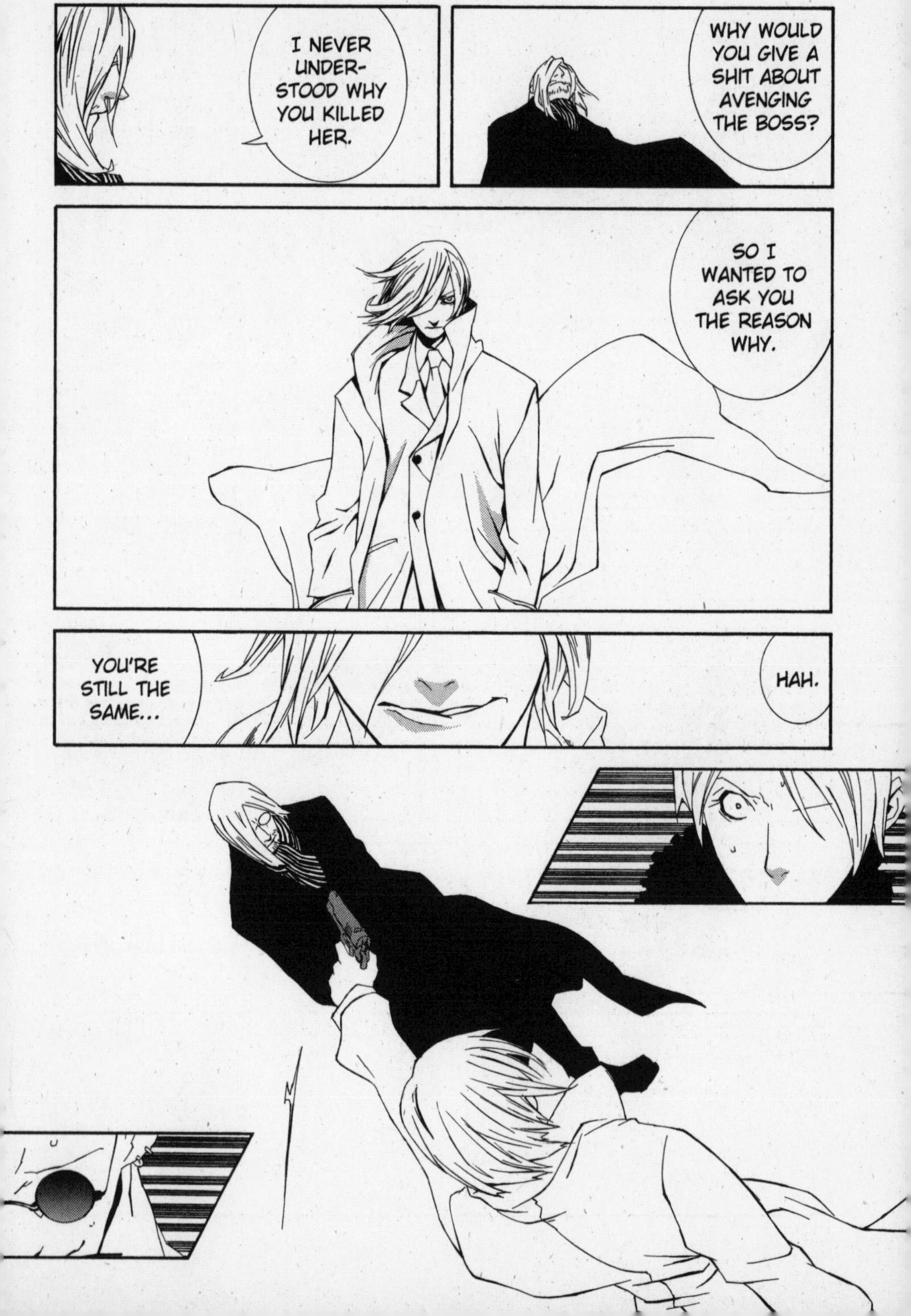
WHY WOULD YOU GIVE A SHIT ABOUT AVENGING THE BOSS?
I NEVER UNDER-STOOD WHY YOU KILLED HER.
SO I WANTED TO ASK YOU THE REASON WHY.
HAH.
YOU'RE STILL THE SAME...

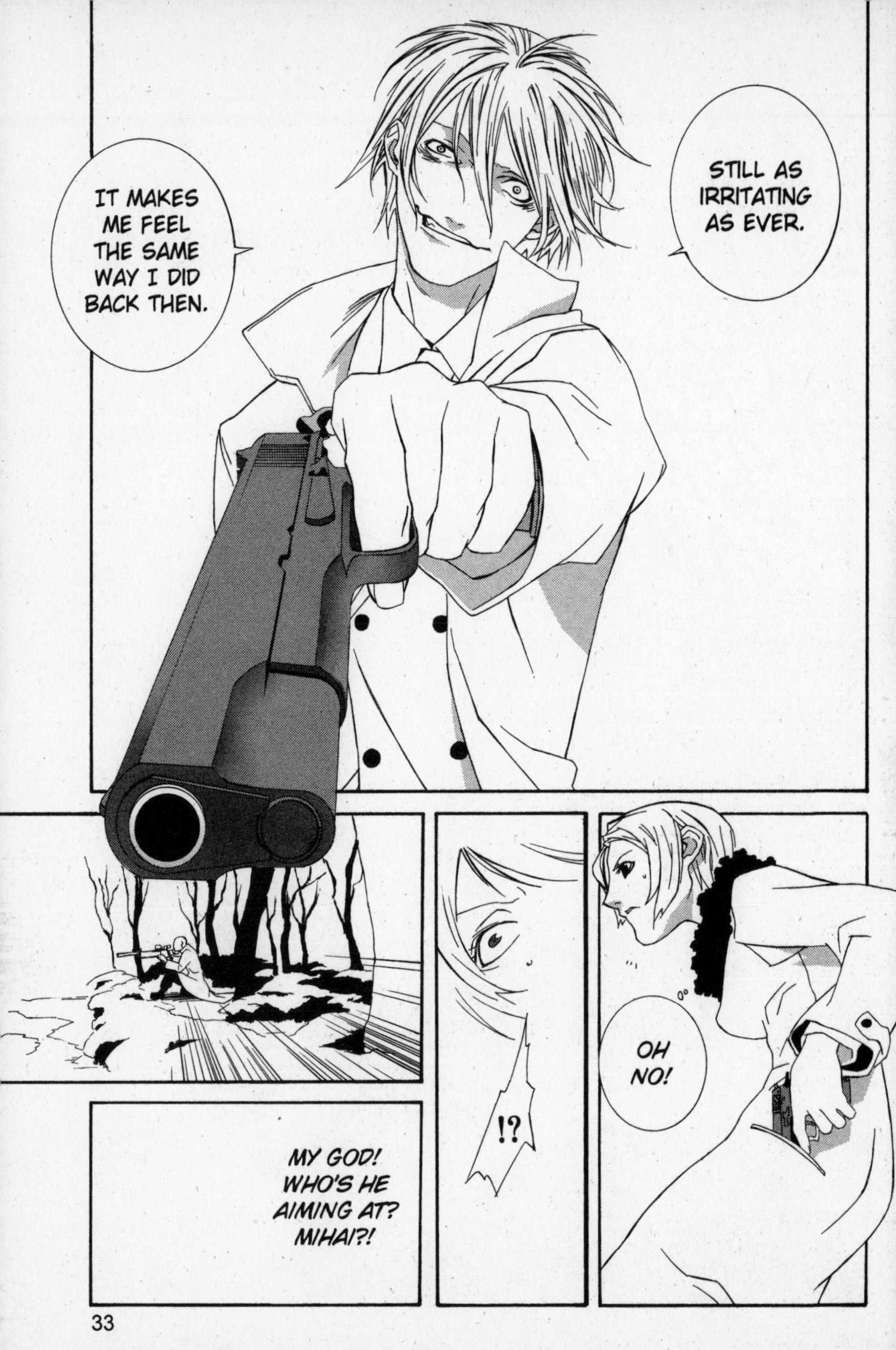
STILL AS IRRITATING AS EVER.
IT MAKES ME FEEL THE SAME WAY I DID BACK THEN.
OH NO!
!?
MY GOD! WHO'S HE AIMING AT? MIHAI?!

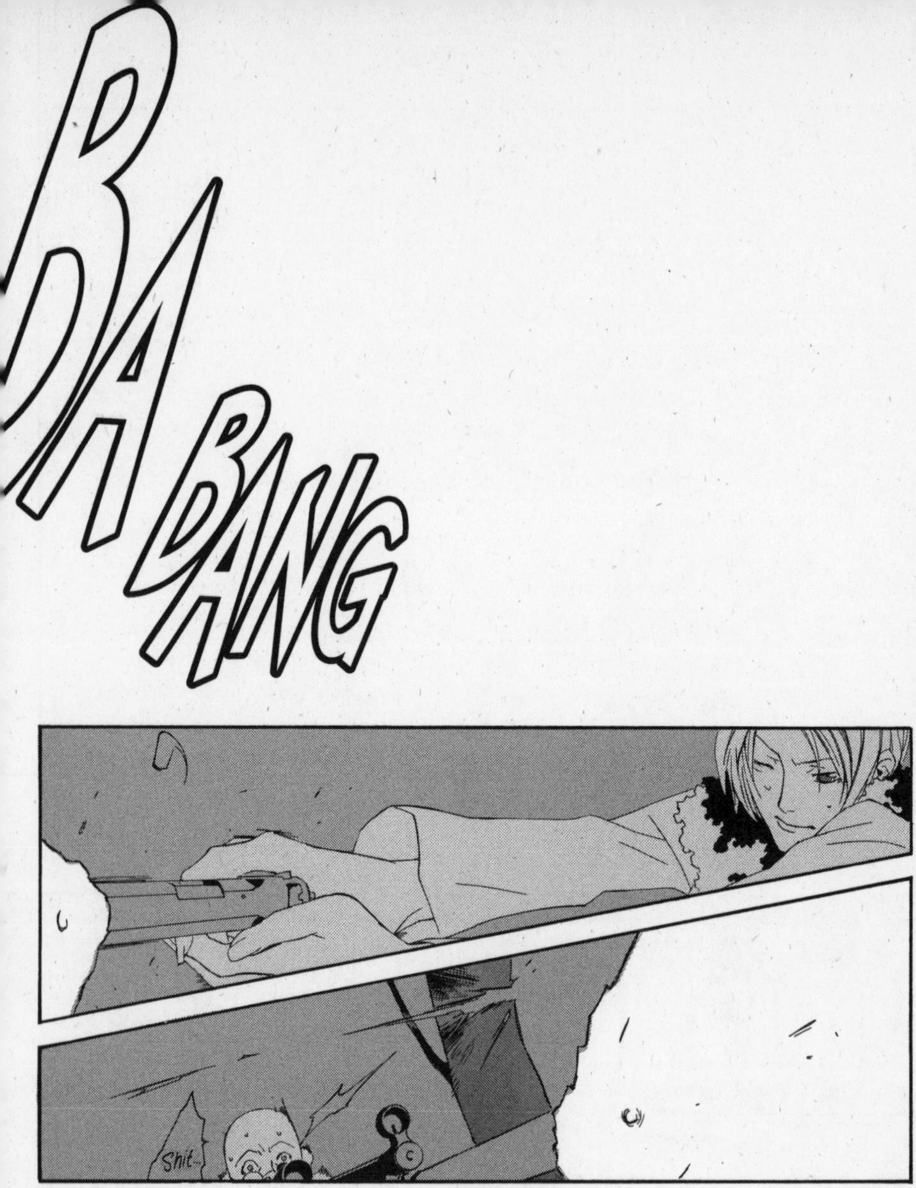
BADABANG
Shit...
NGH... IA—
SPLICK

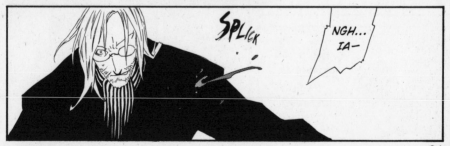

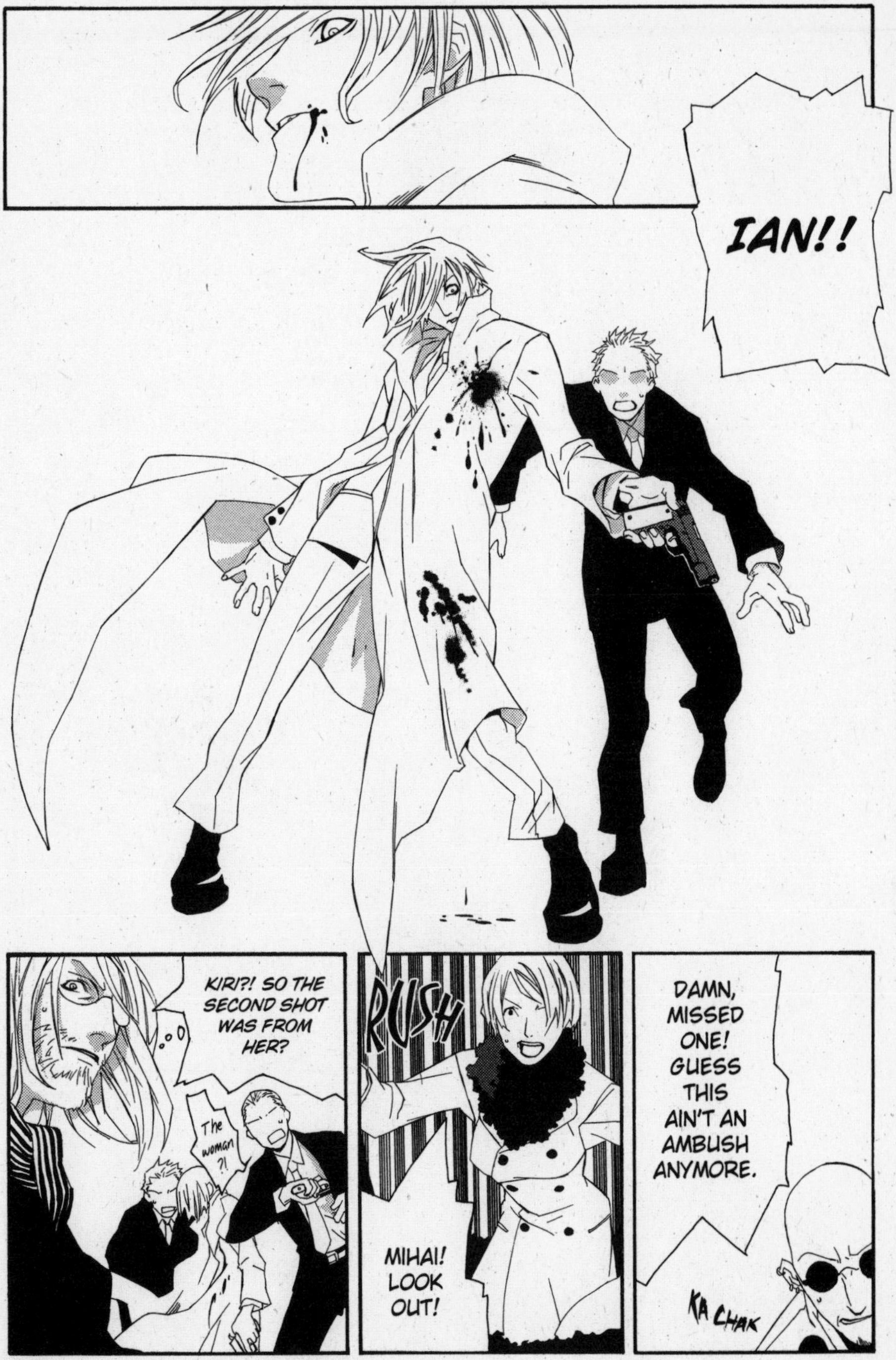
IAN!!
DAMN, MISSED ONE! GUESS THIS AIN'T AN AMBUSH ANYMORE.
KA CHAK
RUSH
MIHAI! LOOK OUT!
KIRI?! SO THE SECOND SHOT WAS FROM HER?
The woman ?!

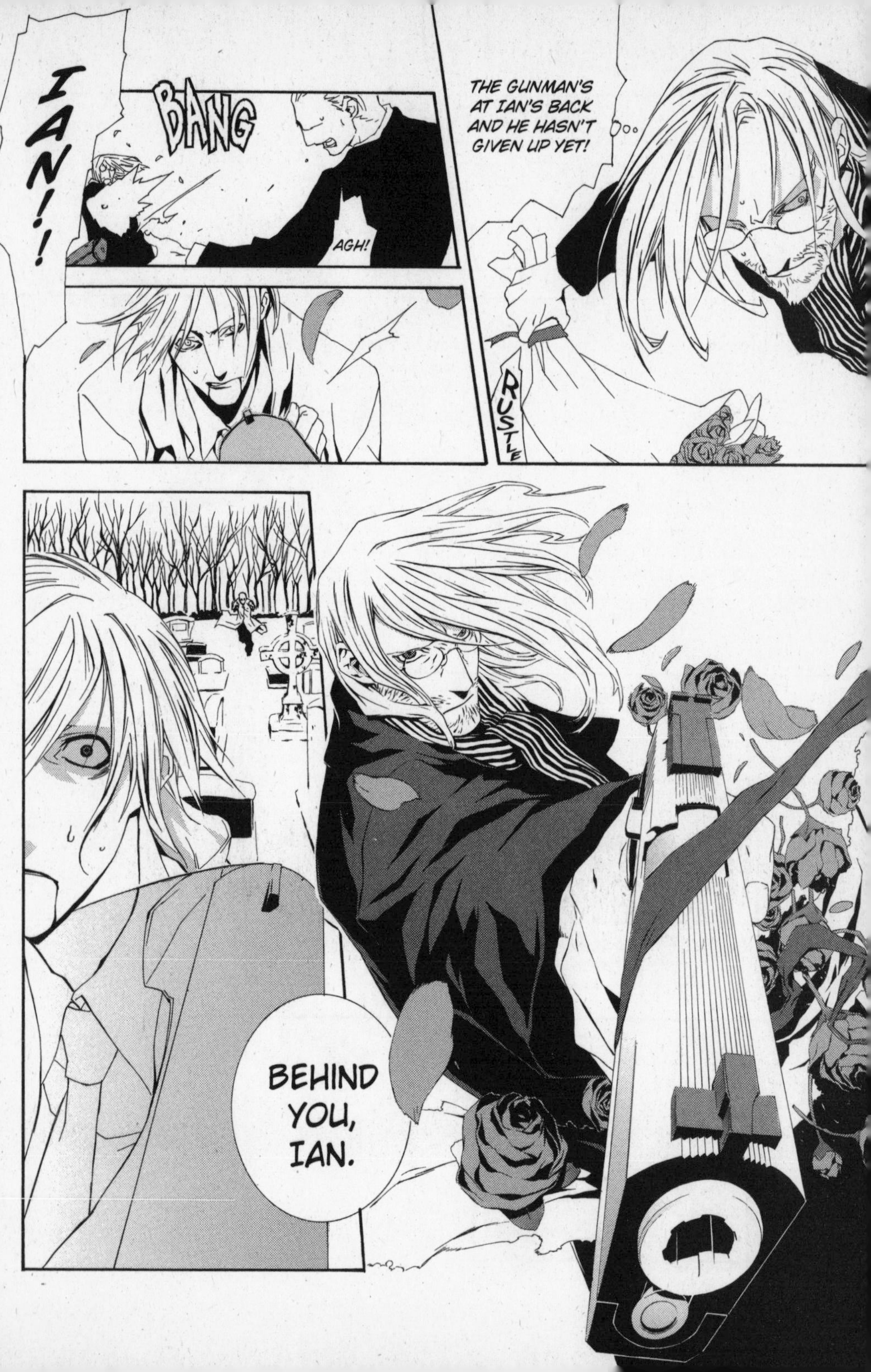
THE GUNMAN'S AT IAN'S BACK AND HE HASN'T GIVEN UP YET!
RUSTLE
BANG
AGH!
IAN!!
BEHIND YOU, IAN.

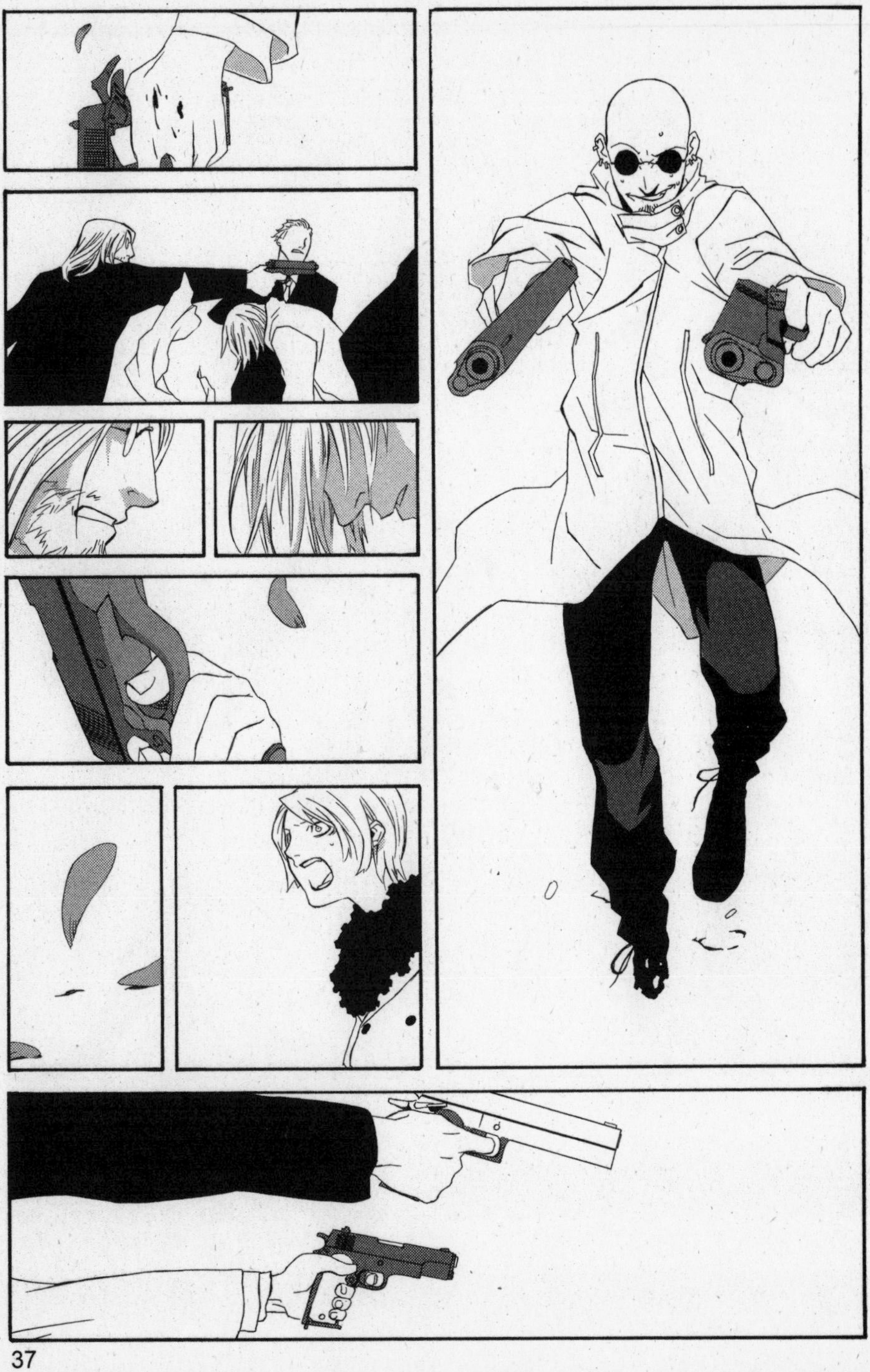

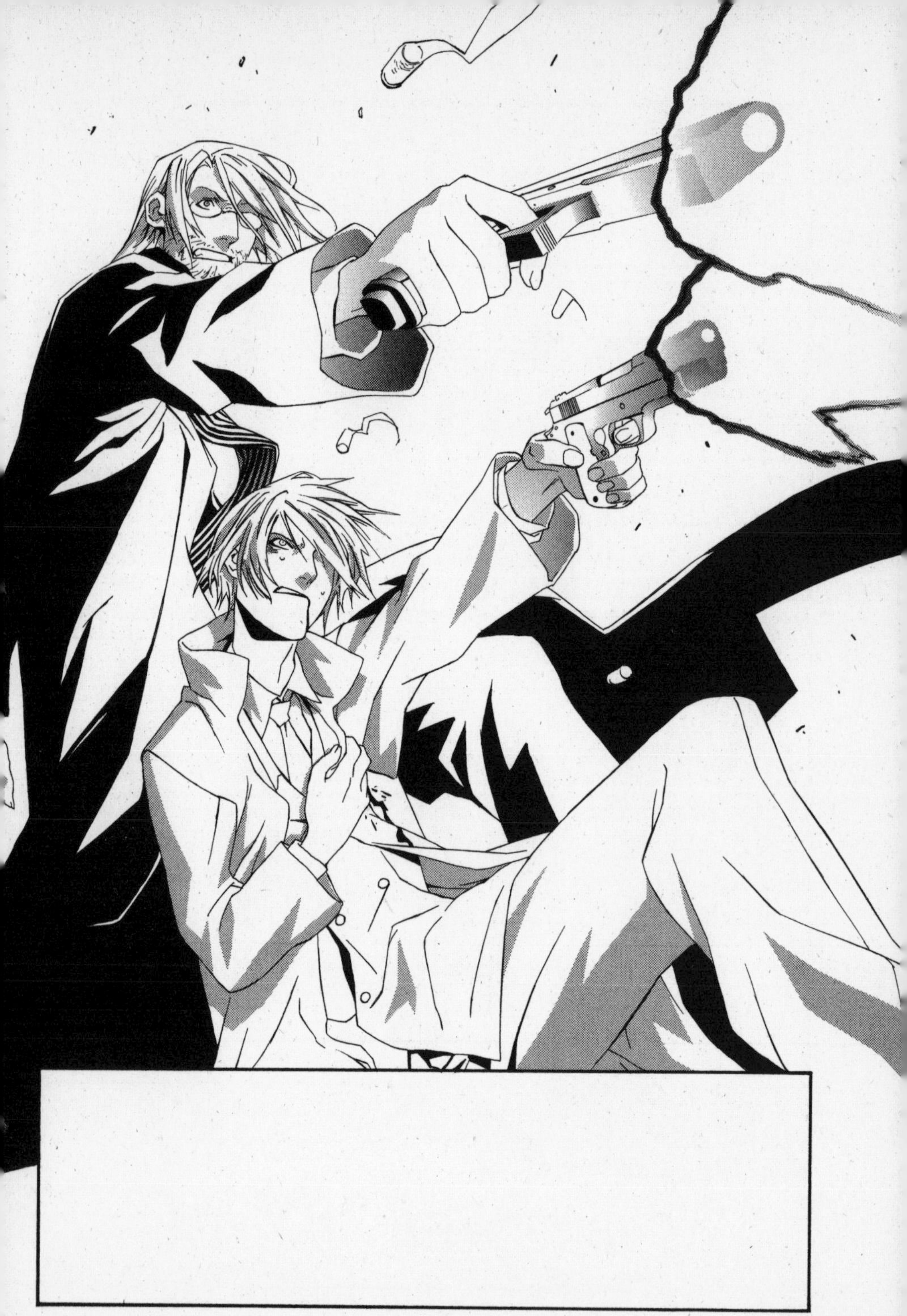

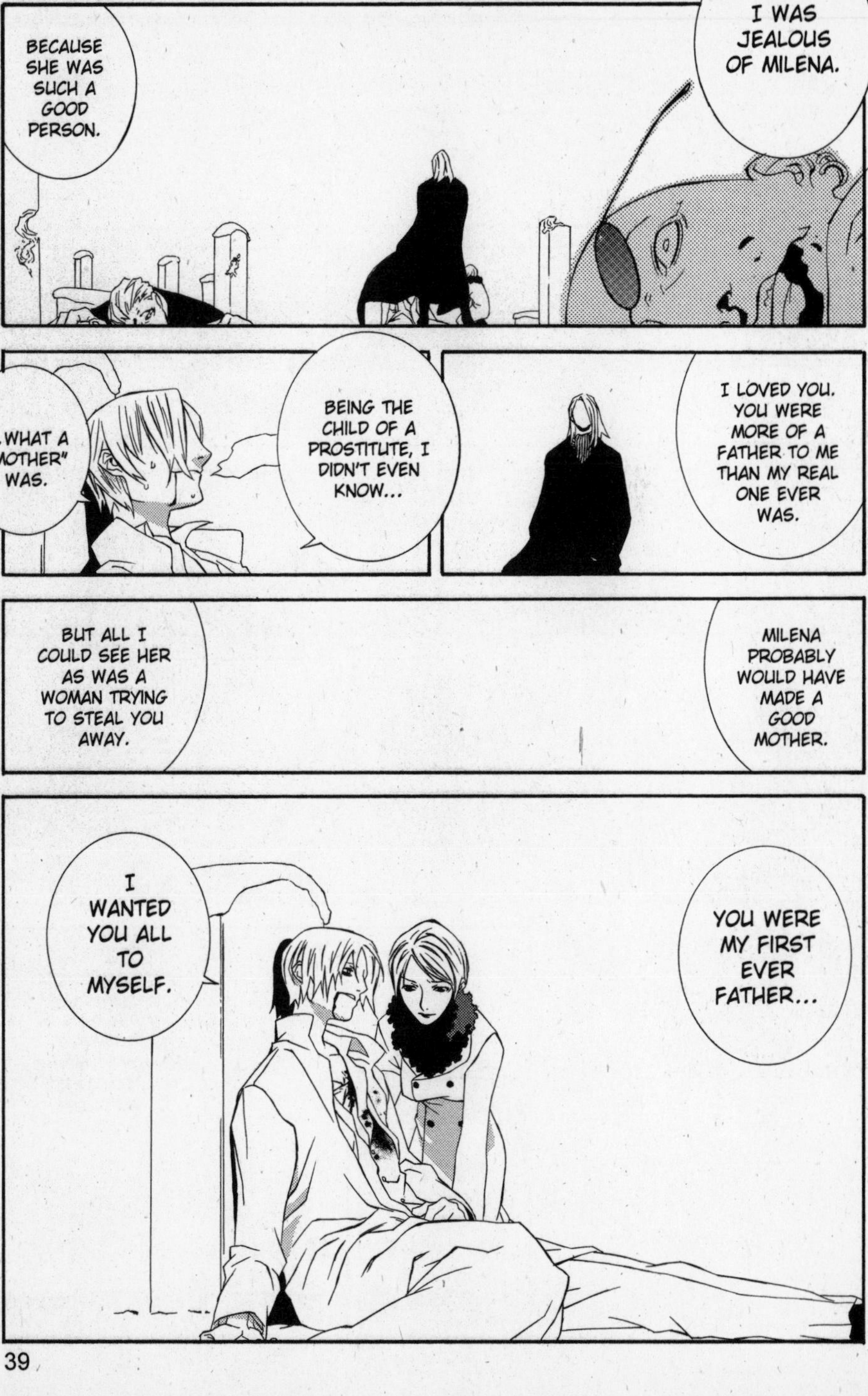
I WAS JEALOUS OF MILENA.
BECAUSE SHE WAS SUCH A GOOD PERSON.
I LOVED YOU. YOU WERE MORE OF A FATHER TO ME THAN MY REAL ONE EVER WAS.
BEING THE CHILD OF A PROSTITUTE, I DIDN'T EVEN KNOW...
...WHAT A "MOTHER" WAS.
MILENA PROBABLY WOULD HAVE MADE A GOOD MOTHER.
BUT ALL I COULD SEE HER AS WAS A WOMAN TRYING TO STEAL YOU AWAY.
YOU WERE MY FIRST EVER FATHER...
I WANTED YOU ALL TO MYSELF.

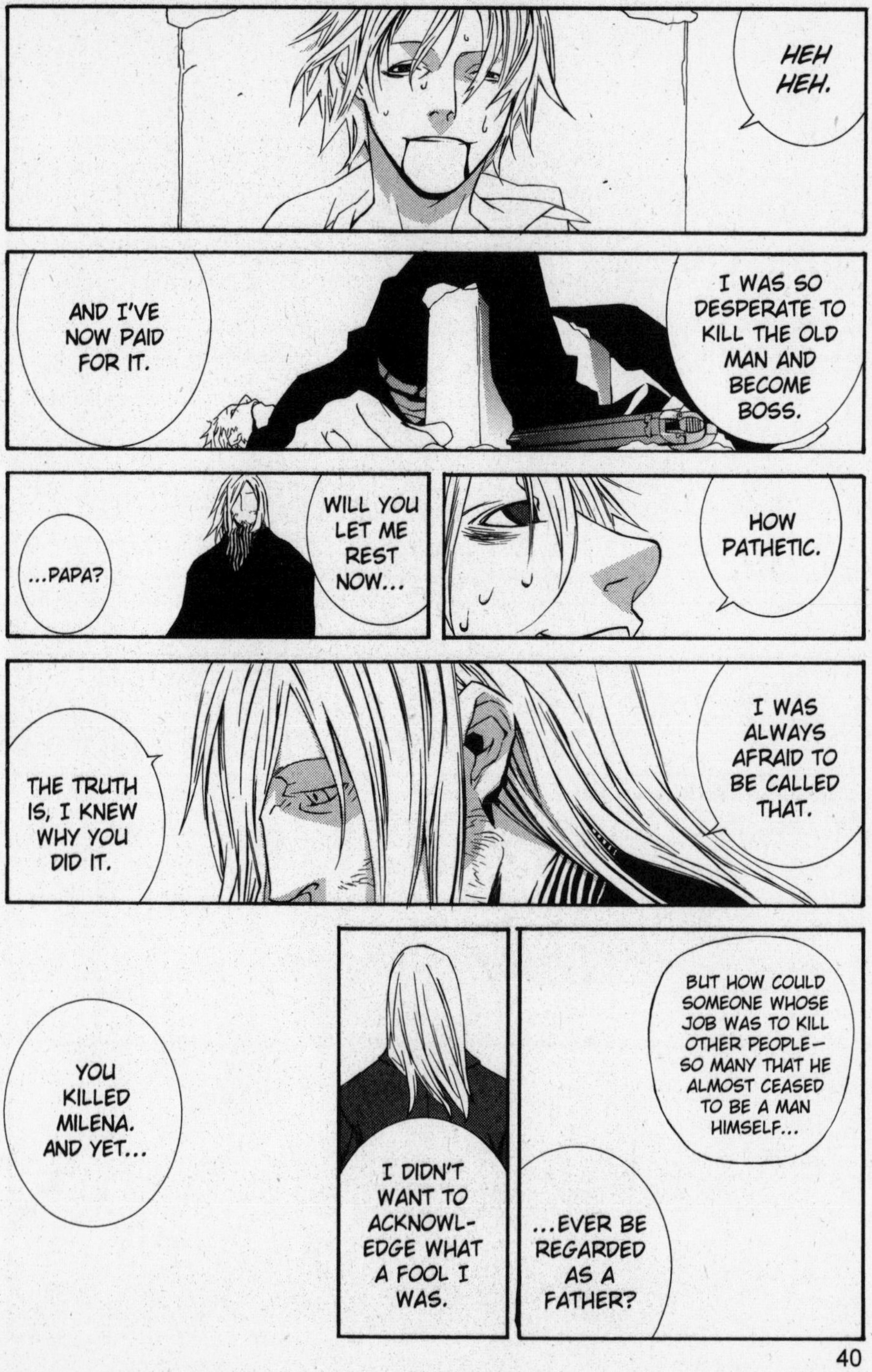
HEH HEH.
I WAS SO DESPERATE TO KILL THE OLD MAN AND BECOME BOSS.
AND I'VE NOW PAID FOR IT.
HOW PATHETIC.
WILL YOU LET ME REST NOW...
...PAPA?
I WAS ALWAYS AFRAID TO BE CALLED THAT.
THE TRUTH IS, I KNEW WHY YOU DID IT.
BUT HOW COULD SOMEONE WHOSE JOB WAS TO KILL OTHER PEOPLE— SO MANY THAT HE ALMOST CEASED TO BE A MAN HIMSELF...
...EVER BE REGARDED AS A FATHER?
YOU KILLED MILENA. AND YET...
I DIDN'T WANT TO ACKNOWL-EDGE WHAT A FOOL I WAS.

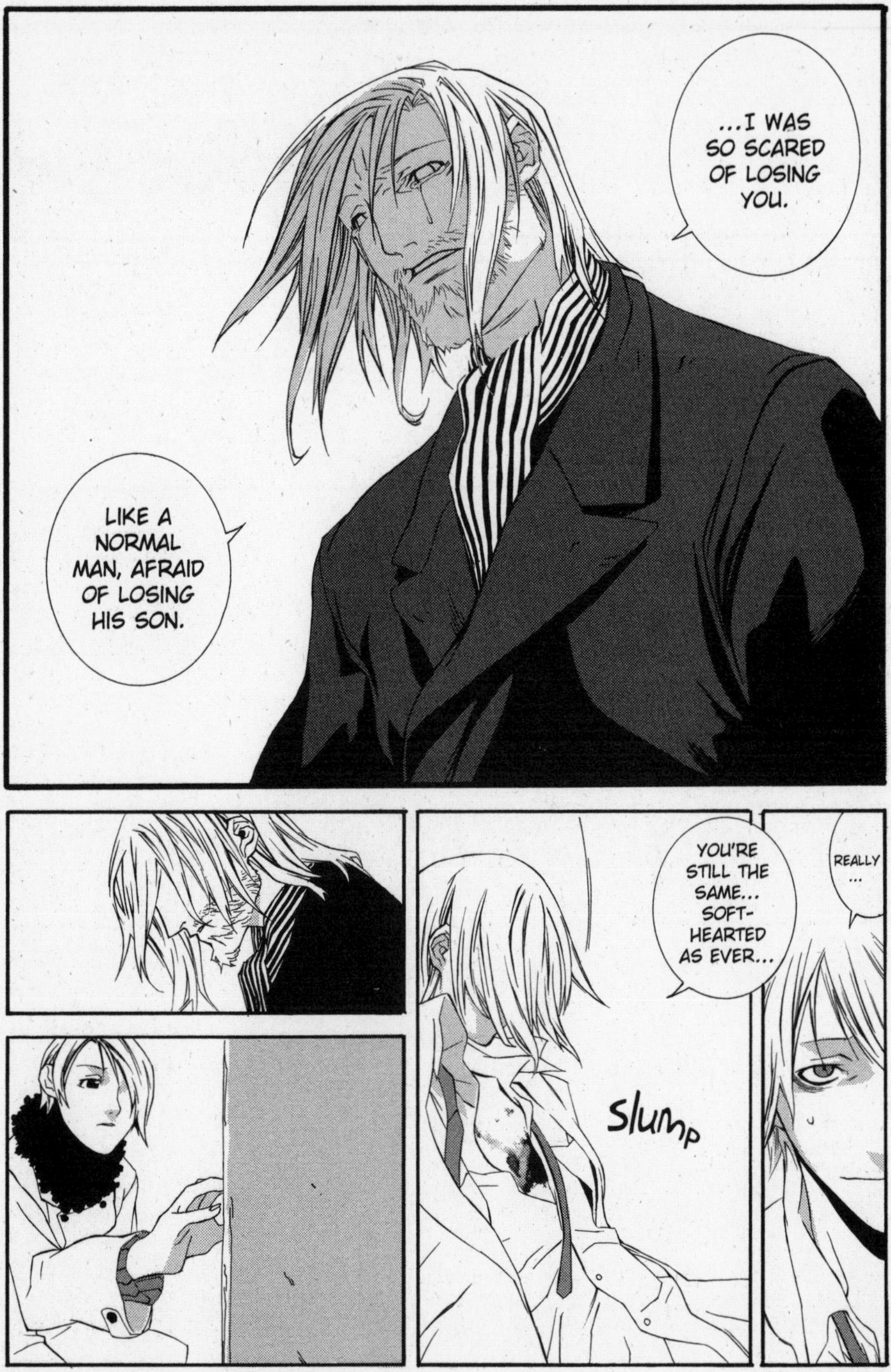
...I WAS SO SCARED OF LOSING YOU.
LIKE A NORMAL MAN, AFRAID OF LOSING HIS SON.
REALLY ...
YOU'RE STILL THE SAME... SOFT-HEARTED AS EVER...
Slump

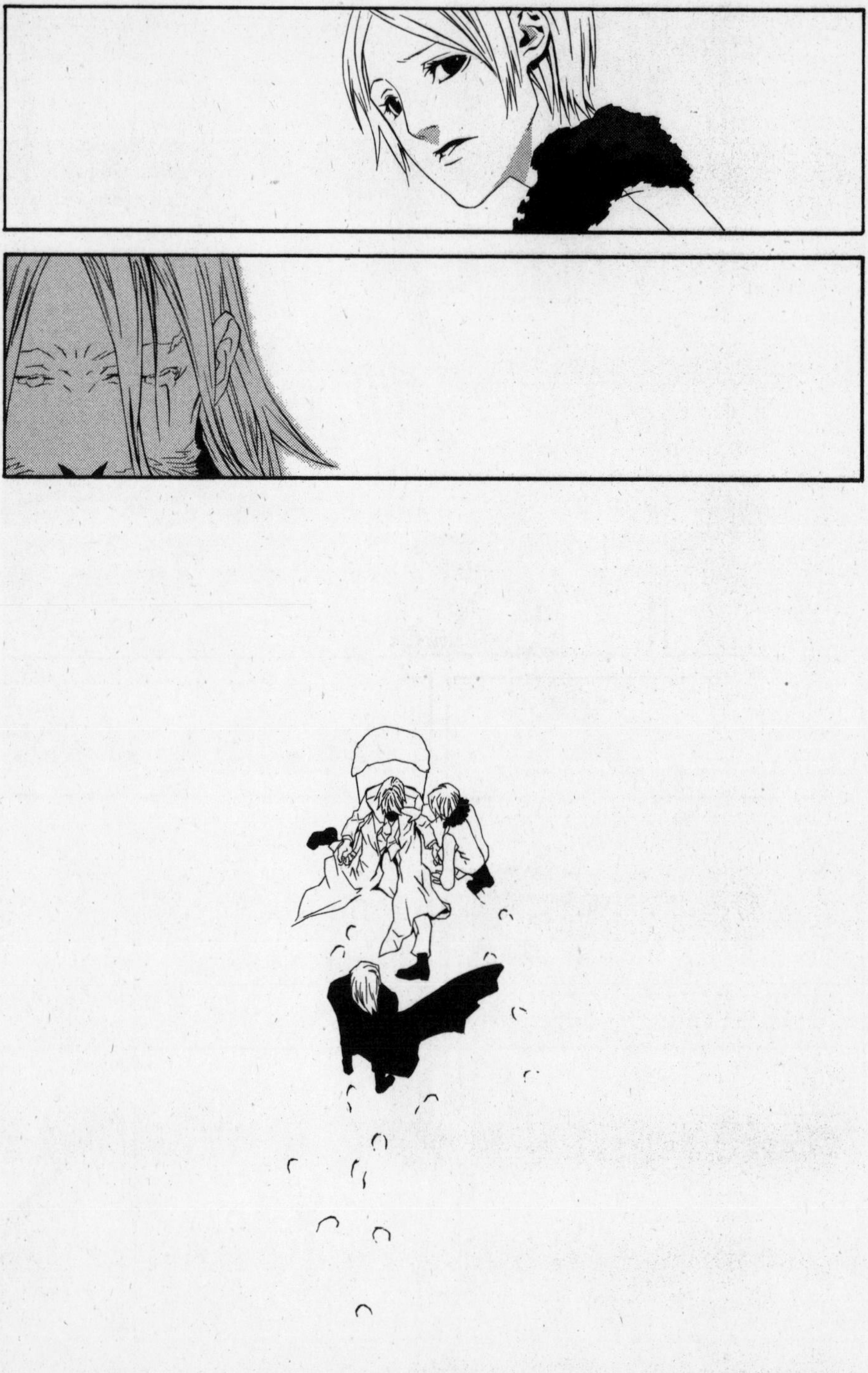

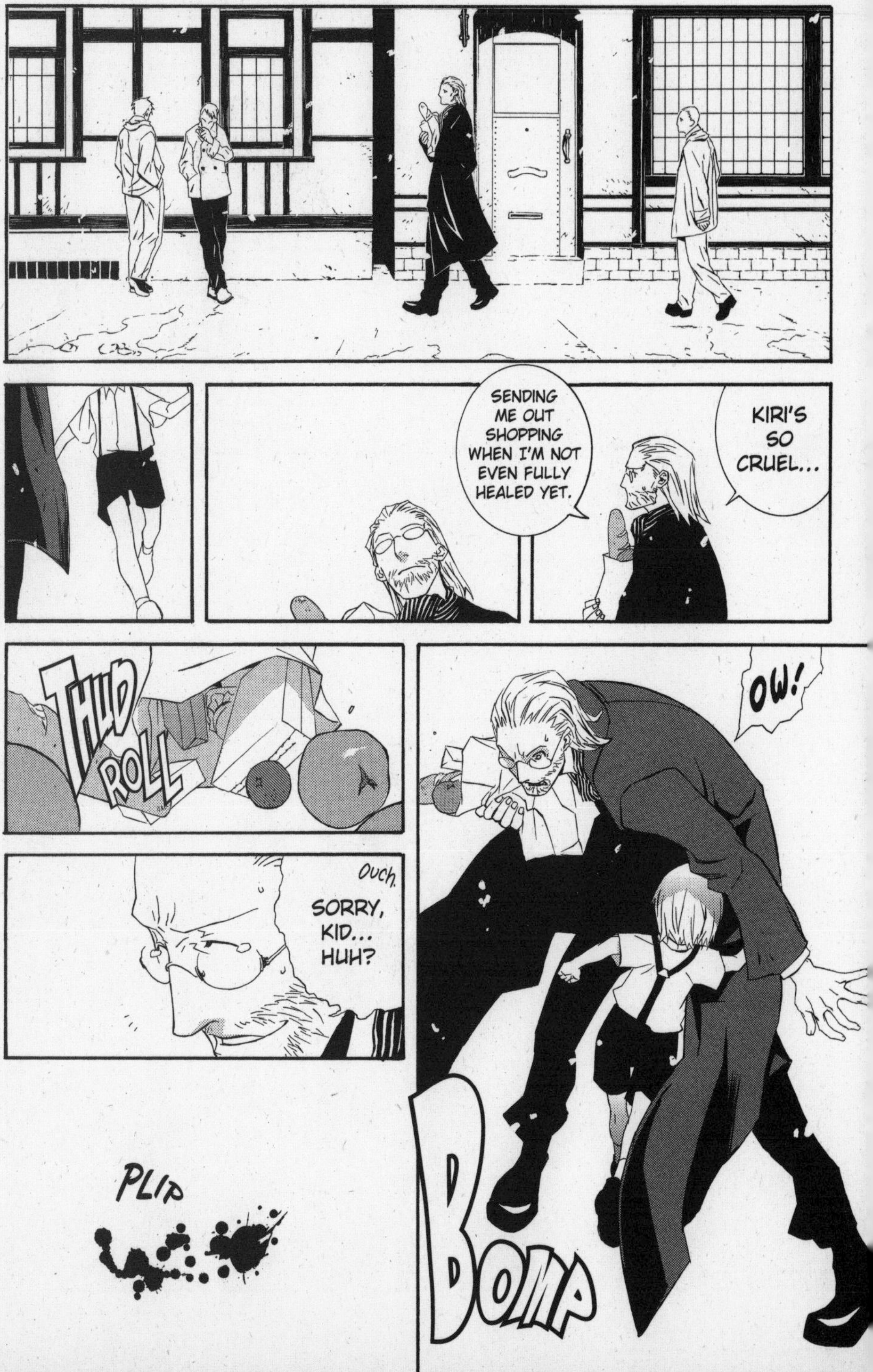
KIRI'S SO CRUEL...
SENDING ME OUT SHOPPING WHEN I'M NOT EVEN FULLY HEALED YET.
OW!
BOMP
THUD
ROLL
Ouch.
SORRY, KID... HUH?
PLIP

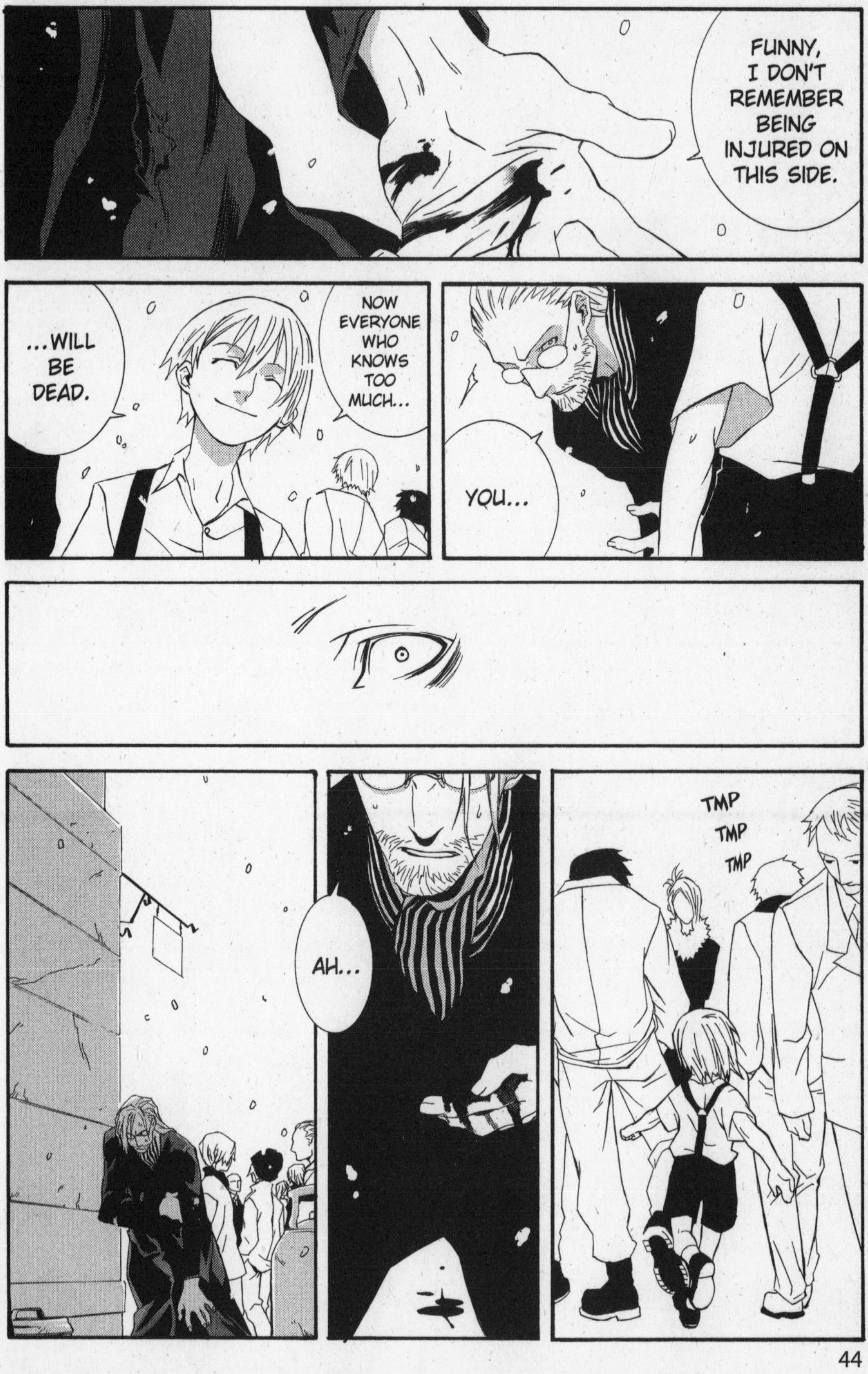
FUNNY, I DON'T REMEMBER BEING INJURED ON THIS SIDE.
YOU...
NOW EVERYONE WHO KNOWS TOO MUCH...
...WILL BE DEAD.
TMP TMP TMP
AH...

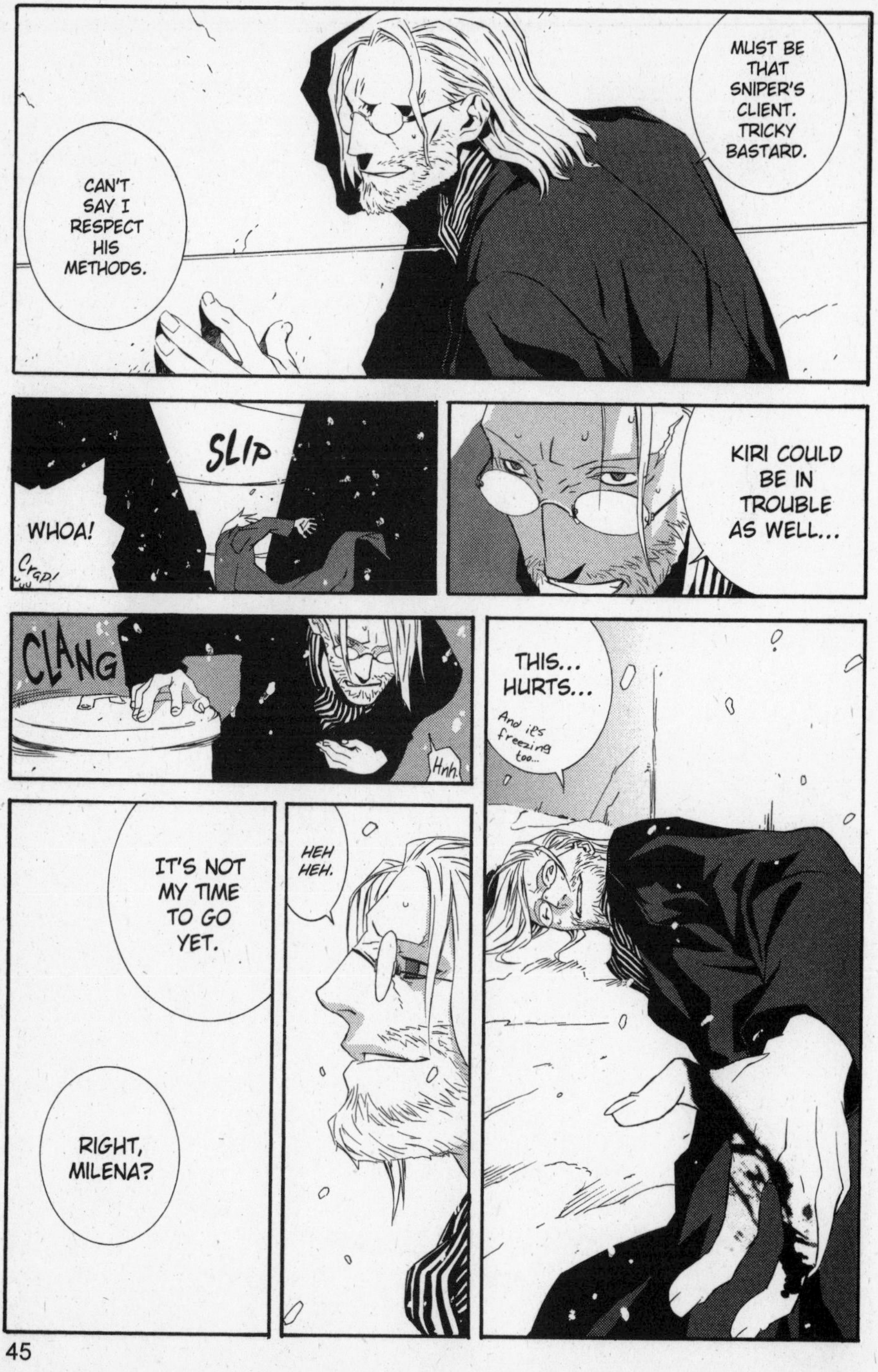
MUST BE THAT SNIPER'S CLIENT. TRICKY BASTARD.
CAN'T SAY I RESPECT HIS METHODS.
KIRI COULD BE IN TROUBLE AS WELL...
SLIP
WHOA!
Crap!
THIS... HURTS...
And it's freezing too...
CLANG
Hnh.
HEH HEH.
IT'S NOT MY TIME TO GO YET.
RIGHT, MILENA?

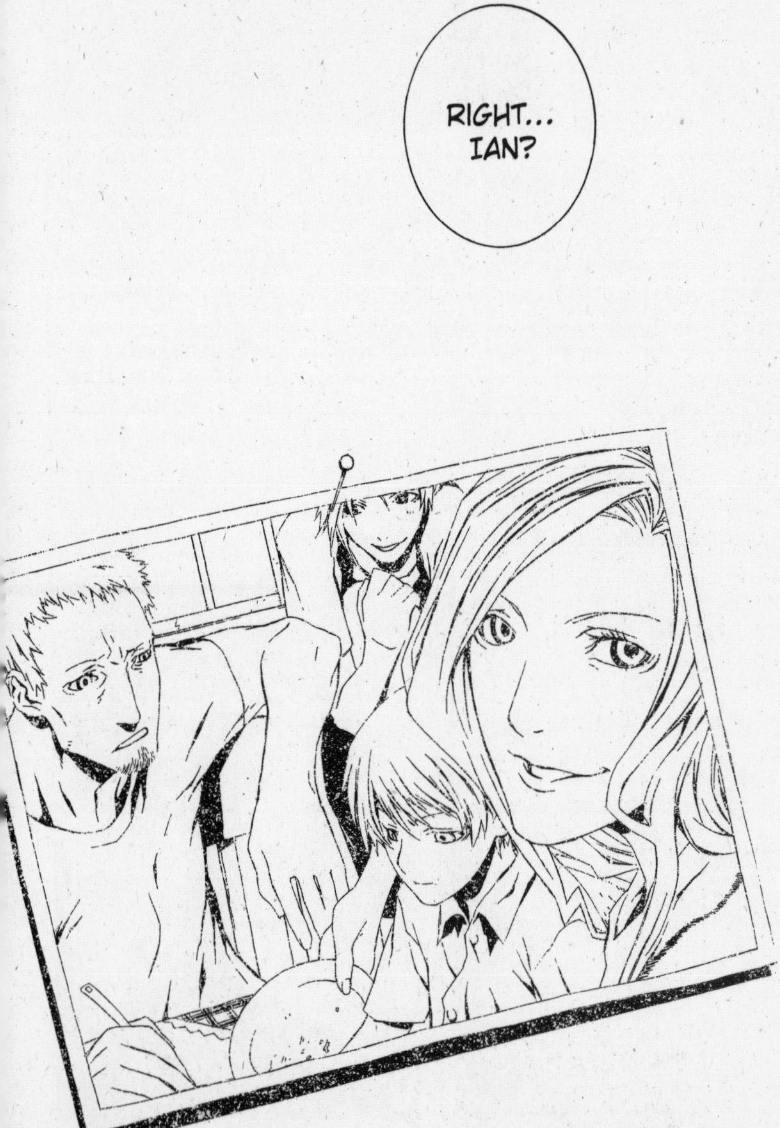
RIGHT... IAN?

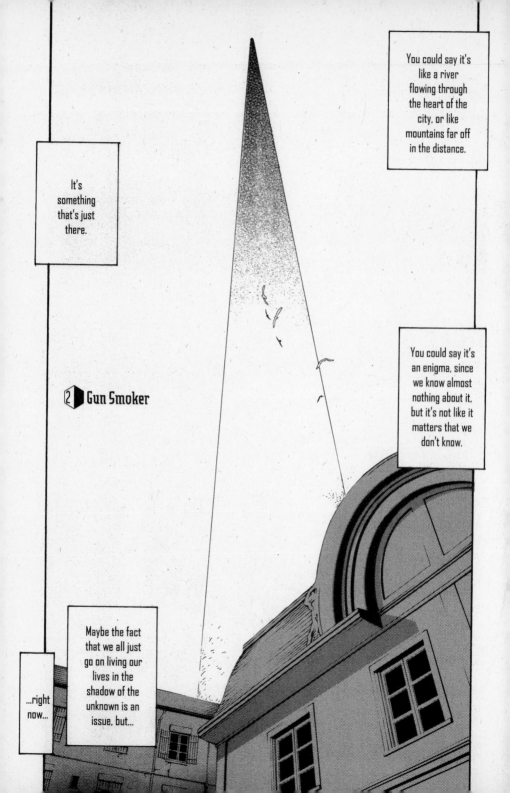

You could say it's like a river flowing through the heart of the city, or like mountains far off in the distance.

It's something that's just there.

② Gun Smoker

You could say it's an enigma, since we know almost nothing about it, but it's not like it matters that we don't know.

Maybe the fact that we all just go on living our lives in the shadow of the unknown is an issue, but...

...right now...

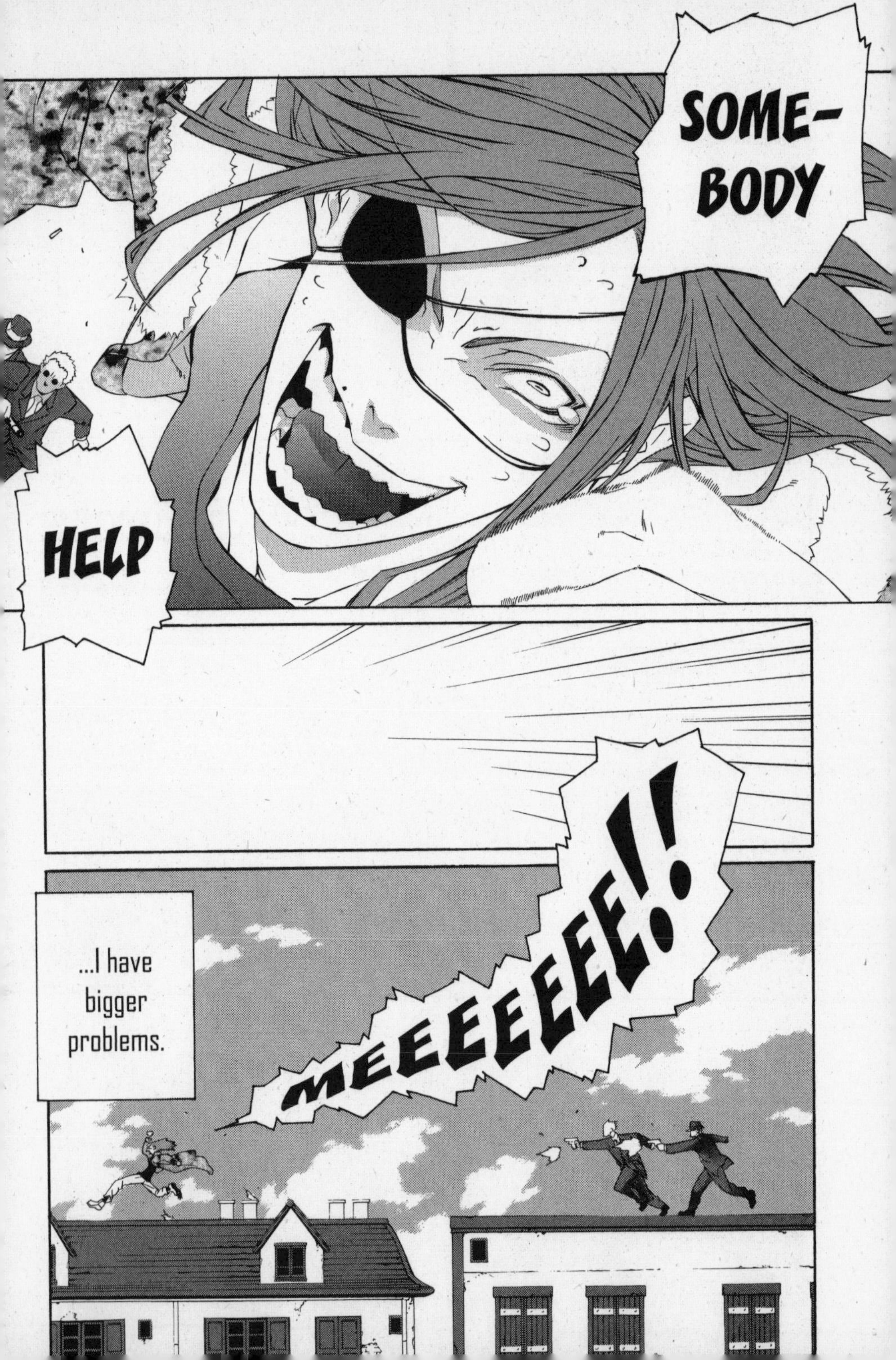
SOME-BODY
HELP
MEEEEEEEE!!
...I have bigger problems.

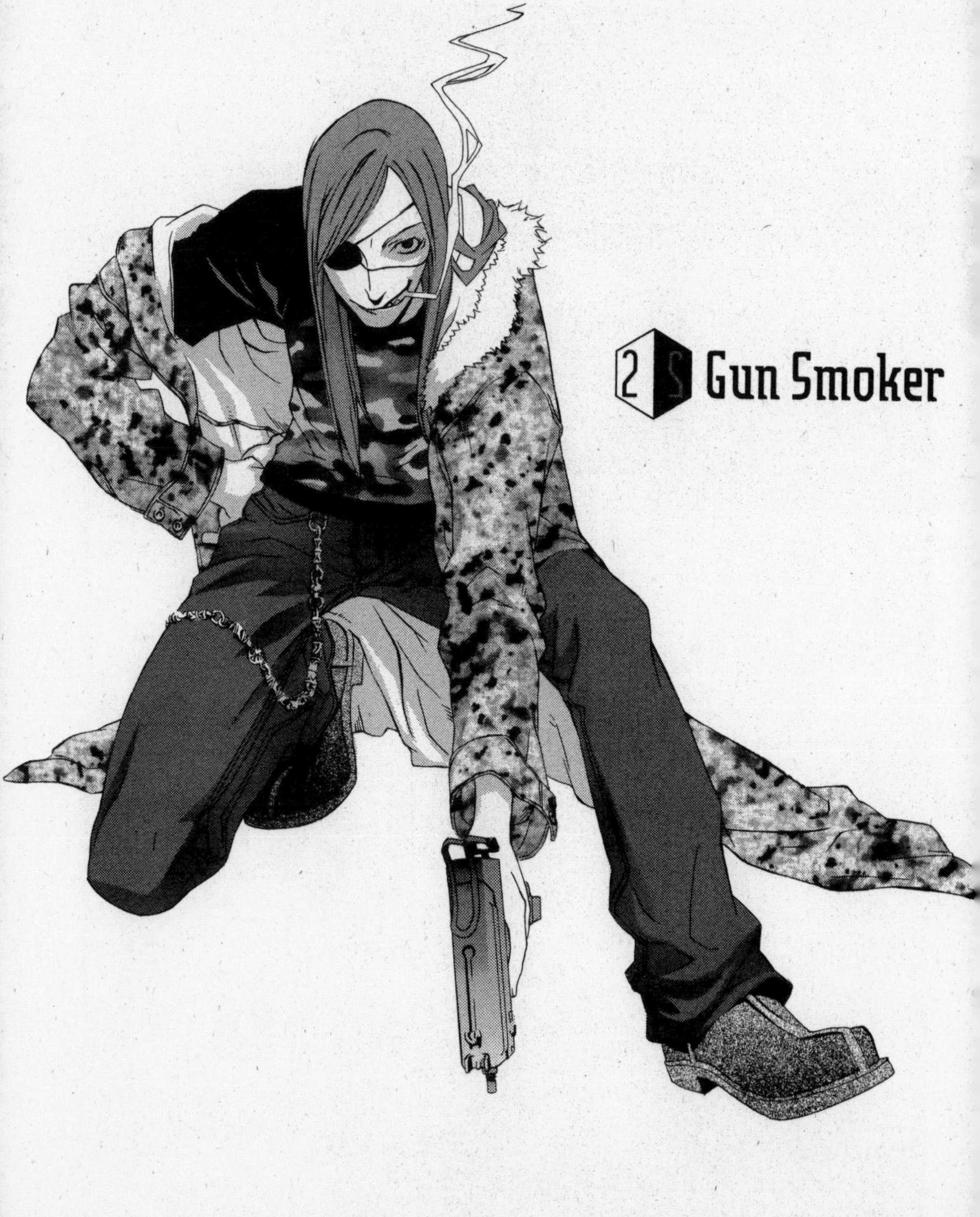

2 Gun Smoker

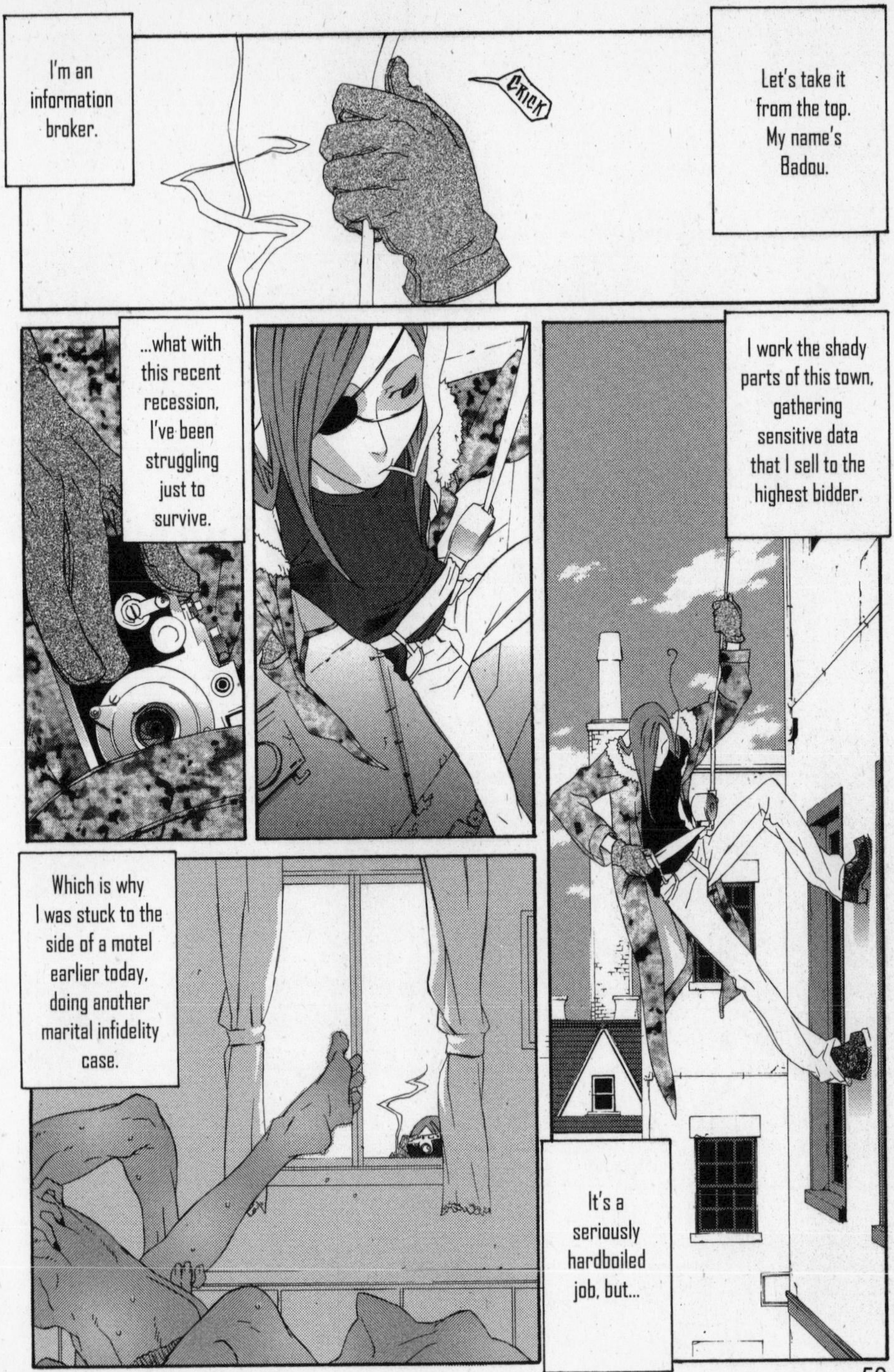
Let's take it from the top. My name's Badou.
CRICK
I'm an information broker.
I work the shady parts of this town, gathering sensitive data that I sell to the highest bidder.
It's a seriously hardboiled job, but...
...what with this recent recession, I've been struggling just to survive.
Which is why I was stuck to the side of a motel earlier today, doing another marital infidelity case.

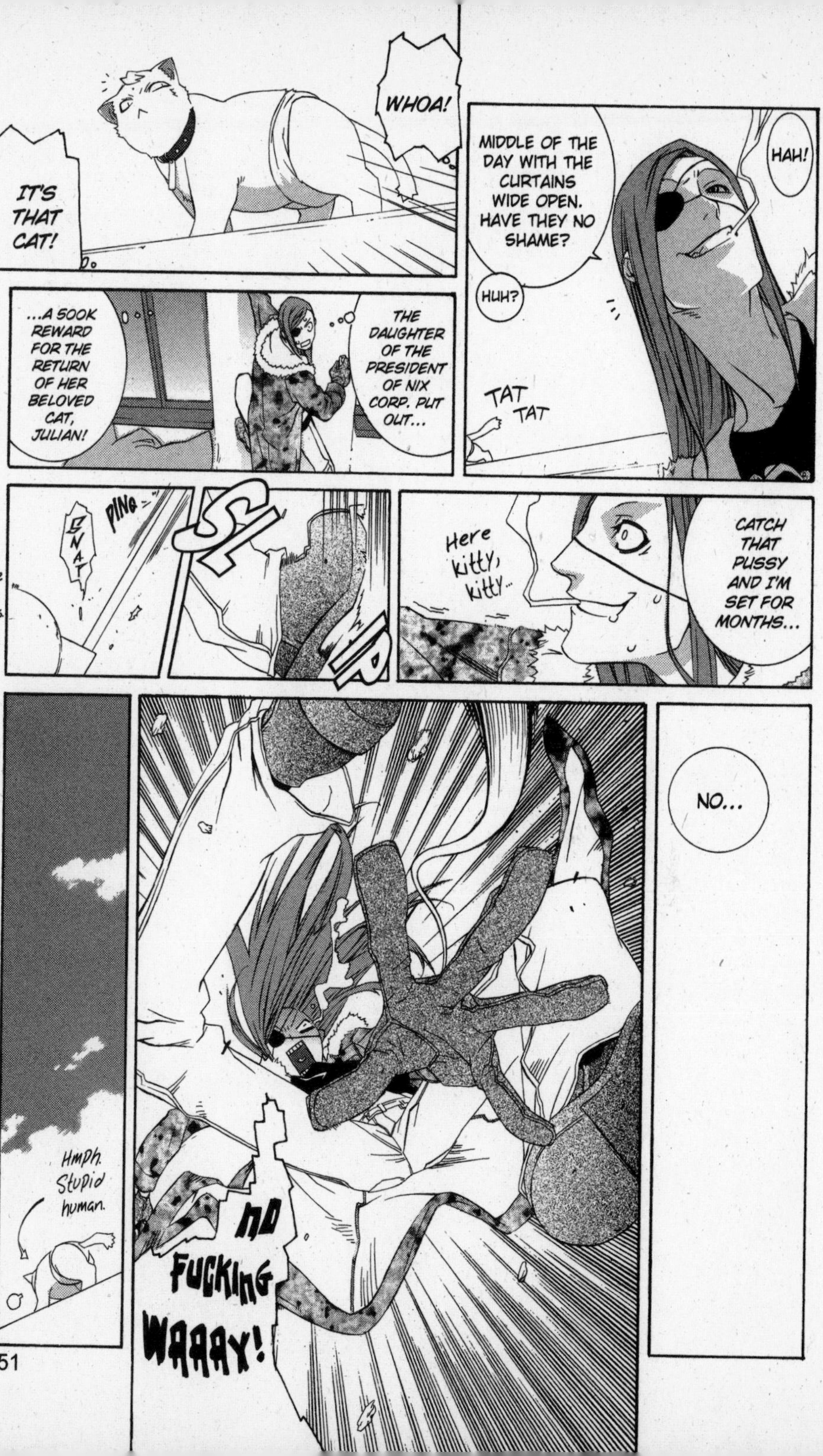

HAH!
MIDDLE OF THE DAY WITH THE CURTAINS WIDE OPEN. HAVE THEY NO SHAME?
HUH?
TAT TAT
WHOA!
IT'S THAT CAT!
THE DAUGHTER OF THE PRESIDENT OF NIX CORP. PUT OUT...
...A 500K REWARD FOR THE RETURN OF HER BELOVED CAT, JULIAN!
CATCH THAT PUSSY AND I'M SET FOR MONTHS...
Here kitty, kitty...
SLIP
PING
SNAT
Broke his harness.
NO...
NO FUCKING WAAAY!
Hmph. Stupid human.

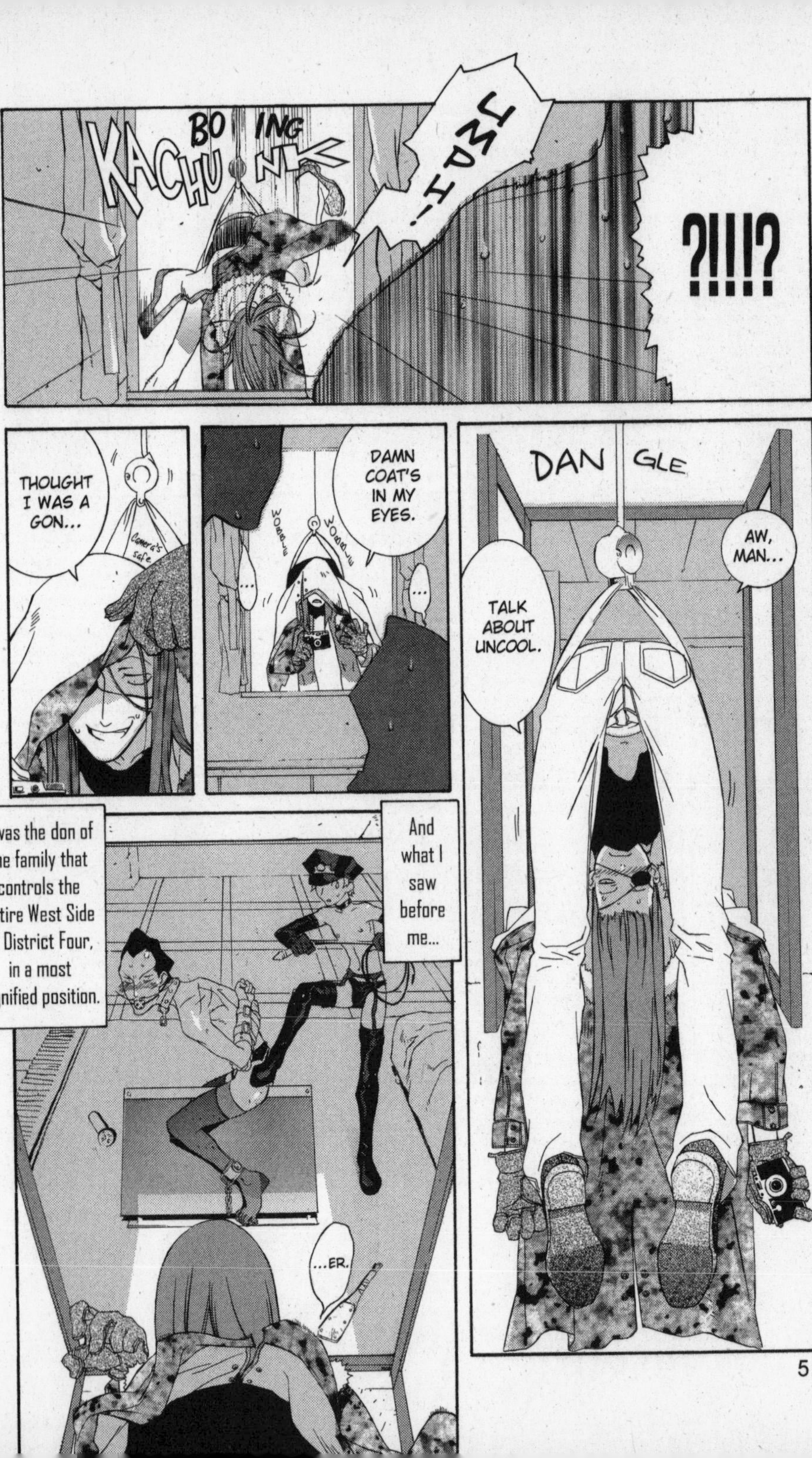
?!!!?
UMPH!
BOING
KACHUNK
DAN GLE
AW, MAN...
TALK ABOUT UNCOOL.
DAMN COAT'S IN MY EYES.
WOBBLE WOBBLE
...
...
THOUGHT I WAS A GON...
Camera's safe.
And what I saw before me...
...was the don of the family that controls the entire West Side of District Four, in a most dignified position.
...ER.

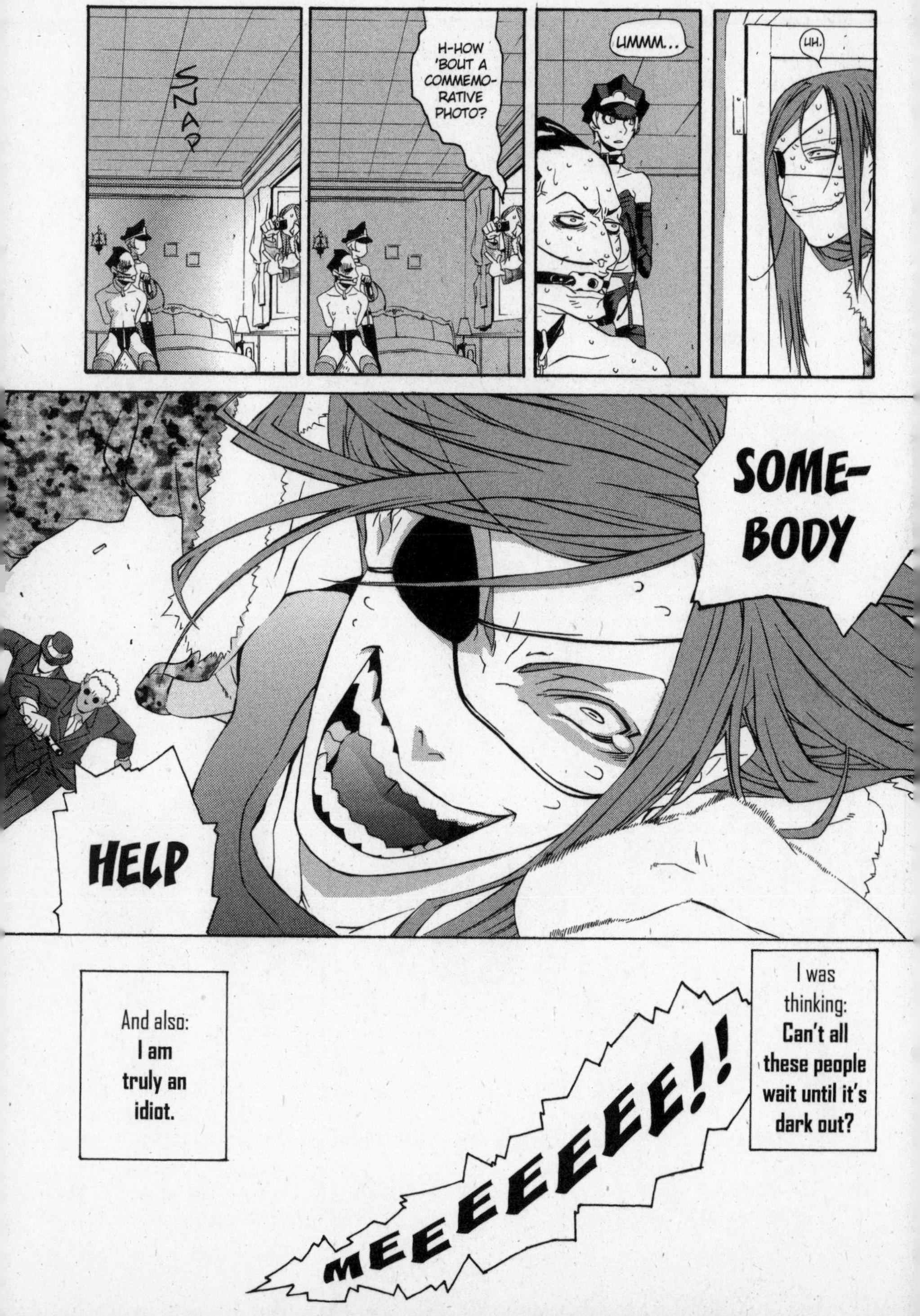
UH.
UMMM...
H-HOW 'BOUT A COMMEMO-RATIVE PHOTO?
SNAP
SOME-BODY
HELP
I was thinking: Can't all these people wait until it's dark out?
MEEEEEEEE!!
And also: I am truly an idiot.

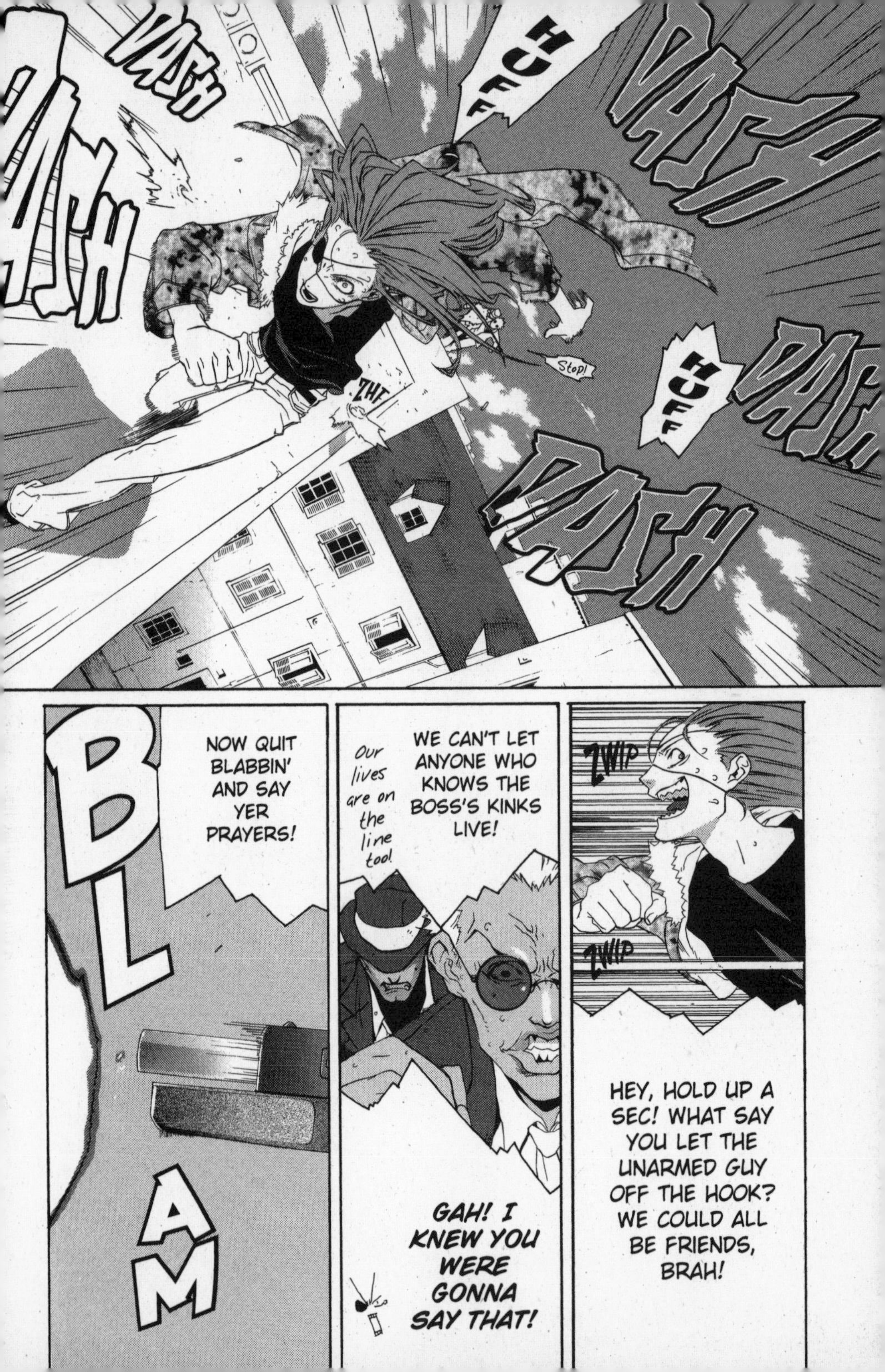
HUFF
HUFF
Stop!
DASH
ZWIP
ZWIP
HEY, HOLD UP A SEC! WHAT SAY YOU LET THE UNARMED GUY OFF THE HOOK? WE COULD ALL BE FRIENDS, BRAH!
WE CAN'T LET ANYONE WHO KNOWS THE BOSS'S KINKS LIVE!
Our lives are on the line too!
GAH! I KNEW YOU WERE GONNA SAY THAT!
NOW QUIT BLABBIN' AND SAY YER PRAYERS!
BLAM

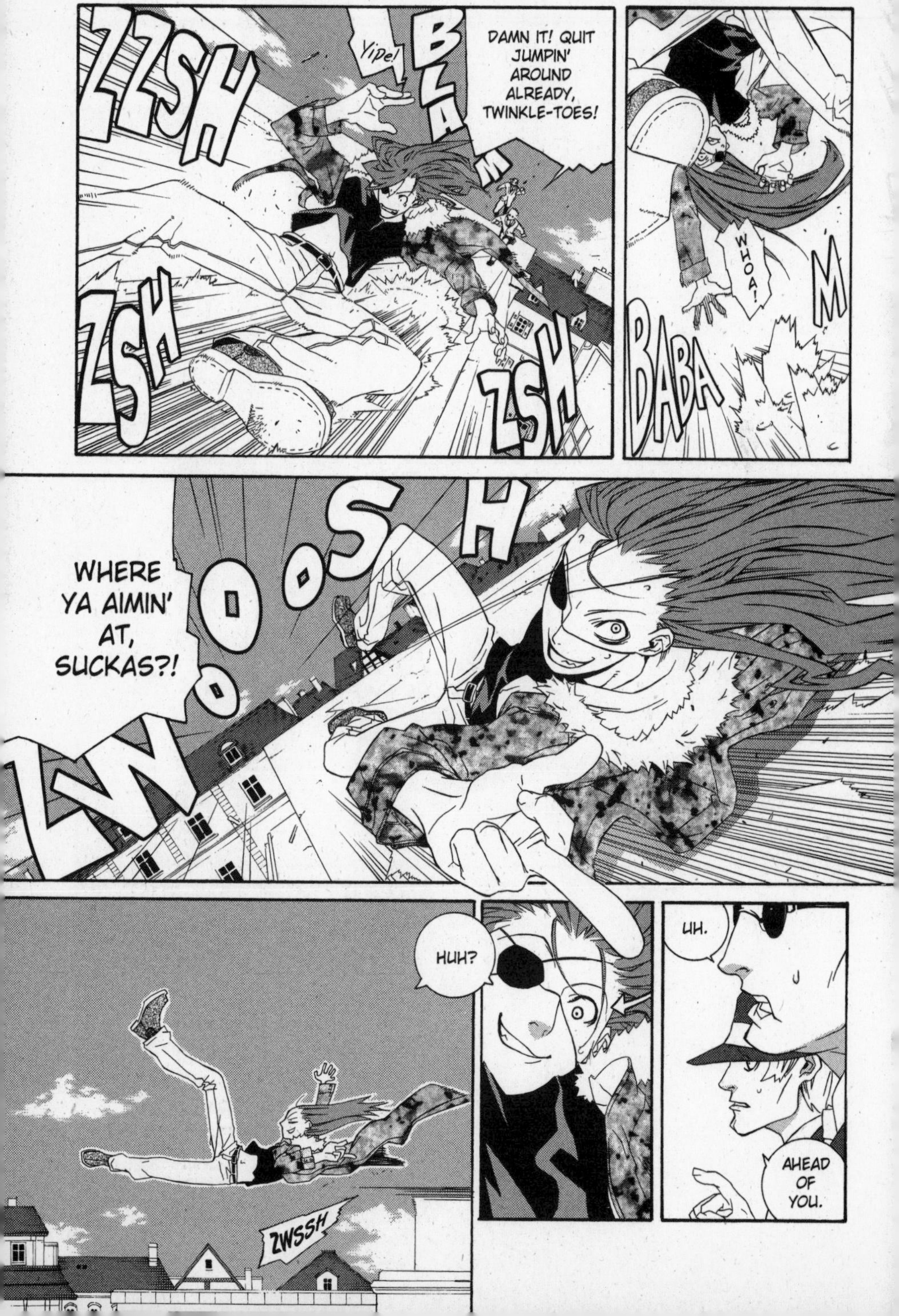
WHOA!
BABAM
DAMN IT! QUIT JUMPIN' AROUND ALREADY, TWINKLE-TOES!
BLAM
Yipe!
ZZSH
ZSH
ZSH
WHOOSH
WHERE YA AIMIN' AT, SUCKAS?!
UH.
AHEAD OF YOU.
HUH?
ZWSSH

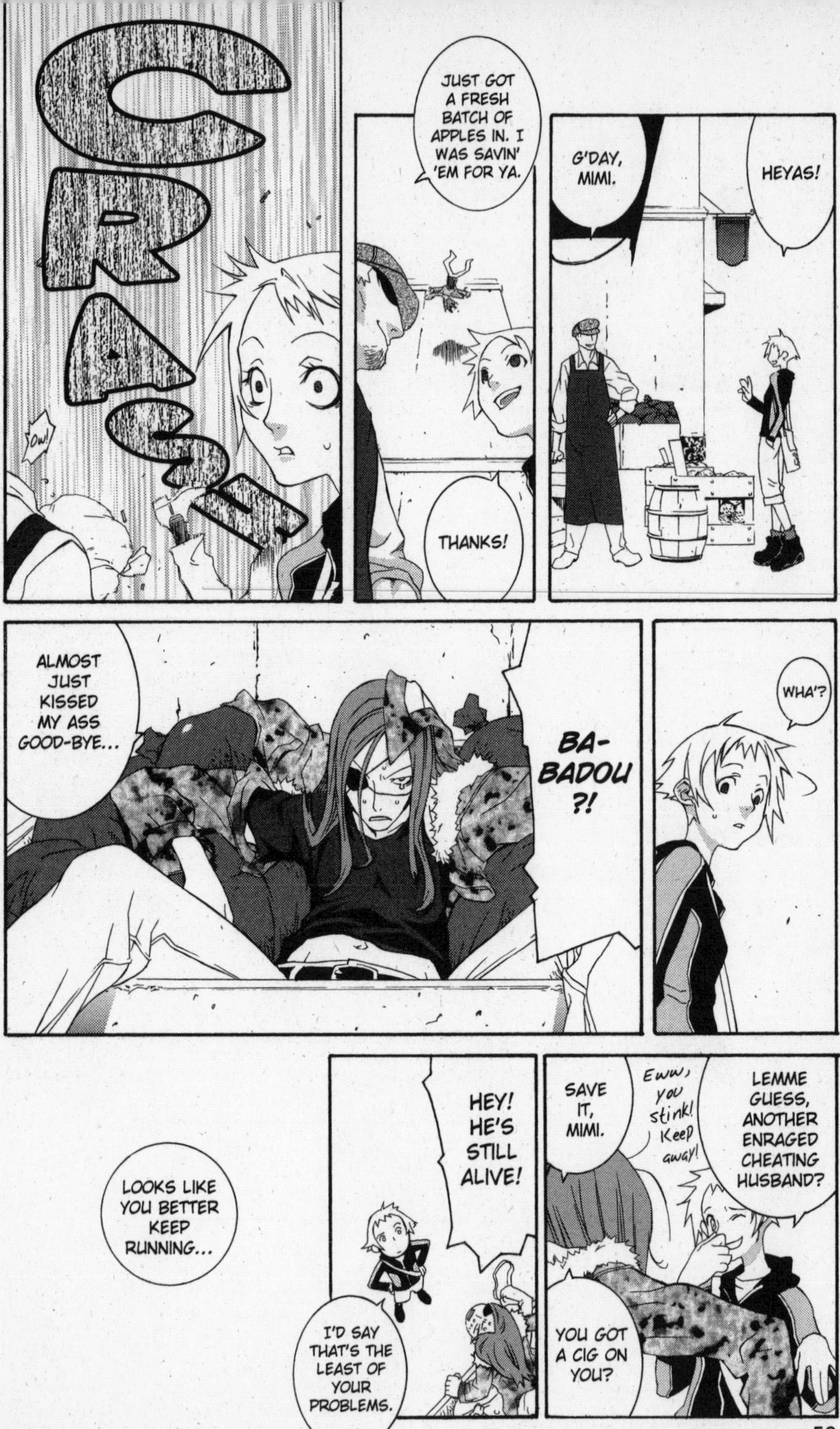
HEYAS!
G'DAY, MIMI.
JUST GOT A FRESH BATCH OF APPLES IN. I WAS SAVIN' 'EM FOR YA.
THANKS!
CRASH
Ow!
WHA'?
BA-BADOU?!
ALMOST JUST KISSED MY ASS GOOD-BYE...
LEMME GUESS, ANOTHER ENRAGED CHEATING HUSBAND?
Eww, you stink! Keep away!
SAVE IT, MIMI.
YOU GOT A CIG ON YOU?
HEY! HE'S STILL ALIVE!
I'D SAY THAT'S THE LEAST OF YOUR PROBLEMS.
LOOKS LIKE YOU BETTER KEEP RUNNING...

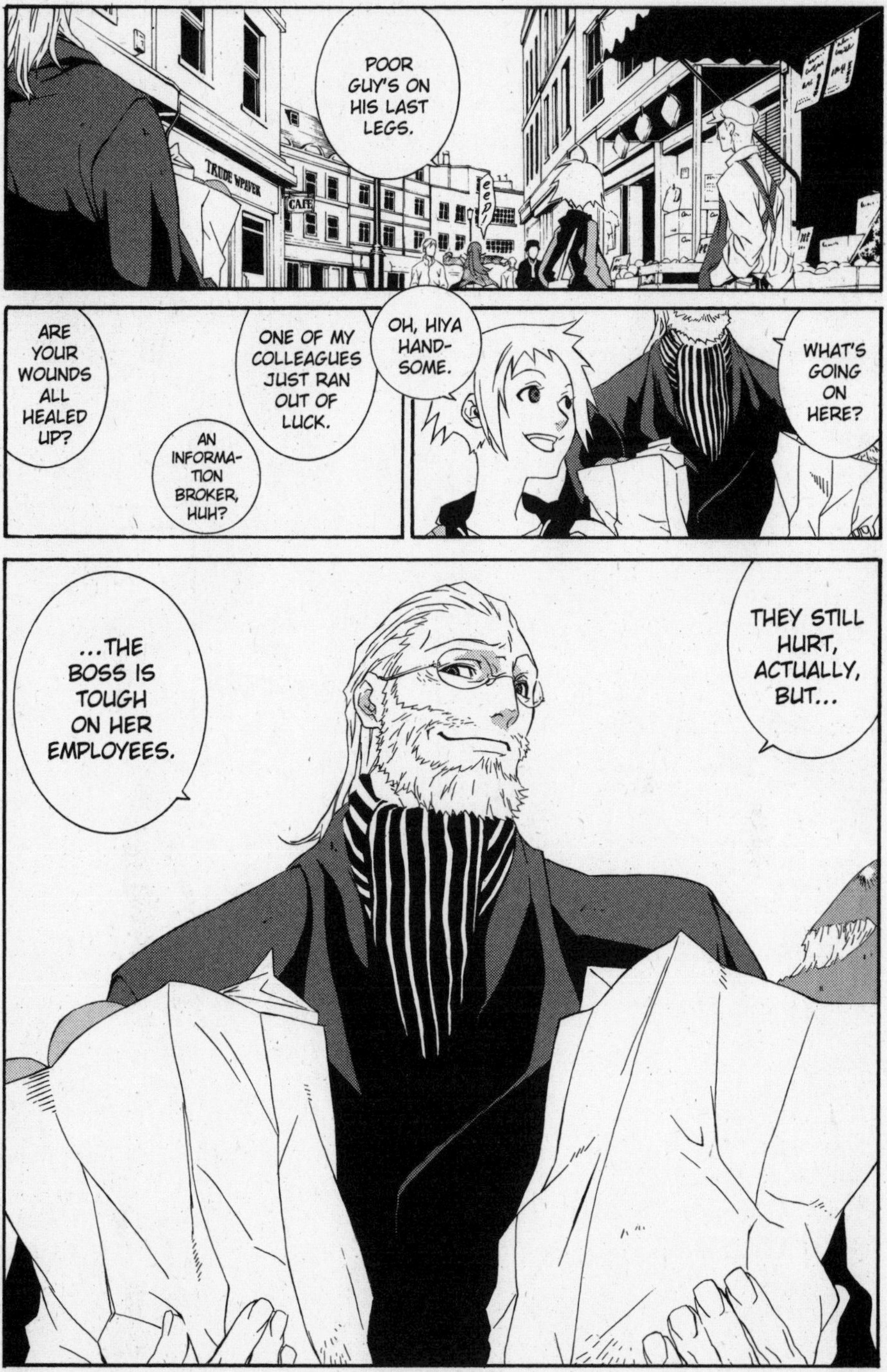
POOR GUY'S ON HIS LAST LEGS.
eep!
CAFE
WHAT'S GOING ON HERE?
OH, HIYA HAND-SOME.
ONE OF MY COLLEAGUES JUST RAN OUT OF LUCK.
AN INFORMATION BROKER, HUH?
ARE YOUR WOUNDS ALL HEALED UP?
THEY STILL HURT, ACTUALLY, BUT...
...THE BOSS IS TOUGH ON HER EMPLOYEES.

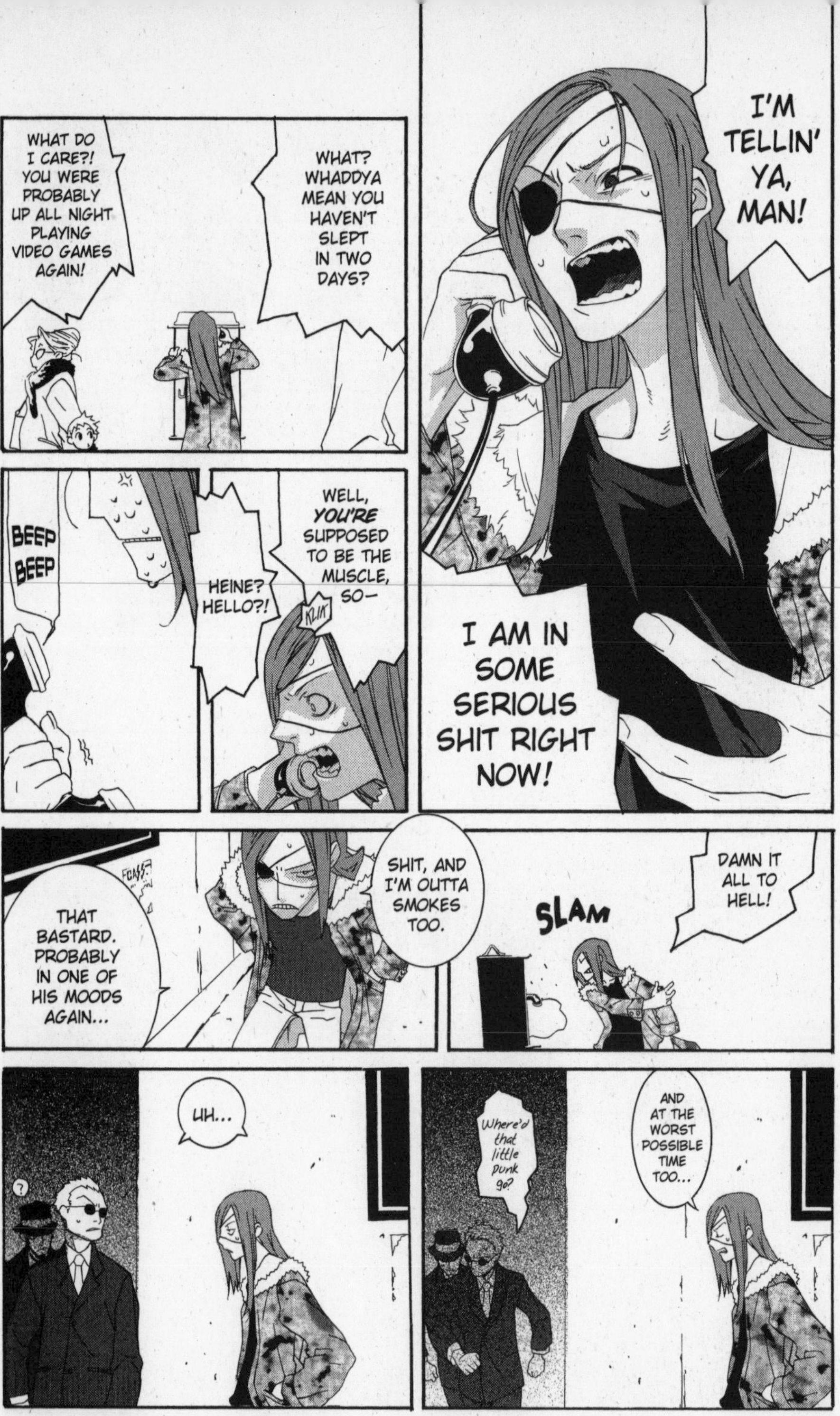
I'M TELLIN' YA, MAN!
I AM IN SOME SERIOUS SHIT RIGHT NOW!
WHAT? WHADDYA MEAN YOU HAVEN'T SLEPT IN TWO DAYS?
WHAT DO I CARE?! YOU WERE PROBABLY UP ALL NIGHT PLAYING VIDEO GAMES AGAIN!
WELL, *YOU'RE* SUPPOSED TO BE THE MUSCLE, SO—
KLIK
HEINE? HELLO?!
BEEP BEEP
DAMN IT ALL TO HELL!
SLAM
SHIT, AND I'M OUTTA SMOKES TOO.
THAT BASTARD. PROBABLY IN ONE OF HIS MOODS AGAIN...
AND AT THE WORST POSSIBLE TIME TOO...
Where'd that little punk go?
UH...

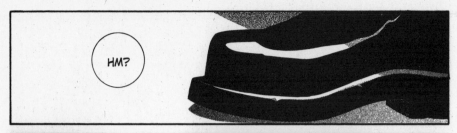

HM?

THAT'S ODD. SHOULD I HAVE GONE RIGHT AT THAT LAST CORNER?

SLAM

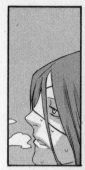

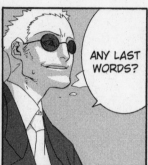

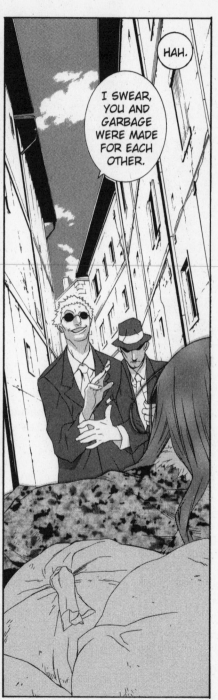

HAH.
I SWEAR, YOU AND GARBAGE WERE MADE FOR EACH OTHER.
ANY LAST WORDS?
GOT A FAG ON YOU?
SORRY, I'M ALL OUT.
HM. NOW...
...I HAVE NO IDEA WHERE I AM...
KLAK
KLAK
RIGHT. TIME TO SAY SAYONARA.
KACHAK

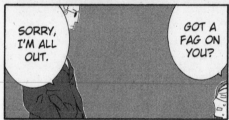

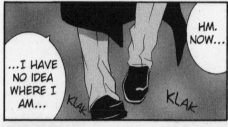

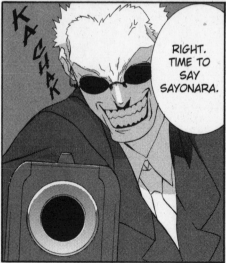

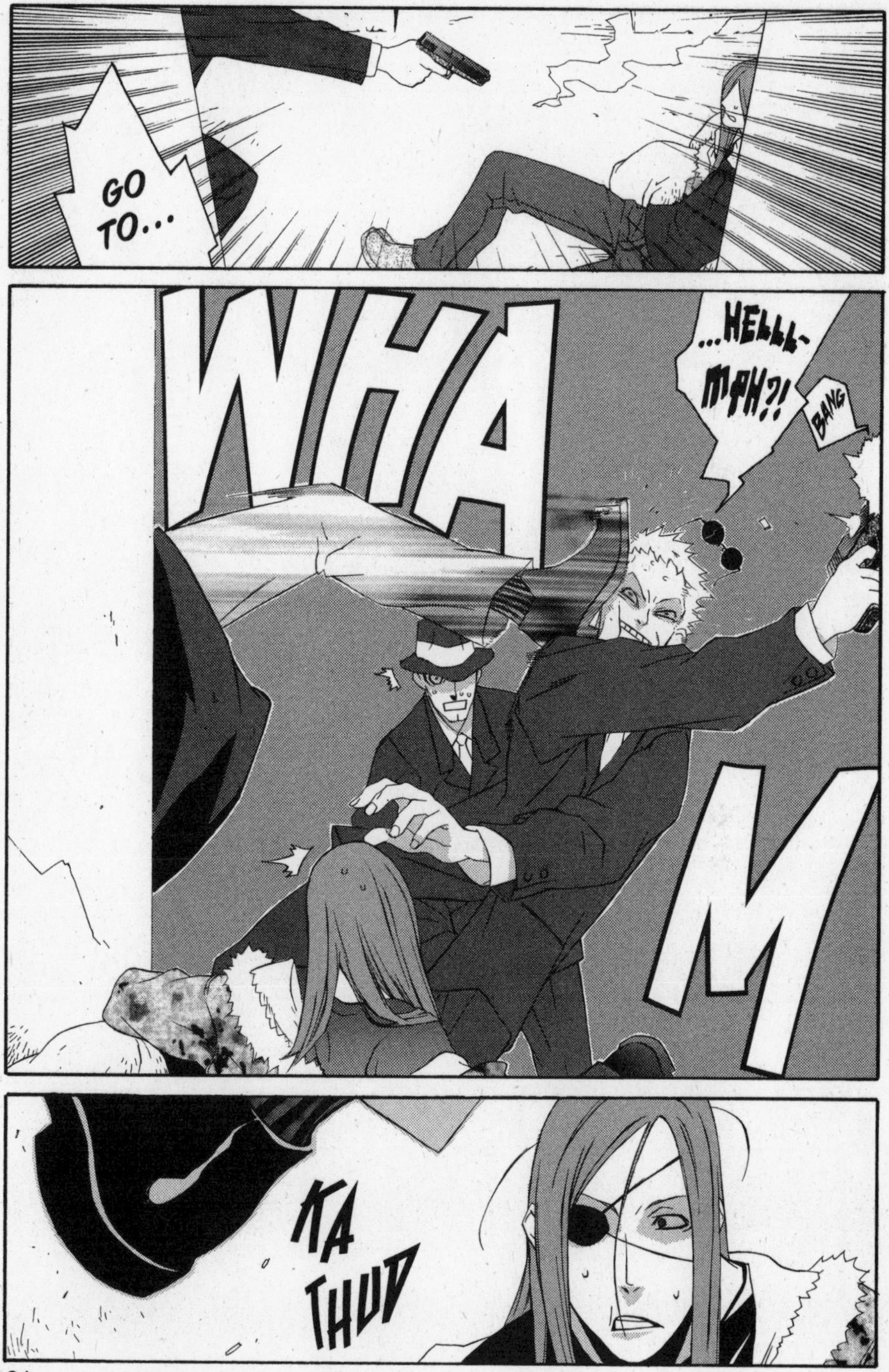
GO TO...
...HELLL-MPH?!
BANG
WHAM
KA THUD

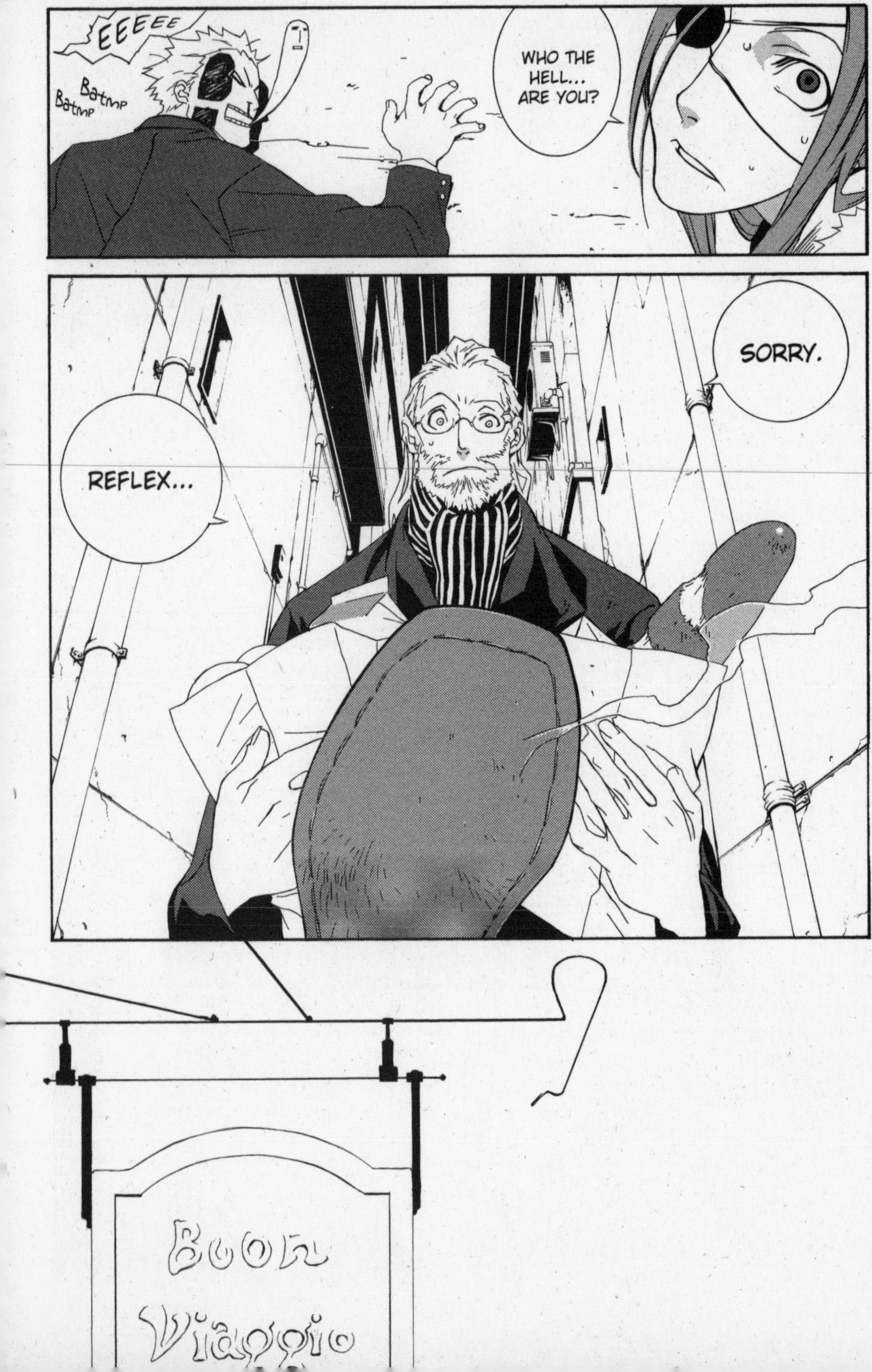
WHO THE HELL... ARE YOU?
EEEEE
Batmp Batmp
SORRY.
REFLEX...
Buon Viaggio

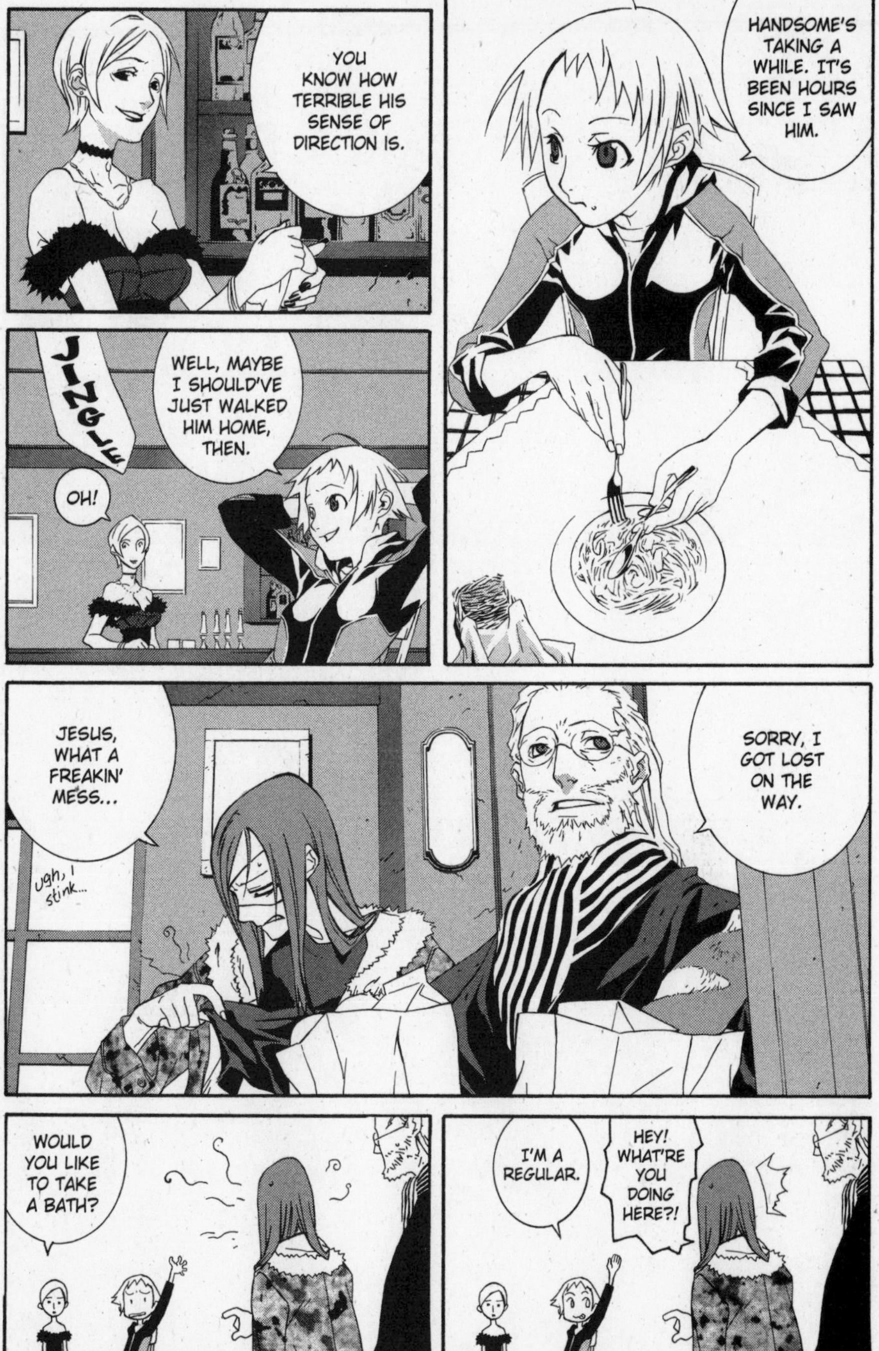
HANDSOME'S TAKING A WHILE. IT'S BEEN HOURS SINCE I SAW HIM.
YOU KNOW HOW TERRIBLE HIS SENSE OF DIRECTION IS.
WELL, MAYBE I SHOULD'VE JUST WALKED HIM HOME, THEN.
JINGLE
OH!
SORRY, I GOT LOST ON THE WAY.
JESUS, WHAT A FREAKIN' MESS...
ugh, I stink...
HEY! WHAT'RE YOU DOING HERE?!
I'M A REGULAR.
WOULD YOU LIKE TO TAKE A BATH?

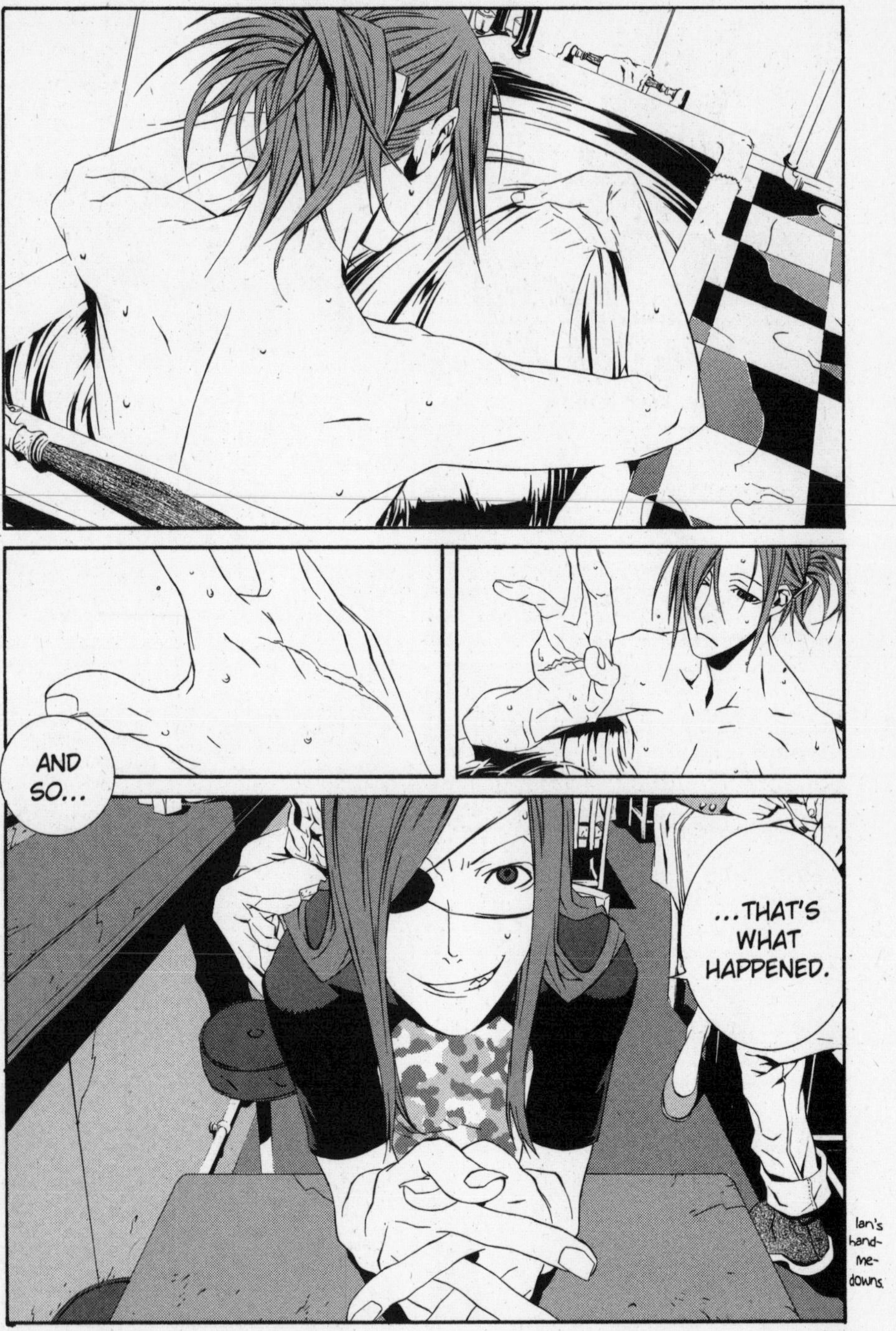
AND SO...
...THAT'S WHAT HAPPENED.
Ian's hand-me-downs.

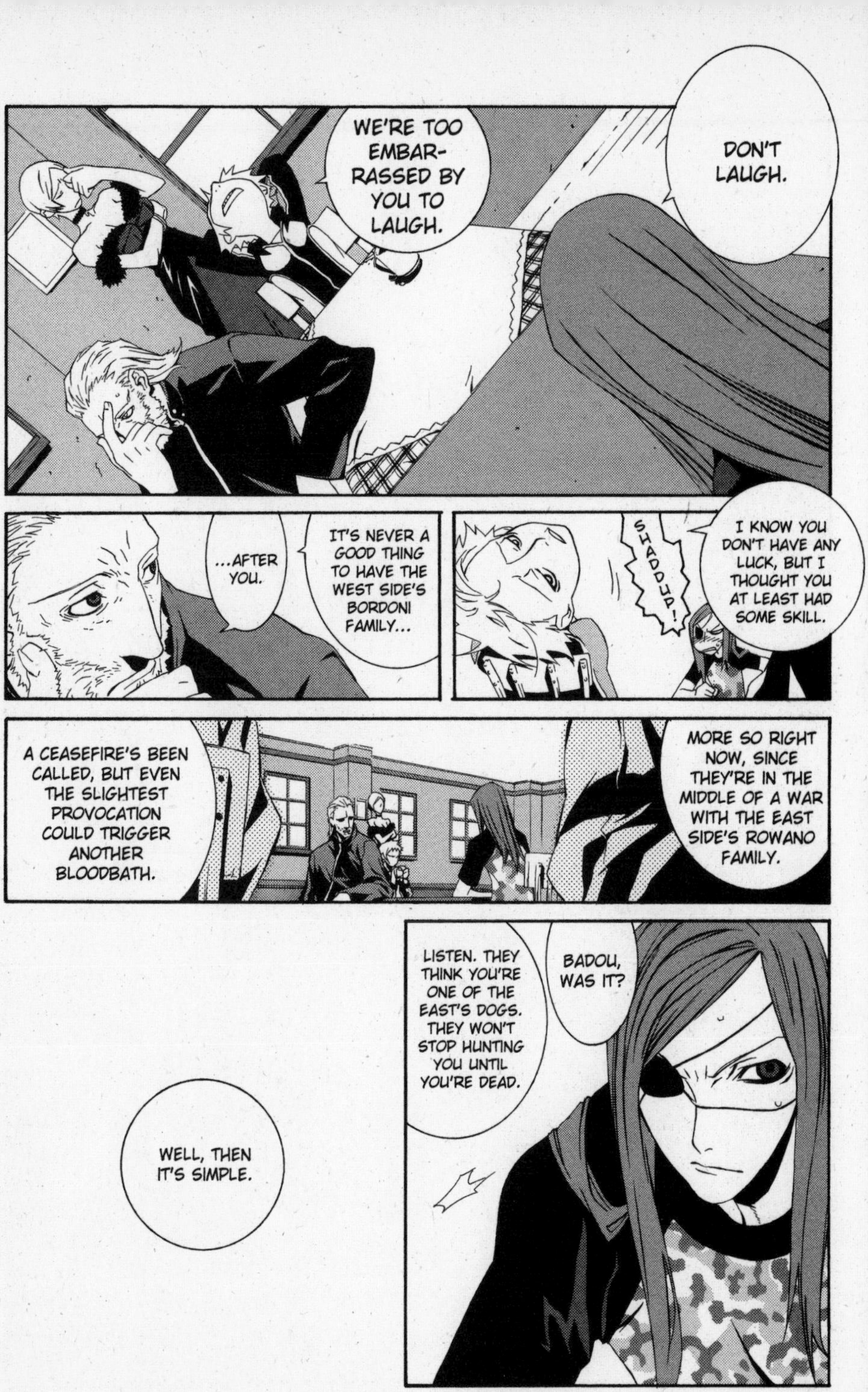
DON'T LAUGH.
WE'RE TOO EMBAR-RASSED BY YOU TO LAUGH.
I KNOW YOU DON'T HAVE ANY LUCK, BUT I THOUGHT YOU AT LEAST HAD SOME SKILL.
SHADDUP!
IT'S NEVER A GOOD THING TO HAVE THE WEST SIDE'S BORDONI FAMILY...
...AFTER YOU.
MORE SO RIGHT NOW, SINCE THEY'RE IN THE MIDDLE OF A WAR WITH THE EAST SIDE'S ROWANO FAMILY.
A CEASEFIRE'S BEEN CALLED, BUT EVEN THE SLIGHTEST PROVOCATION COULD TRIGGER ANOTHER BLOODBATH.
BADOU, WAS IT?
LISTEN. THEY THINK YOU'RE ONE OF THE EAST'S DOGS. THEY WON'T STOP HUNTING YOU UNTIL YOU'RE DEAD.
WELL, THEN IT'S SIMPLE.

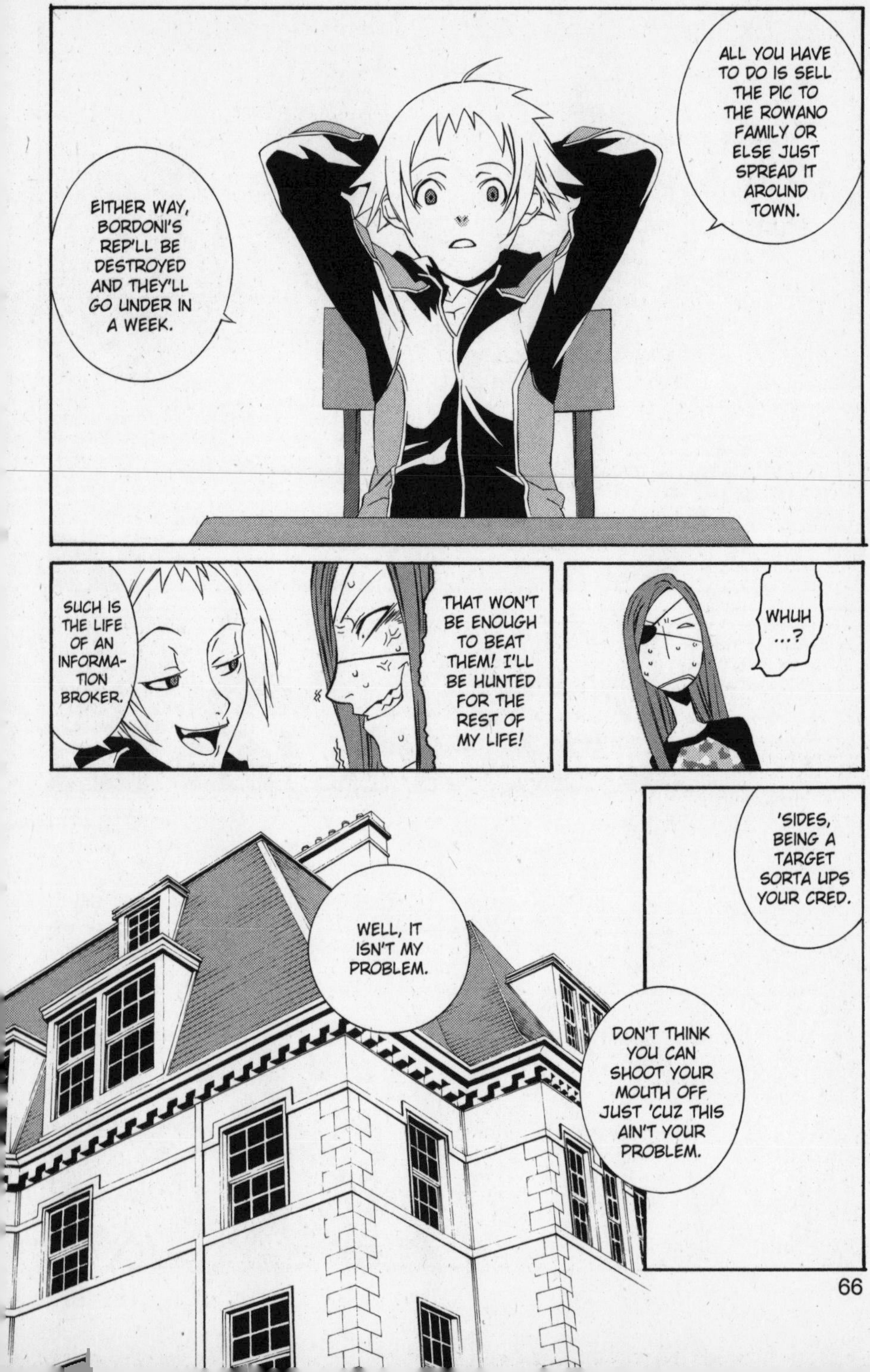
ALL YOU HAVE TO DO IS SELL THE PIC TO THE ROWANO FAMILY OR ELSE JUST SPREAD IT AROUND TOWN.
EITHER WAY, BORDONI'S REP'LL BE DESTROYED AND THEY'LL GO UNDER IN A WEEK.
WHUH ...?
THAT WON'T BE ENOUGH TO BEAT THEM! I'LL BE HUNTED FOR THE REST OF MY LIFE!
SUCH IS THE LIFE OF AN INFORMATION BROKER.
'SIDES, BEING A TARGET SORTA UPS YOUR CRED.
WELL, IT ISN'T MY PROBLEM.
DON'T THINK YOU CAN SHOOT YOUR MOUTH OFF JUST 'CUZ THIS AIN'T YOUR PROBLEM.

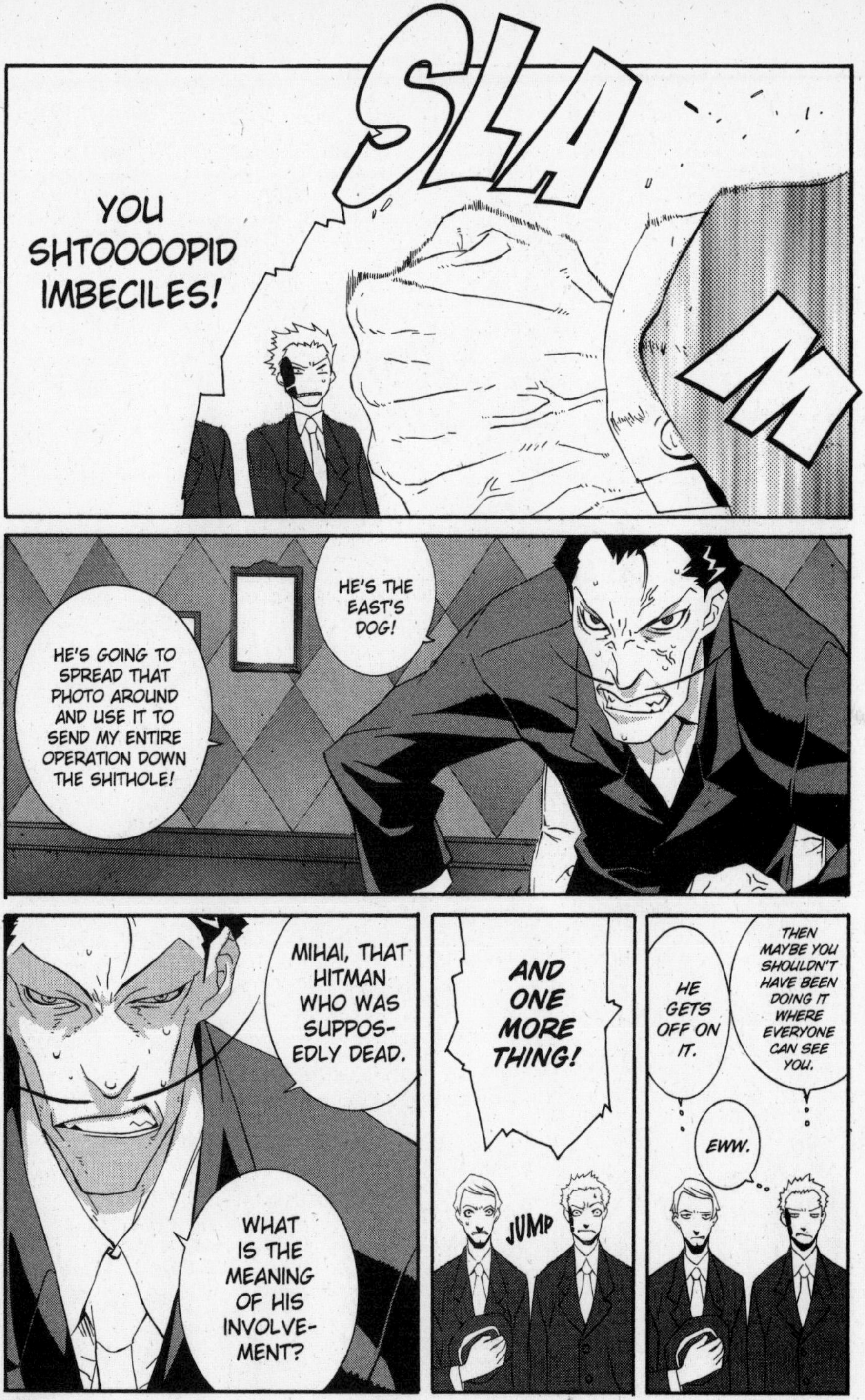
SLAM
YOU SHTOOOOPID IMBECILES!
HE'S THE EAST'S DOG!
HE'S GOING TO SPREAD THAT PHOTO AROUND AND USE IT TO SEND MY ENTIRE OPERATION DOWN THE SHITHOLE!
THEN MAYBE YOU SHOULDN'T HAVE BEEN DOING IT WHERE EVERYONE CAN SEE YOU.
HE GETS OFF ON IT.
EWW.
AND ONE MORE THING!
JUMP
MIHAI, THAT HITMAN WHO WAS SUPPOS-EDLY DEAD.
WHAT IS THE MEANING OF HIS INVOLVE-MENT?

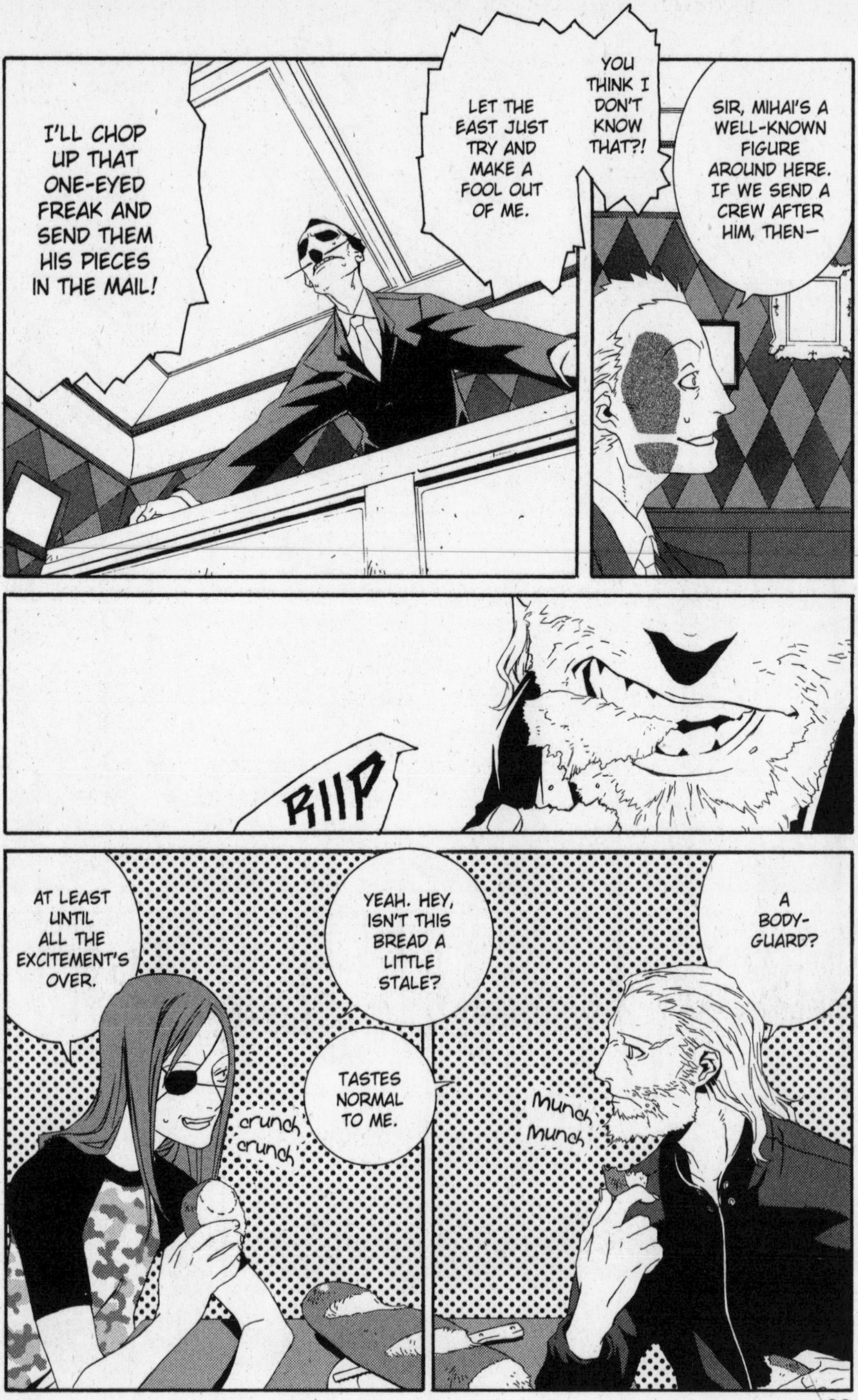
SIR, MIHAI'S A WELL-KNOWN FIGURE AROUND HERE. IF WE SEND A CREW AFTER HIM, THEN—
YOU THINK I DON'T KNOW THAT?!
LET THE EAST JUST TRY AND MAKE A FOOL OUT OF ME.
I'LL CHOP UP THAT ONE-EYED FREAK AND SEND THEM HIS PIECES IN THE MAIL!
RIIP
A BODY-GUARD?
Munch Munch
AT LEAST UNTIL ALL THE EXCITEMENT'S OVER.
YEAH. HEY, ISN'T THIS BREAD A LITTLE STALE?
TASTES NORMAL TO ME.
crunch crunch

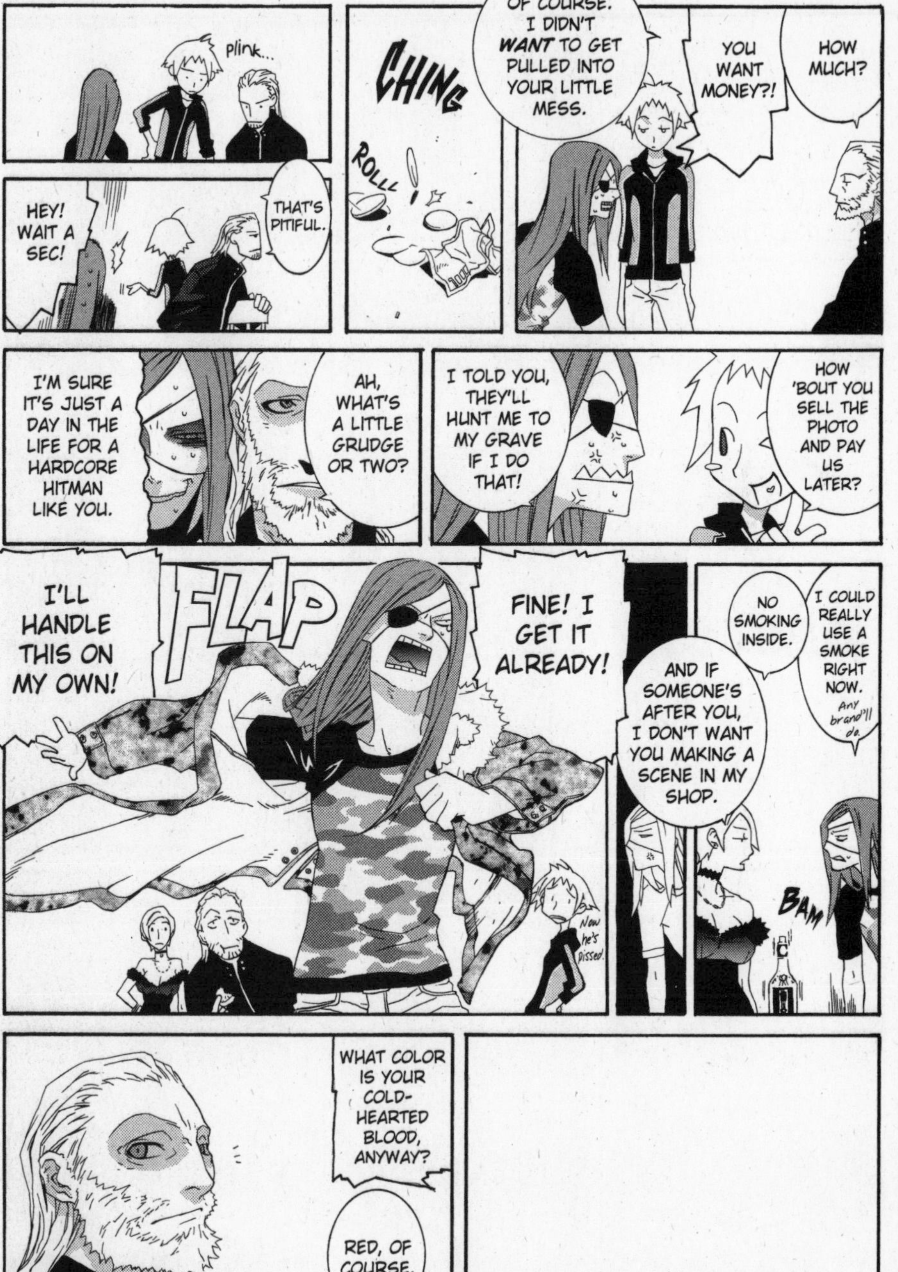
HOW MUCH?
YOU WANT MONEY?!
OF COURSE. I DIDN'T WANT TO GET PULLED INTO YOUR LITTLE MESS.
CHING
ROLLL
plink...
THAT'S PITIFUL.
HEY! WAIT A SEC!
HOW 'BOUT YOU SELL THE PHOTO AND PAY US LATER?
I TOLD YOU, THEY'LL HUNT ME TO MY GRAVE IF I DO THAT!
AH, WHAT'S A LITTLE GRUDGE OR TWO?
I'M SURE IT'S JUST A DAY IN THE LIFE FOR A HARDCORE HITMAN LIKE YOU.
I COULD REALLY USE A SMOKE RIGHT NOW.
Any brand'll do.
NO SMOKING INSIDE.
AND IF SOMEONE'S AFTER YOU, I DON'T WANT YOU MAKING A SCENE IN MY SHOP.
BAM
FINE! I GET IT ALREADY!
FLAP
I'LL HANDLE THIS ON MY OWN!
Now he's pissed!
VMM... VROOM
VROOOOM... SCREECH
WHAT COLOR IS YOUR COLD-HEARTED BLOOD, ANYWAY?
RED, OF COURSE.

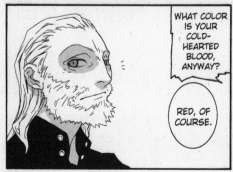

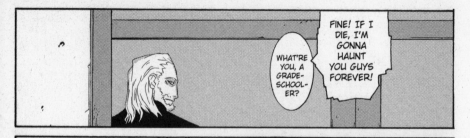

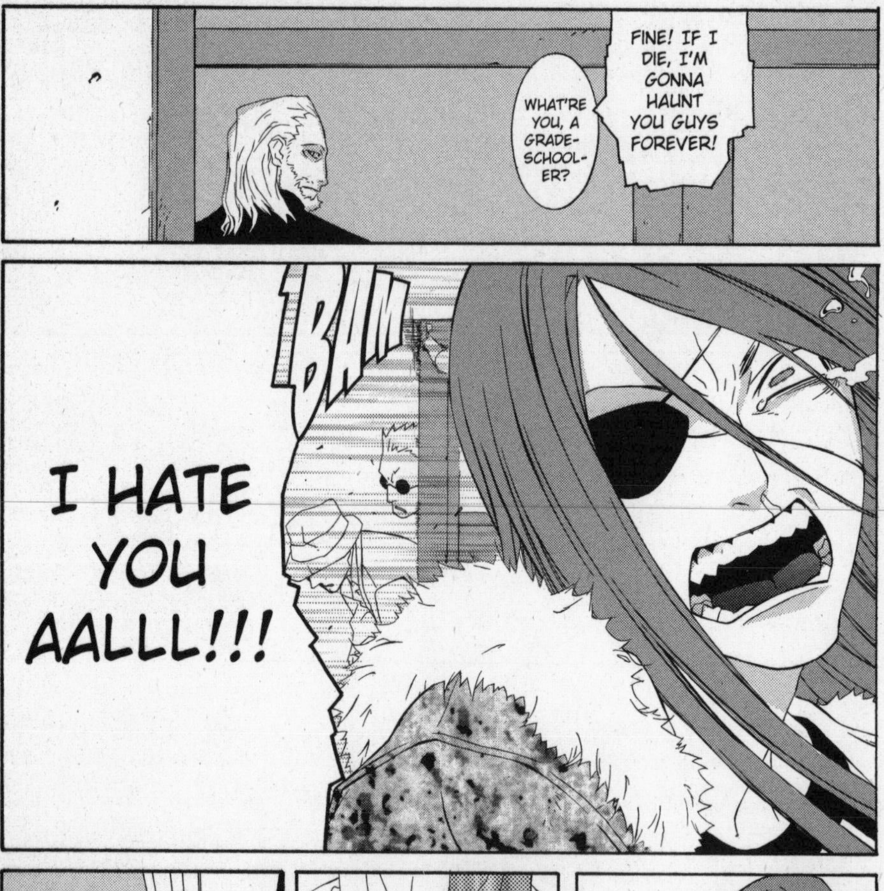

FINE! IF I DIE, I'M GONNA HAUNT YOU GUYS FOREVER!
WHAT'RE YOU, A GRADE-SCHOOLER?
BAM
I HATE YOU AALLL!!!
SHACHAK

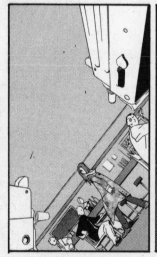

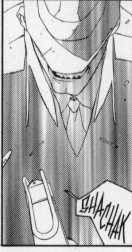

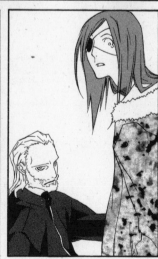

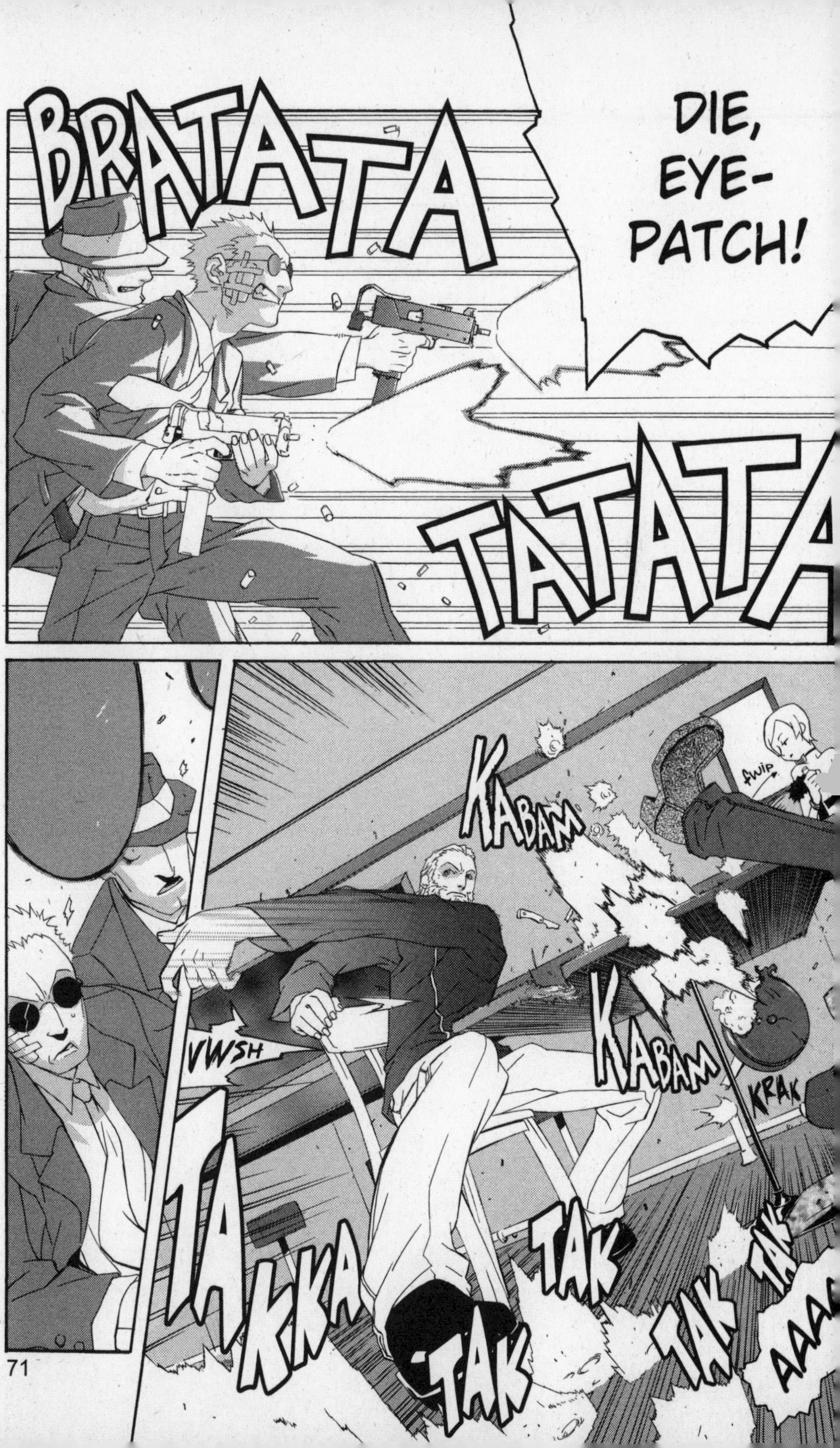
DIE, EYE-PATCH!
BRATATA
TATATA
fwip
KABAM
KABAM
KRAK
TAK
TAK
TAK
TAK
VWSH
TAKKA

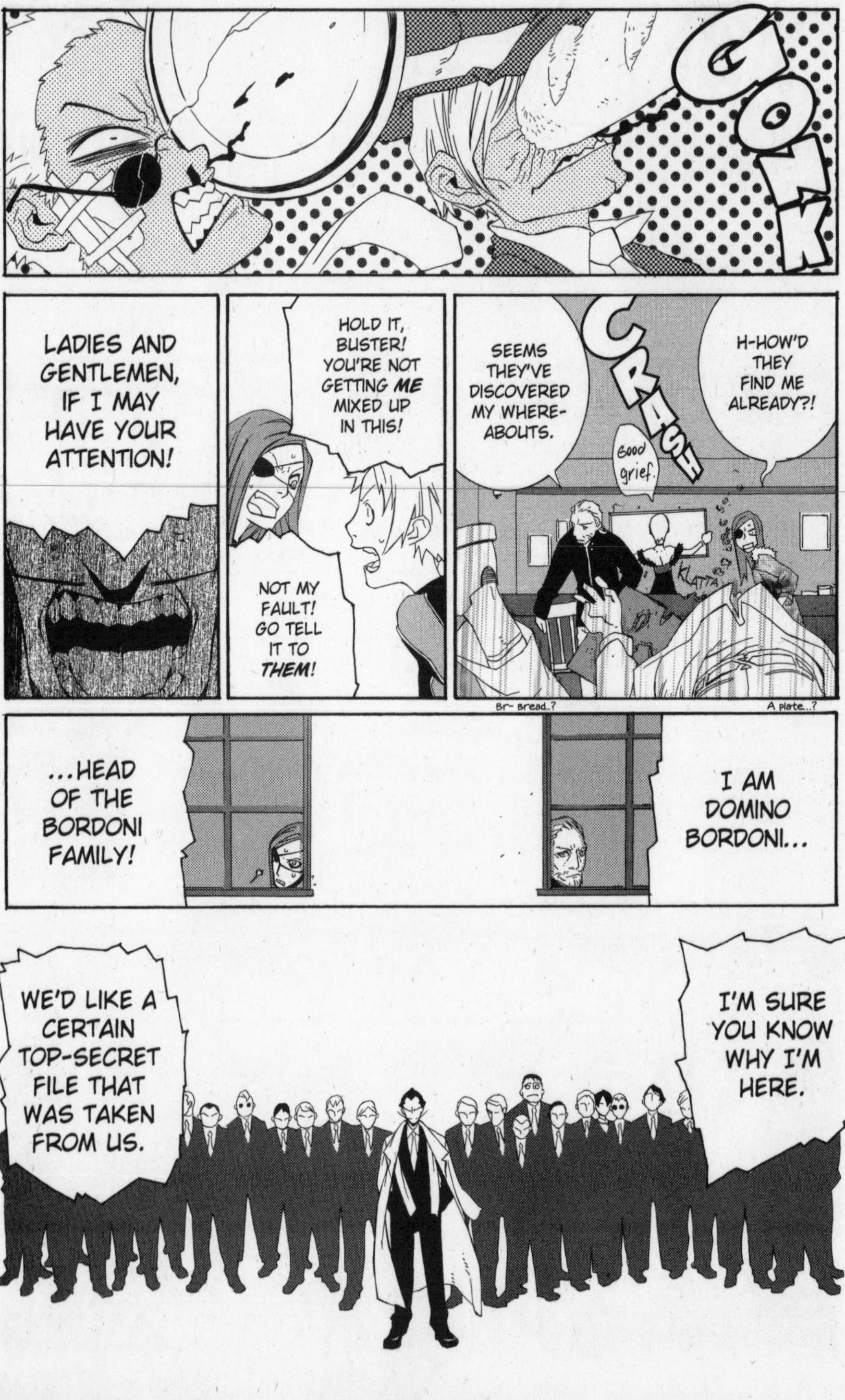
GONK
H-HOW'D THEY FIND ME ALREADY?!
CRASH
SEEMS THEY'VE DISCOVERED MY WHERE-ABOUTS.
Good grief.
KLATTA
A plate...?
Br- bread...?
HOLD IT, BUSTER! YOU'RE NOT GETTING *ME* MIXED UP IN THIS!
NOT MY FAULT! GO TELL IT TO *THEM*!
LADIES AND GENTLEMEN, IF I MAY HAVE YOUR ATTENTION!
I AM DOMINO BORDONI...
...HEAD OF THE BORDONI FAMILY!
I'M SURE YOU KNOW WHY I'M HERE.
WE'D LIKE A CERTAIN TOP-SECRET FILE THAT WAS TAKEN FROM US.

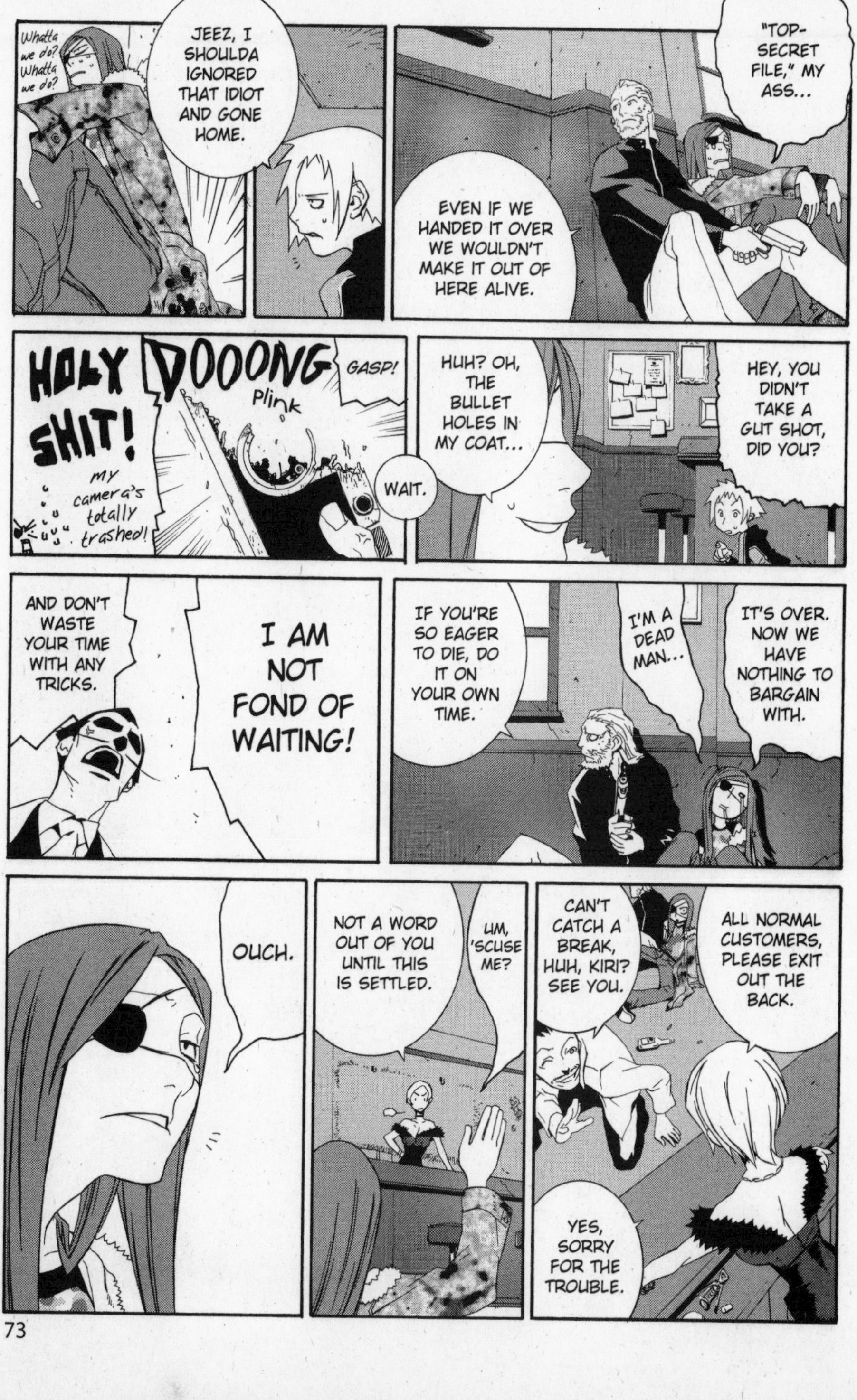
"TOP-SECRET FILE," MY ASS...
EVEN IF WE HANDED IT OVER WE WOULDN'T MAKE IT OUT OF HERE ALIVE.
JEEZ, I SHOULDA IGNORED THAT IDIOT AND GONE HOME.
Whatta we do? Whatta we do?
HEY, YOU DIDN'T TAKE A GUT SHOT, DID YOU?
HUH? OH, THE BULLET HOLES IN MY COAT...
WAIT.
GASP!
DOOONG
plink
HOLY SHIT!
my camera's totally trashed!
IT'S OVER. NOW WE HAVE NOTHING TO BARGAIN WITH.
I'M A DEAD MAN...
IF YOU'RE SO EAGER TO DIE, DO IT ON YOUR OWN TIME.
I AM NOT FOND OF WAITING!
AND DON'T WASTE YOUR TIME WITH ANY TRICKS.
ALL NORMAL CUSTOMERS, PLEASE EXIT OUT THE BACK.
CAN'T CATCH A BREAK, HUH, KIRI? SEE YOU.
YES, SORRY FOR THE TROUBLE.
UM, 'SCUSE ME?
NOT A WORD OUT OF YOU UNTIL THIS IS SETTLED.
OUCH.

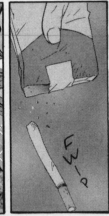

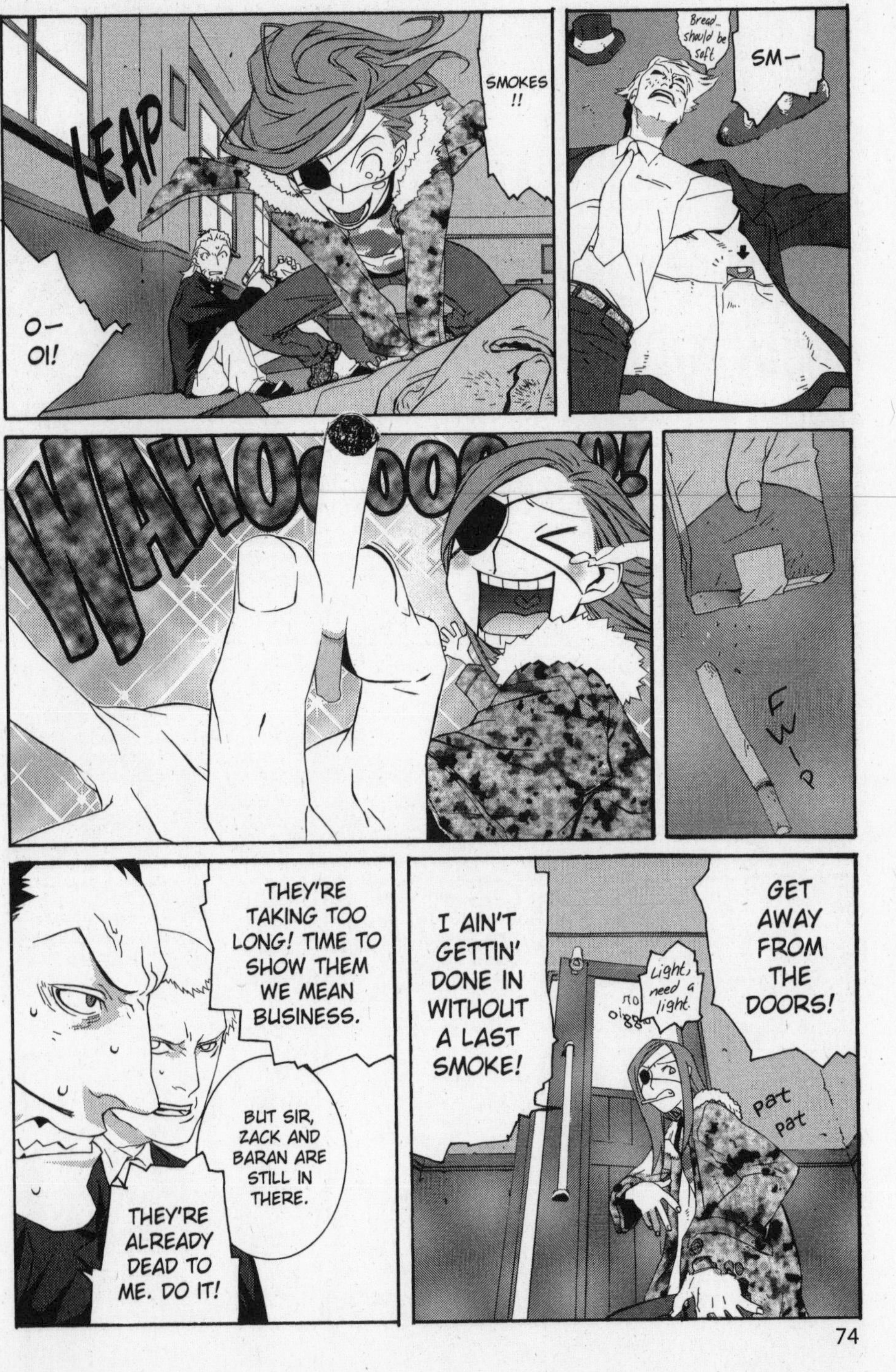
Bread... should be soft.
SM—
SMOKES !!
LEAP
O-OI!
FWIP
GET AWAY FROM THE DOORS!
Light, need a light.
I AIN'T GETTIN' DONE IN WITHOUT A LAST SMOKE!
pat pat
THEY'RE TAKING TOO LONG! TIME TO SHOW THEM WE MEAN BUSINESS.
BUT SIR, ZACK AND BARAN ARE STILL IN THERE.
THEY'RE ALREADY DEAD TO ME. DO IT!

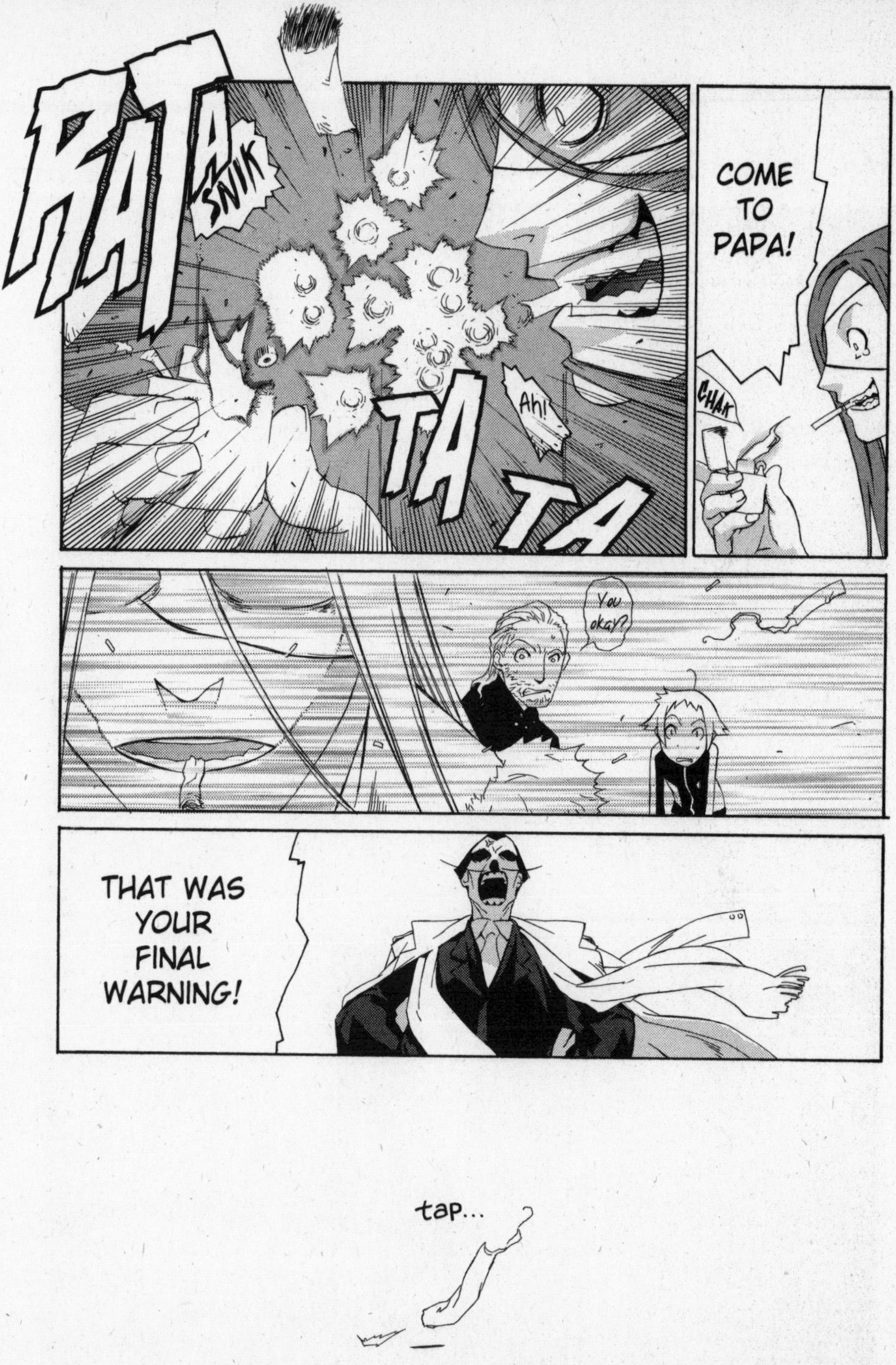
RATA
SNIK
COME TO PAPA!
CHAK
TA
Ah!
TA
You okay?
THAT WAS YOUR FINAL WARNING!
tap...

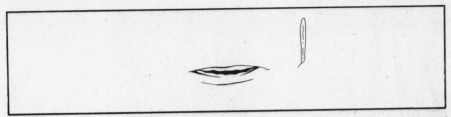

Ah ha ha! Wheee!

PSYCHOLOGICAL PORTRAIT

Just one...

...cig...

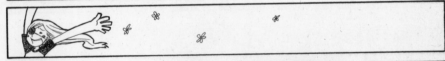

WOBBLE

BADOU?

The plate... the plate... it's flying...

SHAK

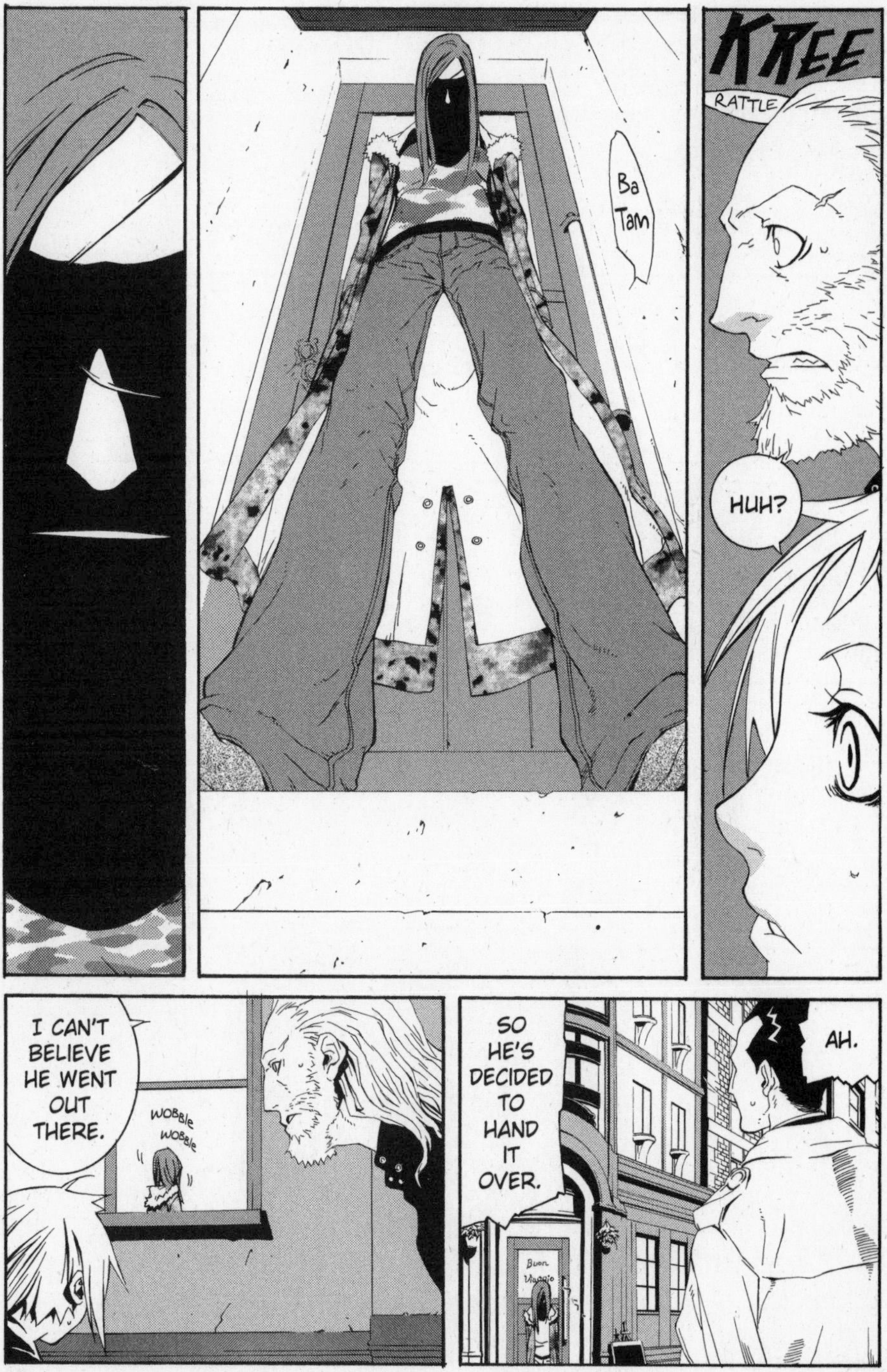
KREE
RATTLE
HUH?
Ba Tam
AH.
SO HE'S DECIDED TO HAND IT OVER.
Buon Viaggio
I CAN'T BELIEVE HE WENT OUT THERE.
WOBBLE WOBBLE

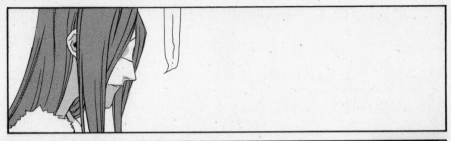

WHAT WAS THAT?

HUH?

SPEAK UP, YOU IDIOT! I CAN'T HEAR YOU!

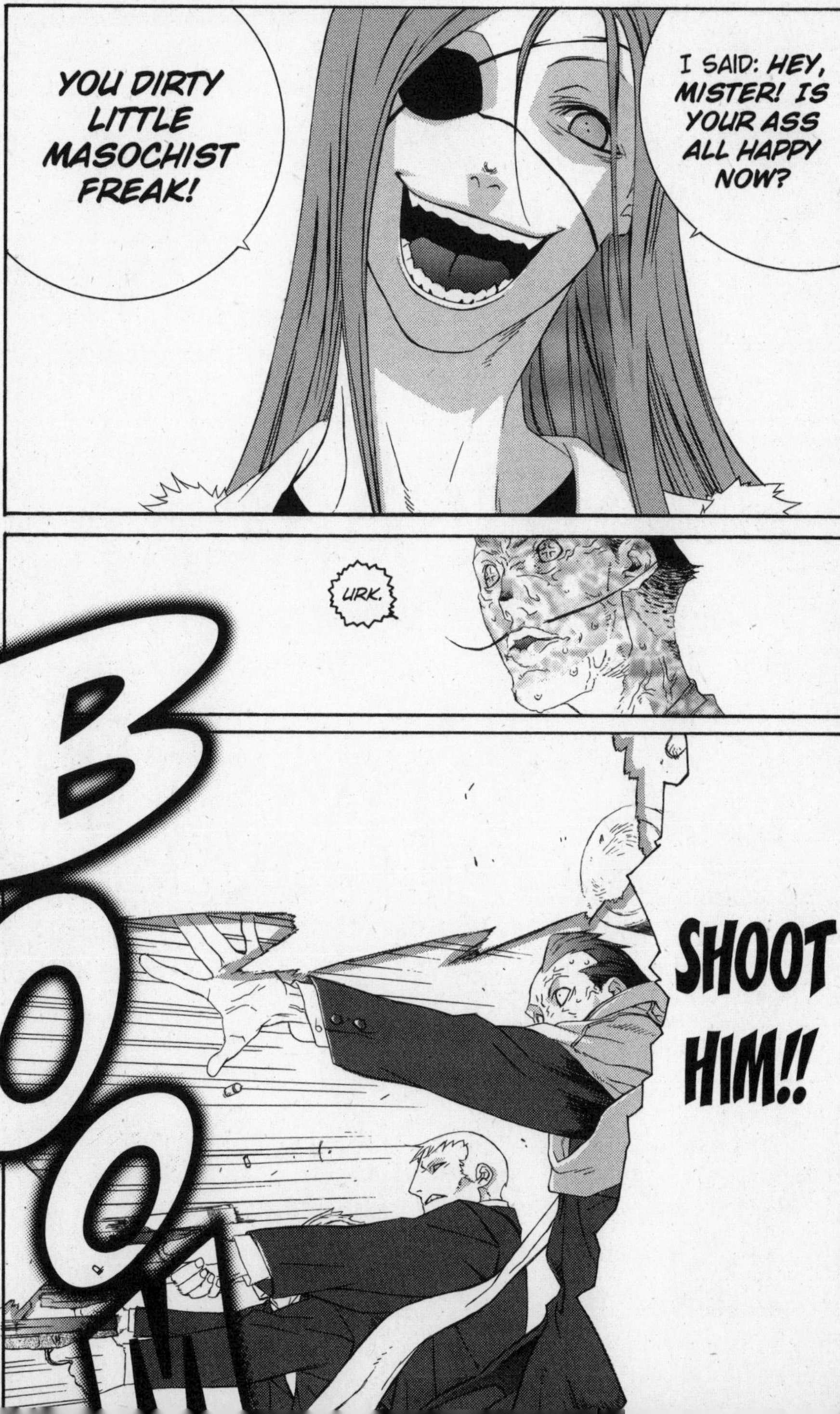
I SAID: HEY, MISTER! IS YOUR ASS ALL HAPPY NOW?
YOU DIRTY LITTLE MASOCHIST FREAK!
URK.
SHOOT HIM!!
BOOM

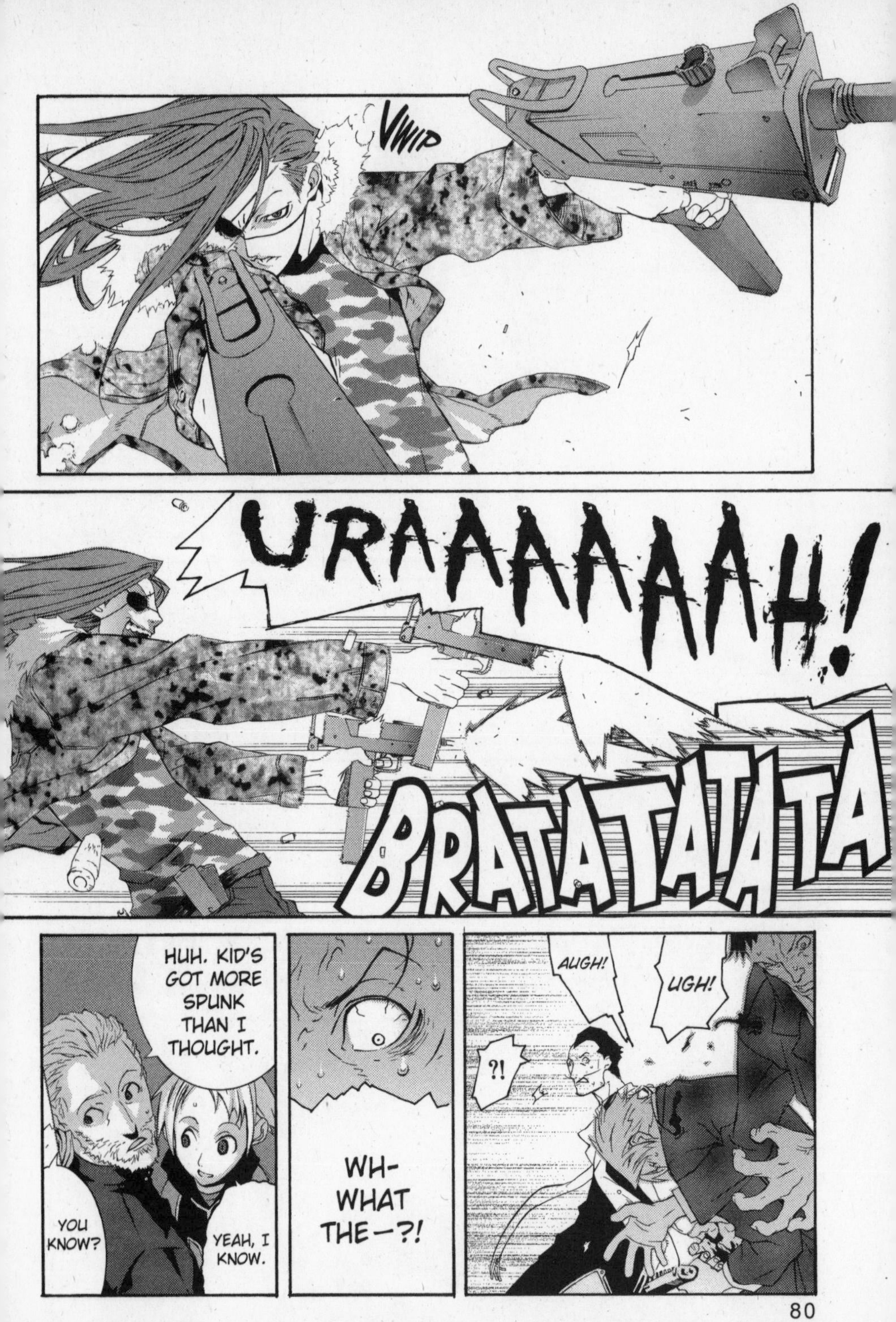
VWIP
URAAAAAAH!
BRATATATATA
UGH!
AUGH!
?!
WH-WHAT THE—?!
HUH. KID'S GOT MORE SPUNK THAN I THOUGHT.
YEAH, I KNOW.
YOU KNOW?

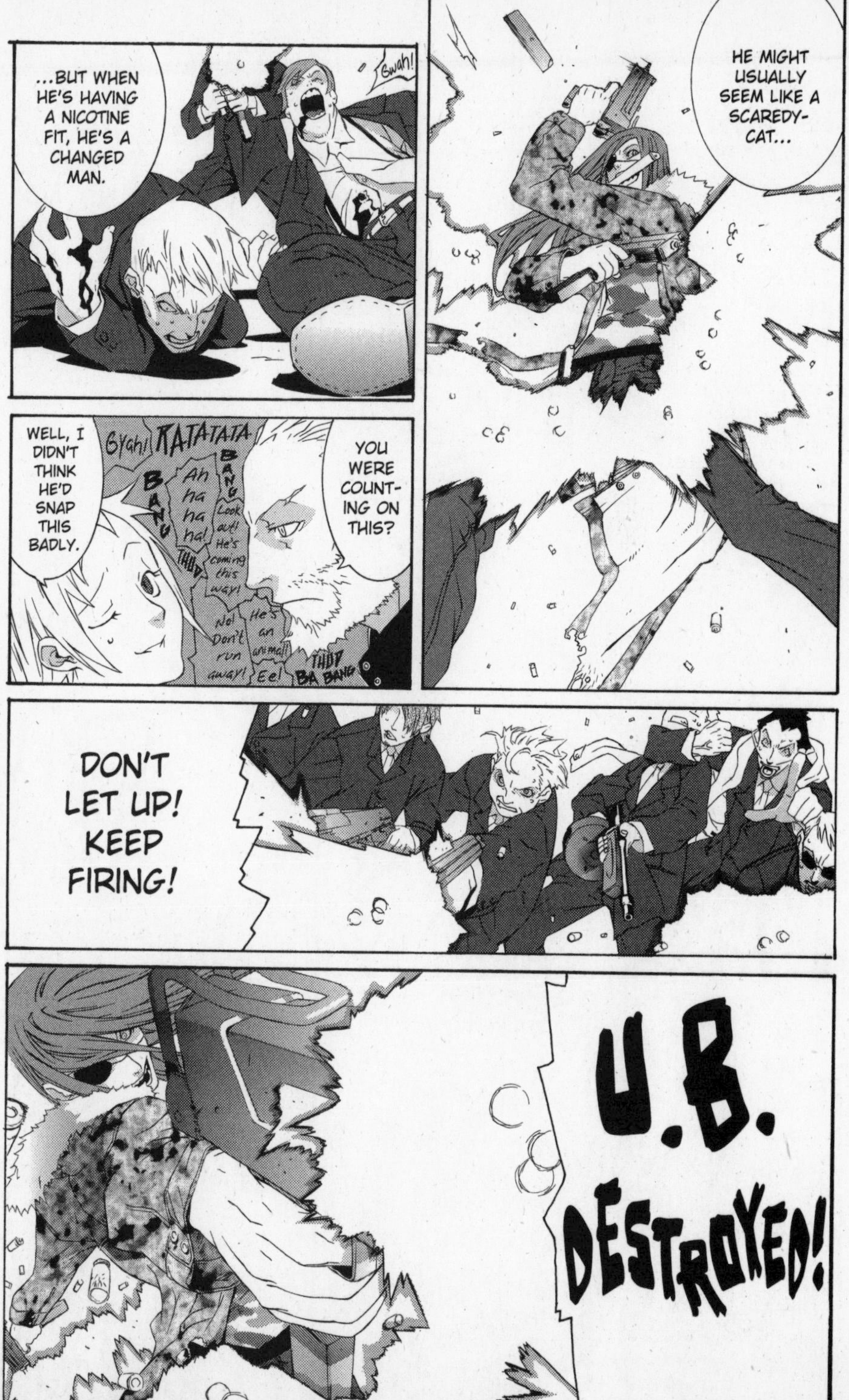
HE MIGHT USUALLY SEEM LIKE A SCAREDY-CAT...
...BUT WHEN HE'S HAVING A NICOTINE FIT, HE'S A CHANGED MAN.
Gwah!
YOU WERE COUNTING ON THIS?
WELL, I DIDN'T THINK HE'D SNAP THIS BADLY.
Gyah!
RATATATA
BANG
BANG
Ah ha ha ha!
Look out! He's coming this way!
THUD
He's an animal!
No! Don't run away!
Ee!
THUD
BA BANG
DON'T LET UP! KEEP FIRING!
U.B. DESTROYED!

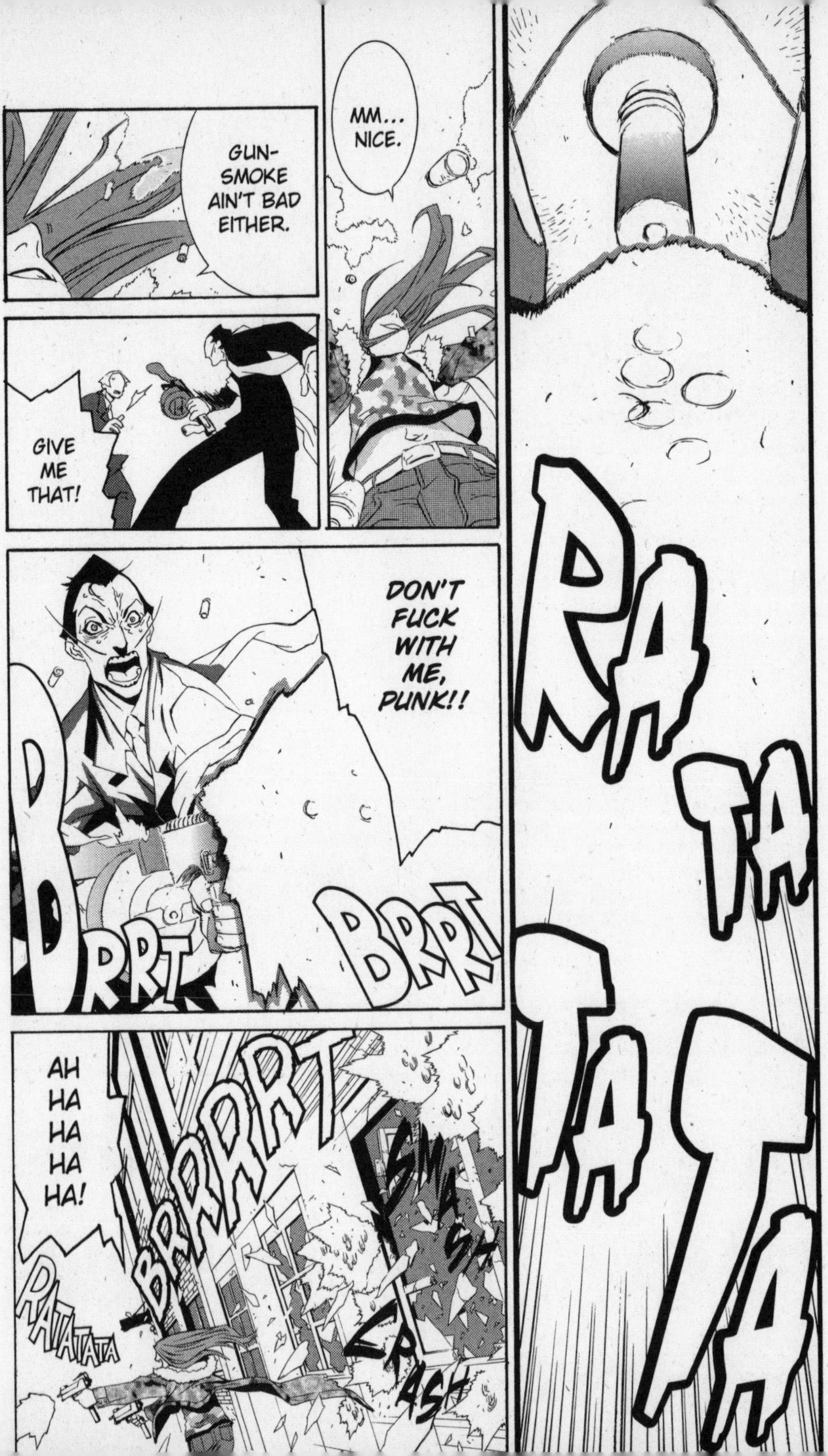
RATATATA
MM... NICE.
GUN-SMOKE AIN'T BAD EITHER.
GIVE ME THAT!
DON'T FUCK WITH ME, PUNK!!
BRRT
BRRT
SMASH
CRASH
BRRRRT
AH HA HA HA HA!
RATATATA

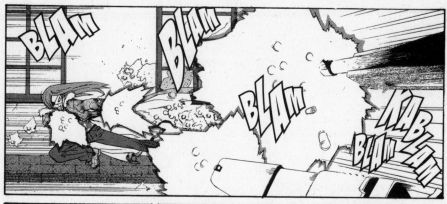

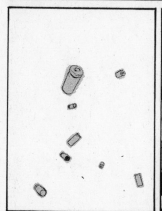

KABLAM
BLAM
BLAM
BLAM
BLAM
SEEMS HE HAS THE SITUATION UNDER CONTROL.
THUD THUD
BRATATA
BLAM BLAM
Four windows, fresh paint for the walls, the food supply...
SMAAASH
KA BANG
Another window...
BEEP BEEP
BRATATA
hisss
RATATATA
THUD
RATATATA
BAM

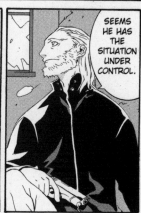

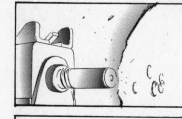

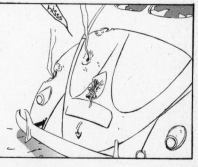

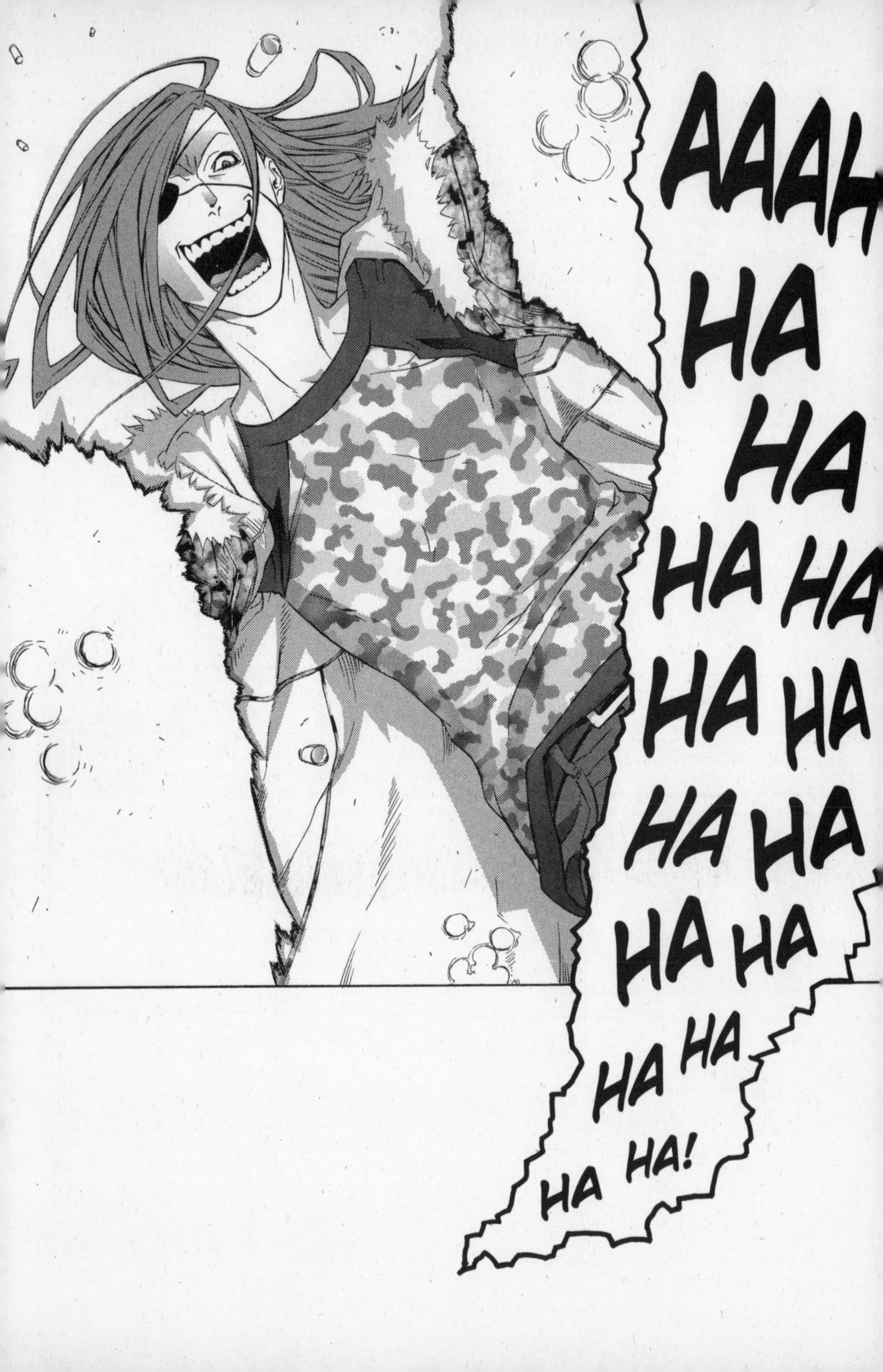
AAAH HA HA HA HA HA HA HA HA HA HA HA HA HA HA HA!

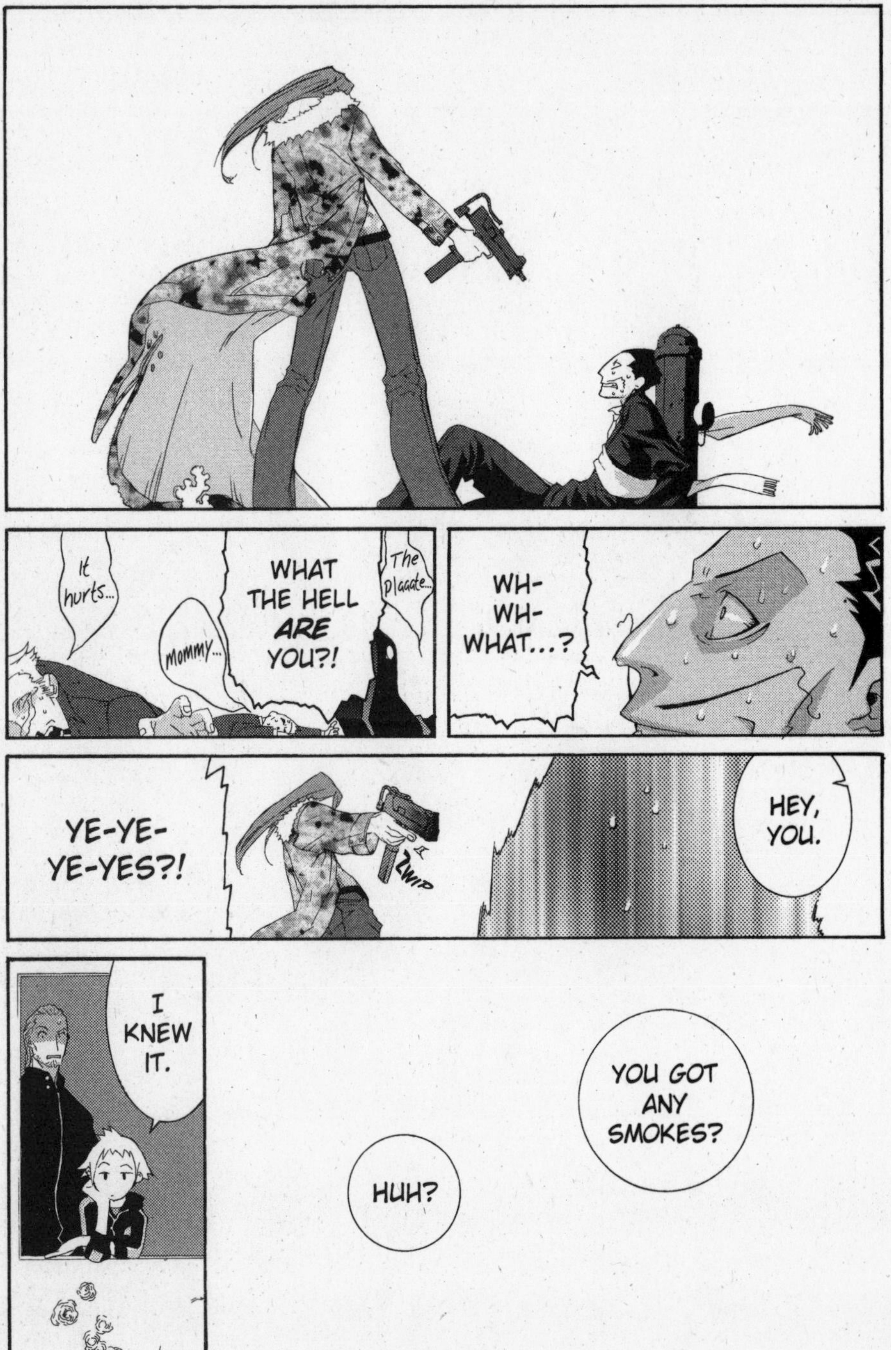
WH- WH- WHAT...?
The plaaate...
WHAT THE HELL ARE YOU?!
mommy...
It hurts...
HEY, YOU.
ZWIP
YE-YE-YE-YES?!
YOU GOT ANY SMOKES?
HUH?
I KNEW IT.

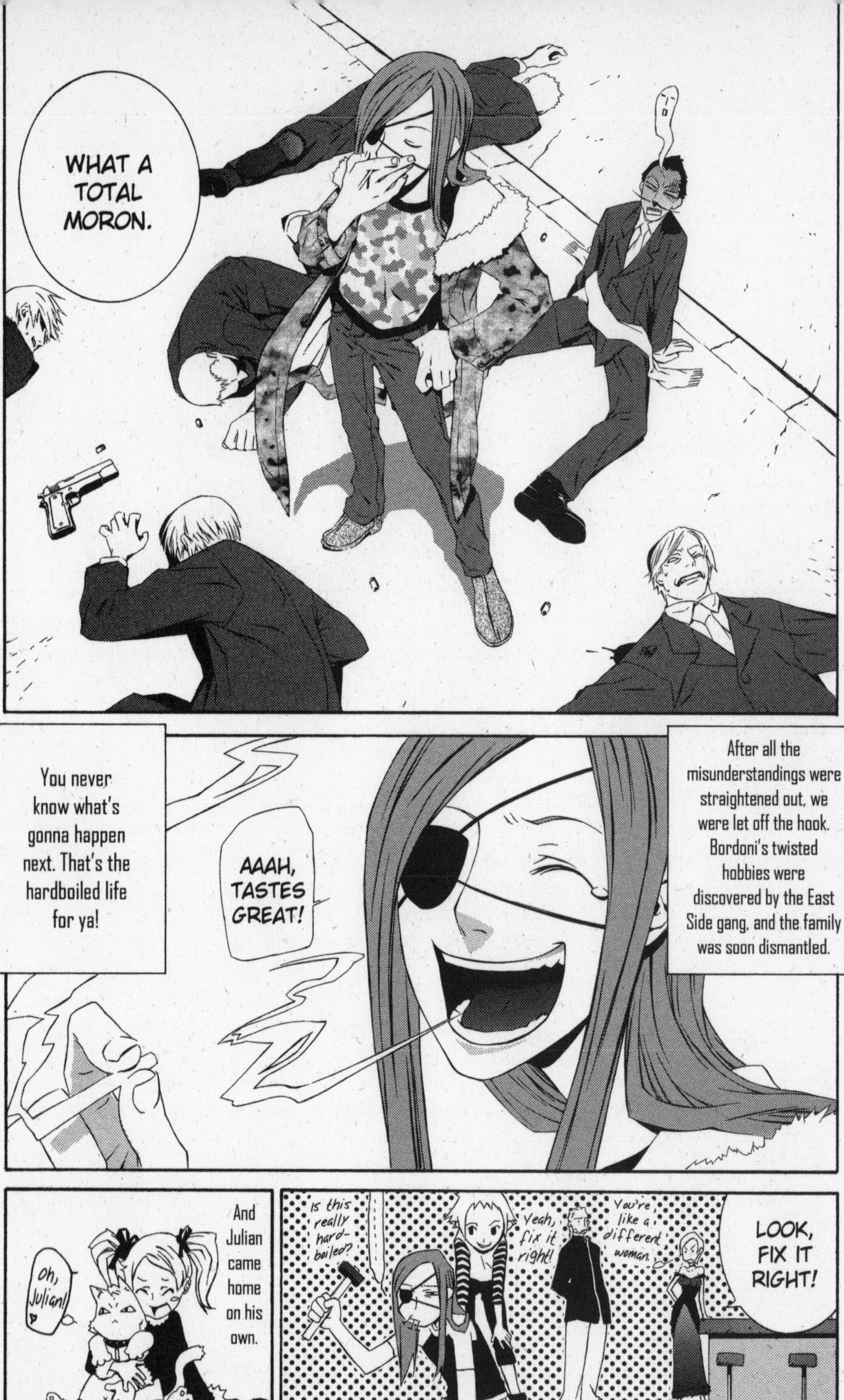
WHAT A TOTAL MORON.
After all the misunderstandings were straightened out, we were let off the hook. Bordoni's twisted hobbies were discovered by the East Side gang, and the family was soon dismantled.
AAAH, TASTES GREAT!
You never know what's gonna happen next. That's the hardboiled life for ya!
LOOK, FIX IT RIGHT!
You're like a different woman.
Yeah, fix it right!
Is this really hard-boiled?
And Julian came home on his own.
Oh, Julian!

3 Blade Maiden [Part 1]

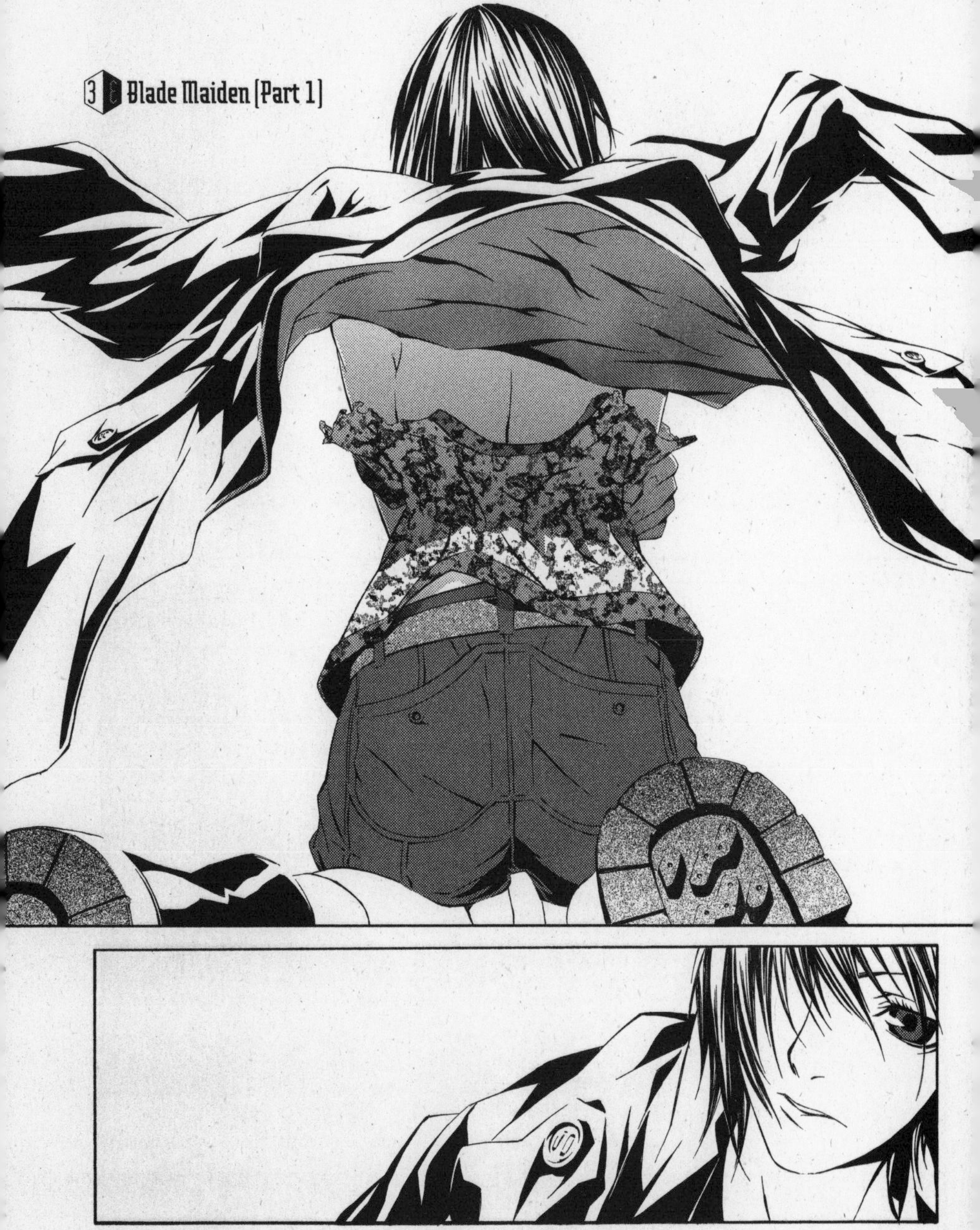

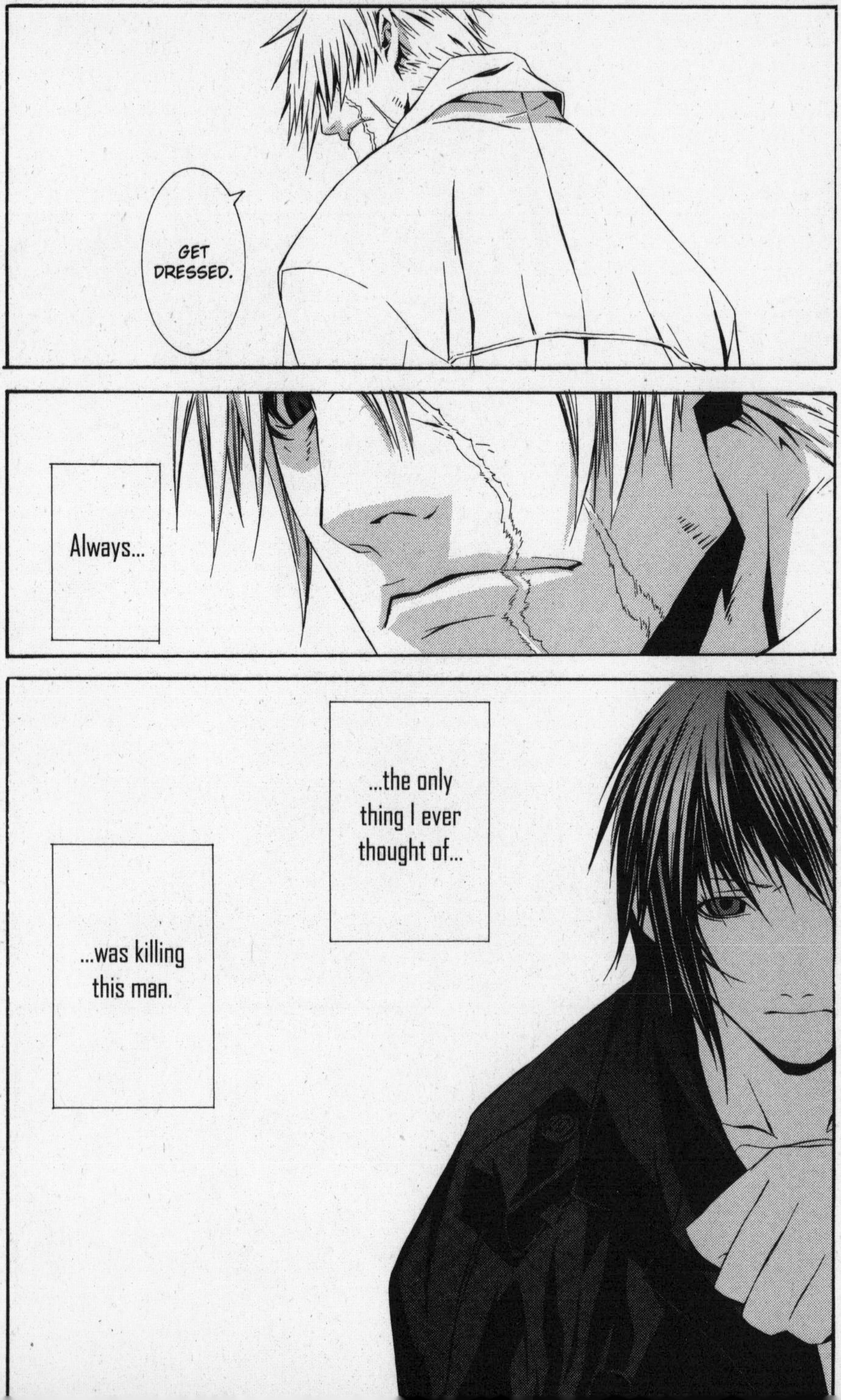
GET DRESSED.
Always...
...the only thing I ever thought of...
...was killing this man.

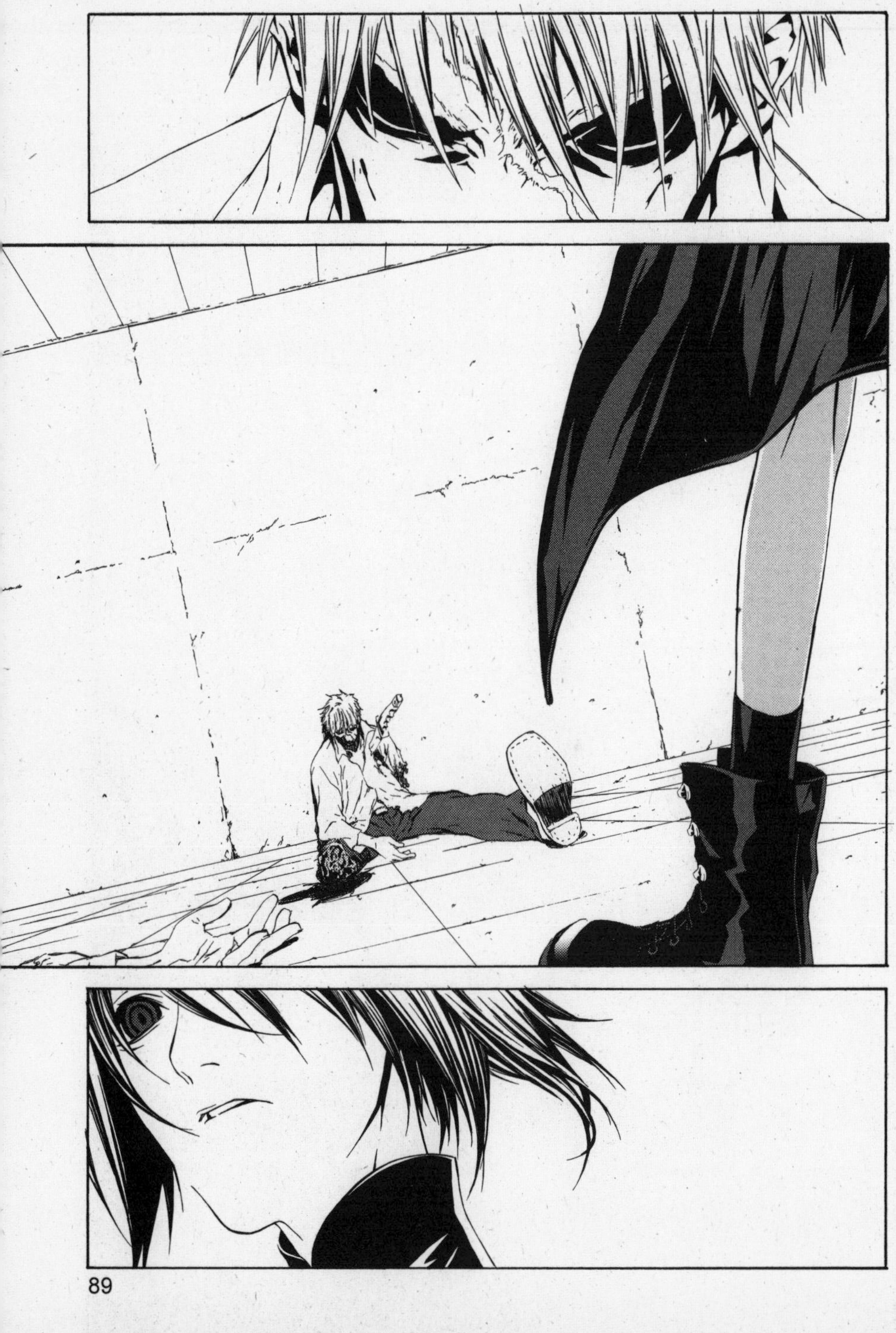

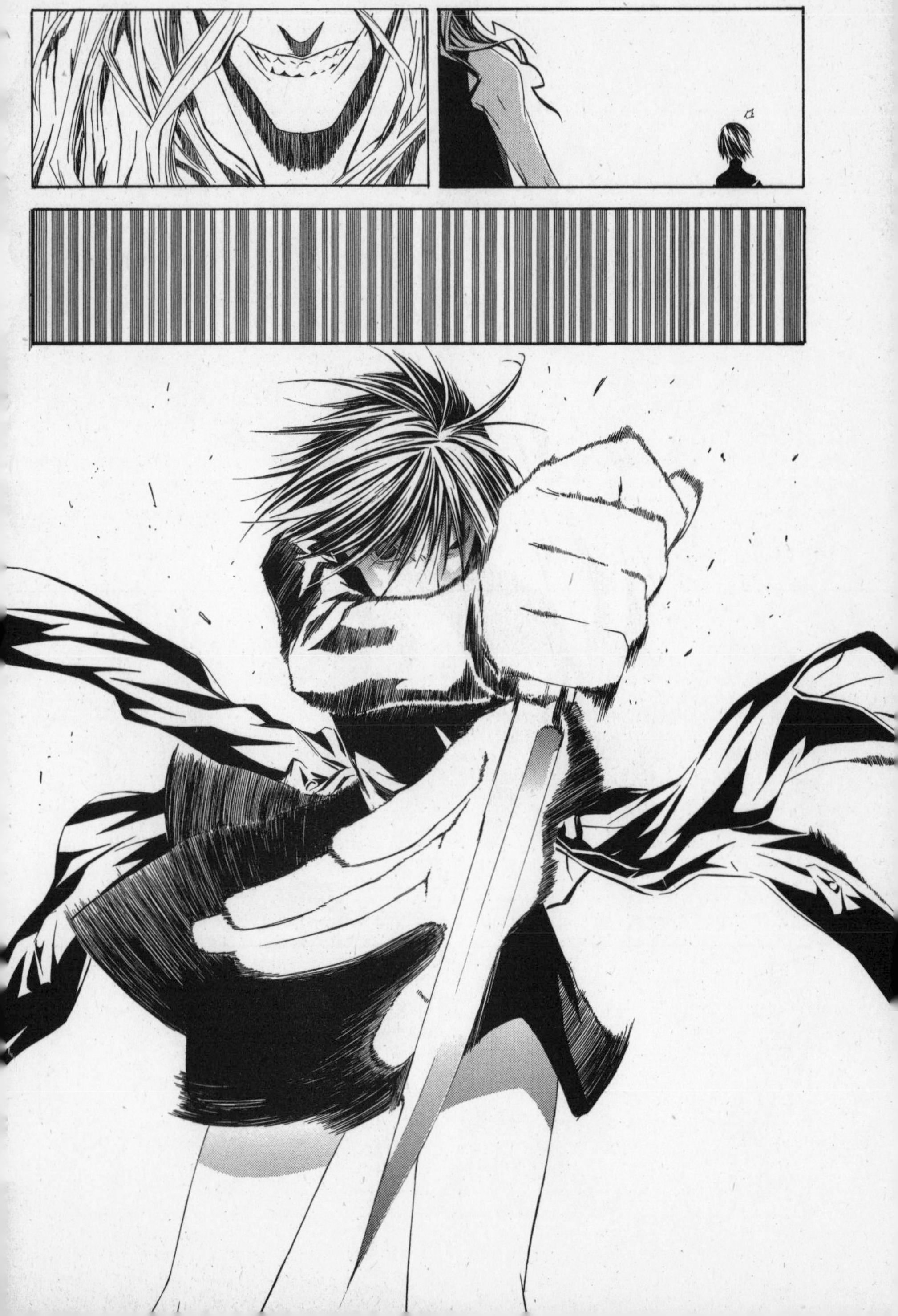

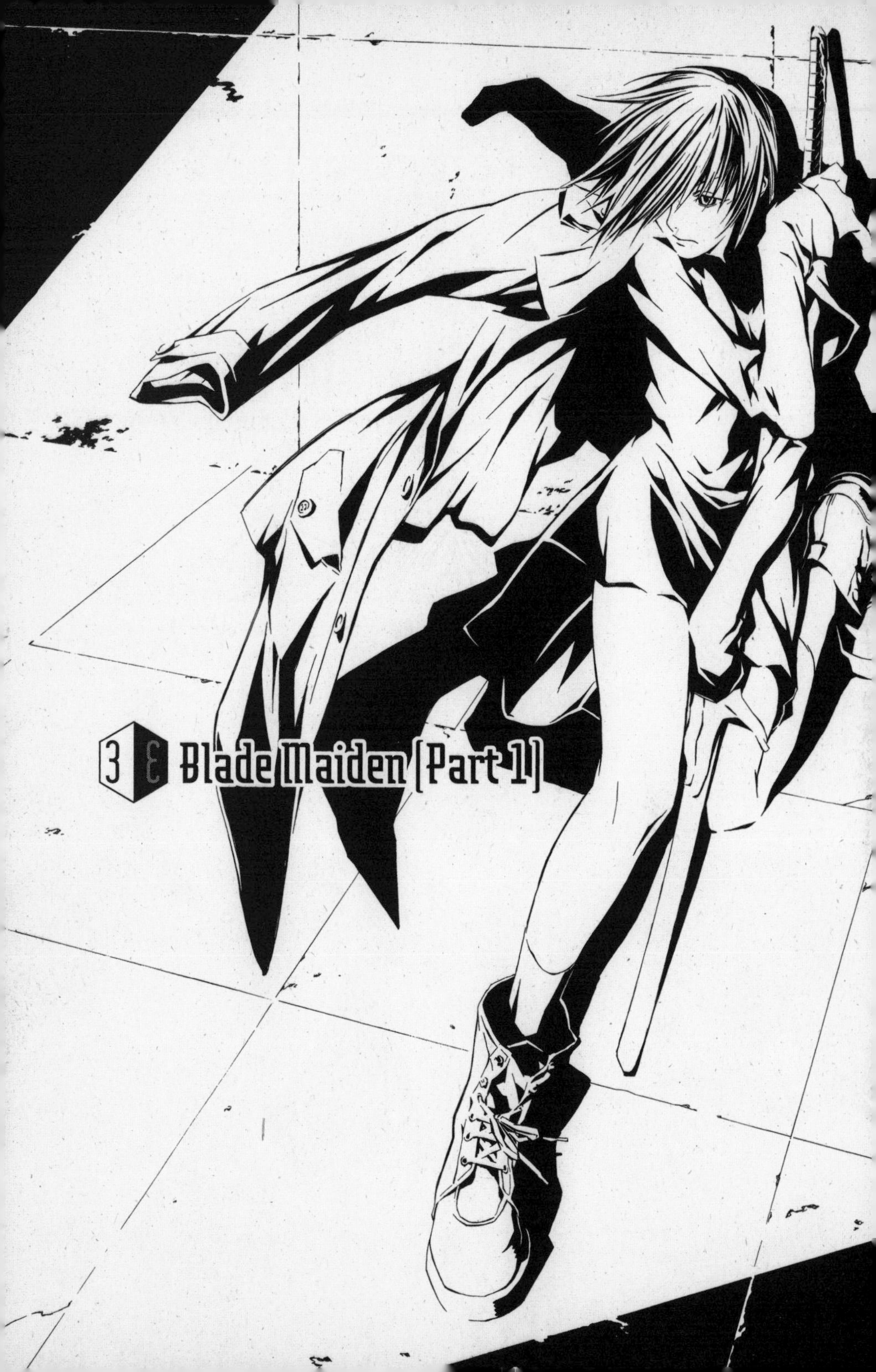
3 Blade Maiden [Part 1]

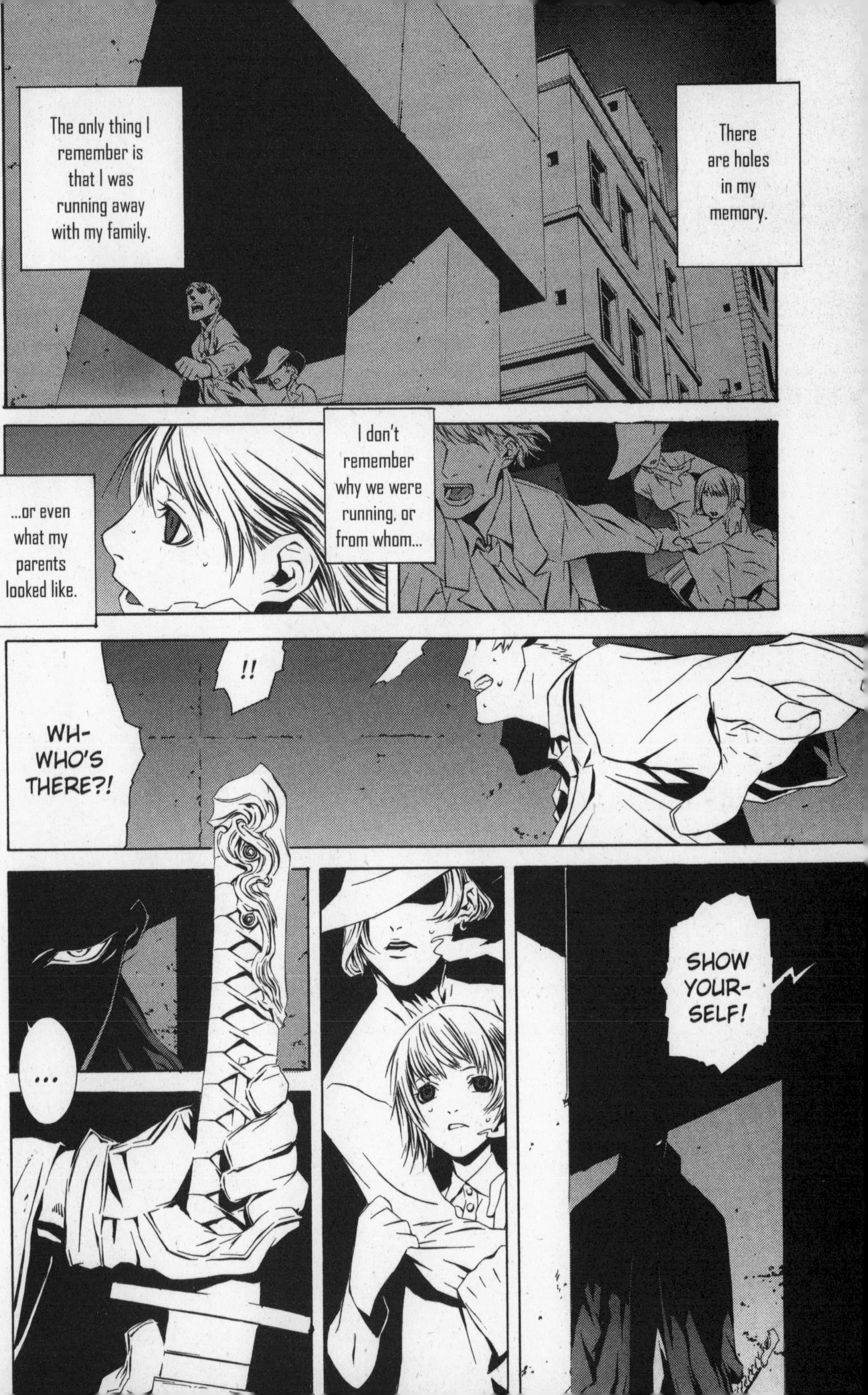

There are holes in my memory.
The only thing I remember is that I was running away with my family.
I don't remember why we were running, or from whom...
...or even what my parents looked like.
!!
WH- WHO'S THERE?!
SHOW YOUR-SELF!
...

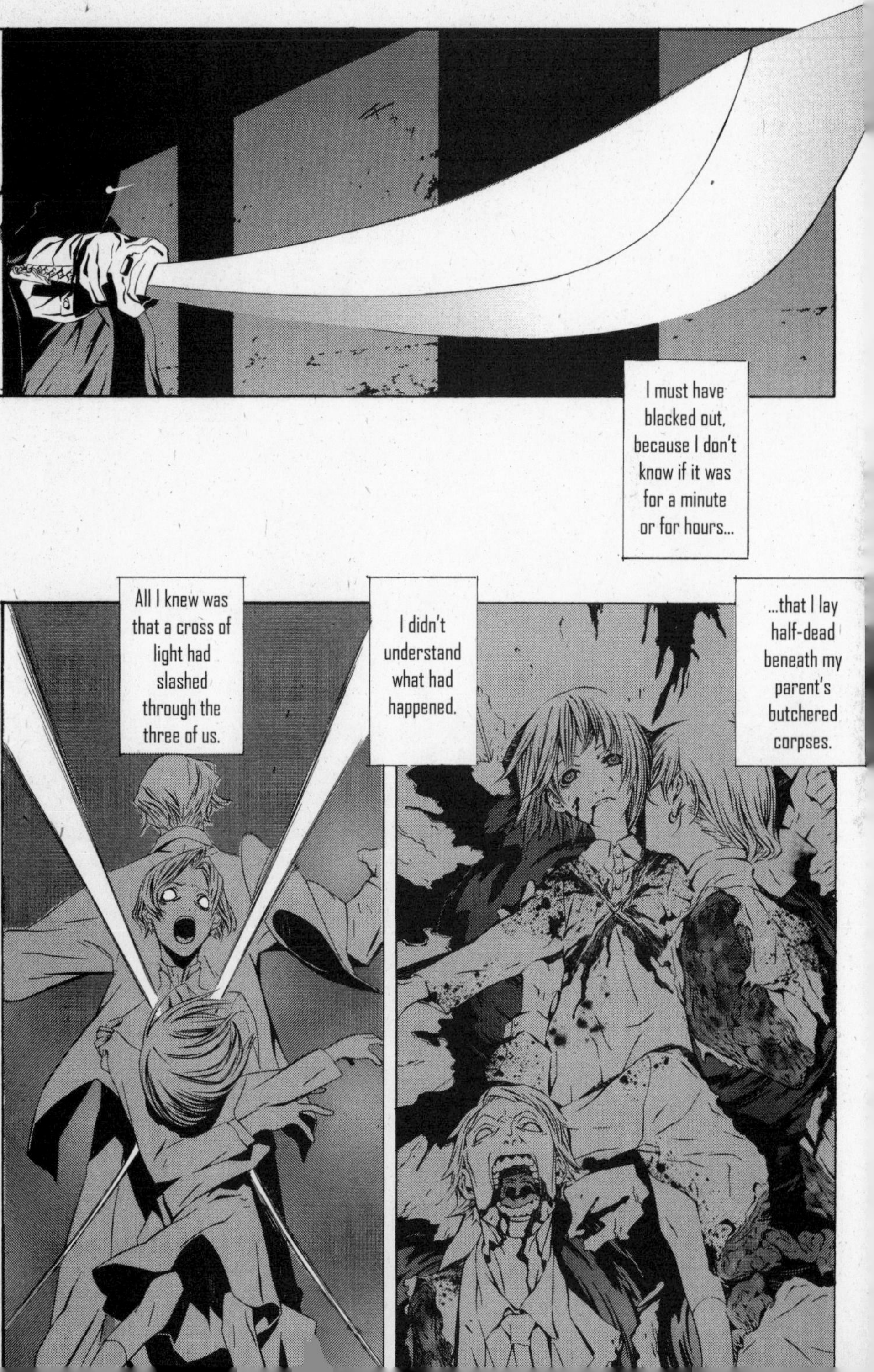
I must have blacked out, because I don't know if it was for a minute or for hours...
...that I lay half-dead beneath my parent's butchered corpses.
I didn't understand what had happened.
All I knew was that a cross of light had slashed through the three of us.

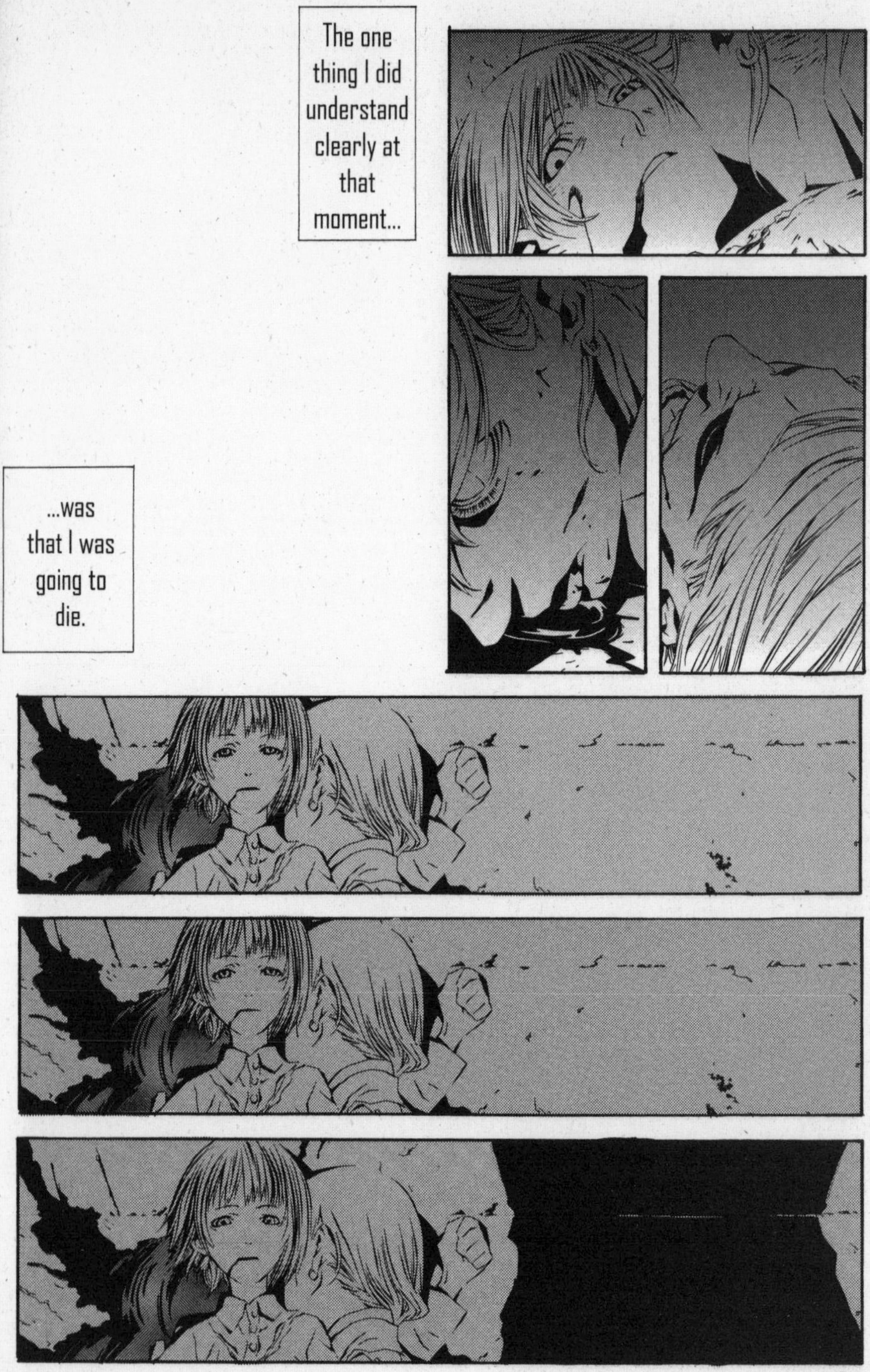
The one thing I did understand clearly at that moment...
...was that I was going to die.

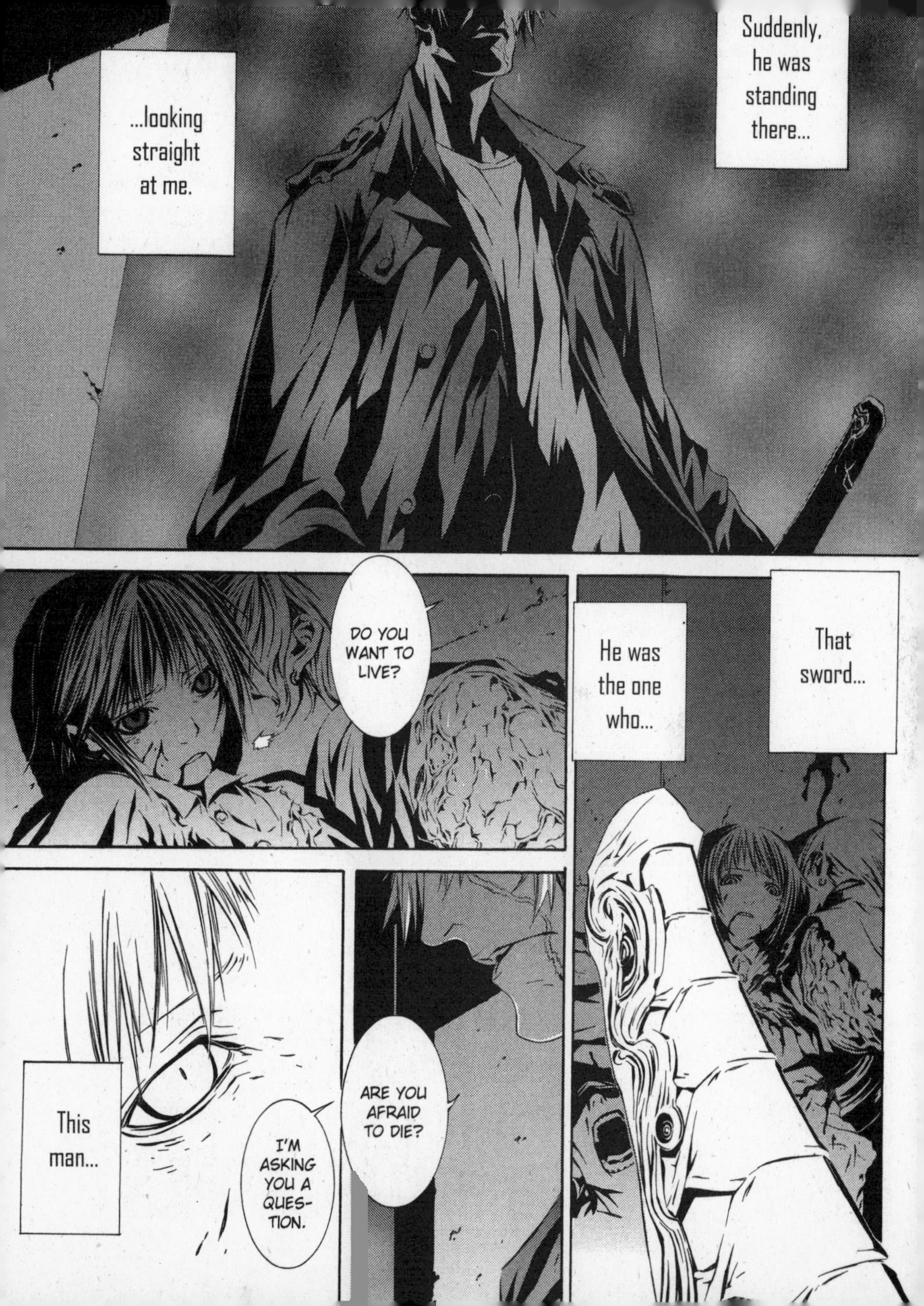
Suddenly, he was standing there...
...looking straight at me.
That sword...
He was the one who...
DO YOU WANT TO LIVE?
ARE YOU AFRAID TO DIE?
I'M ASKING YOU A QUES-TION.
This man...

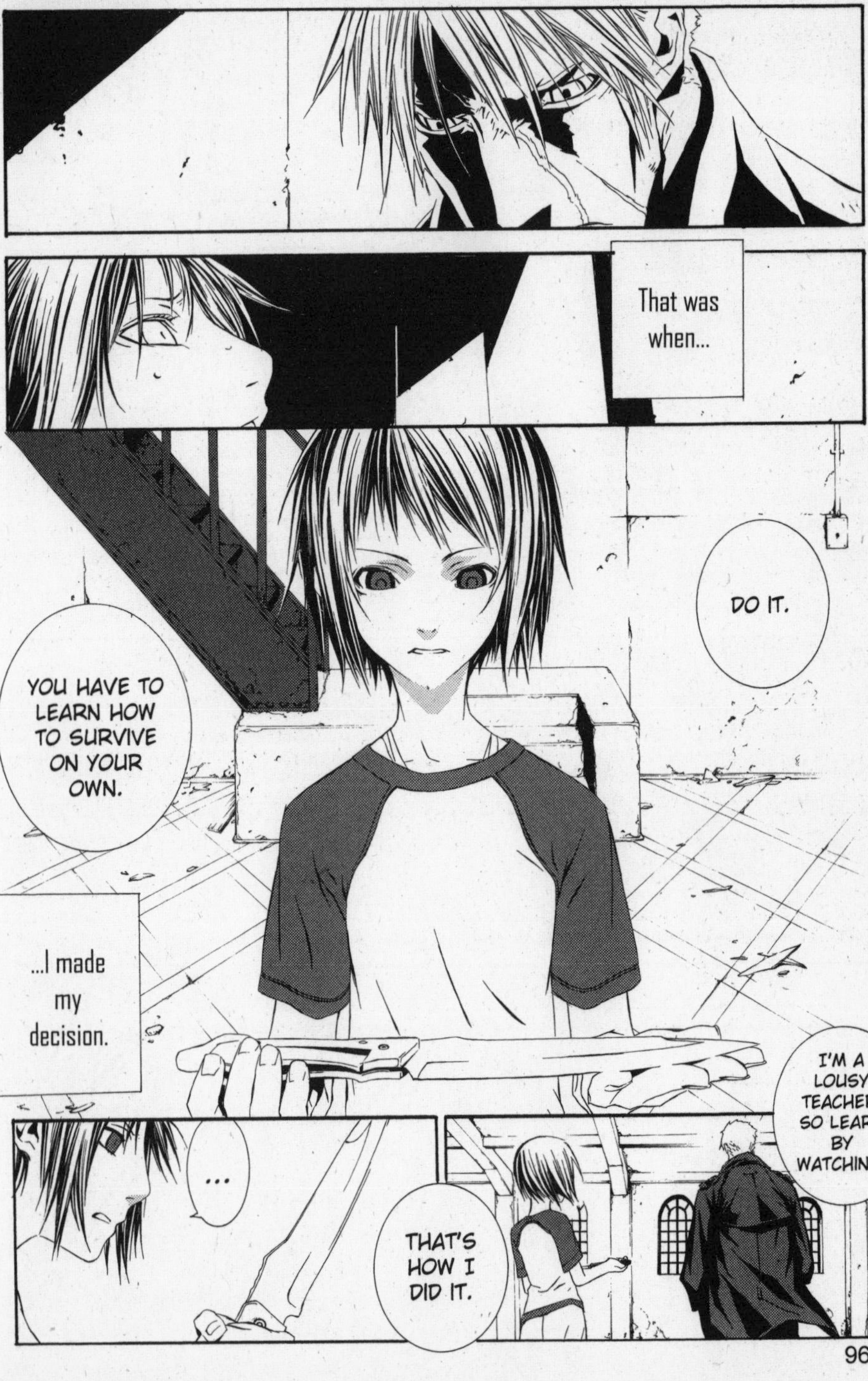

That was when...
DO IT.
YOU HAVE TO LEARN HOW TO SURVIVE ON YOUR OWN.
...I made my decision.
I'M A LOUSY TEACHER, SO LEARN BY WATCHING.
THAT'S HOW I DID IT.
...

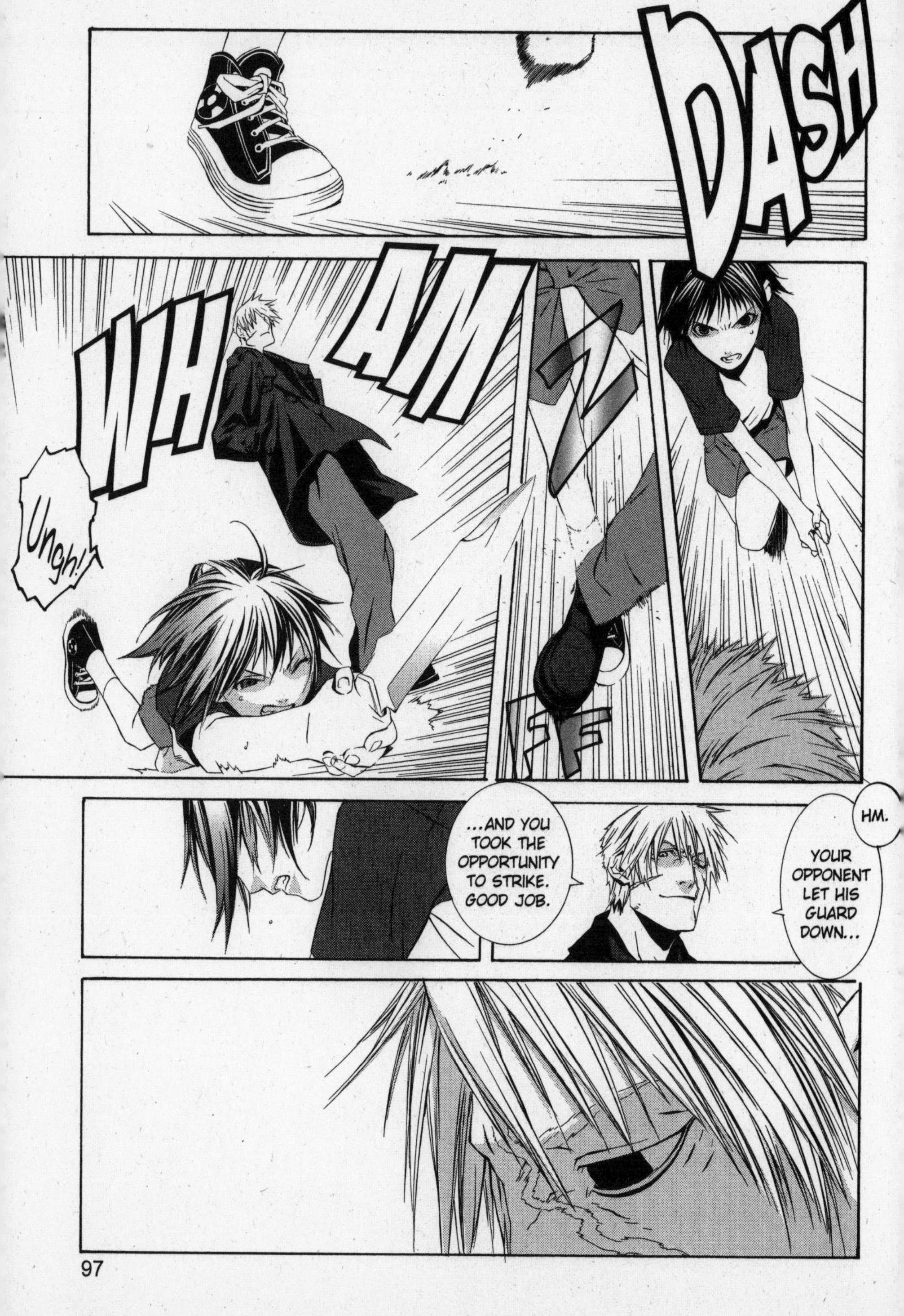
DASH
WHAM
Ungh!
HM.
YOUR OPPONENT LET HIS GUARD DOWN...
...AND YOU TOOK THE OPPORTUNITY TO STRIKE. GOOD JOB.

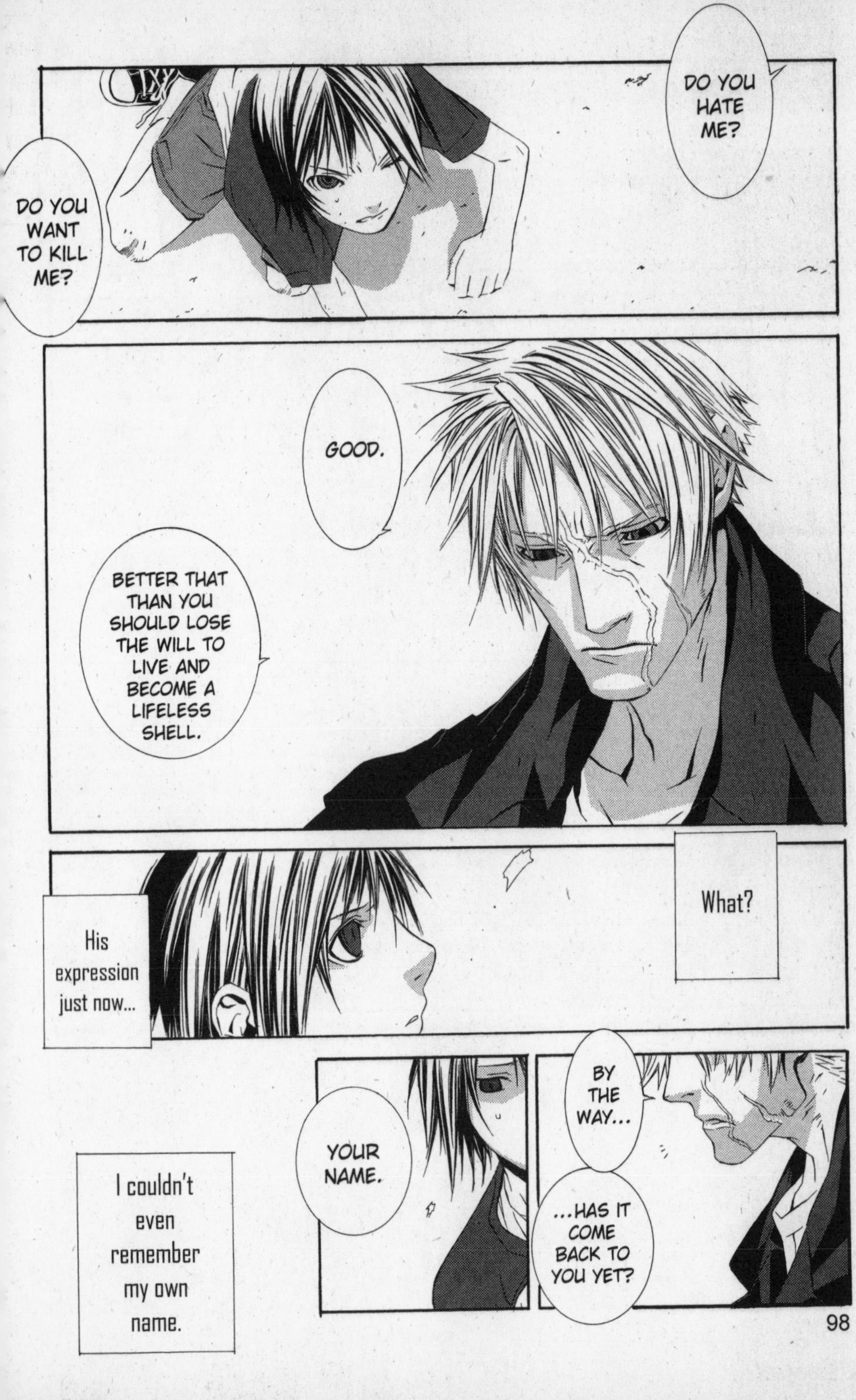
DO YOU HATE ME?
DO YOU WANT TO KILL ME?
GOOD.
BETTER THAT THAN YOU SHOULD LOSE THE WILL TO LIVE AND BECOME A LIFELESS SHELL.
What?
His expression just now...
BY THE WAY...
...HAS IT COME BACK TO YOU YET?
YOUR NAME.
I couldn't even remember my own name.

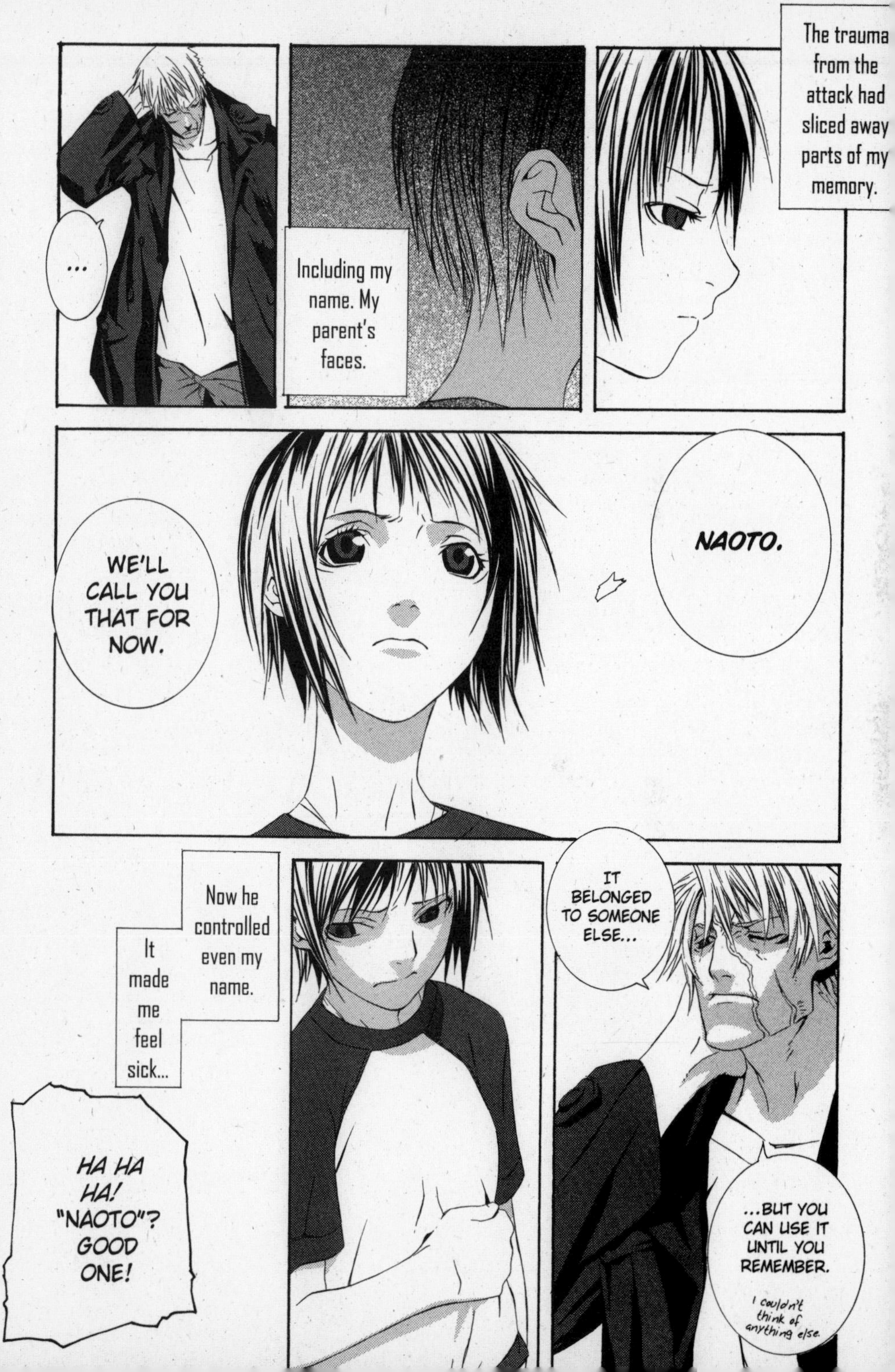
The trauma from the attack had sliced away parts of my memory.
Including my name. My parent's faces.
...
NAOTO.
WE'LL CALL YOU THAT FOR NOW.
IT BELONGED TO SOMEONE ELSE...
...BUT YOU CAN USE IT UNTIL YOU REMEMBER.
I couldn't think of anything else.
Now he controlled even my name.
It made me feel sick...
HA HA HA! "NAOTO"? GOOD ONE!

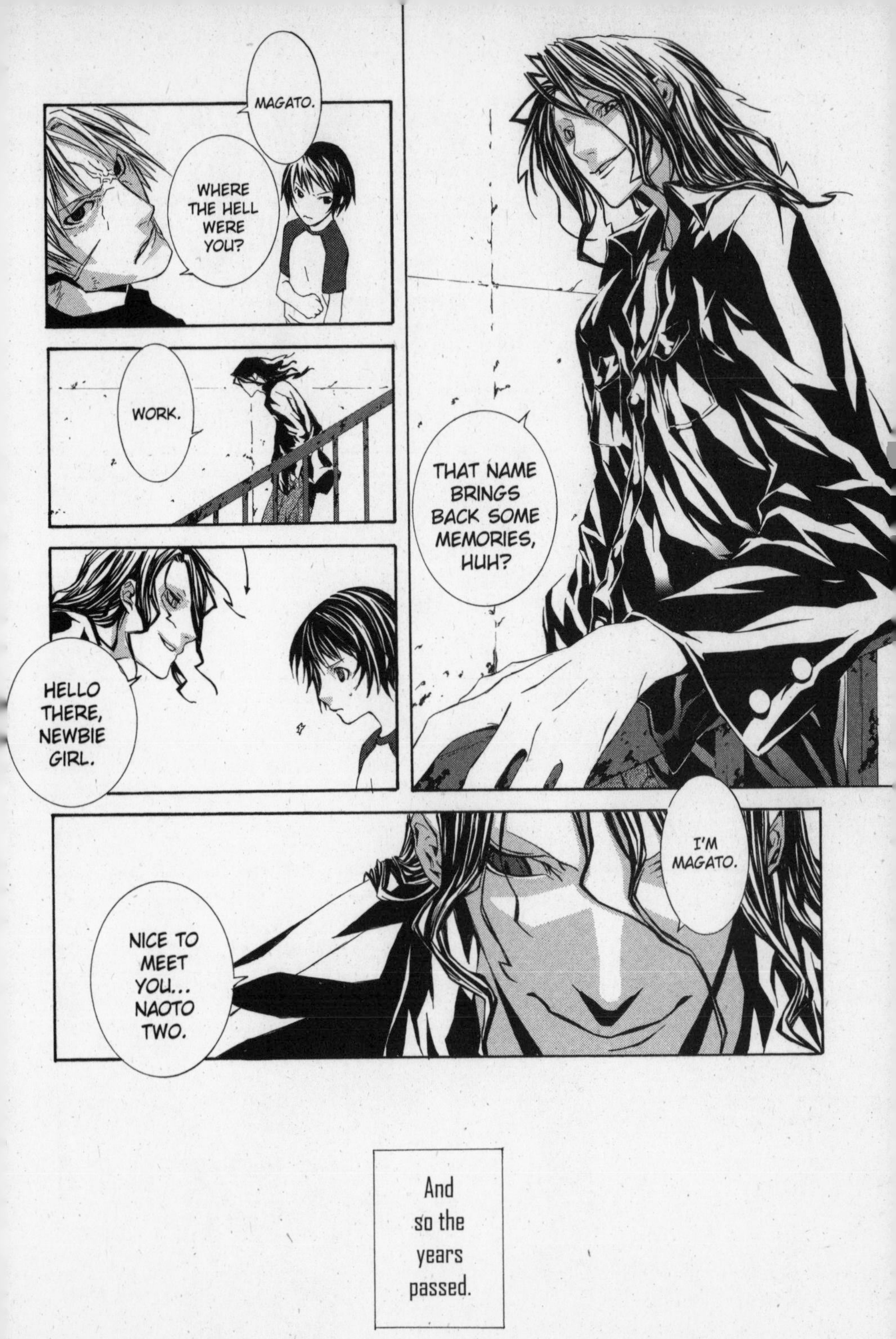
THAT NAME BRINGS BACK SOME MEMORIES, HUH?
MAGATO.
WHERE THE HELL WERE YOU?
WORK.
HELLO THERE, NEWBIE GIRL.
I'M MAGATO.
NICE TO MEET YOU... NAOTO TWO.
And so the years passed.

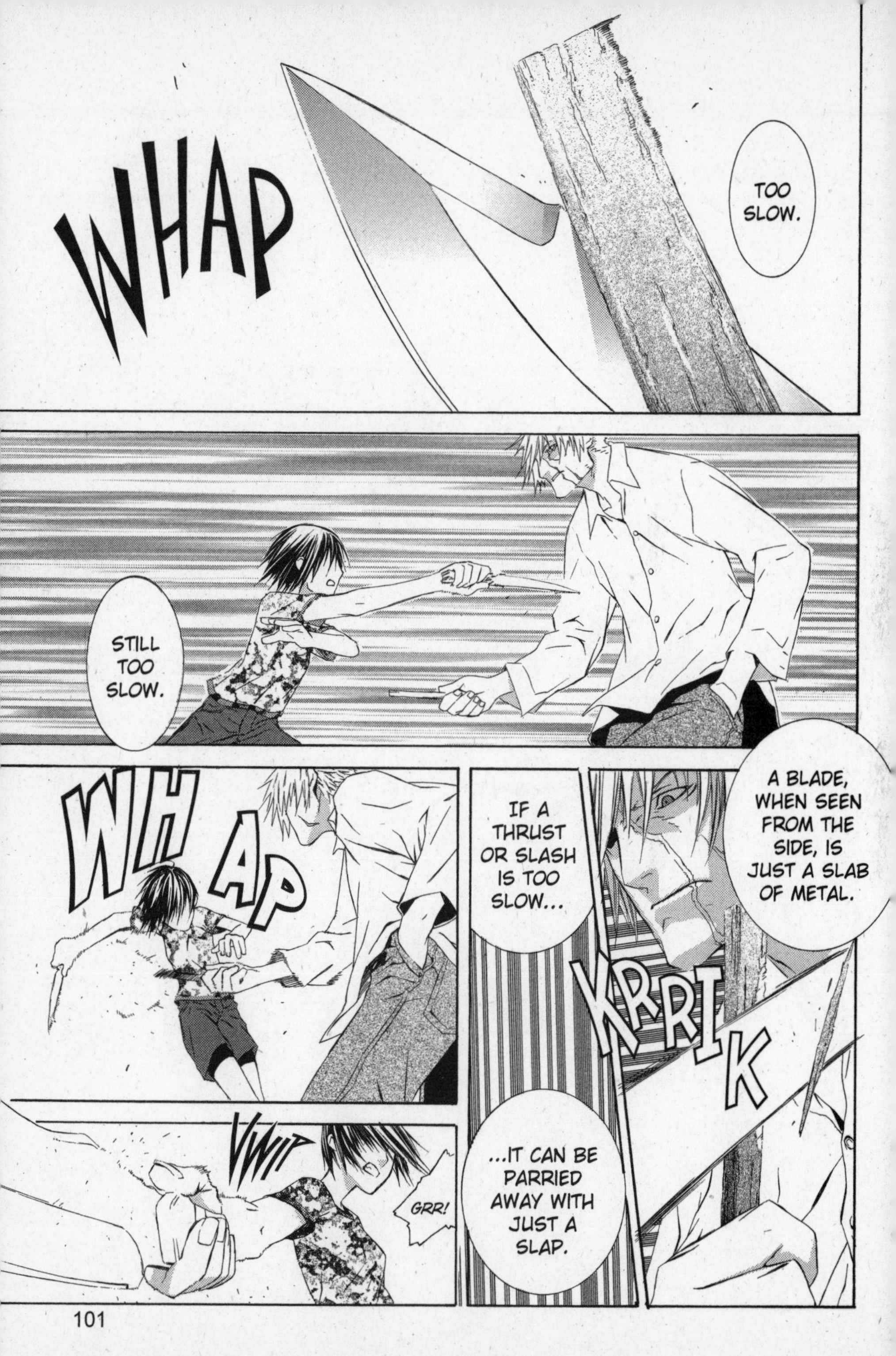
TOO SLOW.
WHAP
STILL TOO SLOW.
A BLADE, WHEN SEEN FROM THE SIDE, IS JUST A SLAB OF METAL.
IF A THRUST OR SLASH IS TOO SLOW...
KRRIK
...IT CAN BE PARRIED AWAY WITH JUST A SLAP.
WHAP
VWIP
GRR!

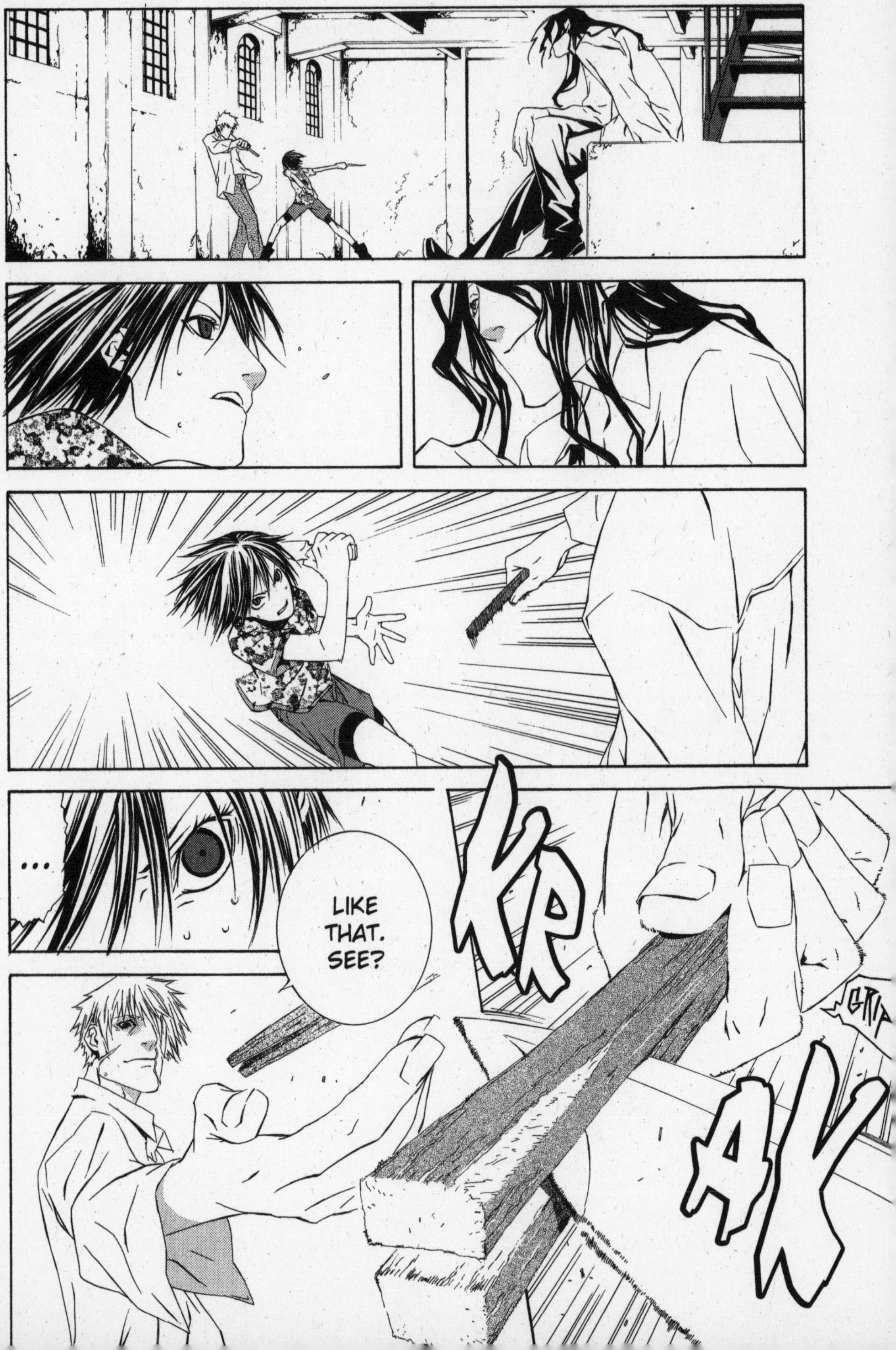
...
LIKE THAT. SEE?
KR
GRIP
AK

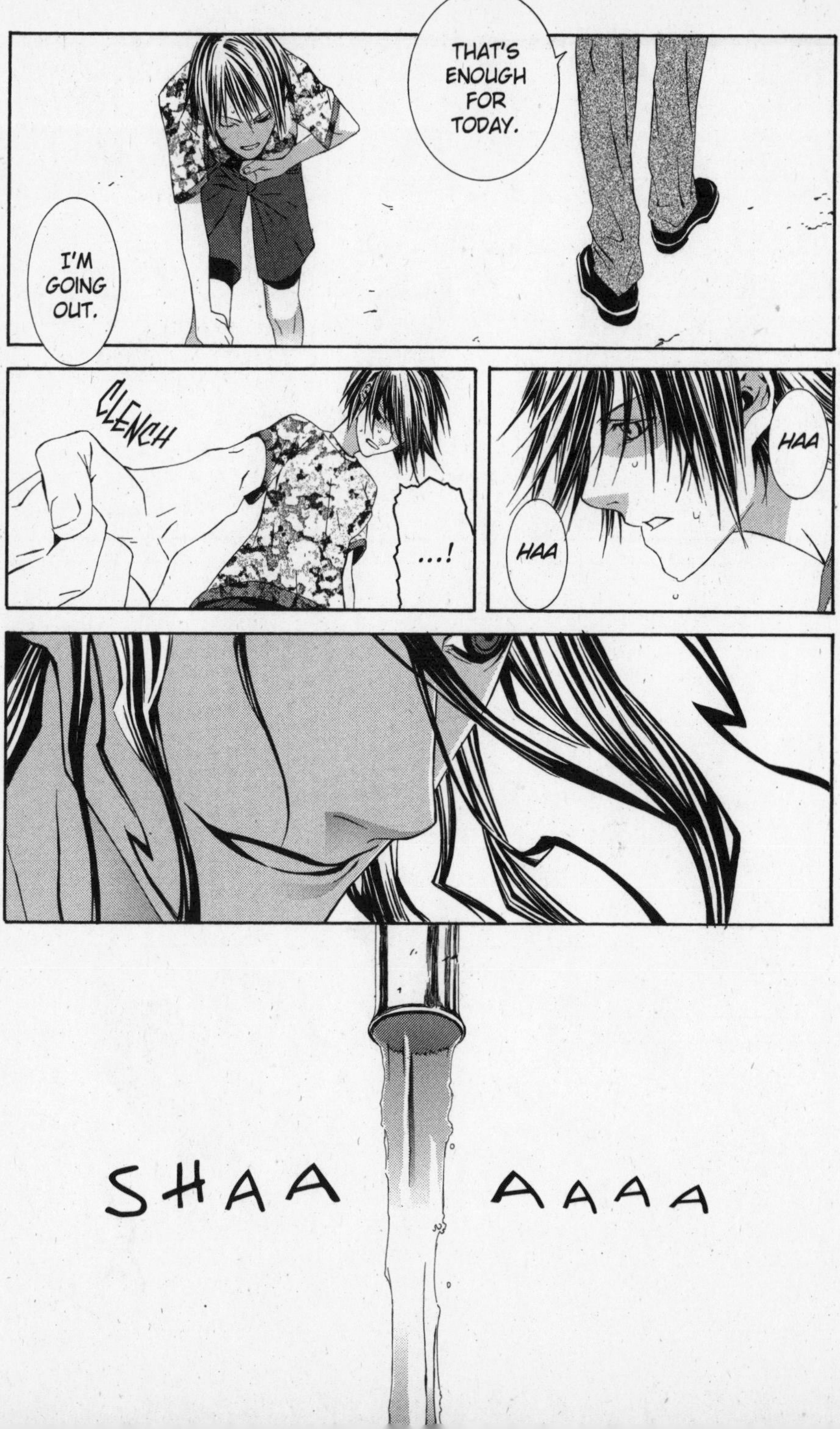
THAT'S ENOUGH FOR TODAY.
I'M GOING OUT.
HAA
HAA
CLENCH
...!
SHAA AAAA

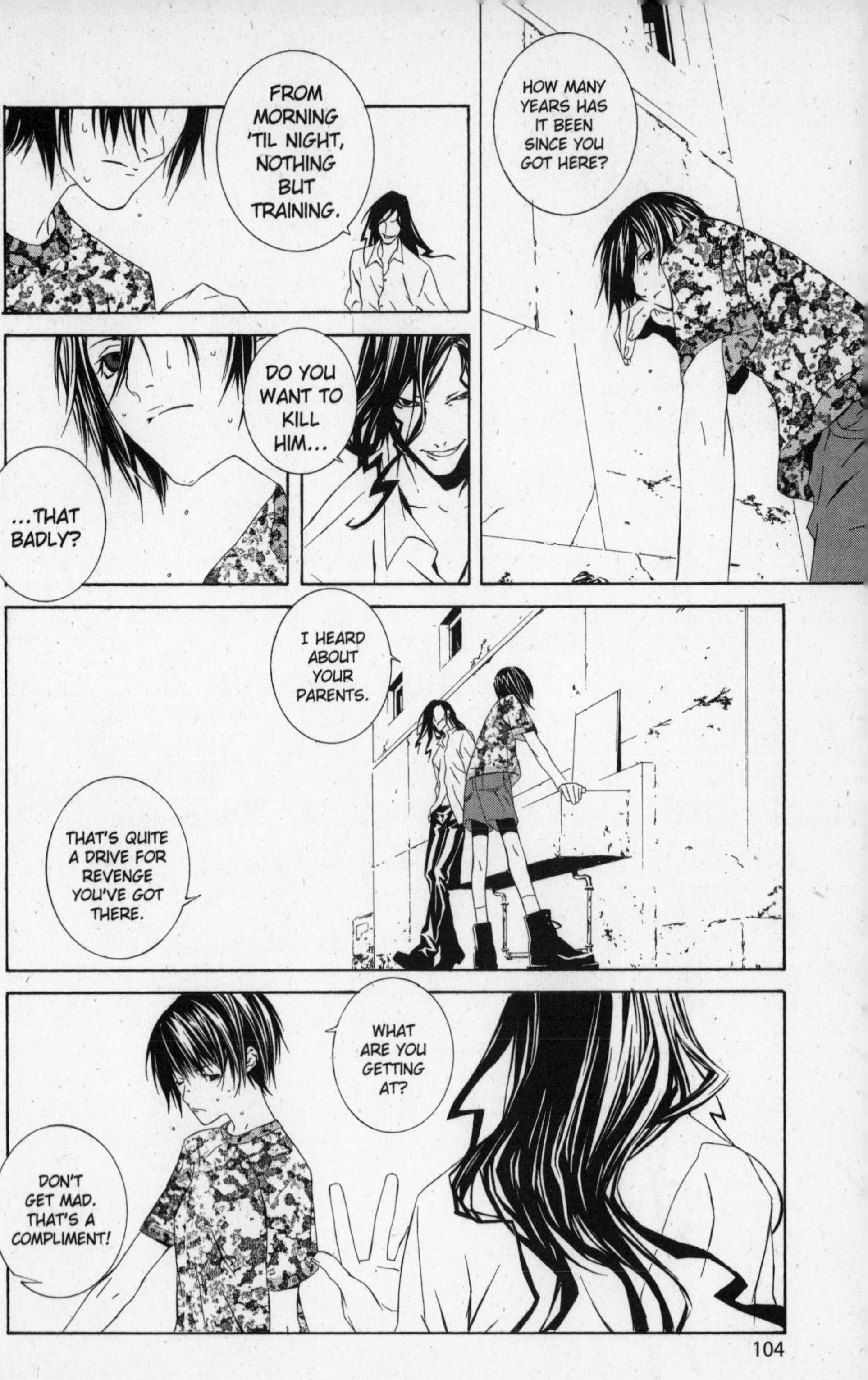
HOW MANY YEARS HAS IT BEEN SINCE YOU GOT HERE?
FROM MORNING 'TIL NIGHT, NOTHING BUT TRAINING.
DO YOU WANT TO KILL HIM...
...THAT BADLY?
I HEARD ABOUT YOUR PARENTS.
THAT'S QUITE A DRIVE FOR REVENGE YOU'VE GOT THERE.
WHAT ARE YOU GETTING AT?
DON'T GET MAD. THAT'S A COMPLIMENT!

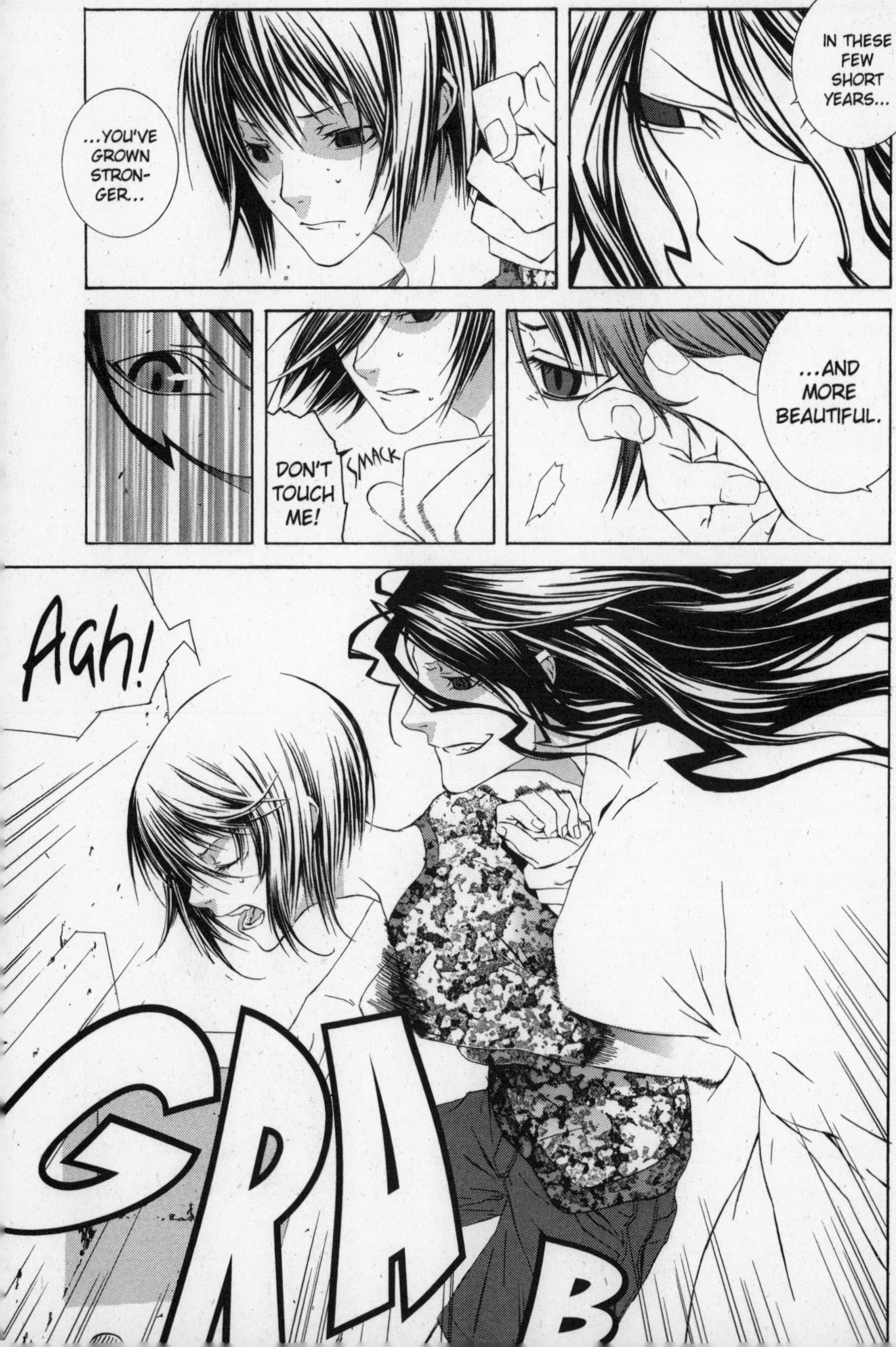
IN THESE FEW SHORT YEARS...
...YOU'VE GROWN STRONGER...
...AND MORE BEAUTIFUL.
SMACK
DON'T TOUCH ME!
Aah!
GRAB

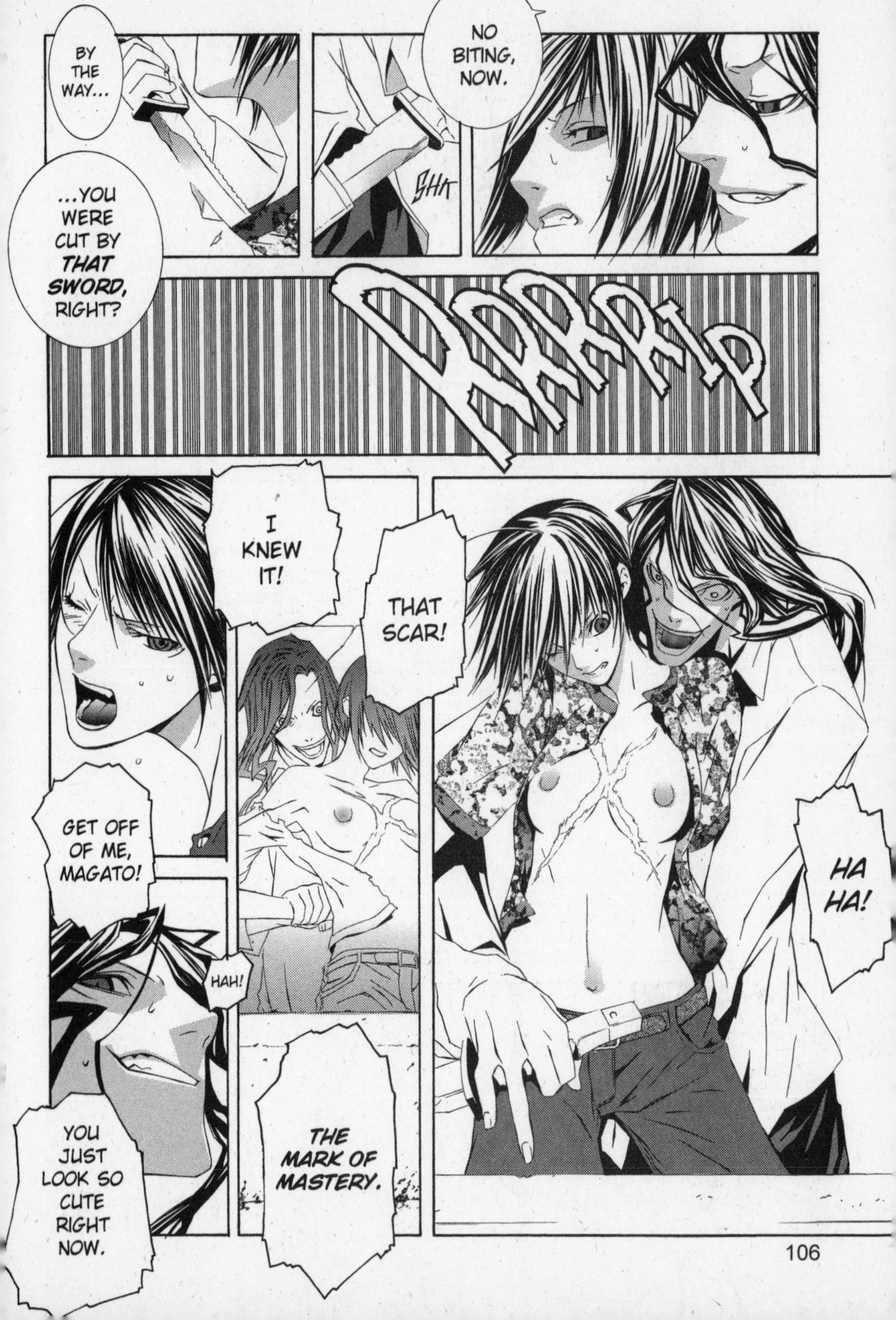
NO BITING, NOW.
SHK
BY THE WAY...
...YOU WERE CUT BY *THAT SWORD*, RIGHT?
DRRRIP
HA HA!
I KNEW IT!
THAT SCAR!
GET OFF OF ME, MAGATO!
THE MARK OF MASTERY.
HAH!
YOU JUST LOOK SO CUTE RIGHT NOW.

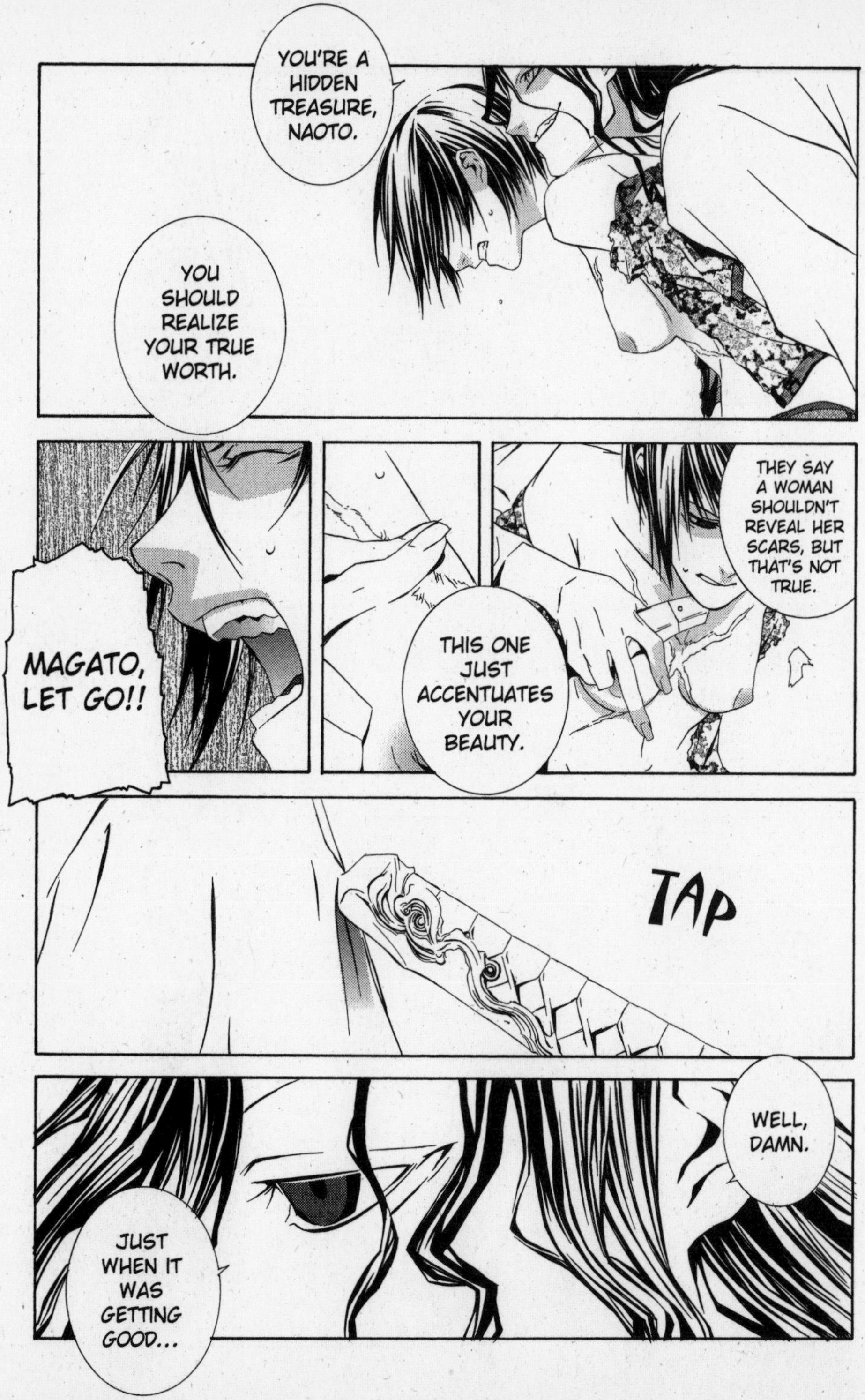
YOU'RE A HIDDEN TREASURE, NAOTO.
YOU SHOULD REALIZE YOUR TRUE WORTH.
THEY SAY A WOMAN SHOULDN'T REVEAL HER SCARS, BUT THAT'S NOT TRUE.
THIS ONE JUST ACCENTUATES YOUR BEAUTY.
MAGATO, LET GO!!
TAP
WELL, DAMN.
JUST WHEN IT WAS GETTING GOOD...

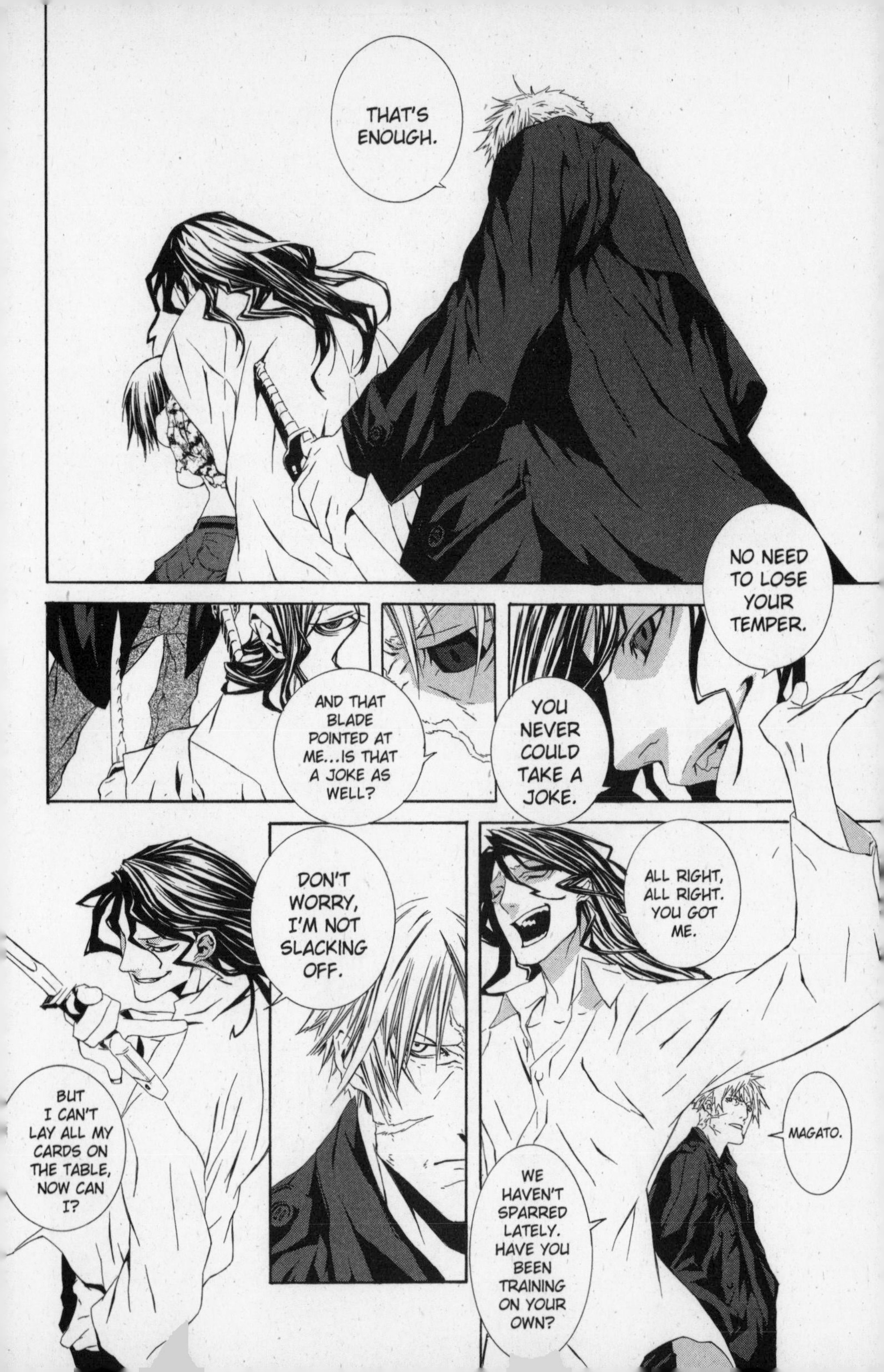
THAT'S ENOUGH.
NO NEED TO LOSE YOUR TEMPER.
YOU NEVER COULD TAKE A JOKE.
AND THAT BLADE POINTED AT ME...IS THAT A JOKE AS WELL?
ALL RIGHT, ALL RIGHT. YOU GOT ME.
MAGATO.
WE HAVEN'T SPARRED LATELY. HAVE YOU BEEN TRAINING ON YOUR OWN?
DON'T WORRY, I'M NOT SLACKING OFF.
BUT I CAN'T LAY ALL MY CARDS ON THE TABLE, NOW CAN I?

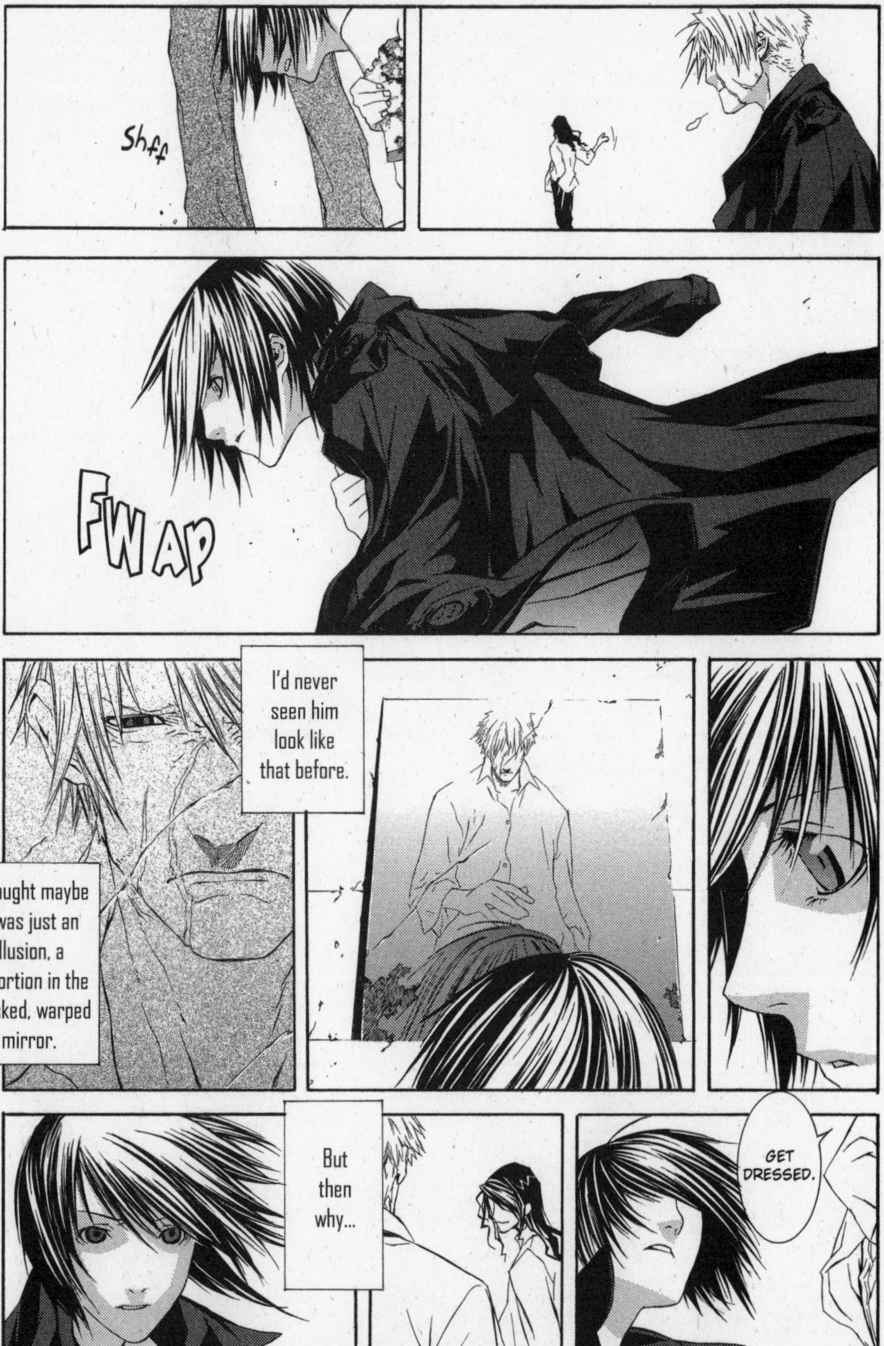
Shff
FWAP
I'd never seen him look like that before.
I thought maybe it was just an illusion, a distortion in the cracked, warped mirror.
GET DRESSED.
But then why...

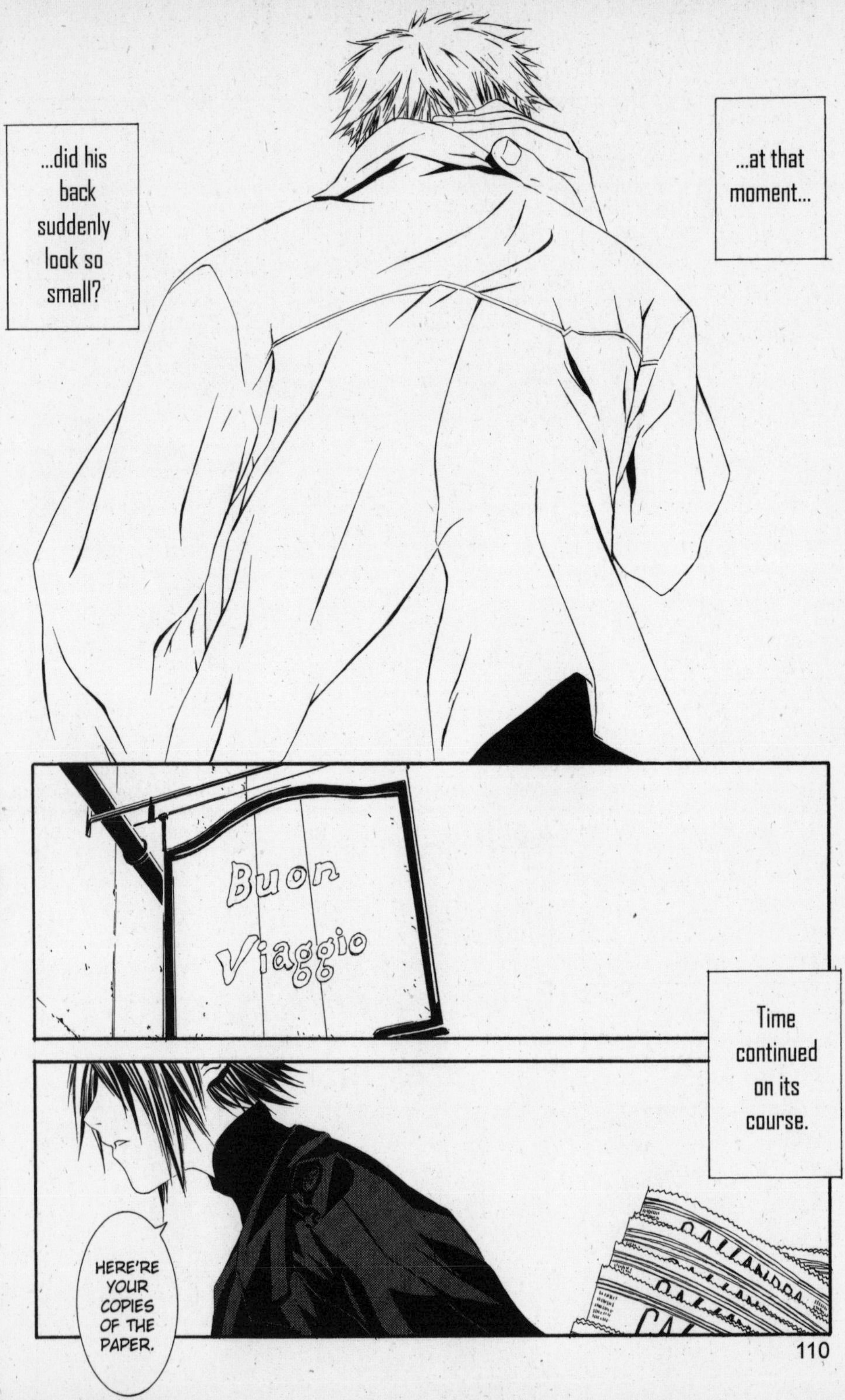
...at that moment...
...did his back suddenly look so small?
Buon Viaggio
Time continued on its course.
HERE'RE YOUR COPIES OF THE PAPER.

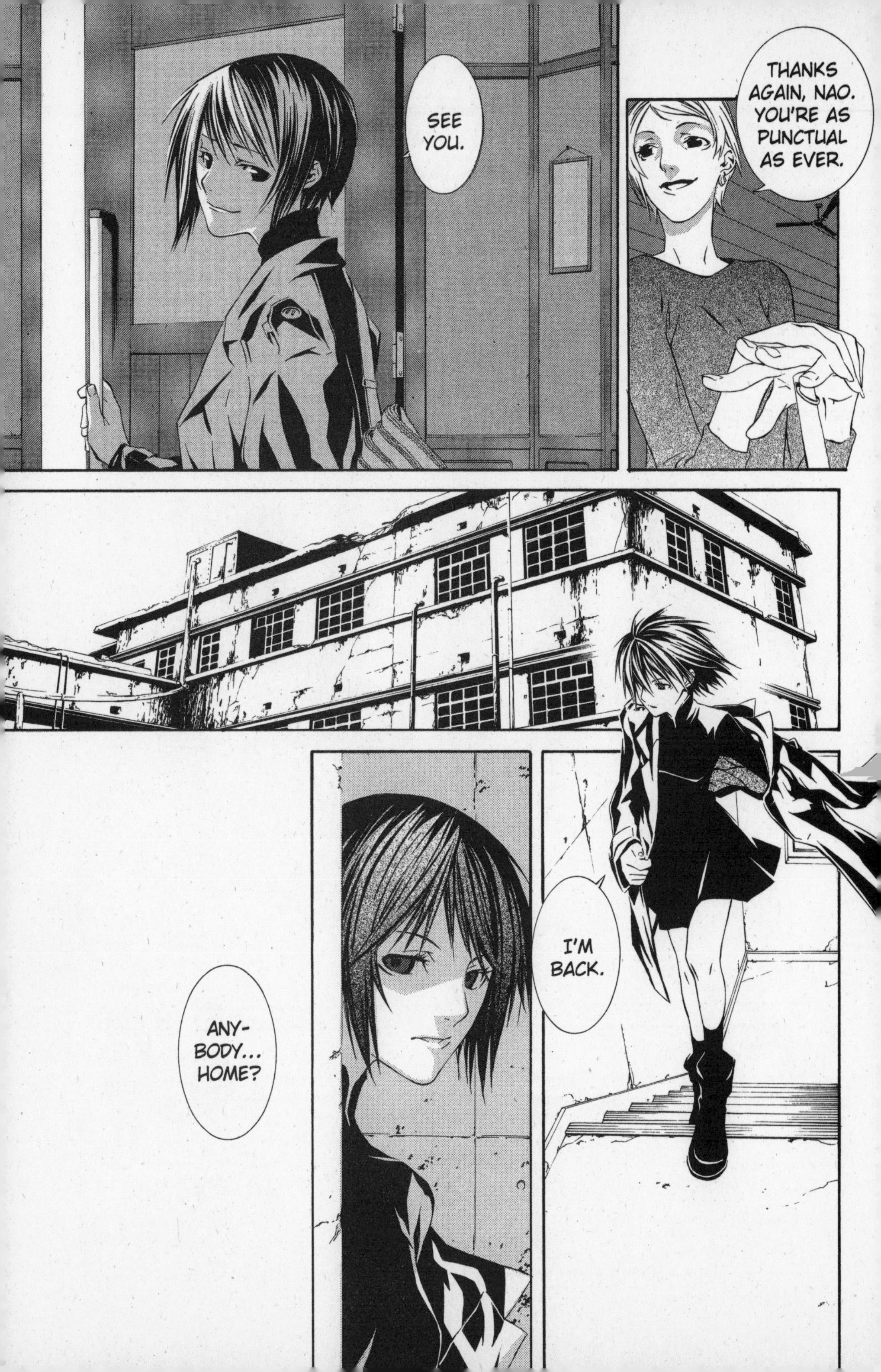
THANKS AGAIN, NAO. YOU'RE AS PUNCTUAL AS EVER.
SEE YOU.
I'M BACK.
ANY-BODY... HOME?

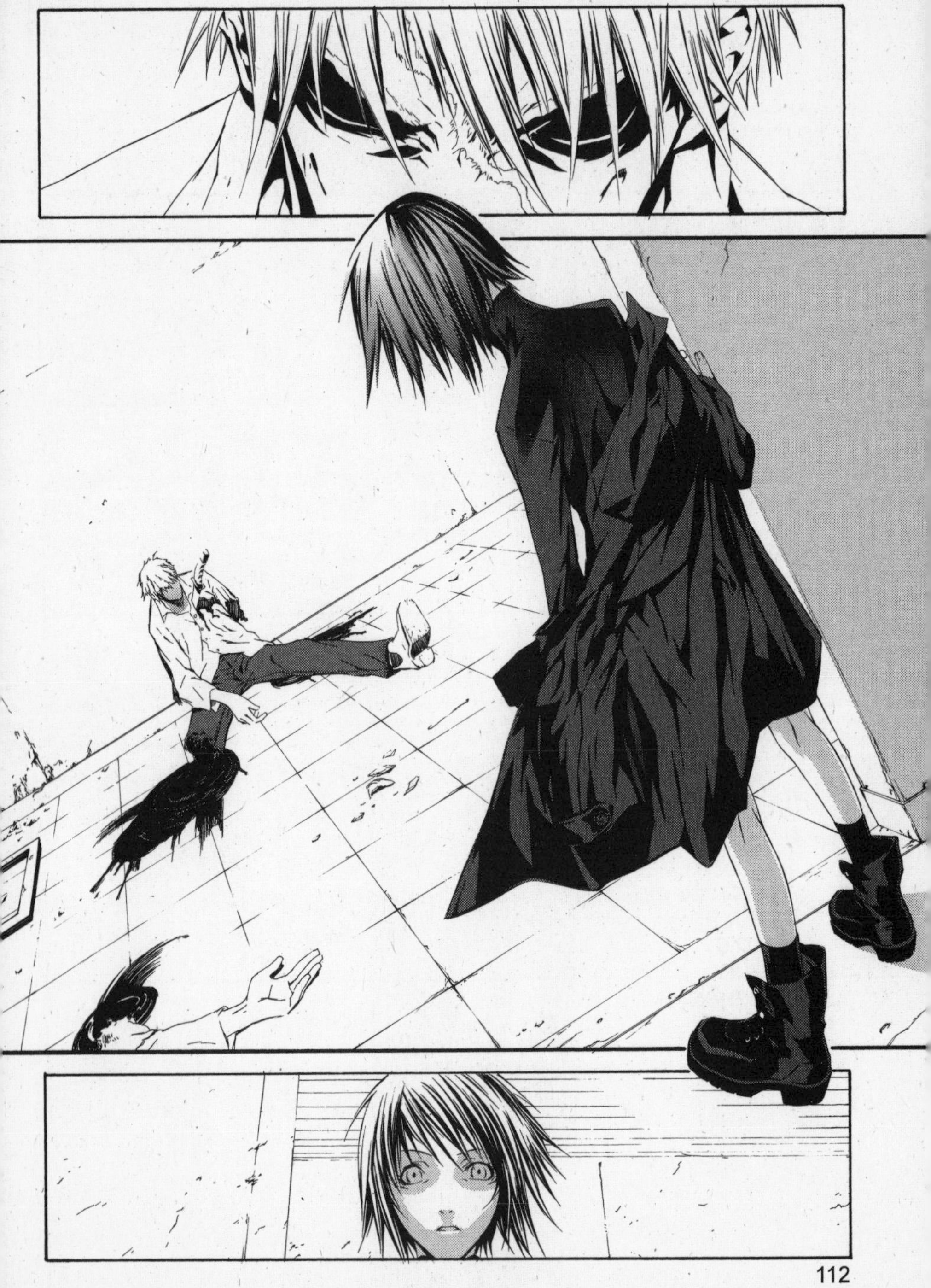

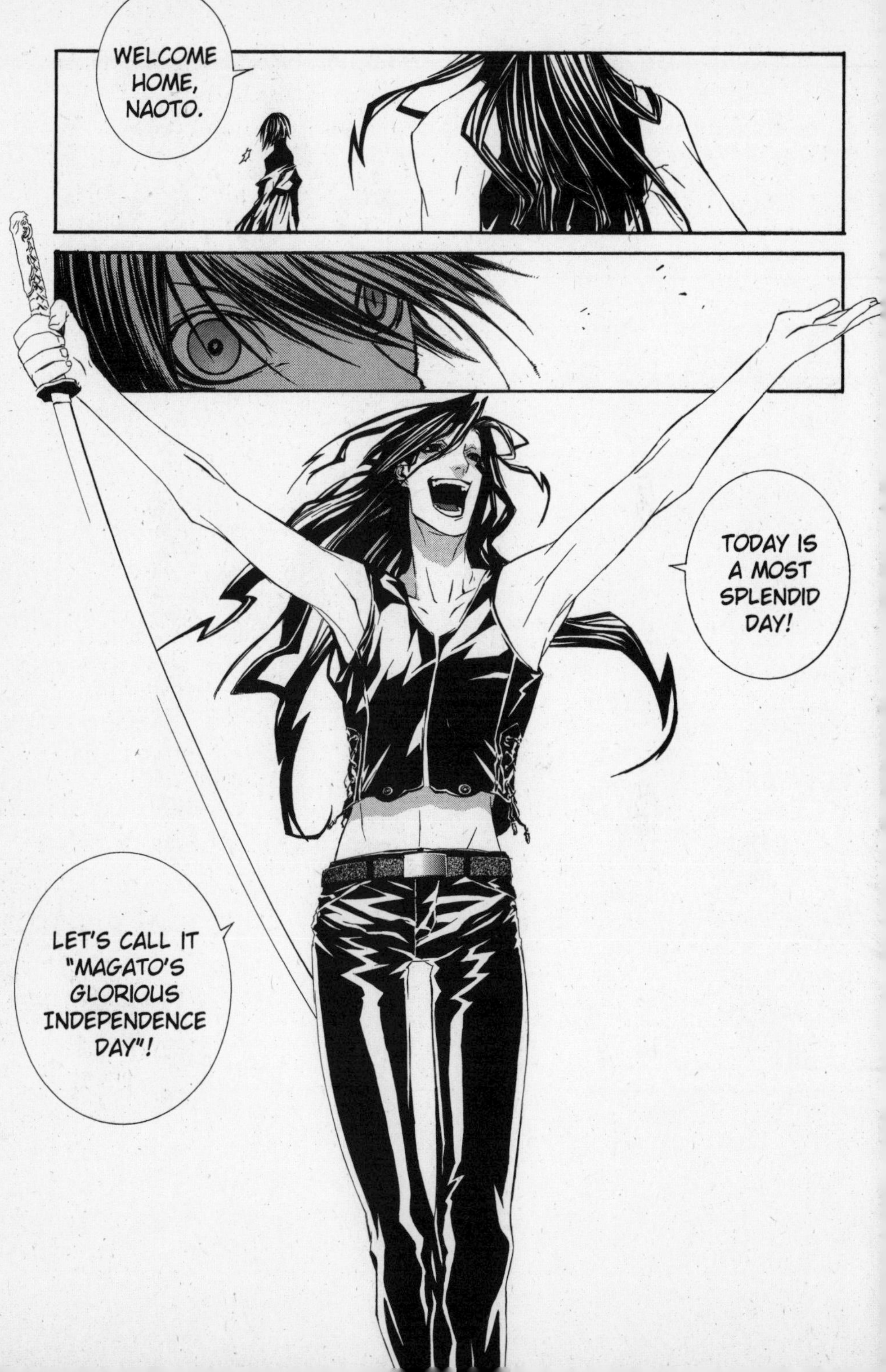
WELCOME HOME, NAOTO.
TODAY IS A MOST SPLENDID DAY!
LET'S CALL IT "MAGATO'S GLORIOUS INDEPENDENCE DAY"!

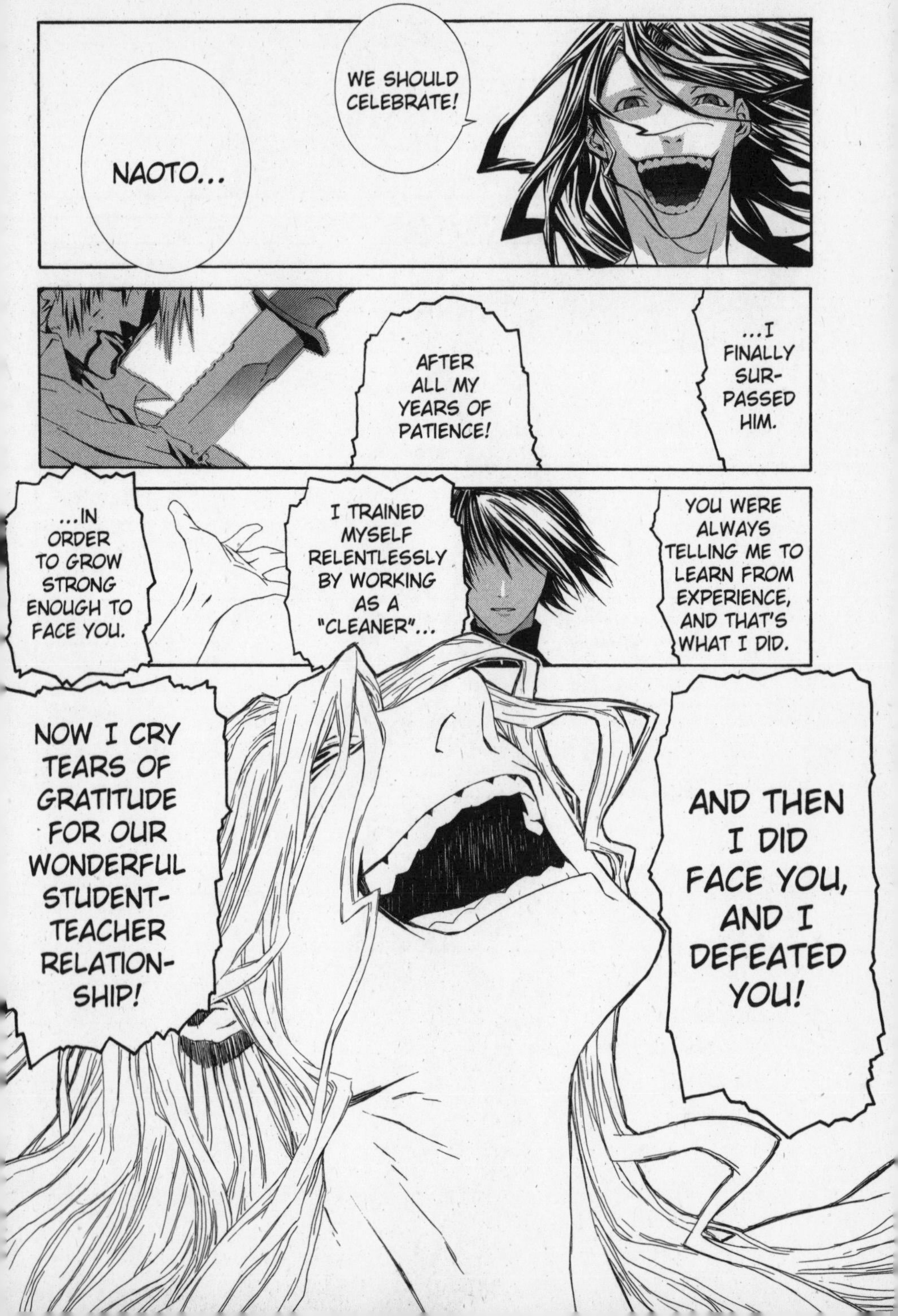
WE SHOULD CELEBRATE!
NAOTO...
...I FINALLY SUR-PASSED HIM.
AFTER ALL MY YEARS OF PATIENCE!
YOU WERE ALWAYS TELLING ME TO LEARN FROM EXPERIENCE, AND THAT'S WHAT I DID.
I TRAINED MYSELF RELENTLESSLY BY WORKING AS A "CLEANER"...
...IN ORDER TO GROW STRONG ENOUGH TO FACE YOU.
AND THEN I DID FACE YOU, AND I DEFEATED YOU!
NOW I CRY TEARS OF GRATITUDE FOR OUR WONDERFUL STUDENT-TEACHER RELATION-SHIP!

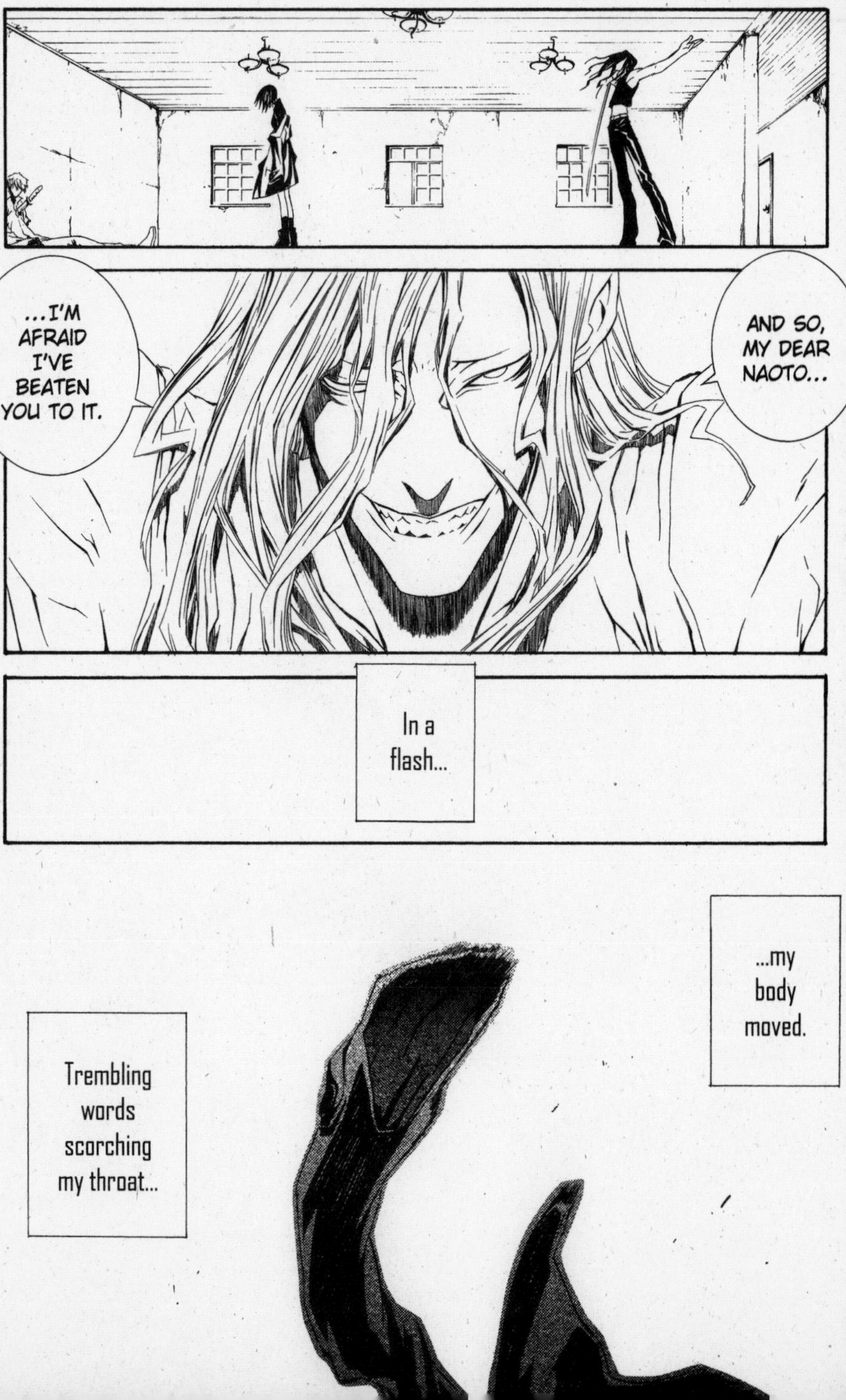
AND SO, MY DEAR NAOTO...
...I'M AFRAID I'VE BEATEN YOU TO IT.
In a flash...
...my body moved.
Trembling words scorching my throat...

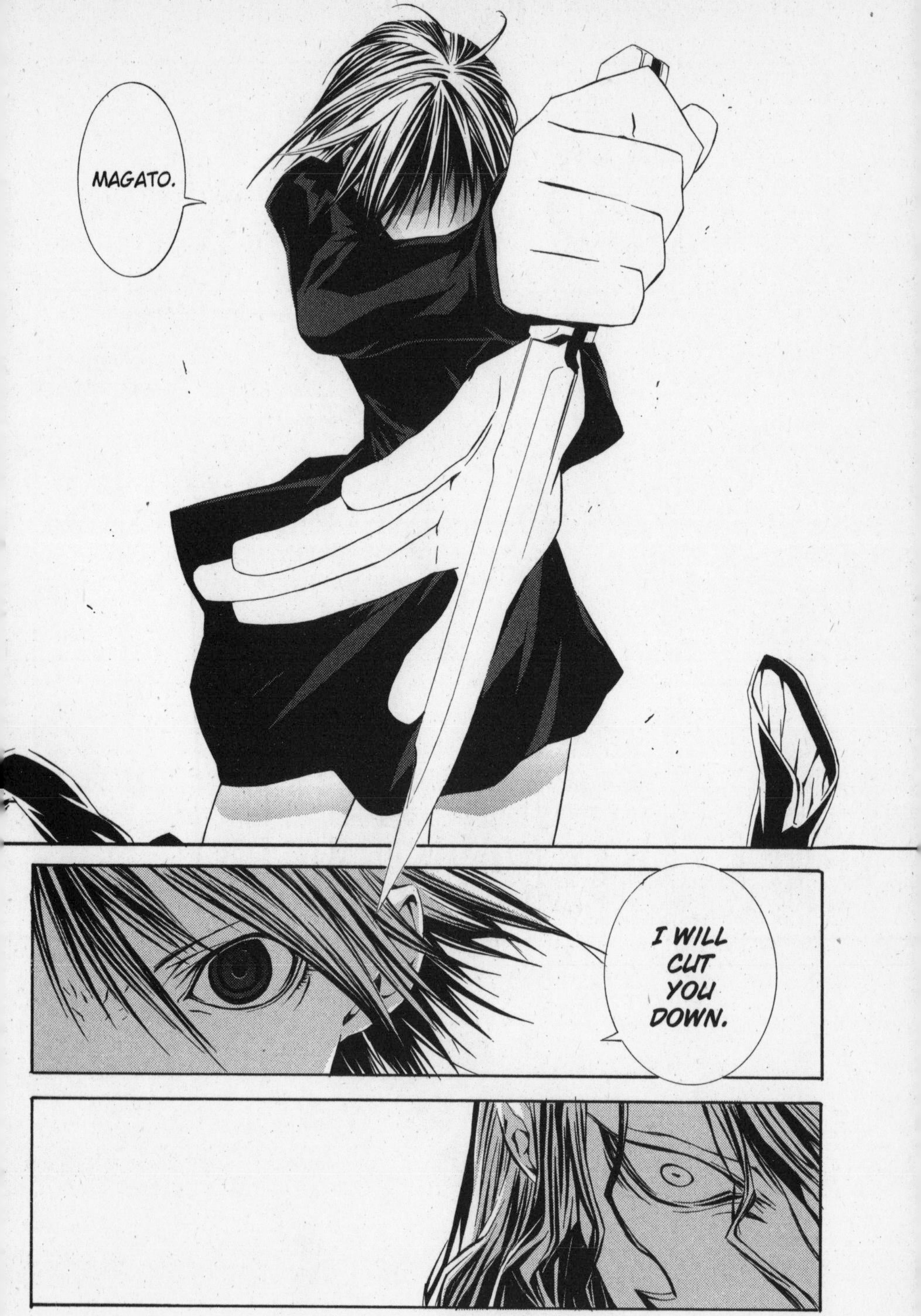
MAGATO.
I WILL CUT YOU DOWN.

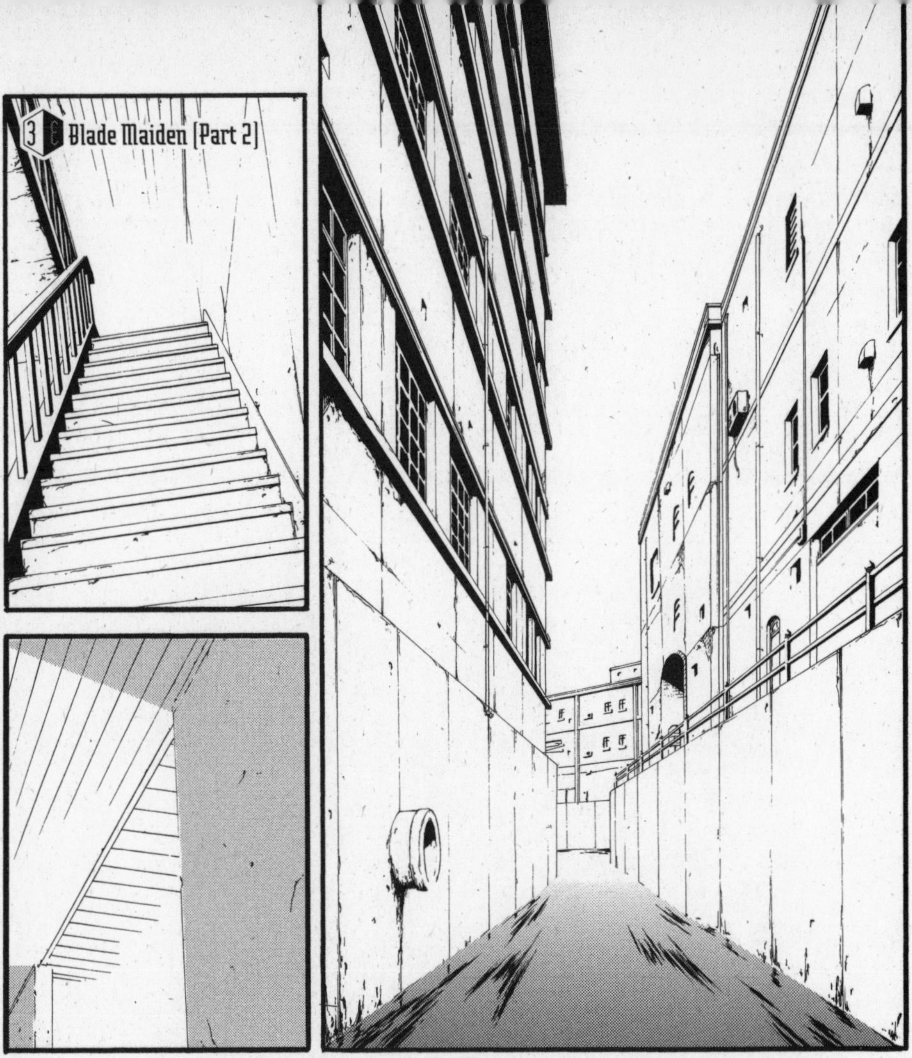
3 Blade Maiden [Part 2]

My mind was overwhelmed by a storm of emotions.

When I came back to my senses, I was just swinging my blade around wildly.

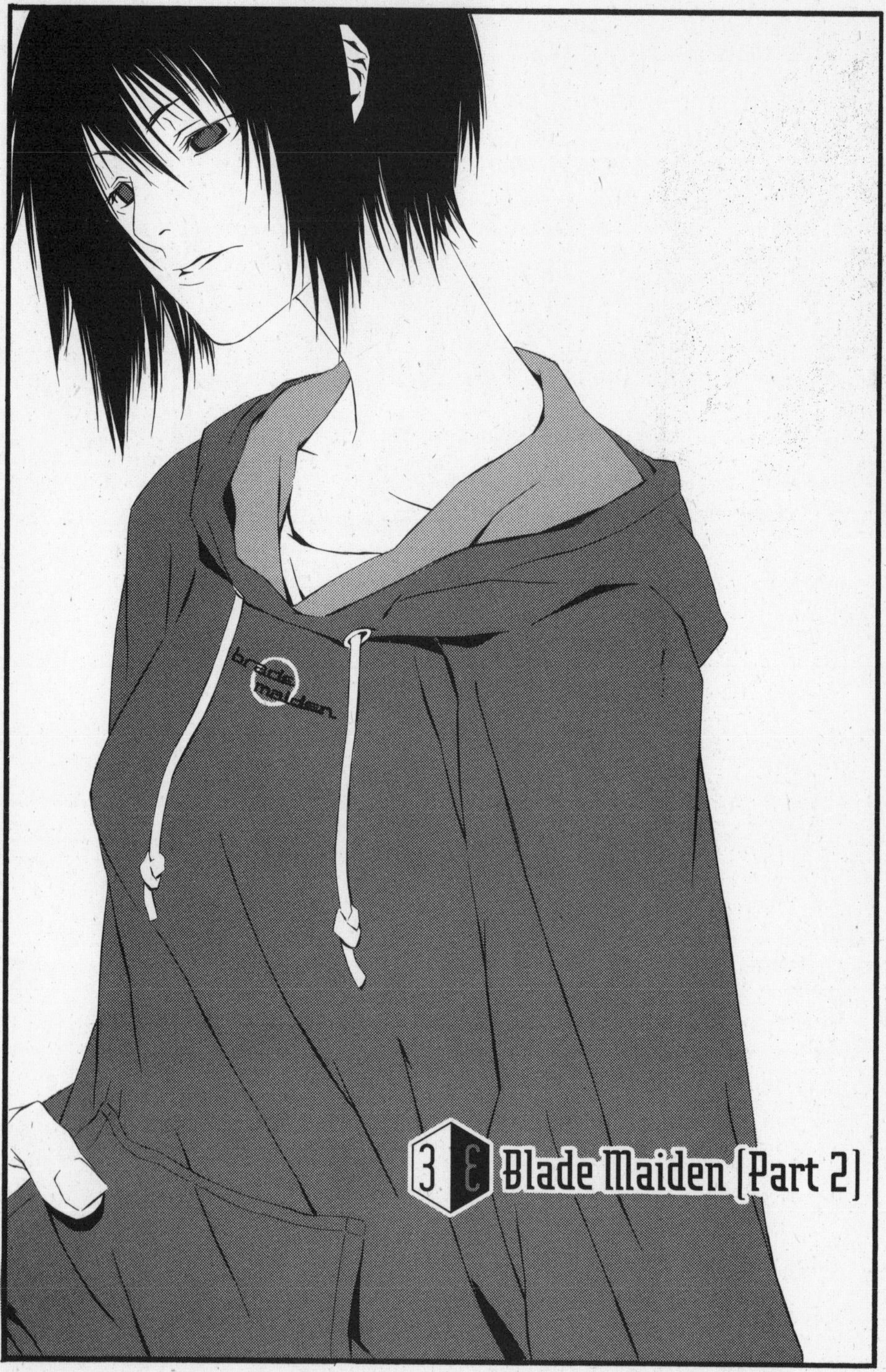
3 Blade Maiden [Part 2]

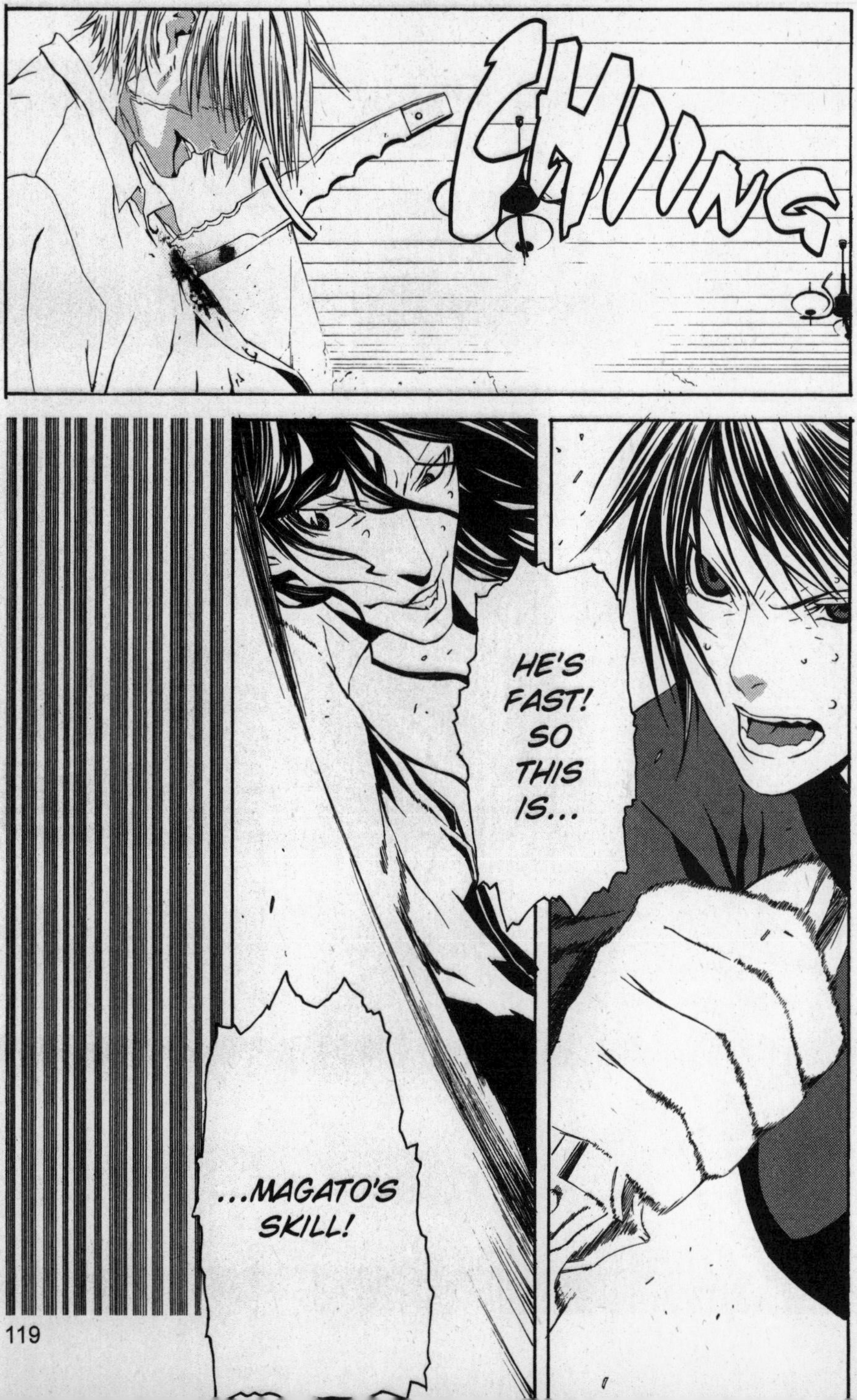
CHING
HE'S FAST! SO THIS IS...
...MAGATO'S SKILL!

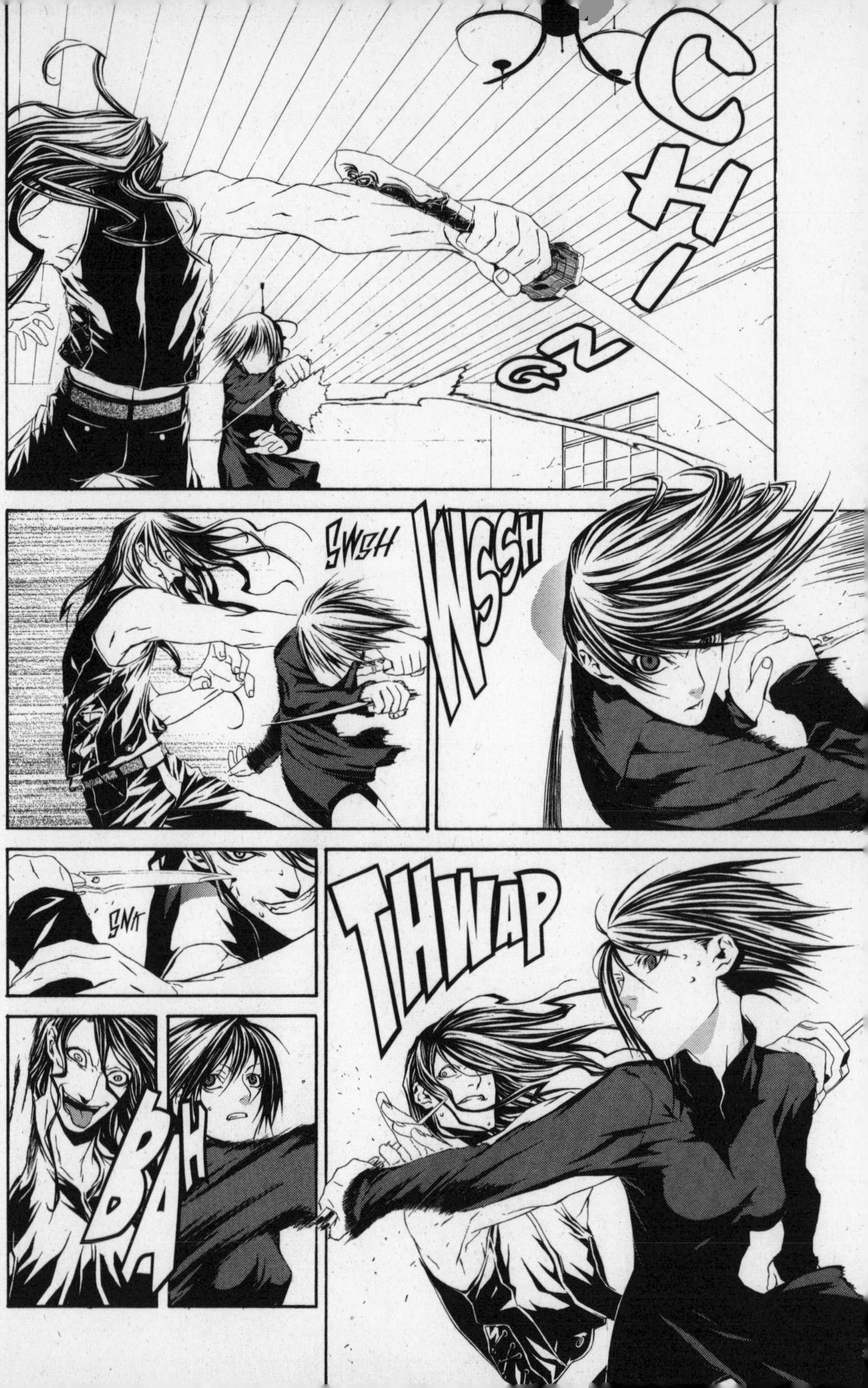
CHING
WSSH
SWSH
THWAP
SNK
BAH

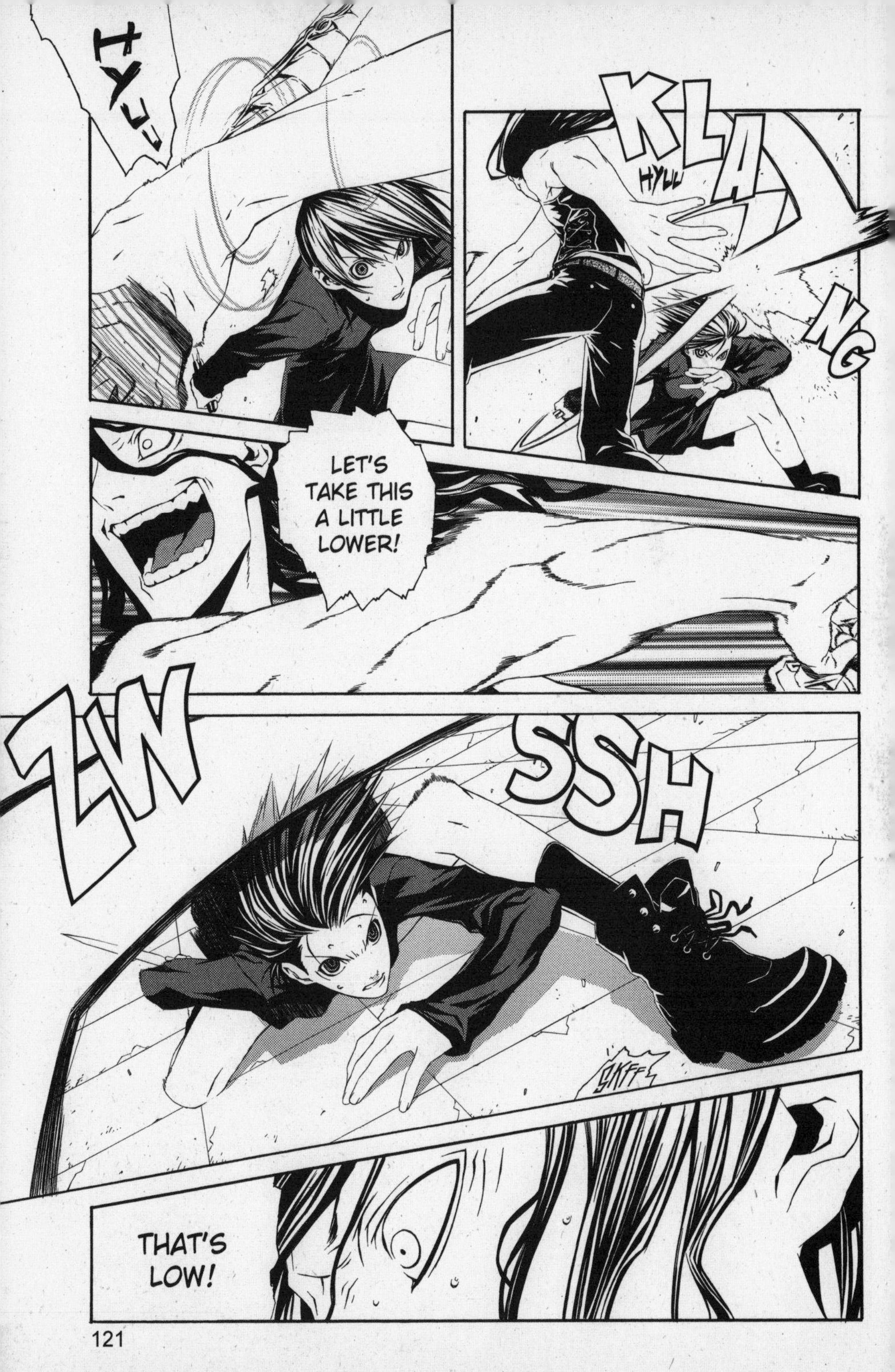
KLANG
HYUU
HYUU
LET'S TAKE THIS A LITTLE LOWER!
ZWSSH
SKFF
THAT'S LOW!

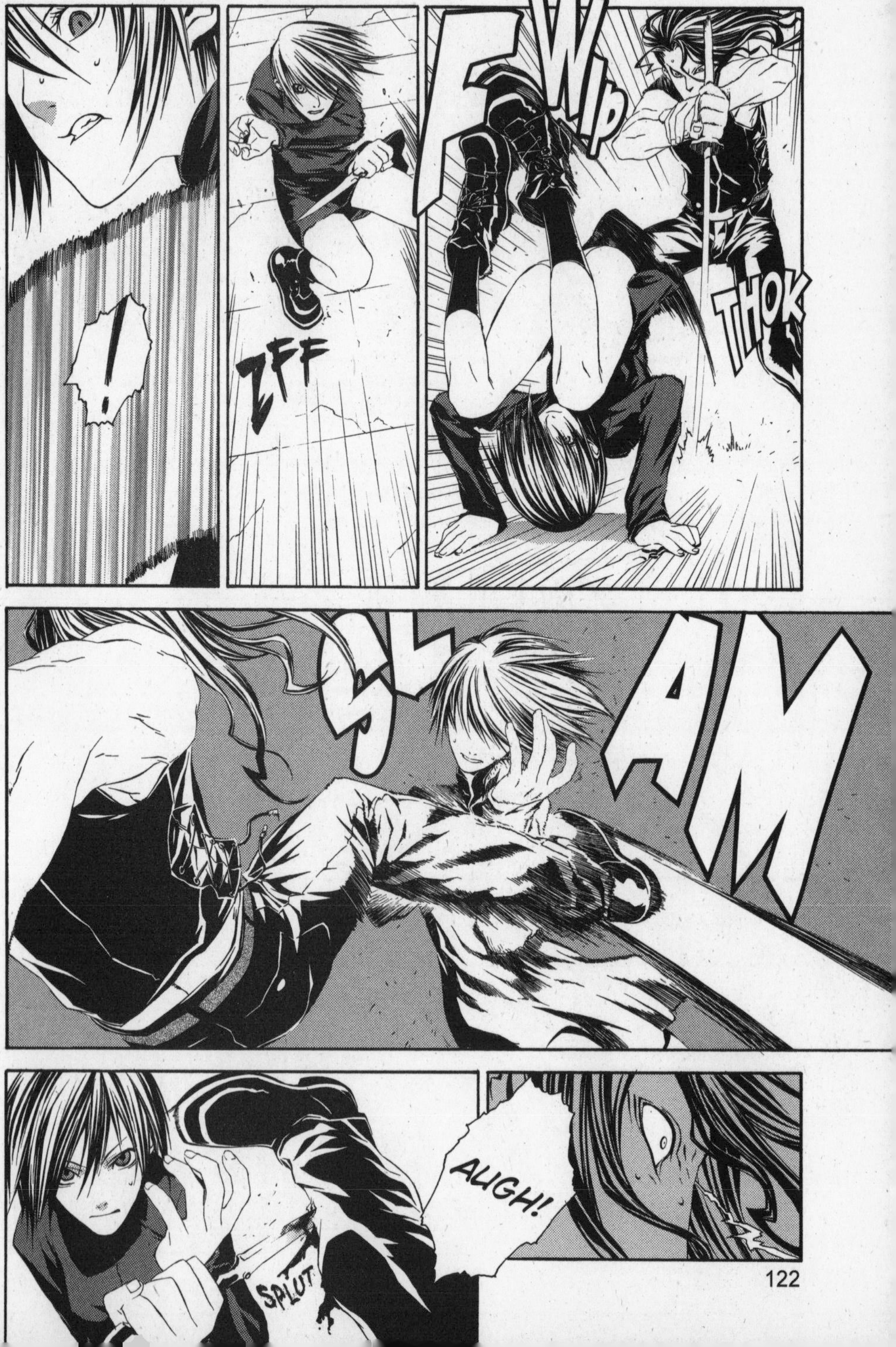
FWIP
THOK
ZFF
!
SLAM
AUGH!
SPLUT

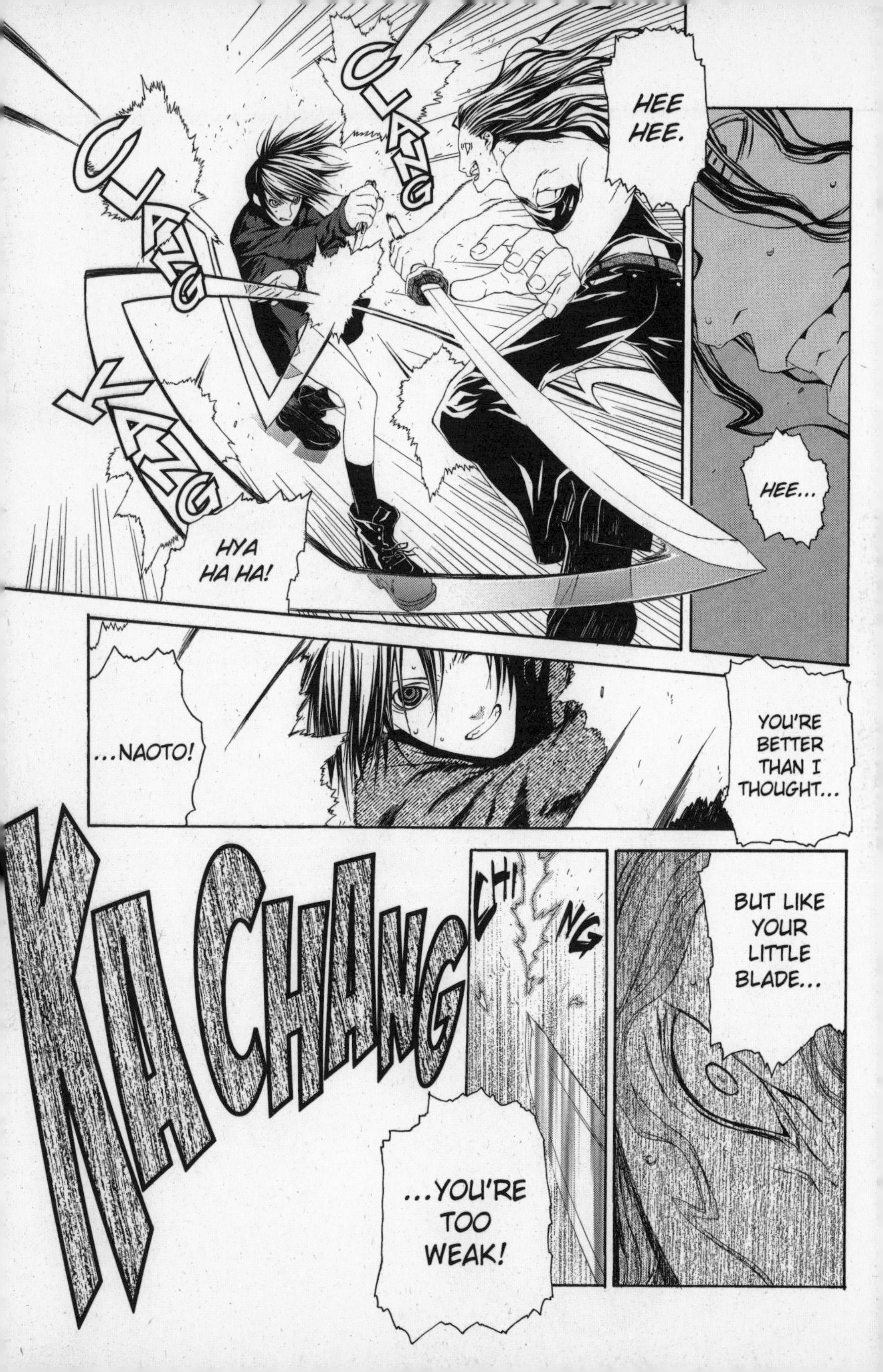
HEE HEE.
HEE...
CLANG
CLANG
YANG
HYA HA HA!
YOU'RE BETTER THAN I THOUGHT...
...NAOTO!
BUT LIKE YOUR LITTLE BLADE...
CHING
KA CHANG
...YOU'RE TOO WEAK!

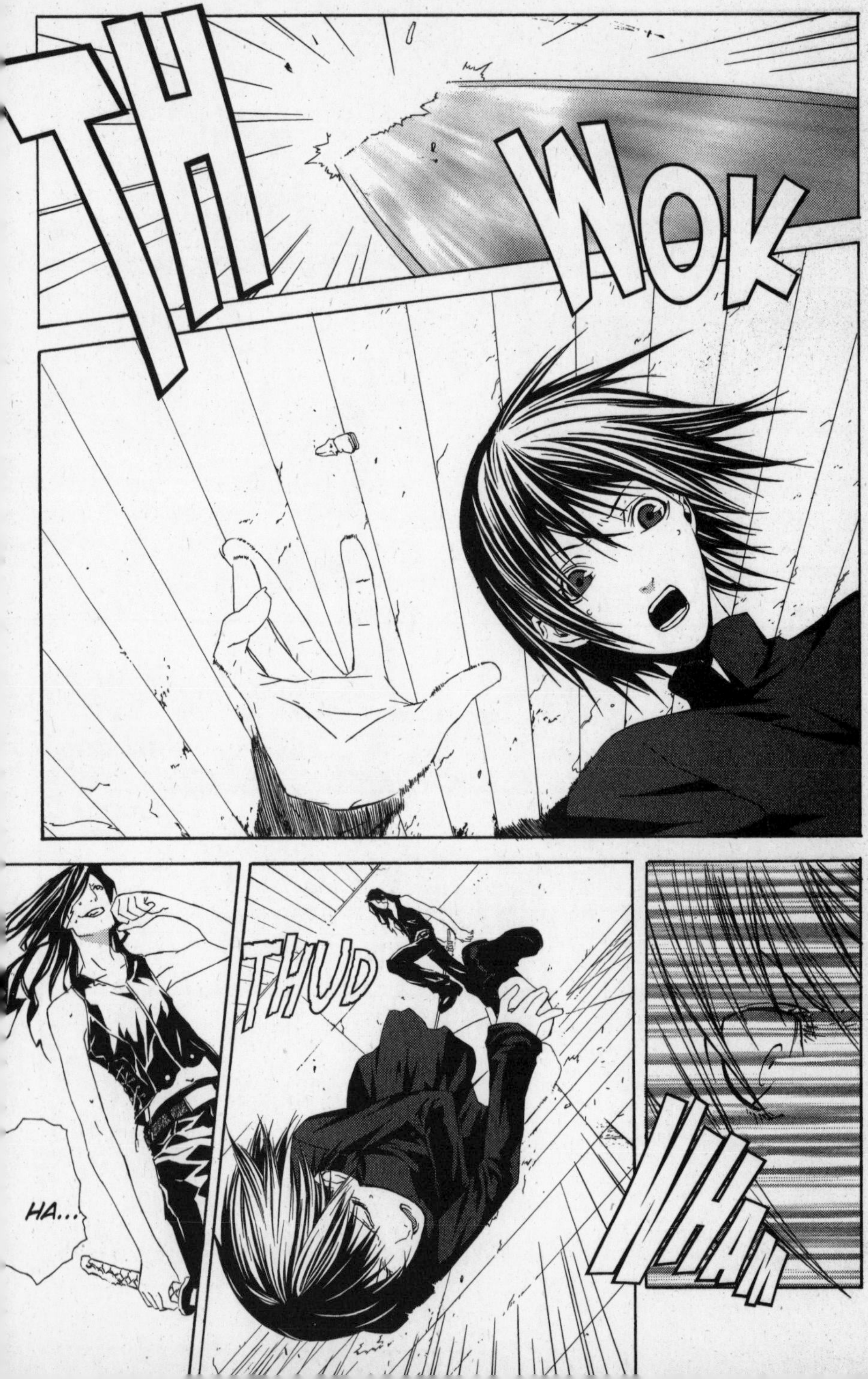
THWOK
WHAM
THUD
HA...

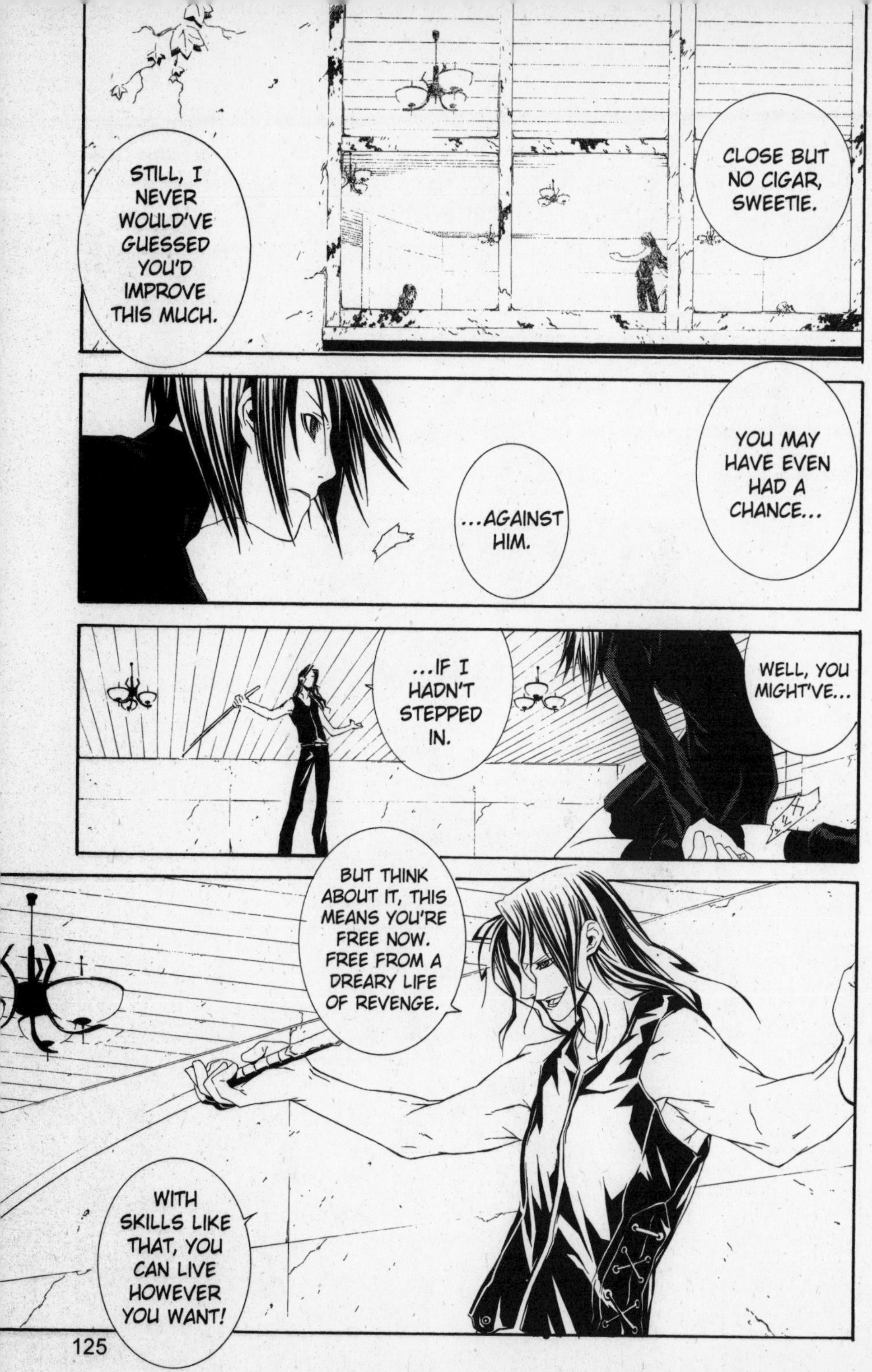
CLOSE BUT NO CIGAR, SWEETIE.
STILL, I NEVER WOULD'VE GUESSED YOU'D IMPROVE THIS MUCH.
YOU MAY HAVE EVEN HAD A CHANCE...
...AGAINST HIM.
WELL, YOU MIGHT'VE...
...IF I HADN'T STEPPED IN.
BUT THINK ABOUT IT, THIS MEANS YOU'RE FREE NOW. FREE FROM A DREARY LIFE OF REVENGE.
WITH SKILLS LIKE THAT, YOU CAN LIVE HOWEVER YOU WANT!

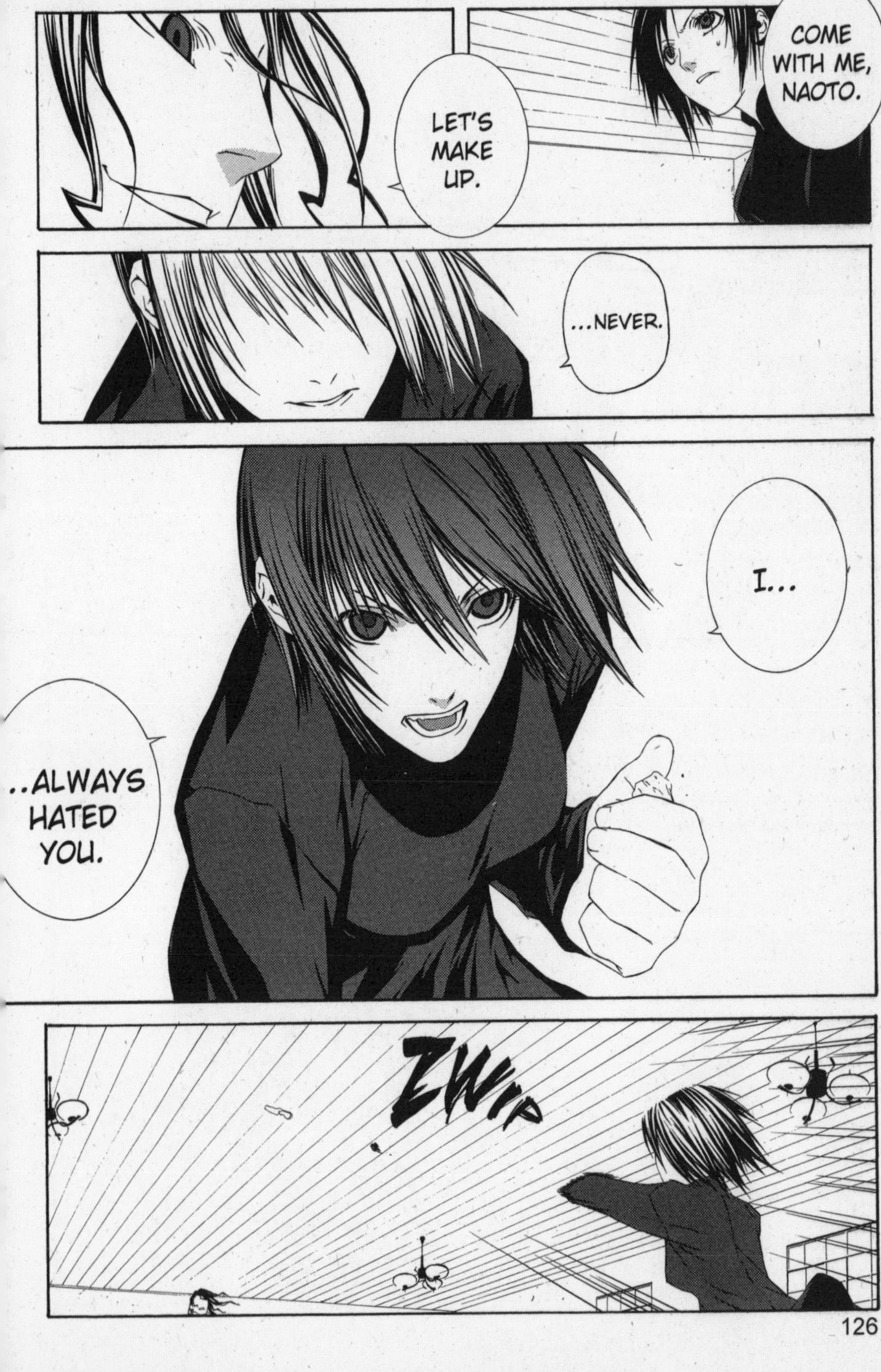
COME WITH ME, NAOTO.
LET'S MAKE UP.
...NEVER.
I...
..ALWAYS HATED YOU.
ZWIP

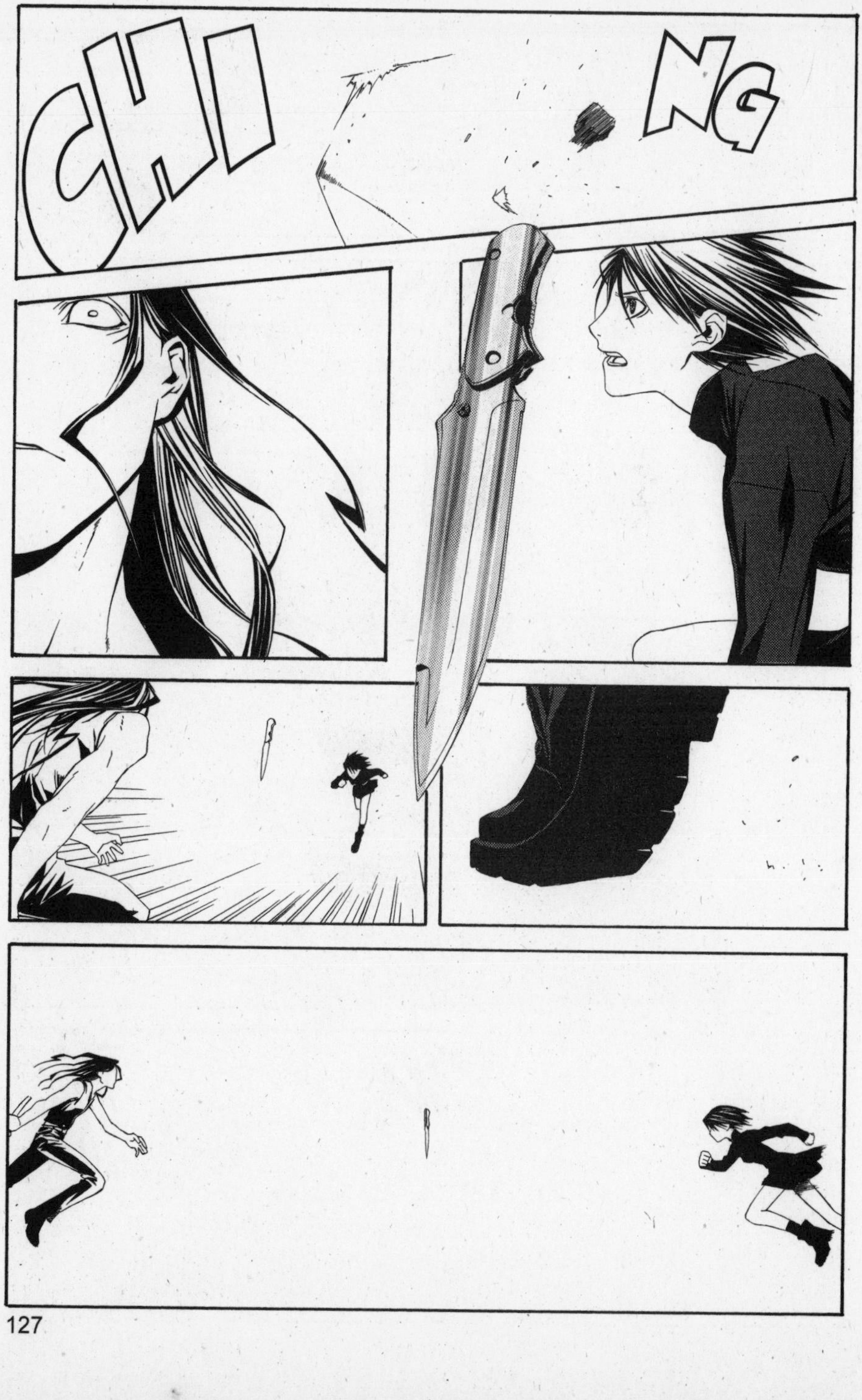
CHI
NG

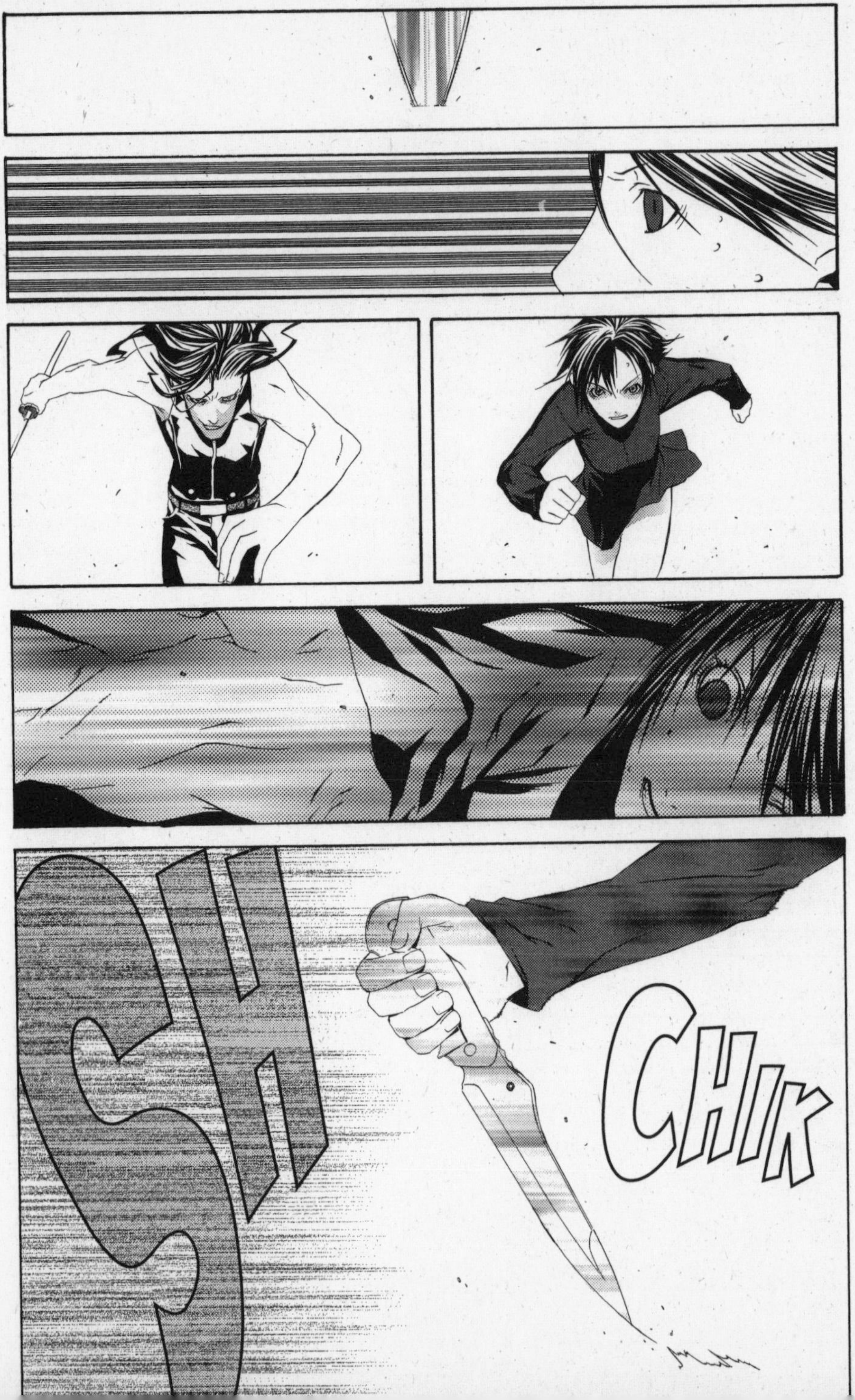
CHIK
SH

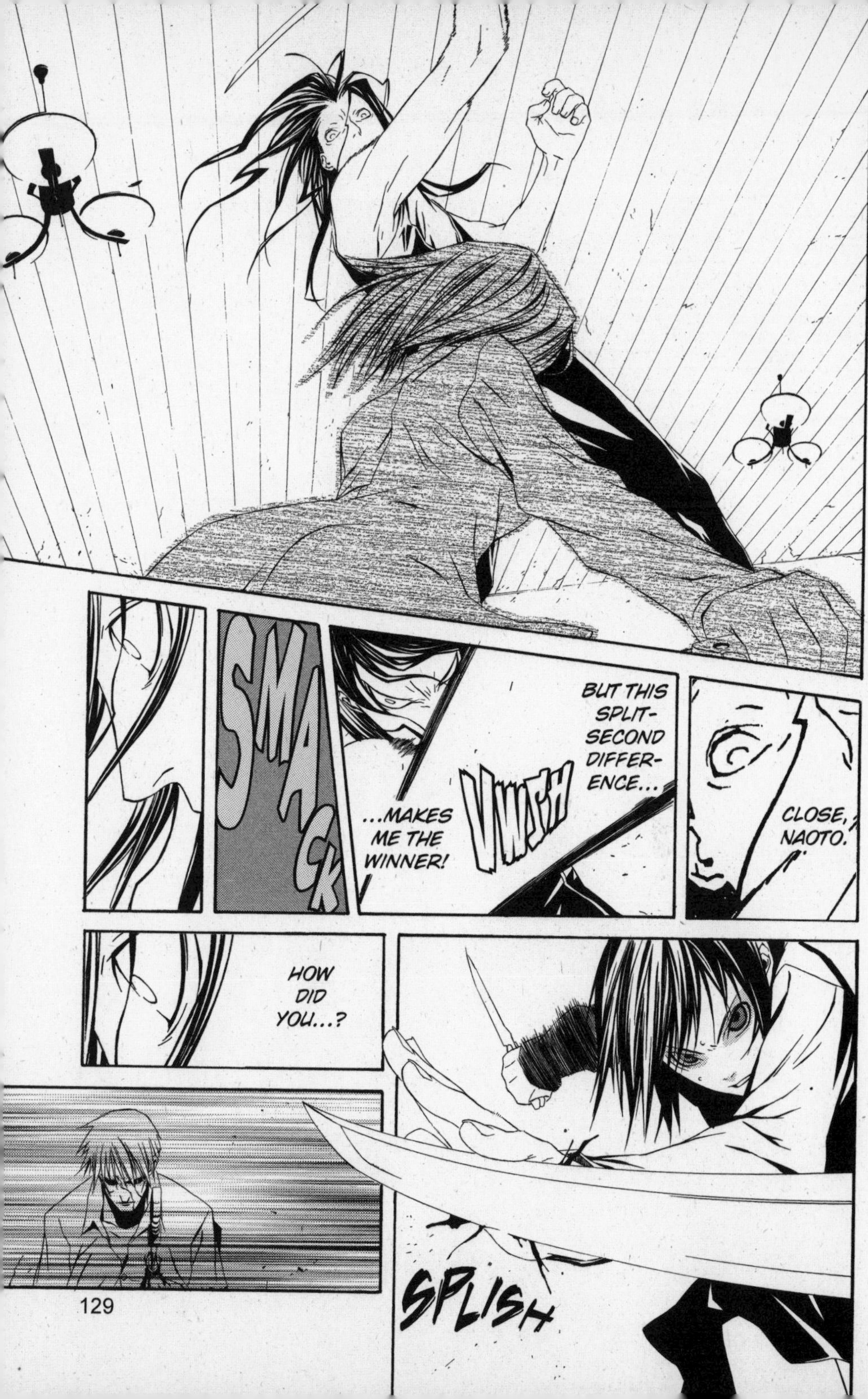
CLOSE, NAOTO.
BUT THIS SPLIT-SECOND DIFFERENCE...
VWISH
...MAKES ME THE WINNER!
SMACK
SPLISH
HOW DID YOU...?

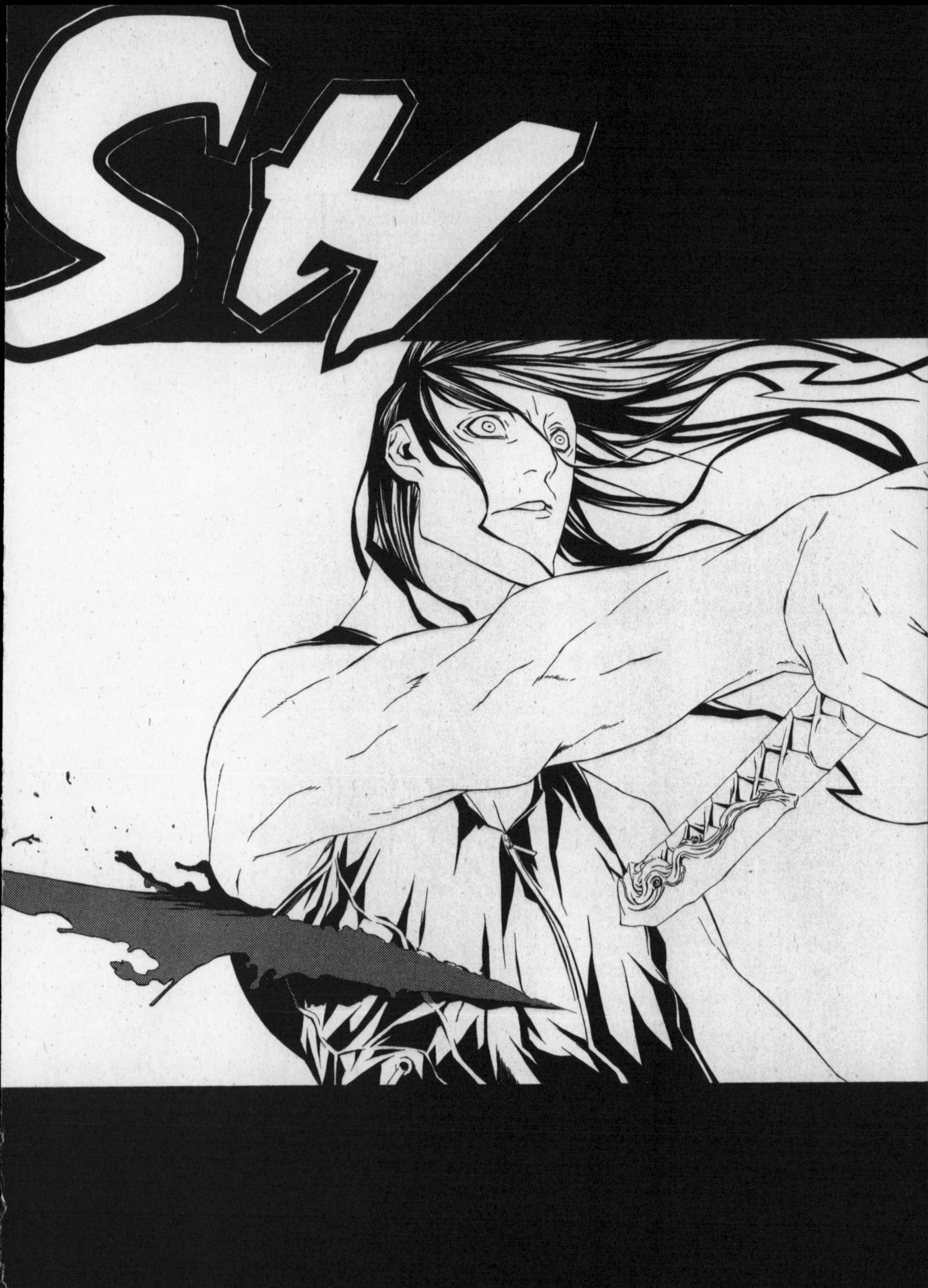
SH

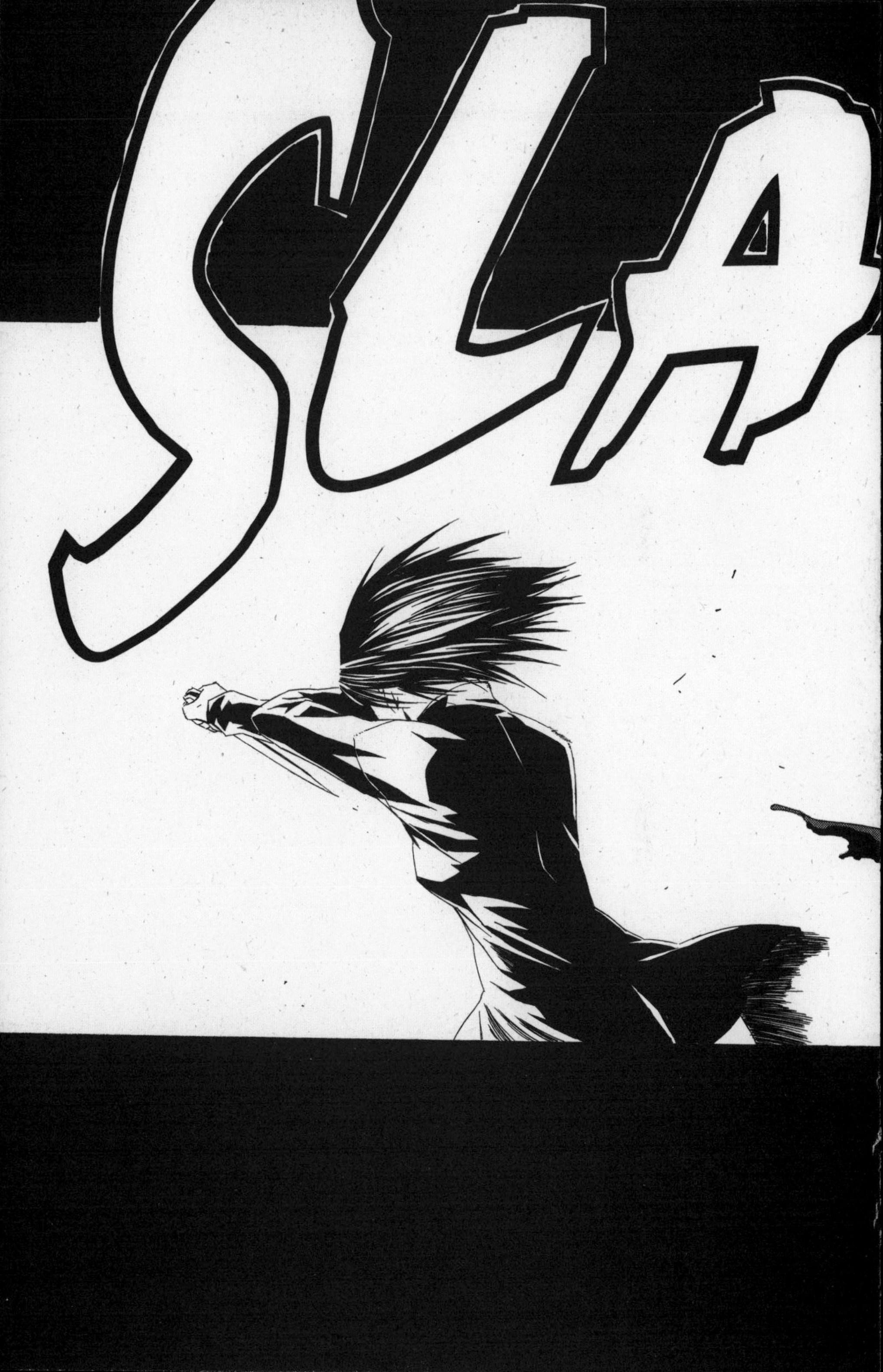
SLA

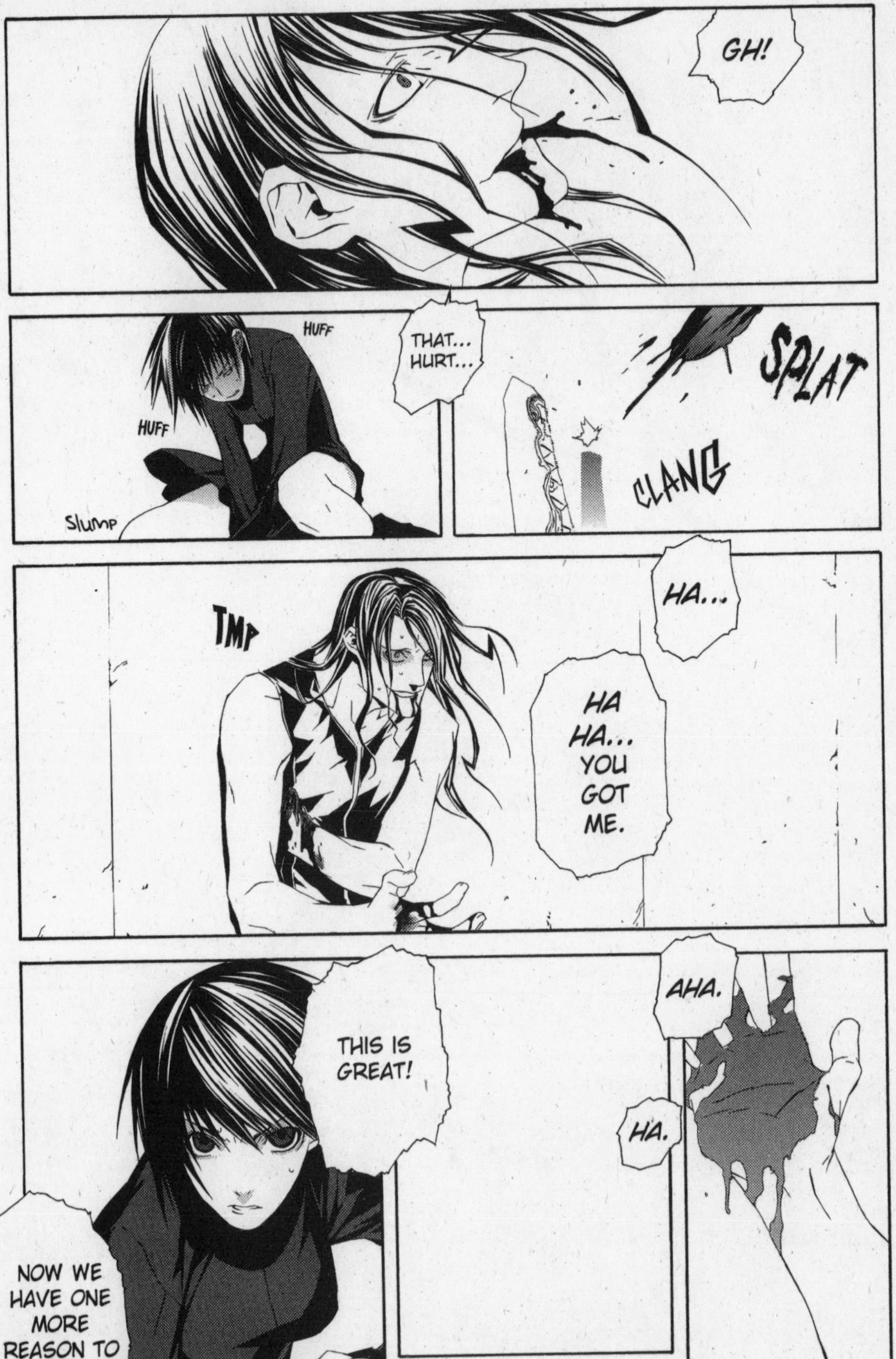
GH!
SPLAT
CLANG
THAT... HURT...
HUFF
HUFF
Slump
HA...
HA HA... YOU GOT ME.
TMP
AHA.
HA.
THIS IS GREAT!
NOW WE HAVE ONE MORE REASON TO CELEBRATE.

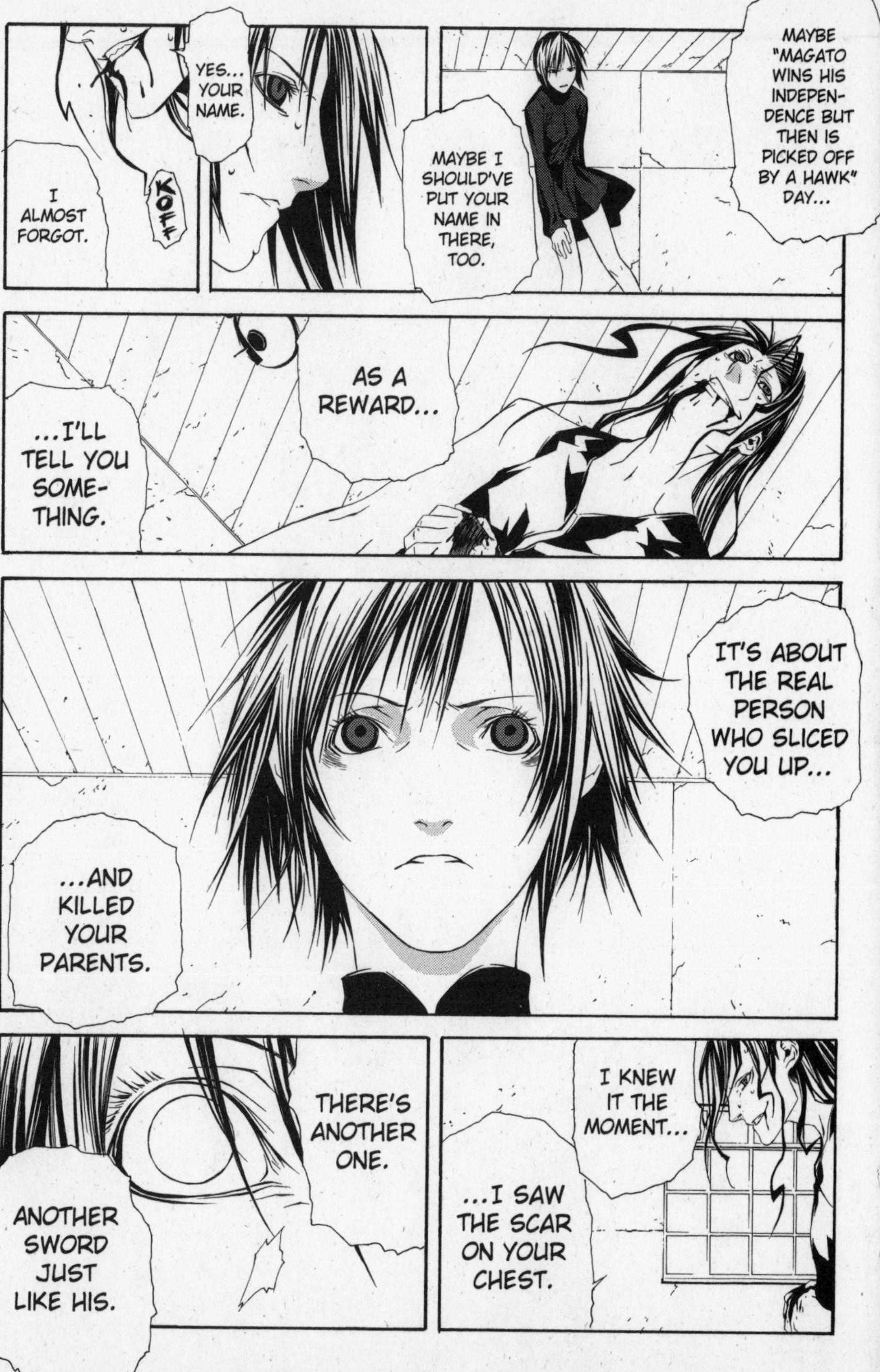
MAYBE "MAGATO WINS HIS INDEPEN-DENCE BUT THEN IS PICKED OFF BY A HAWK" DAY...
MAYBE I SHOULD'VE PUT YOUR NAME IN THERE, TOO.
YES... YOUR NAME.
KOFF
I ALMOST FORGOT.
AS A REWARD...
...I'LL TELL YOU SOME-THING.
IT'S ABOUT THE REAL PERSON WHO SLICED YOU UP...
...AND KILLED YOUR PARENTS.
I KNEW IT THE MOMENT...
...I SAW THE SCAR ON YOUR CHEST.
THERE'S ANOTHER ONE.
ANOTHER SWORD JUST LIKE HIS.

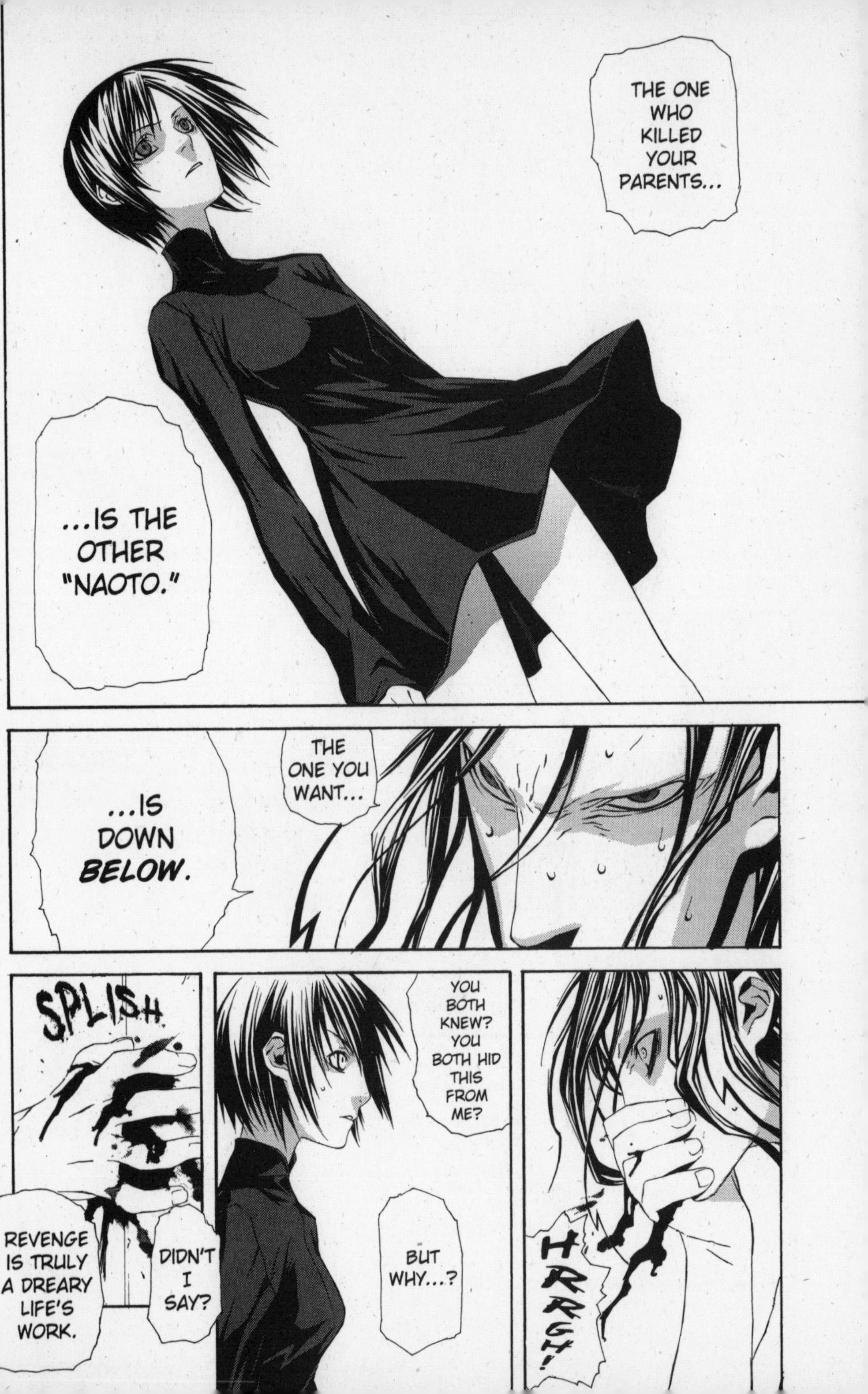
THE ONE WHO KILLED YOUR PARENTS...
...IS THE OTHER "NAOTO."
THE ONE YOU WANT...
...IS DOWN BELOW.
HRRGH!
YOU BOTH KNEW? YOU BOTH HID THIS FROM ME?
BUT WHY...?
SPLISH
DIDN'T I SAY?
REVENGE IS TRULY A DREARY LIFE'S WORK.

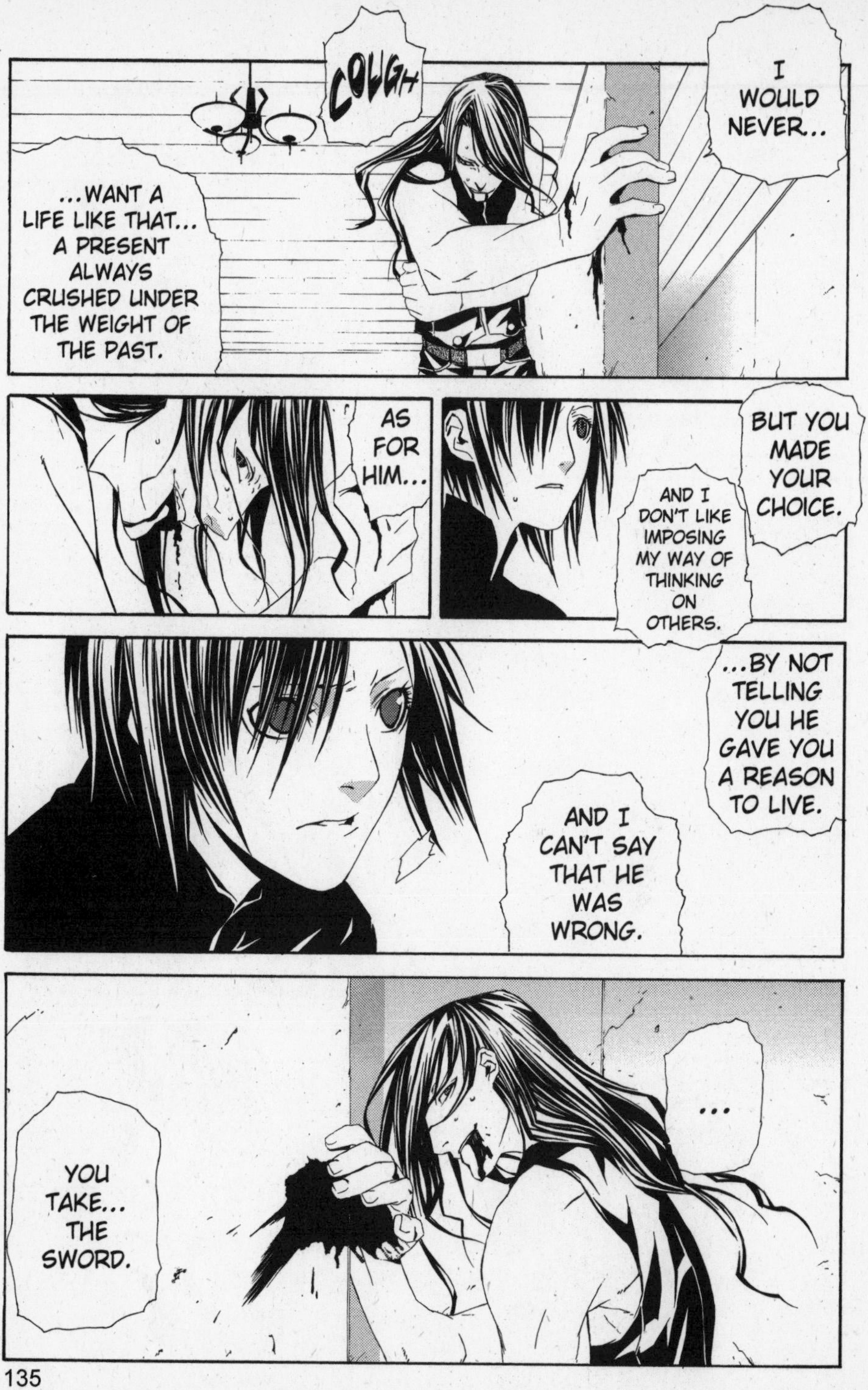
I WOULD NEVER...
COUGH
...WANT A LIFE LIKE THAT... A PRESENT ALWAYS CRUSHED UNDER THE WEIGHT OF THE PAST.
BUT YOU MADE YOUR CHOICE.
AND I DON'T LIKE IMPOSING MY WAY OF THINKING ON OTHERS.
AS FOR HIM...
...BY NOT TELLING YOU HE GAVE YOU A REASON TO LIVE.
AND I CAN'T SAY THAT HE WAS WRONG.
...
YOU TAKE... THE SWORD.

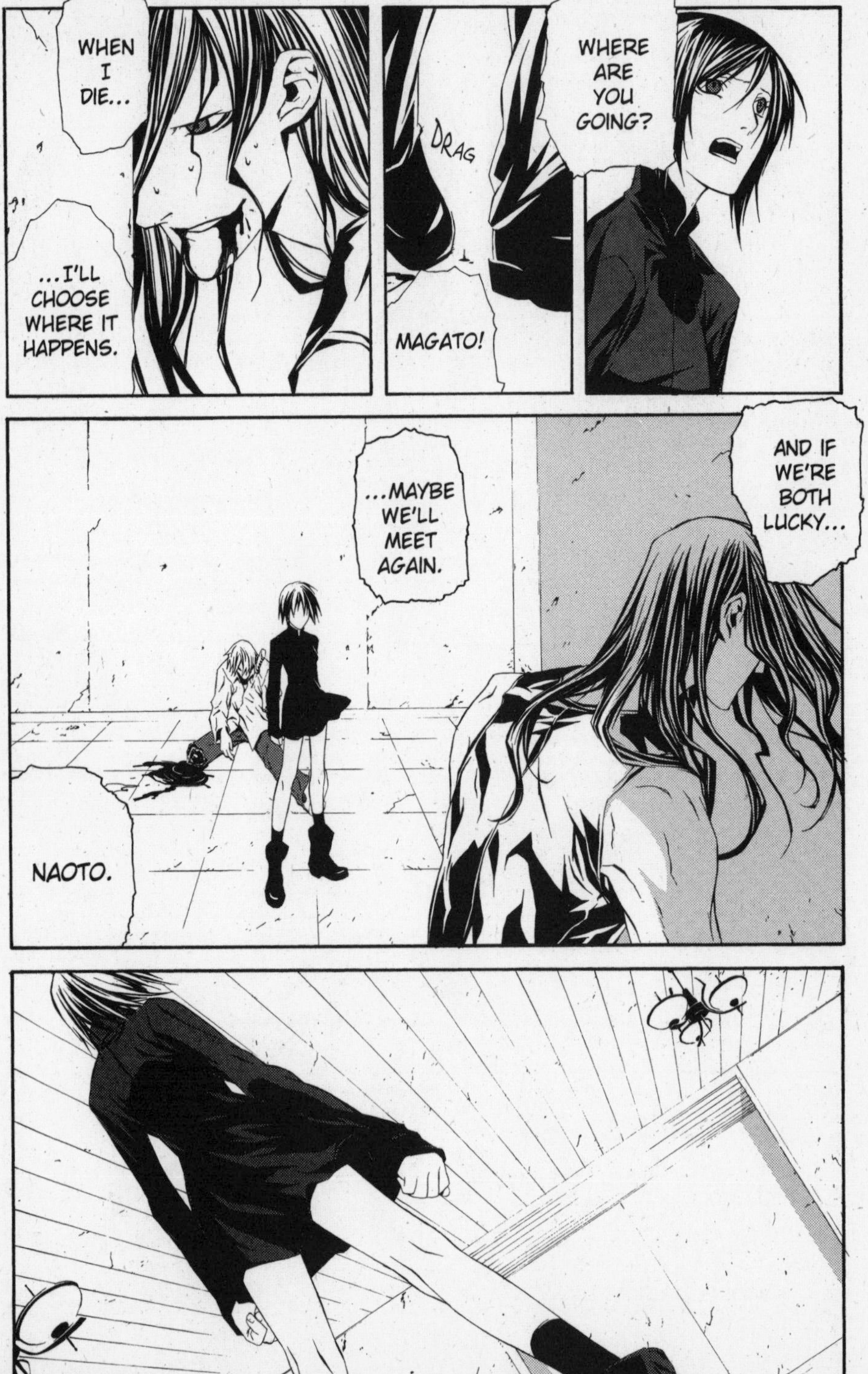
WHERE ARE YOU GOING?
DRAG
MAGATO!
WHEN I DIE...
...I'LL CHOOSE WHERE IT HAPPENS.
AND IF WE'RE BOTH LUCKY...
...MAYBE WE'LL MEET AGAIN.
NAOTO.

UNH!

NNGH!

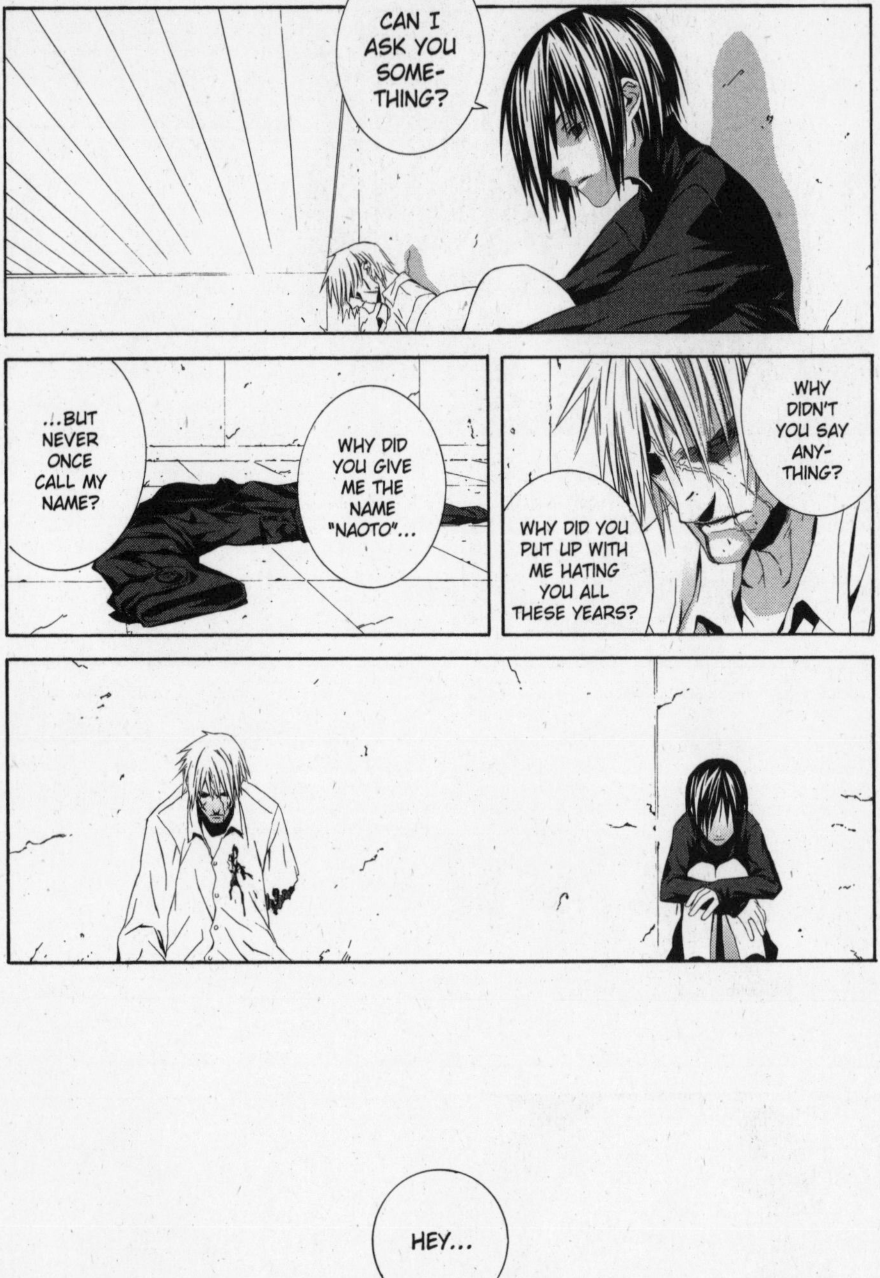
CAN I ASK YOU SOME-THING?
WHY DIDN'T YOU SAY ANY-THING?
WHY DID YOU PUT UP WITH ME HATING YOU ALL THESE YEARS?
WHY DID YOU GIVE ME THE NAME "NAOTO"...
...BUT NEVER ONCE CALL MY NAME?
HEY...

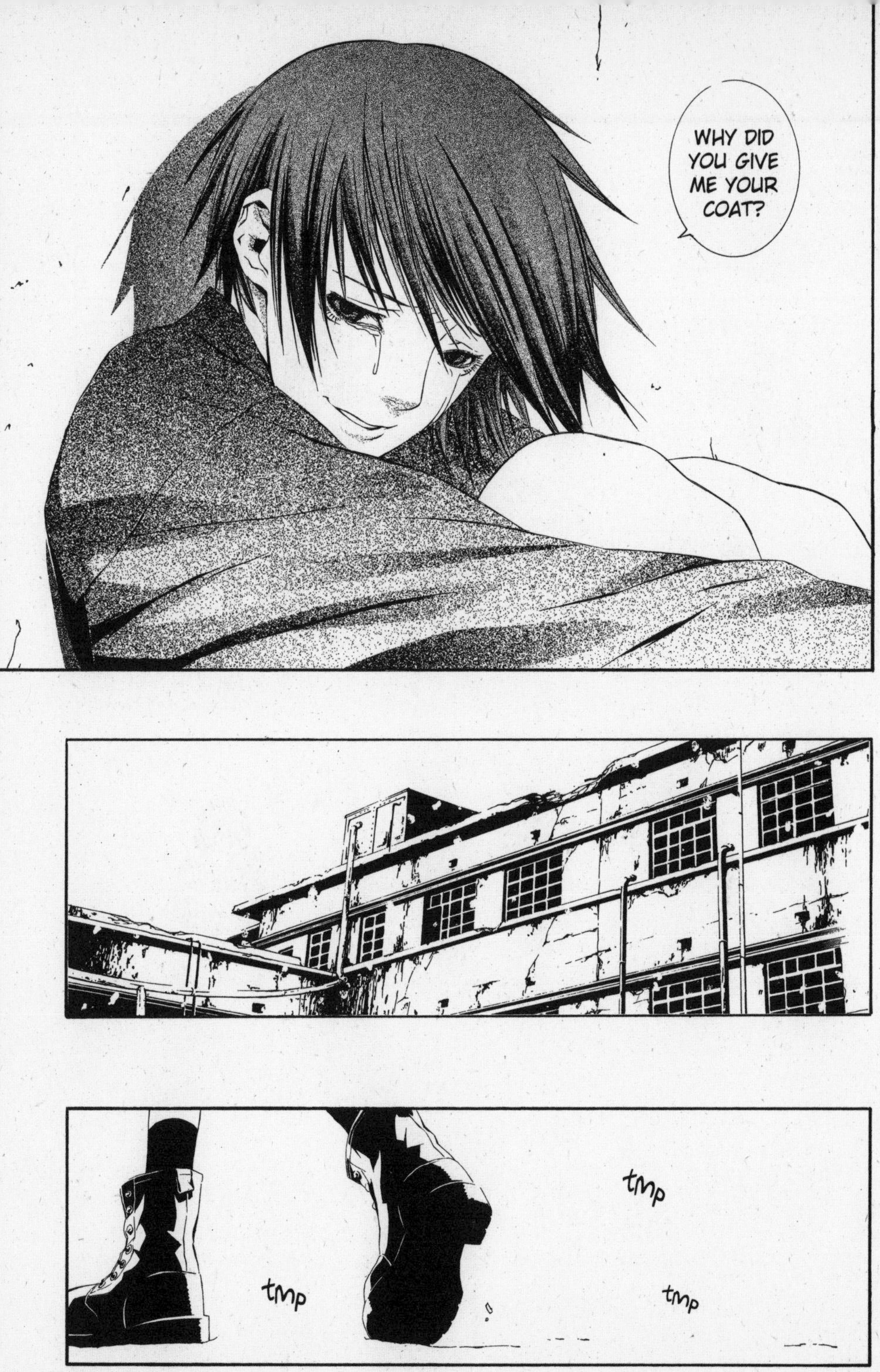
WHY DID YOU GIVE ME YOUR COAT?
tmp
tmp
tmp

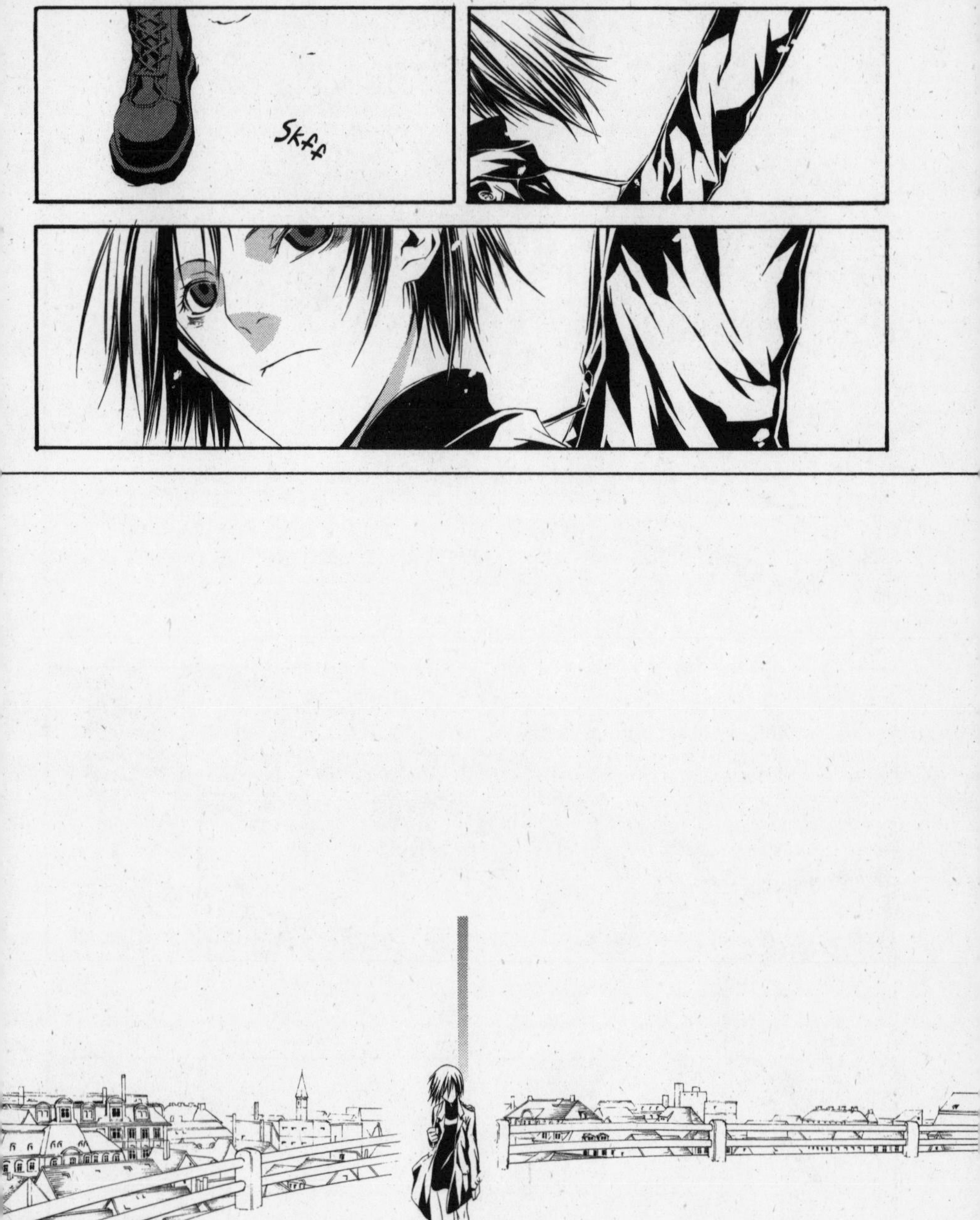
Skff

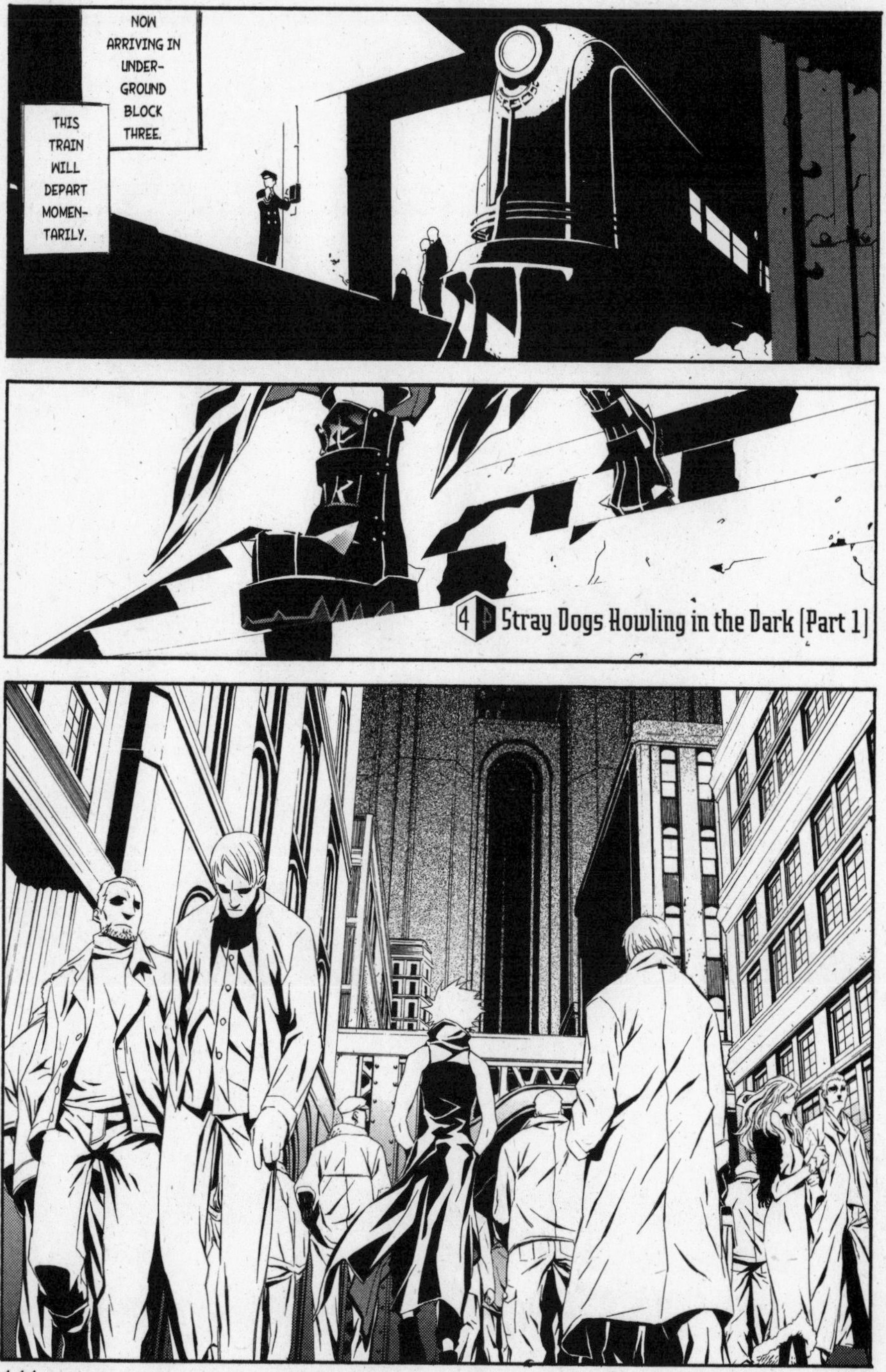
NOW ARRIVING IN UNDER-GROUND BLOCK THREE.
THIS TRAIN WILL DEPART MOMEN-TARILY.
4 Stray Dogs Howling in the Dark [Part 1]

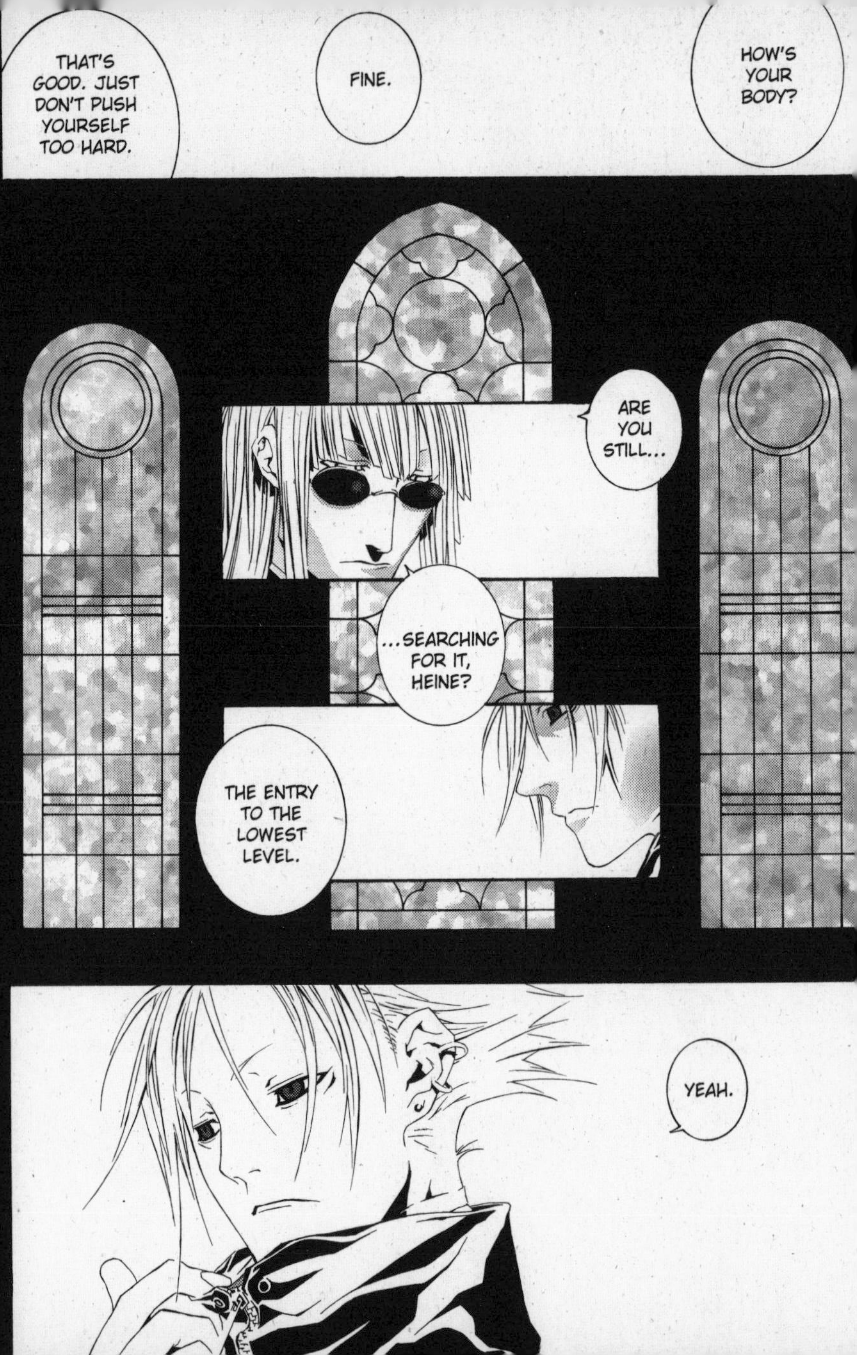
HOW'S YOUR BODY?
FINE.
THAT'S GOOD. JUST DON'T PUSH YOURSELF TOO HARD.
ARE YOU STILL...
...SEARCHING FOR IT, HEINE?
THE ENTRY TO THE LOWEST LEVEL.
YEAH.

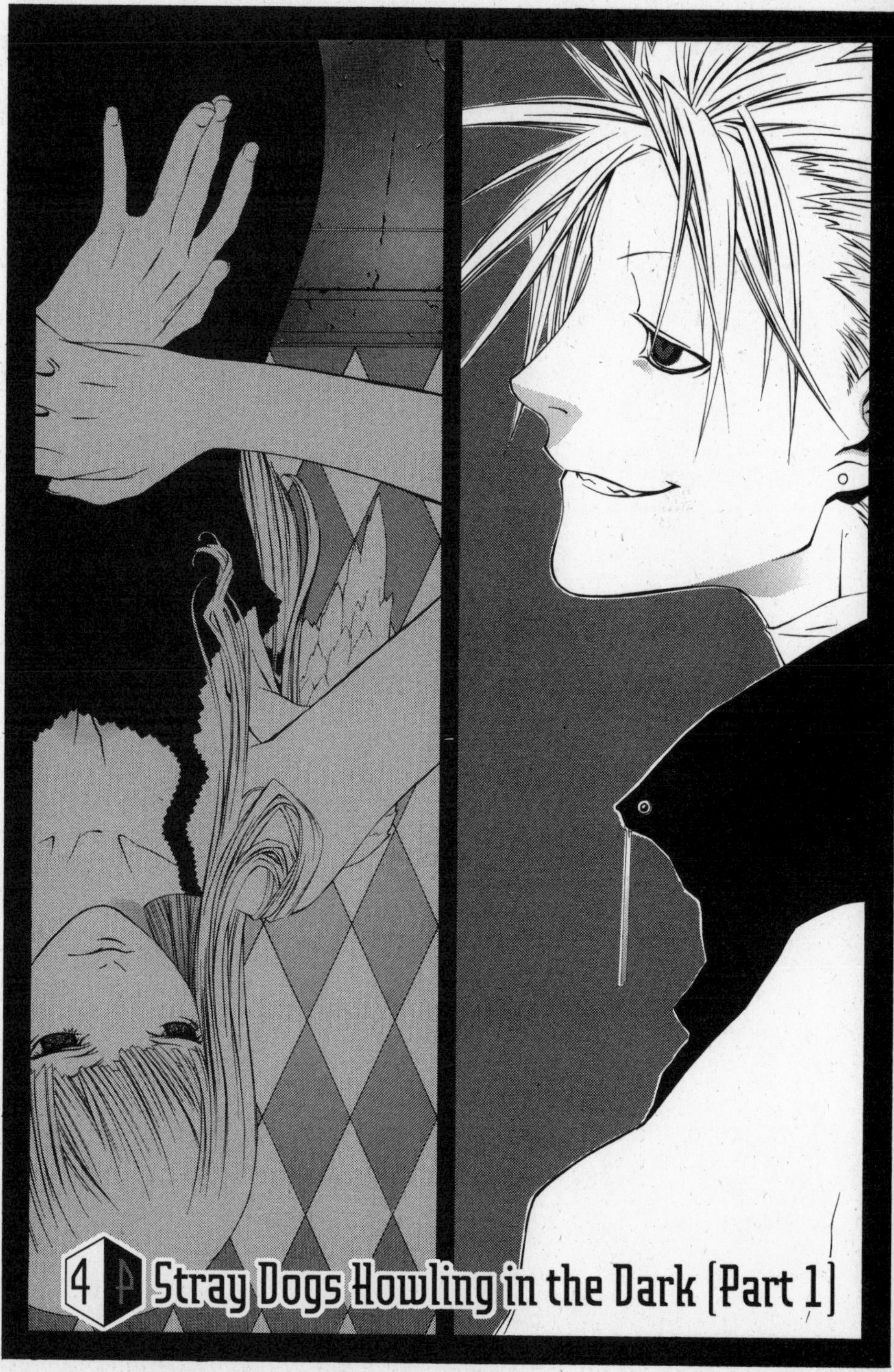
4
Stray Dogs Howling in the Dark (Part 1)

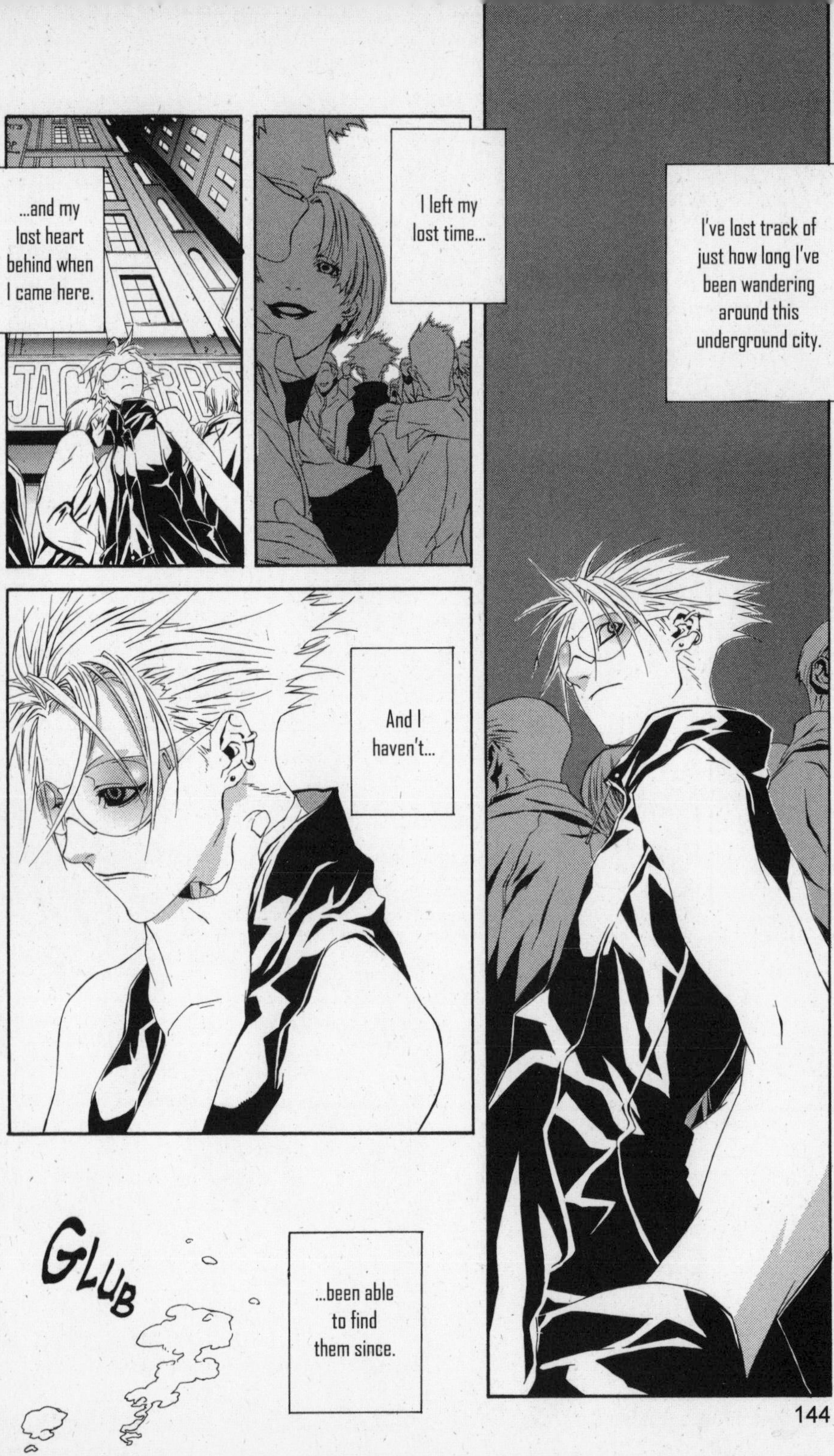
I've lost track of just how long I've been wandering around this underground city.
I left my lost time...
...and my lost heart behind when I came here.
JACKRABBIT
And I haven't...
...been able to find them since.
GLUB

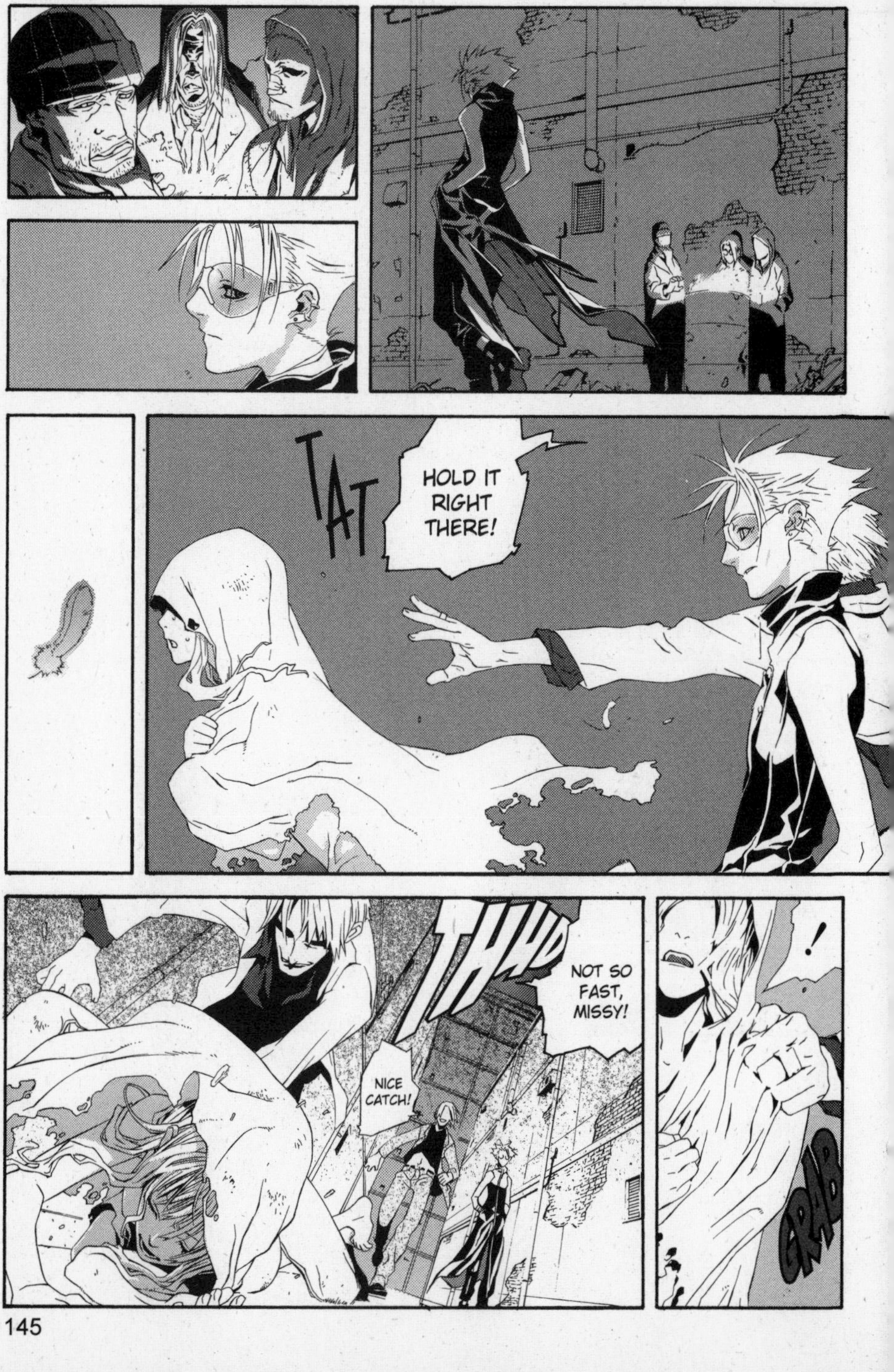
HOLD IT RIGHT THERE!
TAT
!
GRAB
NOT SO FAST, MISSY!
NICE CATCH!

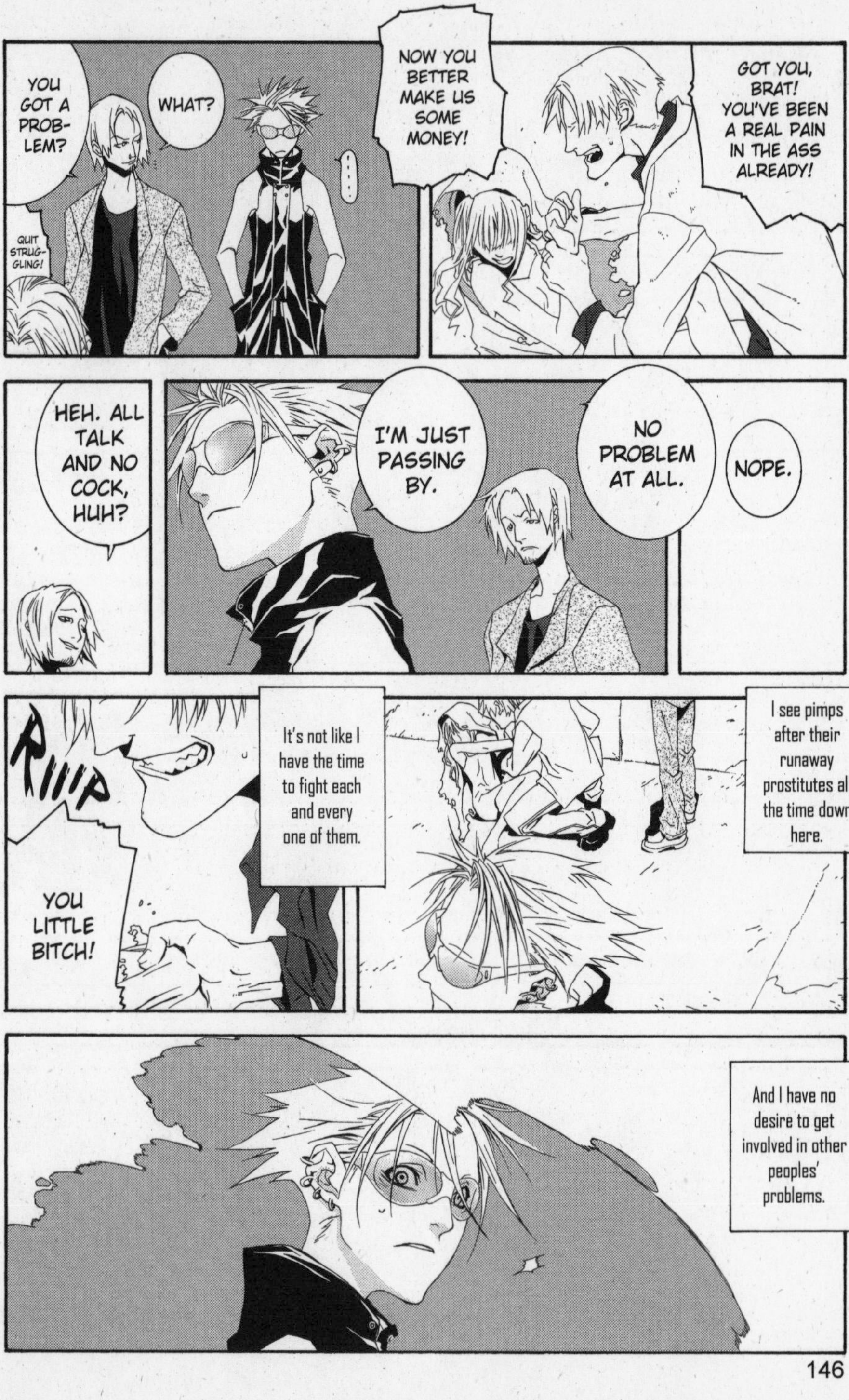
GOT YOU, BRAT! YOU'VE BEEN A REAL PAIN IN THE ASS ALREADY!
NOW YOU BETTER MAKE US SOME MONEY!
WHAT?
YOU GOT A PROB-LEM?
QUIT STRUG-GLING!
NOPE.
NO PROBLEM AT ALL.
I'M JUST PASSING BY.
HEH. ALL TALK AND NO COCK, HUH?
I see pimps after their runaway prostitutes all the time down here.
It's not like I have the time to fight each and every one of them.
RIIIP
YOU LITTLE BITCH!
And I have no desire to get involved in other peoples' problems.

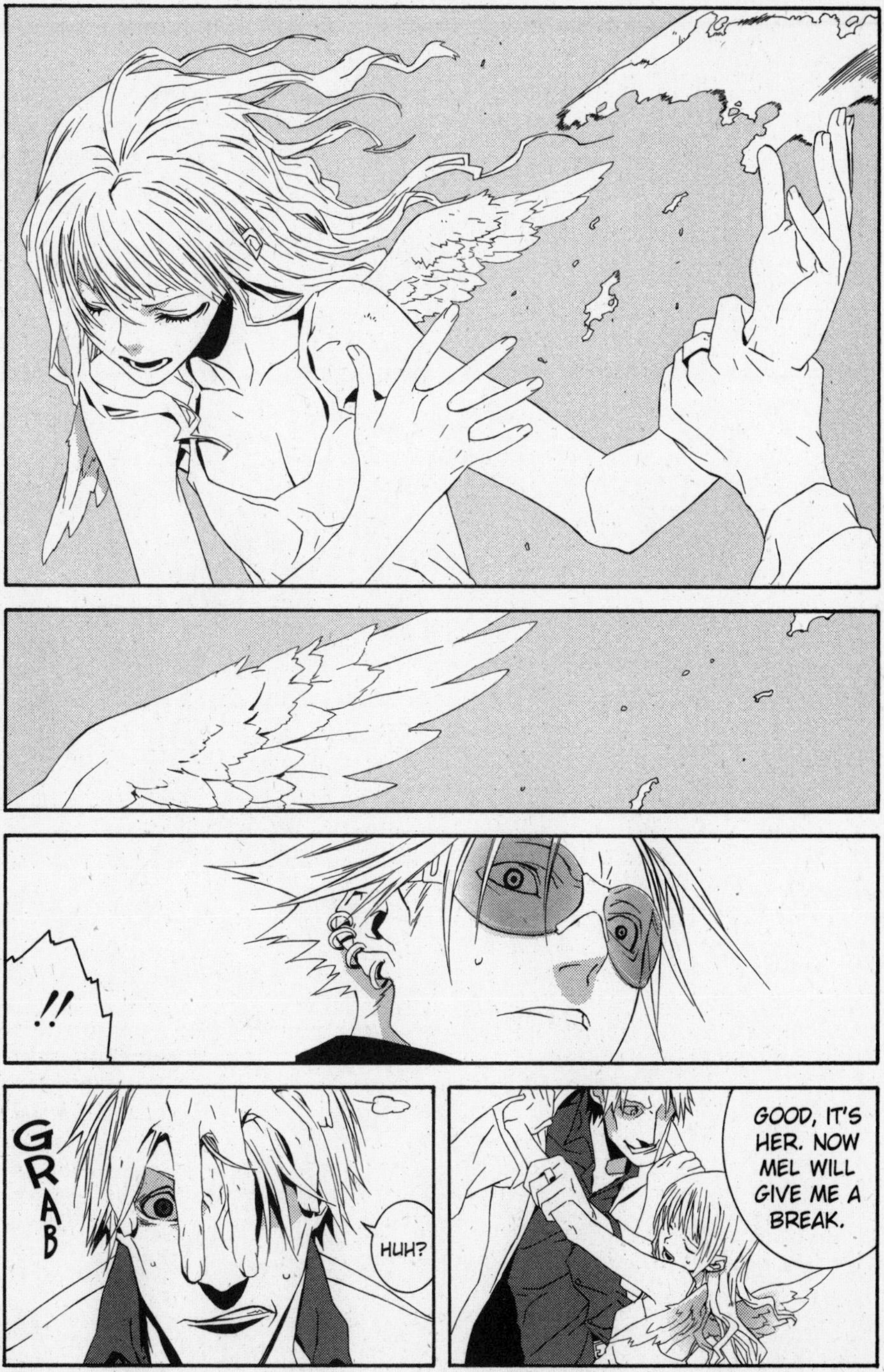
!!
GOOD, IT'S HER. NOW MEL WILL GIVE ME A BREAK.
HUH?
GRAB

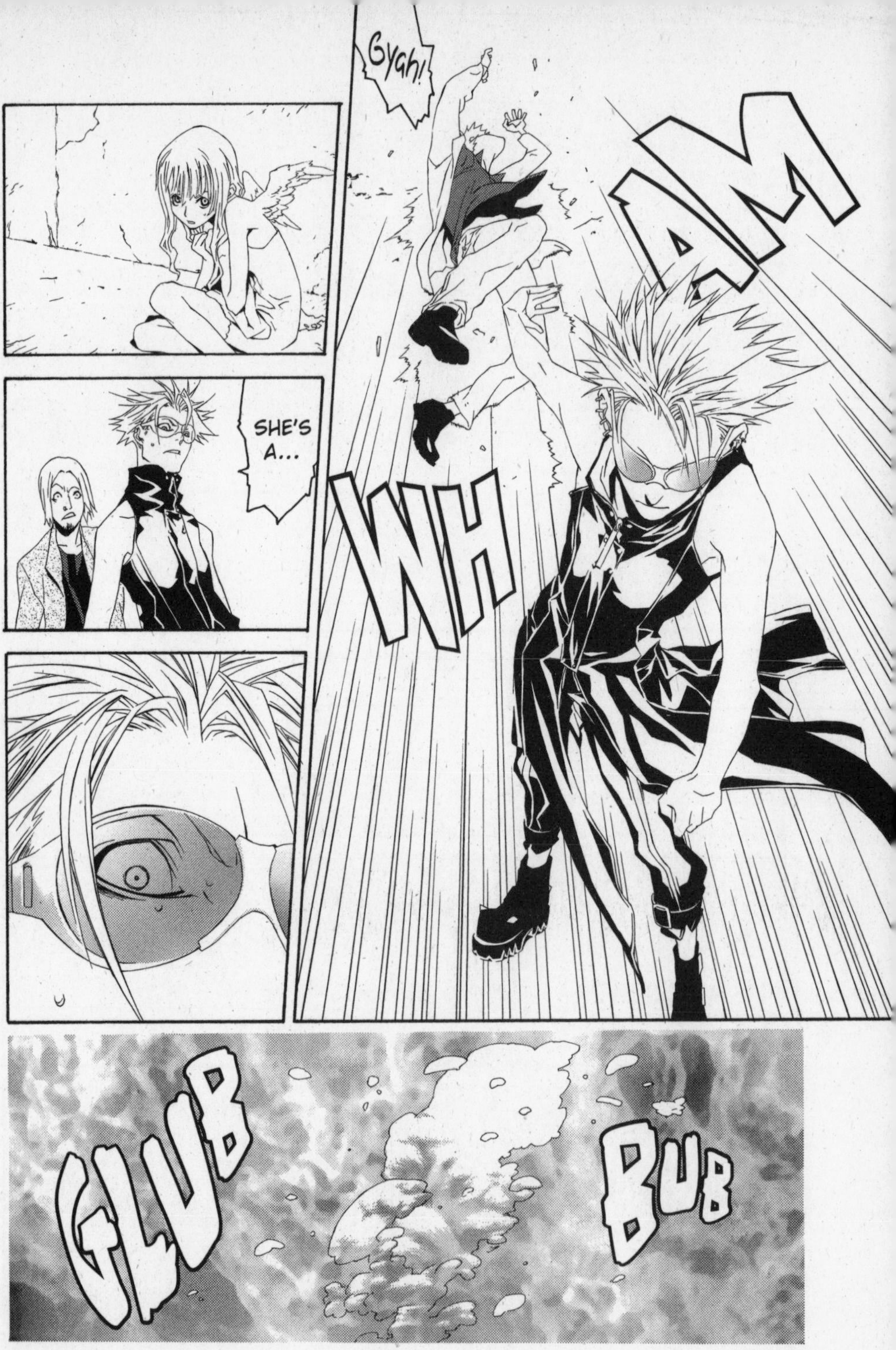
Gyah!
WHAM
SHE'S A...
GLUB
BUB

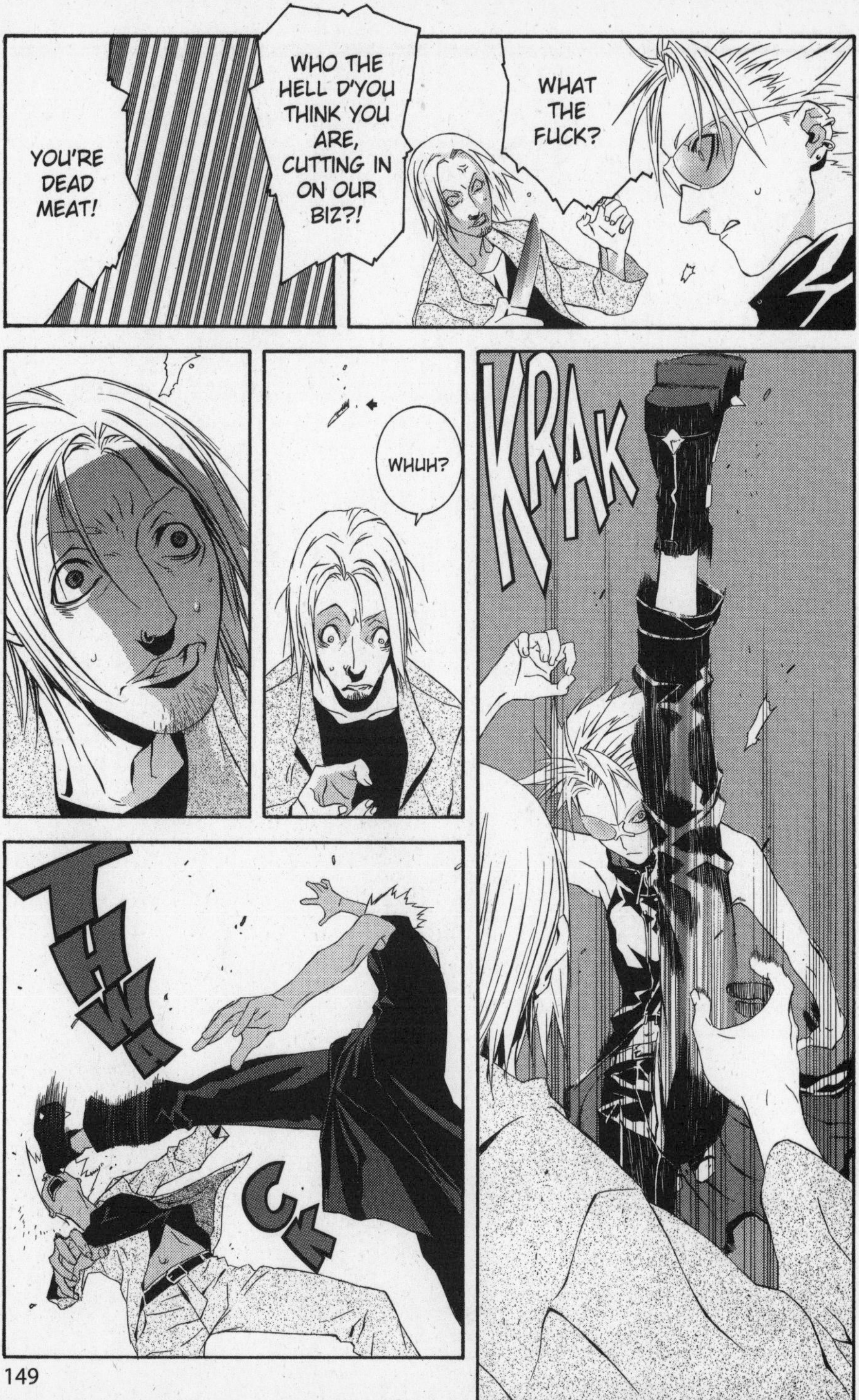
WHAT THE FUCK?
WHO THE HELL D'YOU THINK YOU ARE, CUTTING IN ON OUR BIZ?!
YOU'RE DEAD MEAT!
KRAK
WHUH?
THWACK

Unh. THU Agh!

SORRY ABOUT THAT...

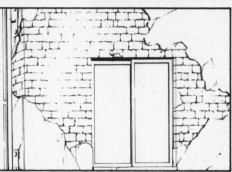

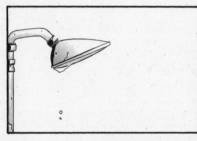

WHAT THE HELL AM I DOING? WHY'D I SAVE HER?

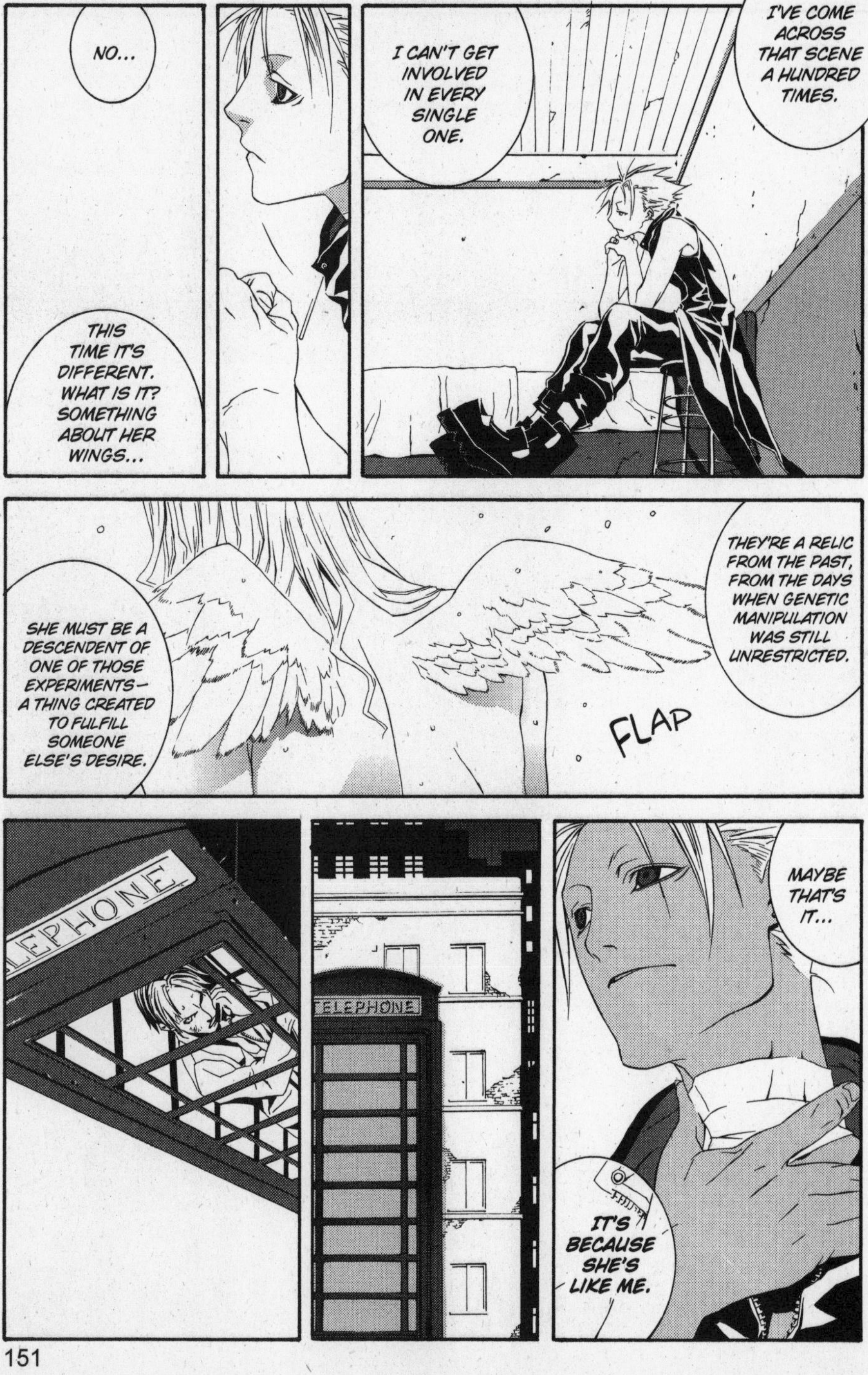
I'VE COME ACROSS THAT SCENE A HUNDRED TIMES.
I CAN'T GET INVOLVED IN EVERY SINGLE ONE.
NO...
THIS TIME IT'S DIFFERENT. WHAT IS IT? SOMETHING ABOUT HER WINGS...
THEY'RE A RELIC FROM THE PAST, FROM THE DAYS WHEN GENETIC MANIPULATION WAS STILL UNRESTRICTED.
FLAP
SHE MUST BE A DESCENDENT OF ONE OF THOSE EXPERIMENTS— A THING CREATED TO FULFILL SOMEONE ELSE'S DESIRE.
MAYBE THAT'S IT...
IT'S BECAUSE SHE'S LIKE ME.
TELEPHONE
ELEPHONE

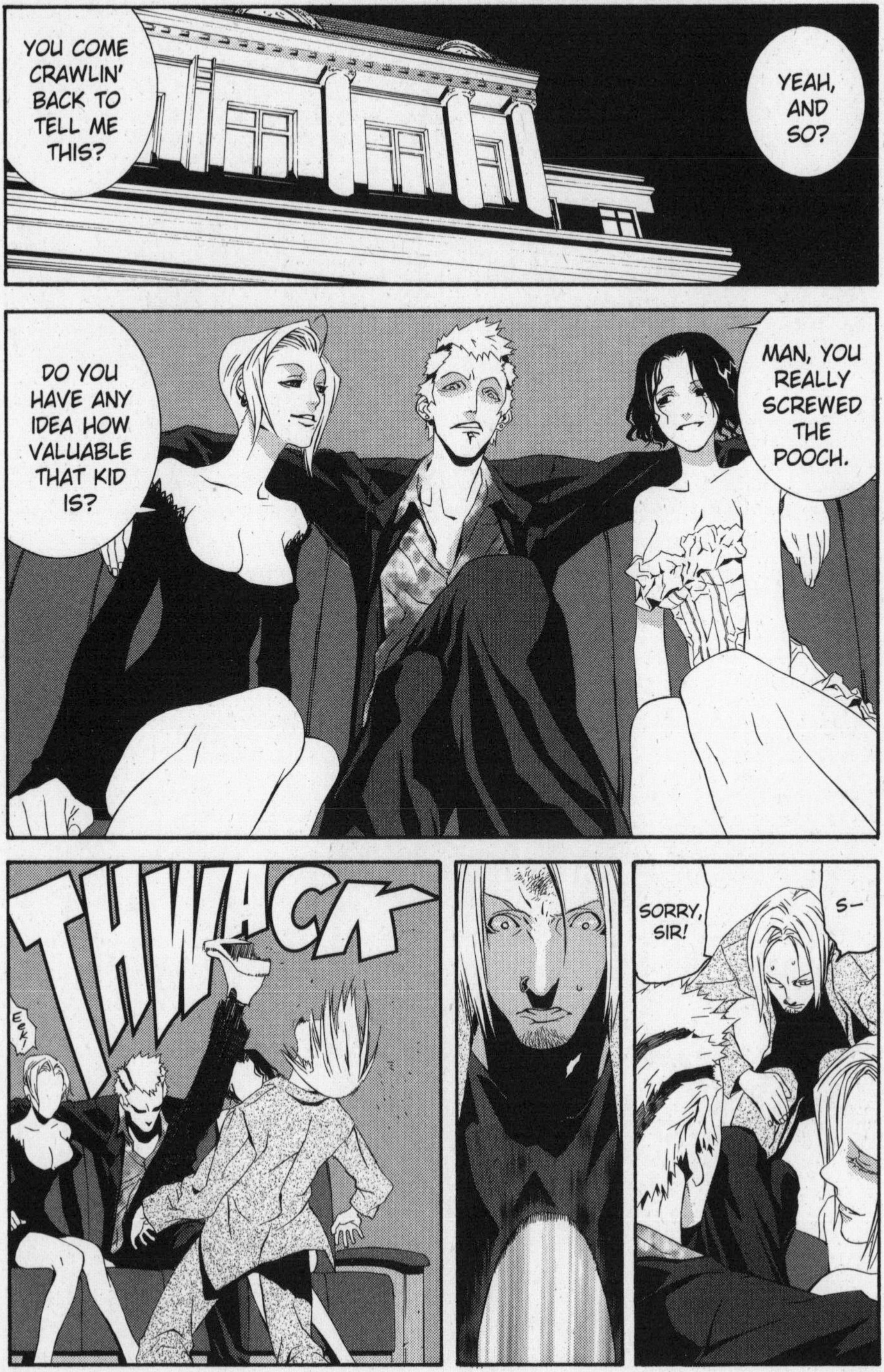
YEAH, AND SO?
YOU COME CRAWLIN' BACK TO TELL ME THIS?
MAN, YOU REALLY SCREWED THE POOCH.
DO YOU HAVE ANY IDEA HOW VALUABLE THAT KID IS?
S—
SORRY, SIR!
THWACK
EEK!

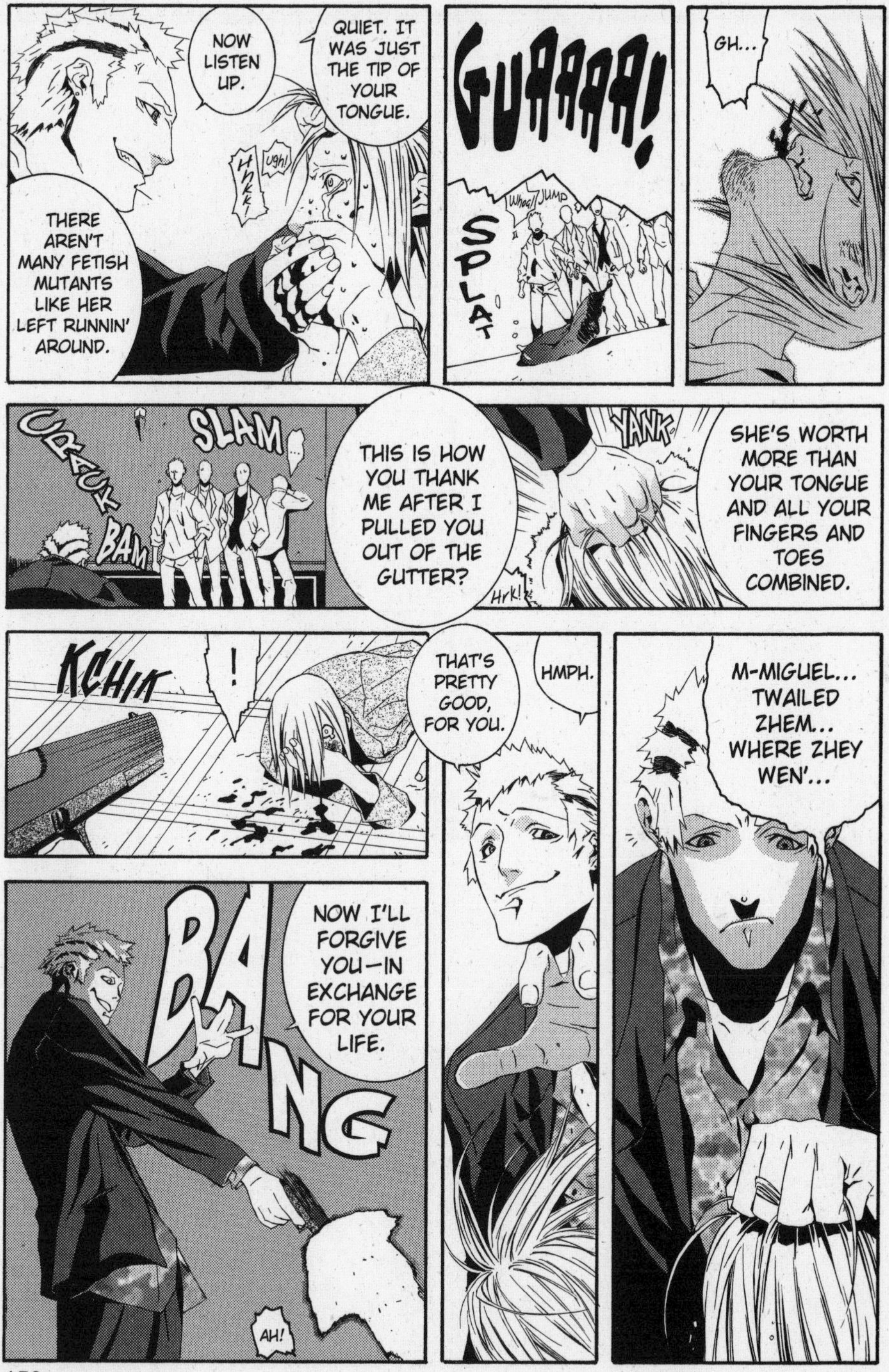
GH...
GUAAAA!
SPLAT
Whoa!
JUMP
QUIET. IT WAS JUST THE TIP OF YOUR TONGUE.
NOW LISTEN UP.
Ugh!
HNKK!
THERE AREN'T MANY FETISH MUTANTS LIKE HER LEFT RUNNIN' AROUND.
SHE'S WORTH MORE THAN YOUR TONGUE AND ALL YOUR FINGERS AND TOES COMBINED.
YANK
Hrk!
THIS IS HOW YOU THANK ME AFTER I PULLED YOU OUT OF THE GUTTER?
SLAM
...
CRACK
BAM
M-MIGUEL... TWAILED ZHEM... WHERE ZHEY WEN'...
HMPH.
THAT'S PRETTY GOOD, FOR YOU.
KCHIK
!
NOW I'LL FORGIVE YOU—IN EXCHANGE FOR YOUR LIFE.
BANG
AH!

RIGHT. LOCK AND LOAD, BOYS.

WE'RE ON THE HUNT FOR ONE FICKLE LITTLE ANGEL.

Ha ha. Just like a water-melon!

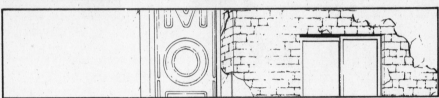

...

WHAT'S YOUR NAME?

A HOME?

CONTACTS?

FRIENDS?

GOT ANY FAMILY?

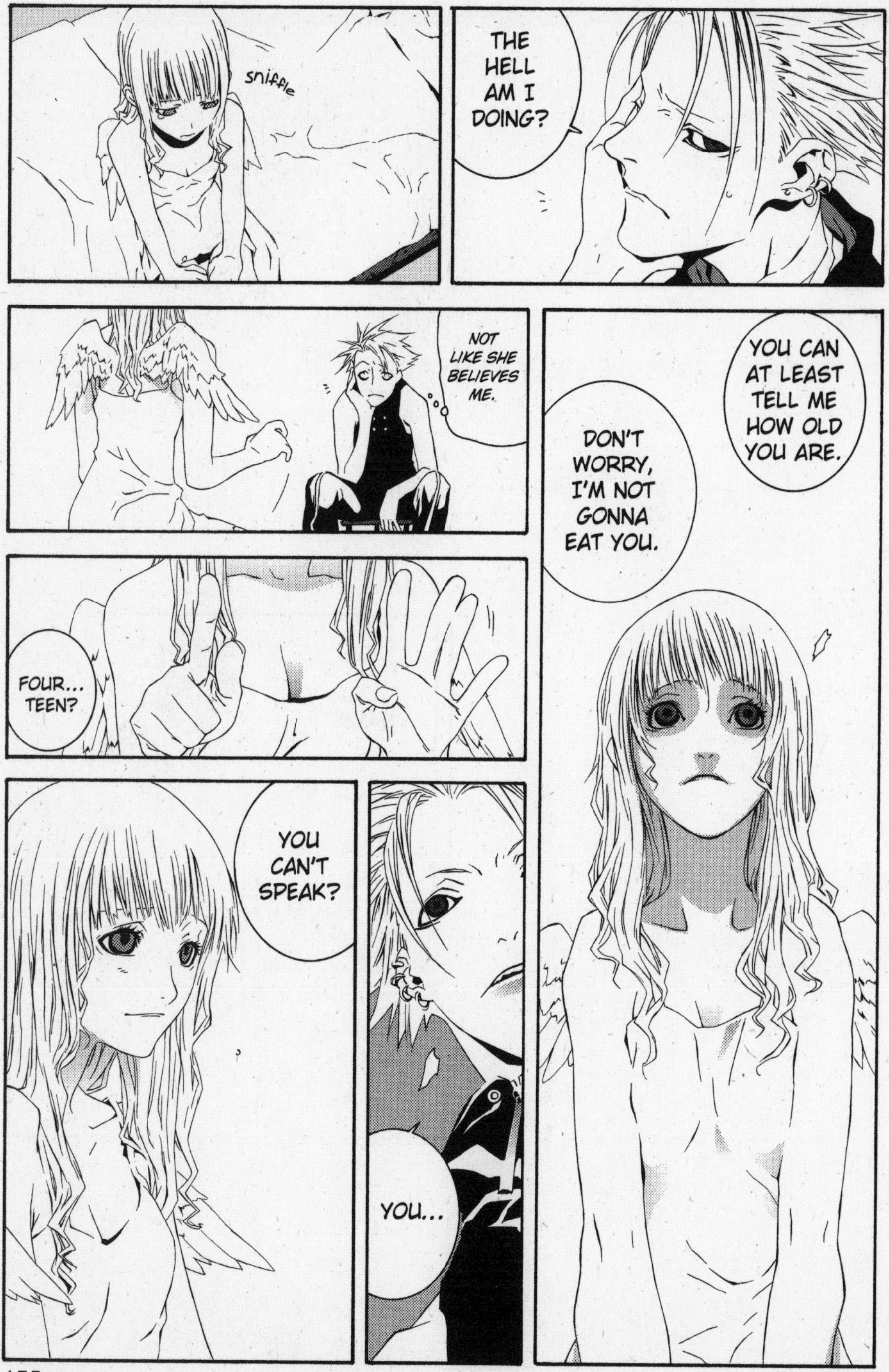
THE HELL AM I DOING?
sniffle
YOU CAN AT LEAST TELL ME HOW OLD YOU ARE.
DON'T WORRY, I'M NOT GONNA EAT YOU.
NOT LIKE SHE BELIEVES ME.
FOUR... TEEN?
YOU...
YOU CAN'T SPEAK?

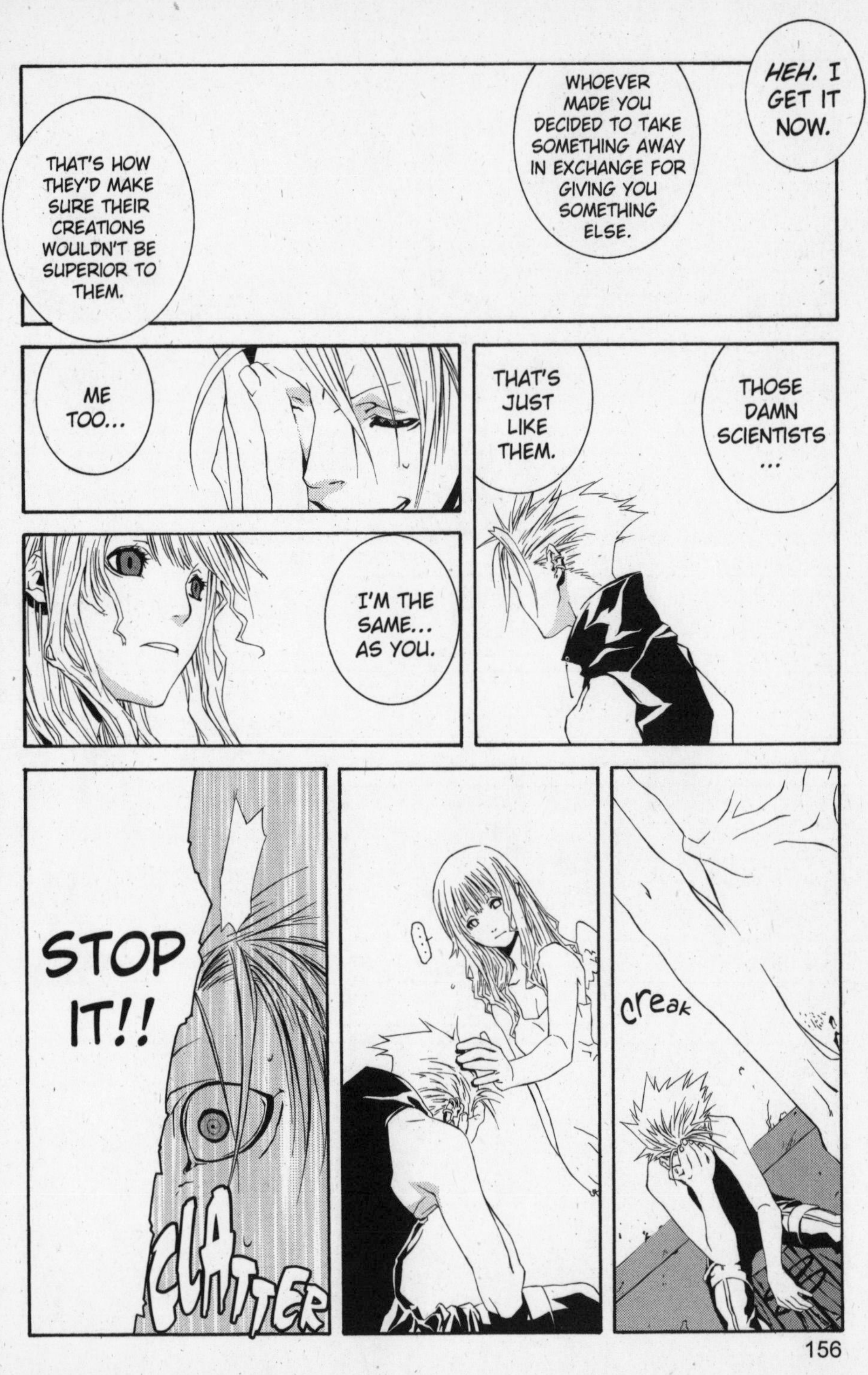
HEH. I GET IT NOW.
WHOEVER MADE YOU DECIDED TO TAKE SOMETHING AWAY IN EXCHANGE FOR GIVING YOU SOMETHING ELSE.
THAT'S HOW THEY'D MAKE SURE THEIR CREATIONS WOULDN'T BE SUPERIOR TO THEM.
THOSE DAMN SCIENTISTS...
THAT'S JUST LIKE THEM.
ME TOO...
I'M THE SAME... AS YOU.
creak
...
STOP IT!!
CLATTER

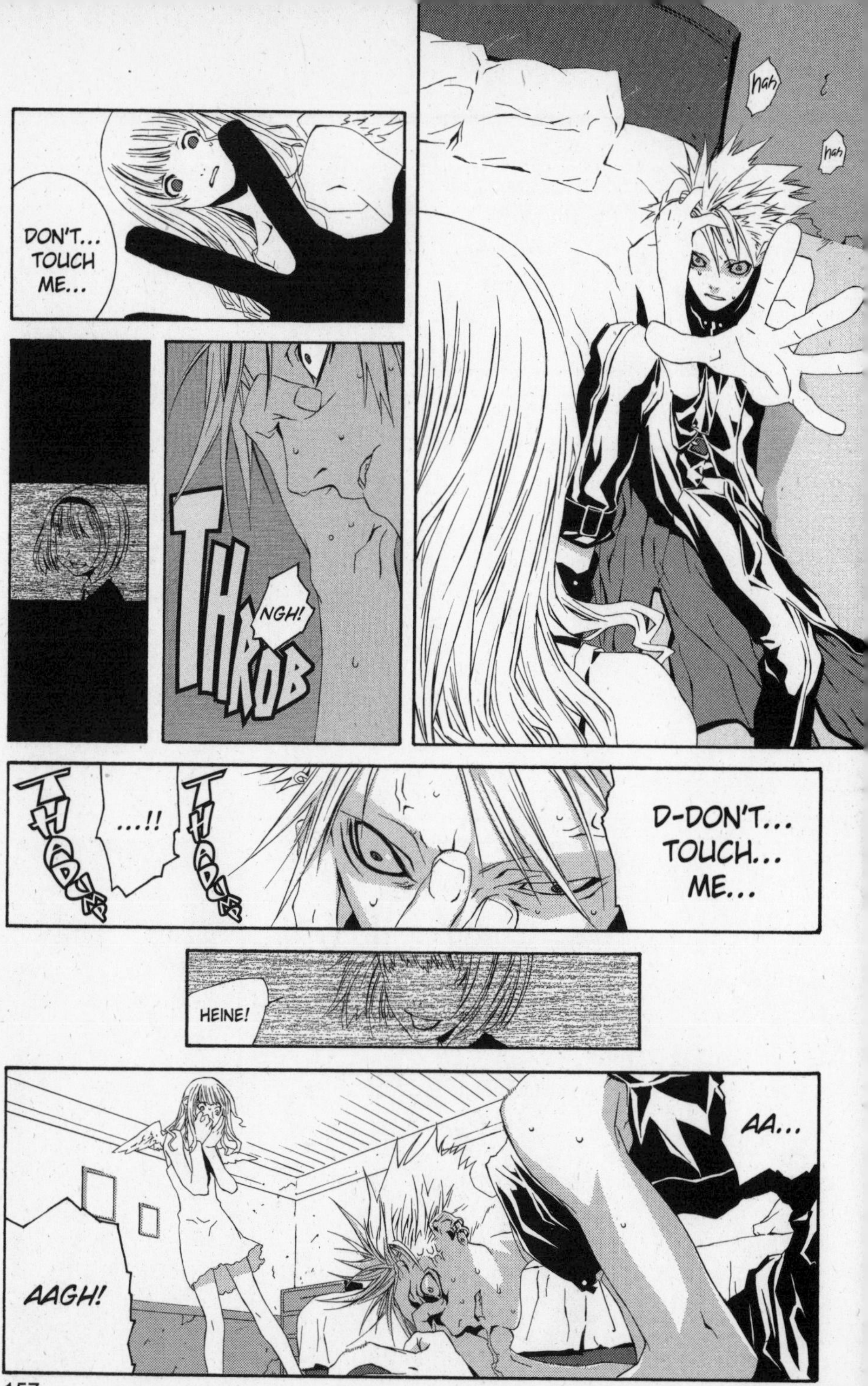
hah
hah
DON'T... TOUCH ME...
THROB
NGH!
D-DON'T... TOUCH... ME...
THADUMP
...!!
THADUMP
HEINE!
AA...
AAGH!

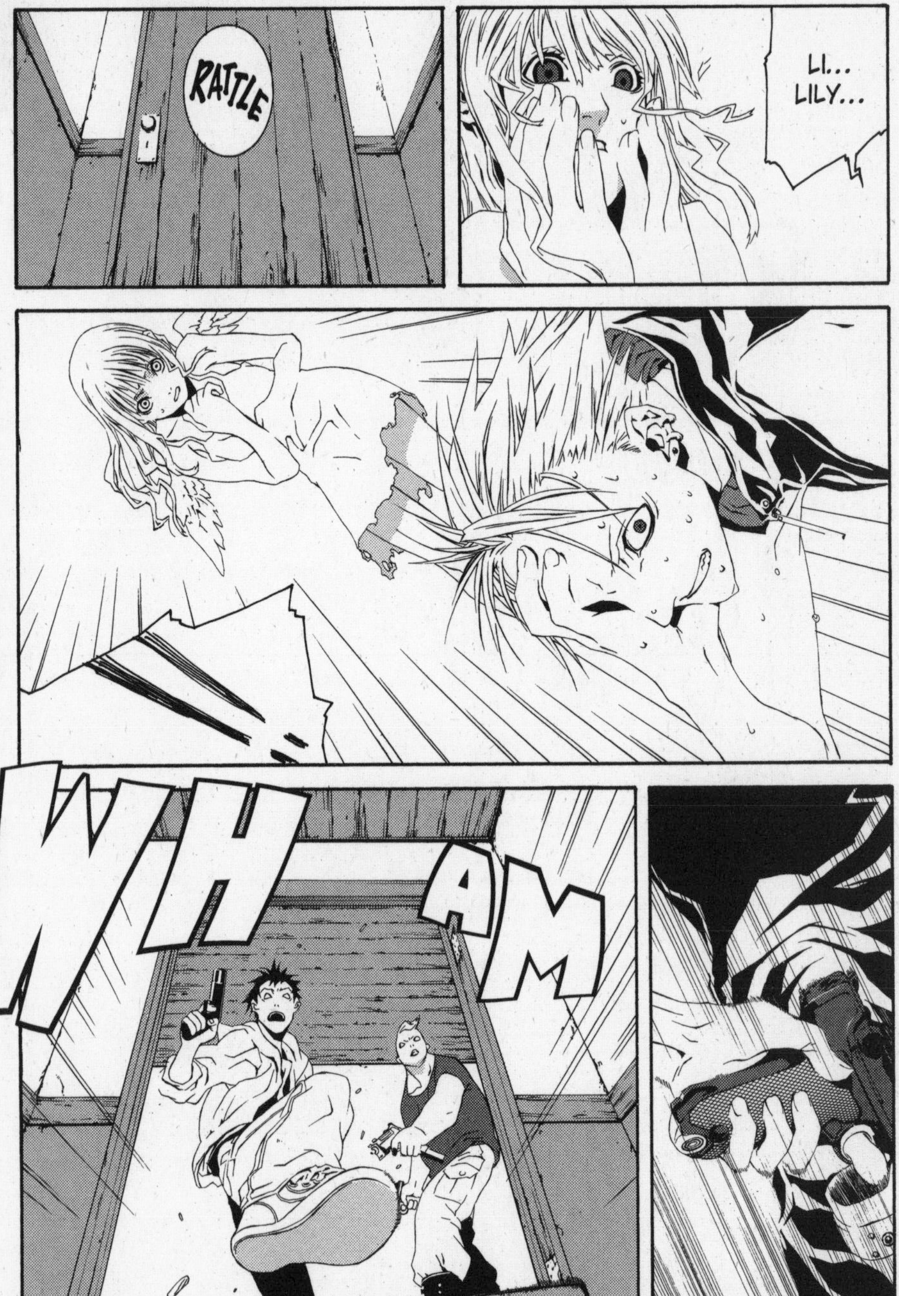
LI... LILY...
RATTLE
WHAM

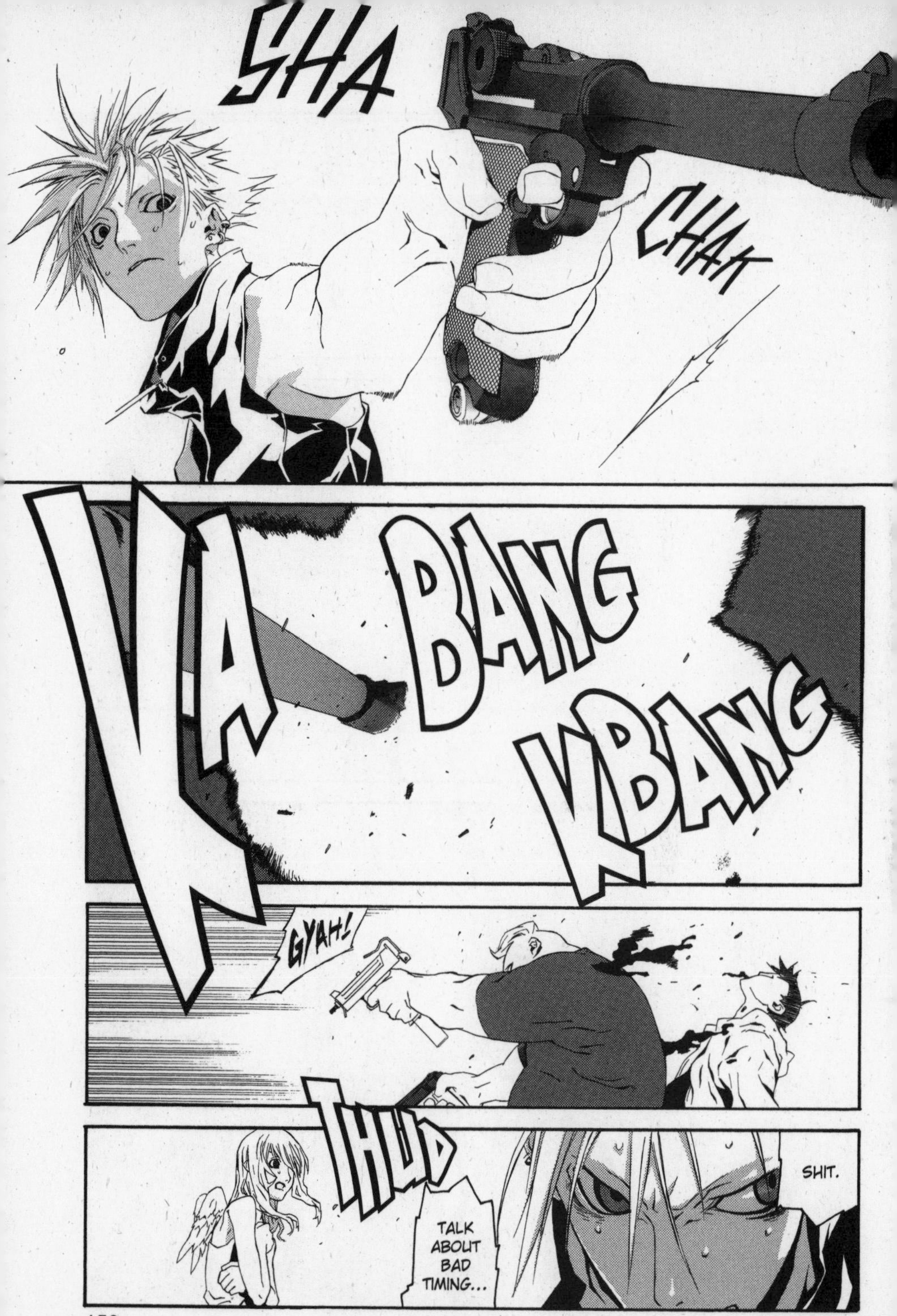
SHA
CHAK
BANG
KBANG
VA
GYAH!
SHIT.
TALK ABOUT BAD TIMING...
THUD

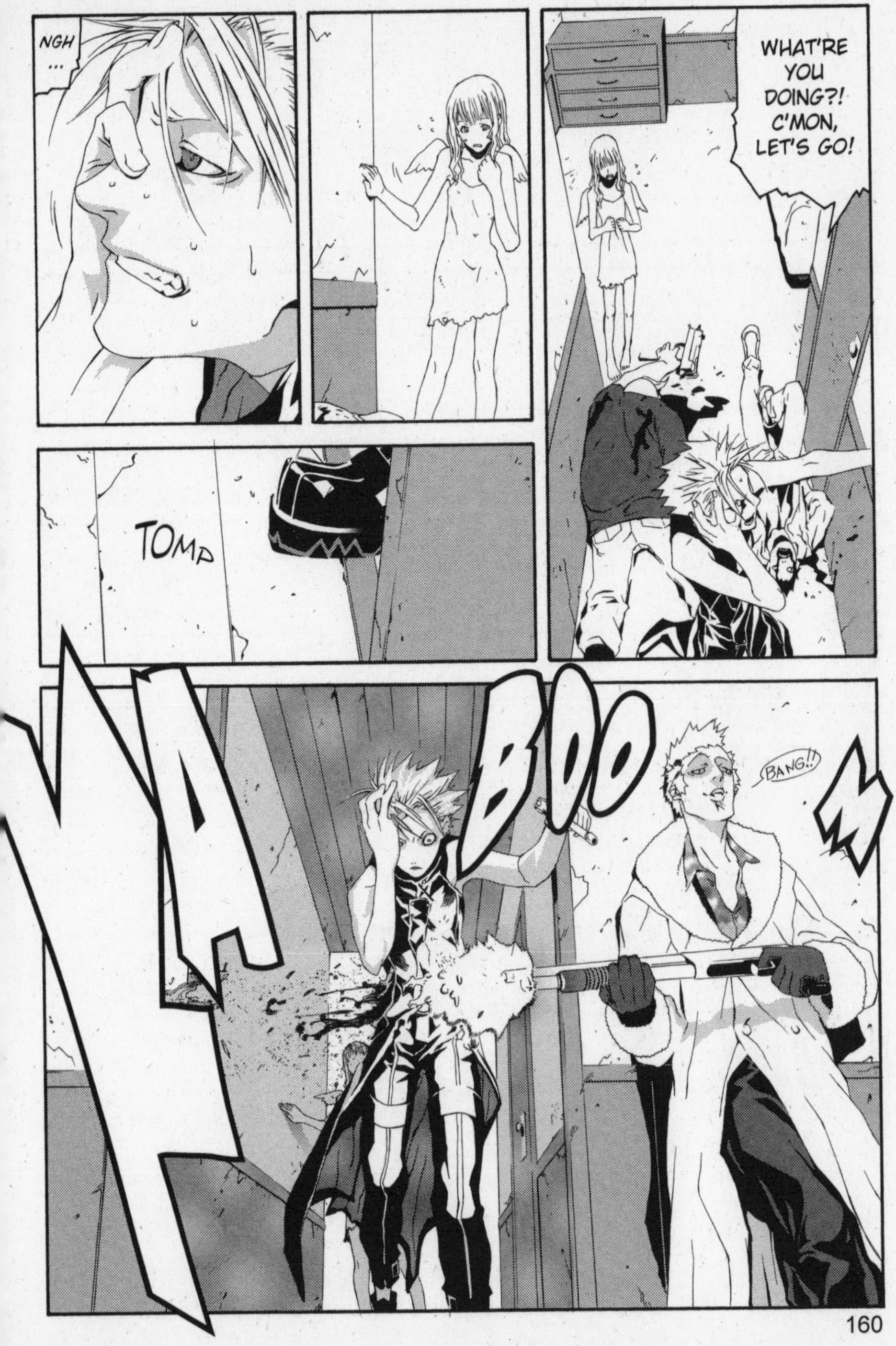
WHAT'RE YOU DOING?! C'MON, LET'S GO!
NGH ...
TOMP
BANG!!
KABOOM

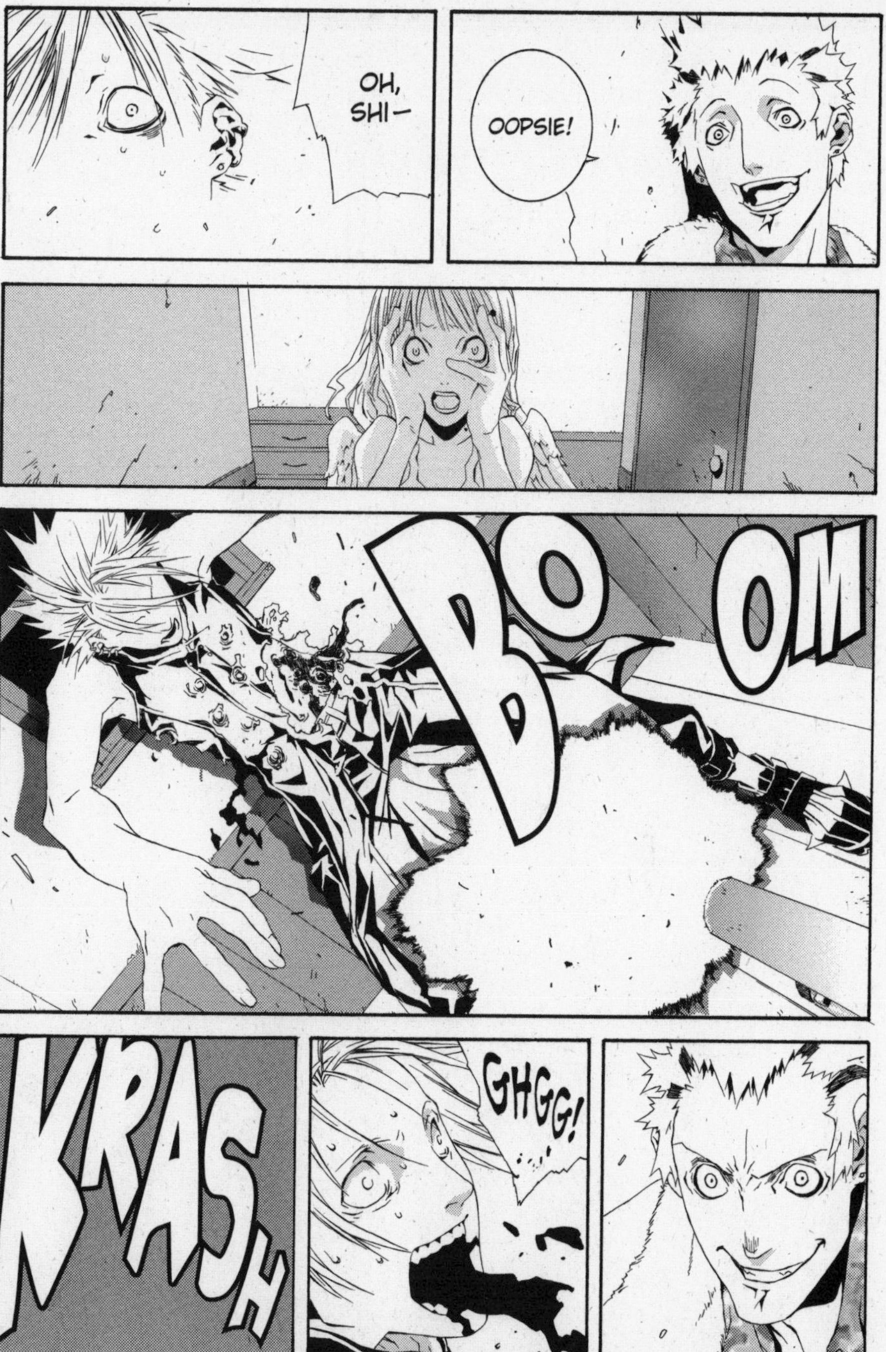
OOPSIE!
OH, SHI—
BOOM
GHGG!
KRASH

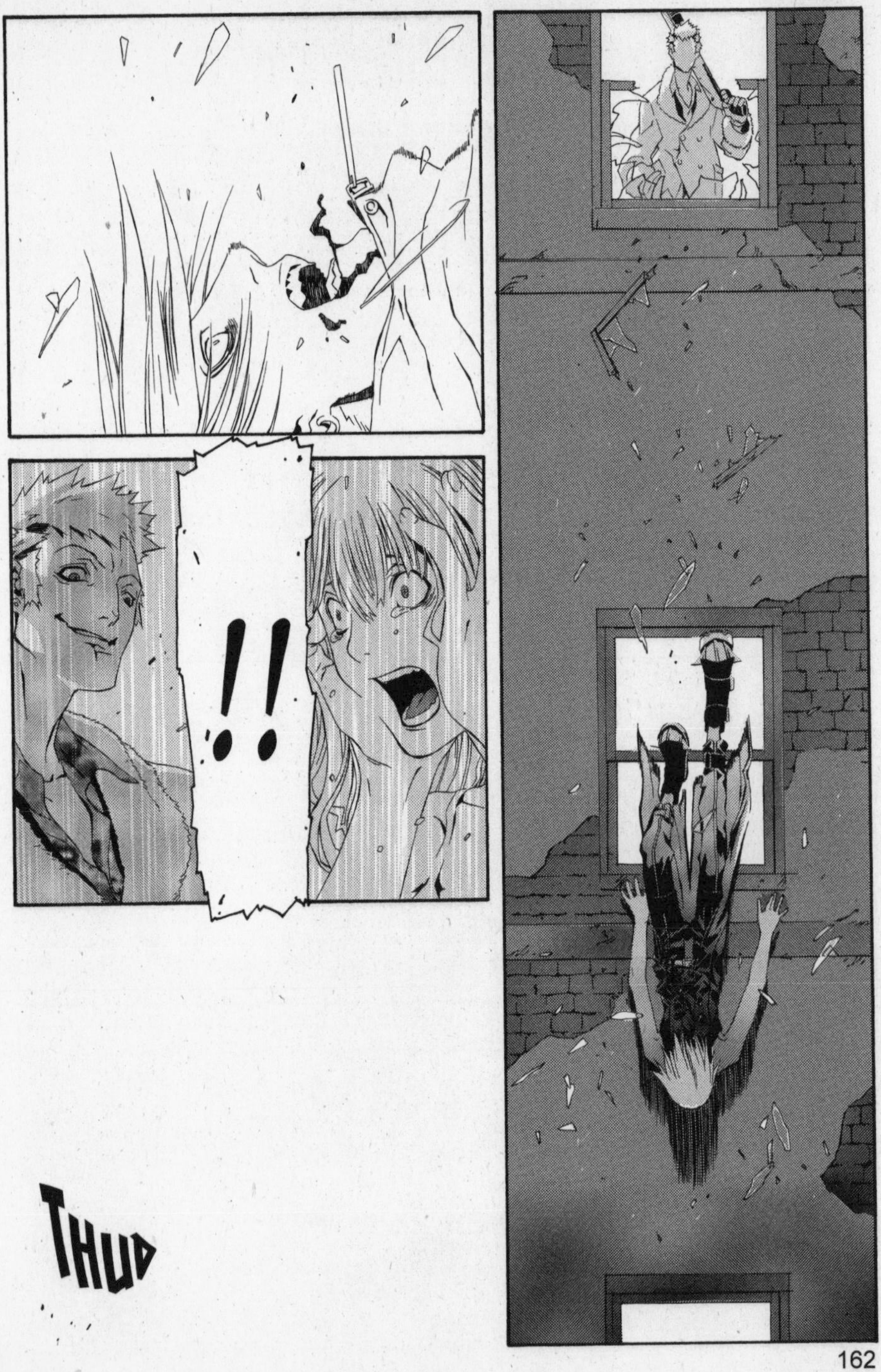
!!
THUD

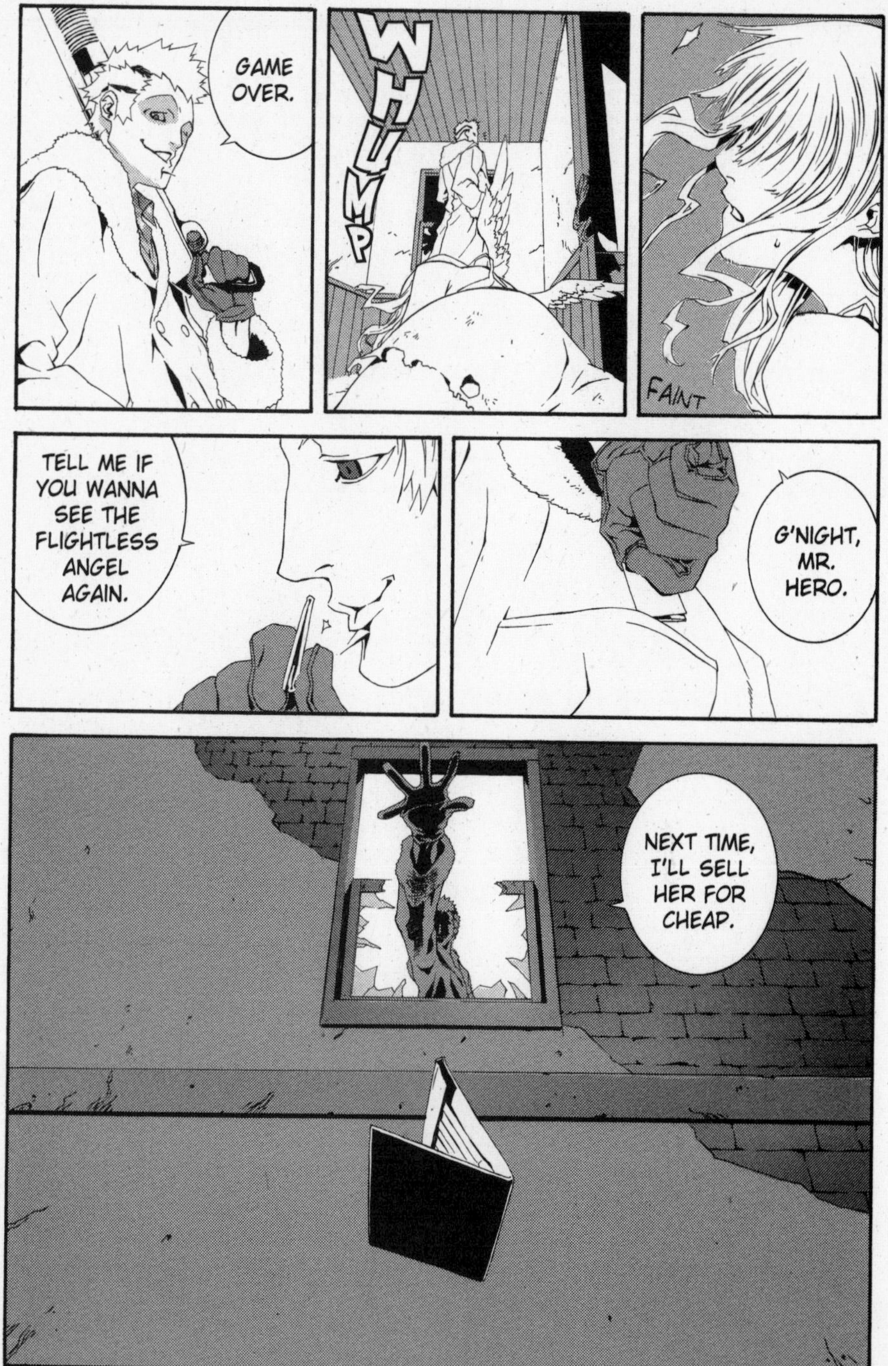
FAINT
WHUMP
GAME OVER.
G'NIGHT, MR. HERO.
TELL ME IF YOU WANNA SEE THE FLIGHTLESS ANGEL AGAIN.
NEXT TIME, I'LL SELL HER FOR CHEAP.

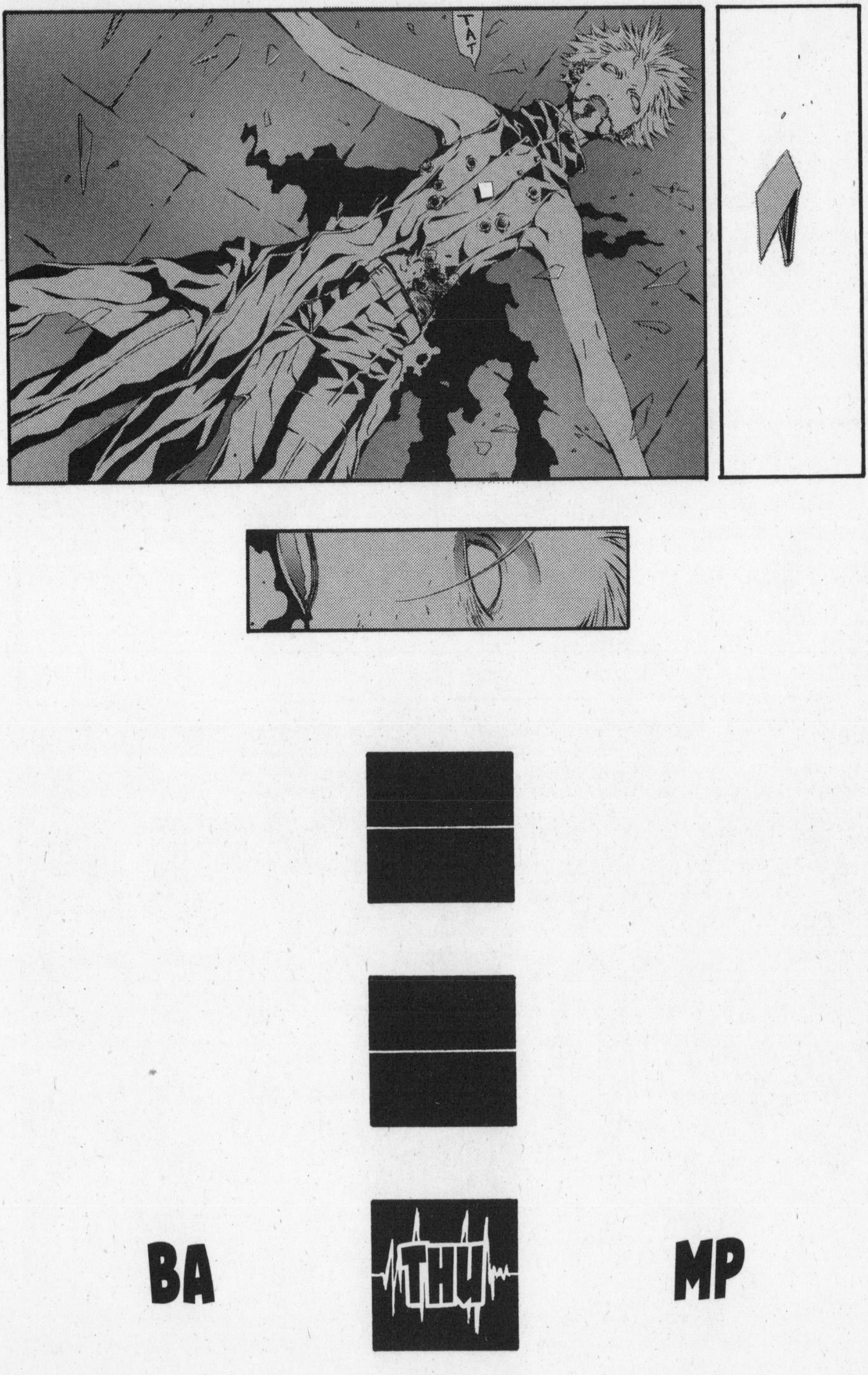
TAT
BA THU MP

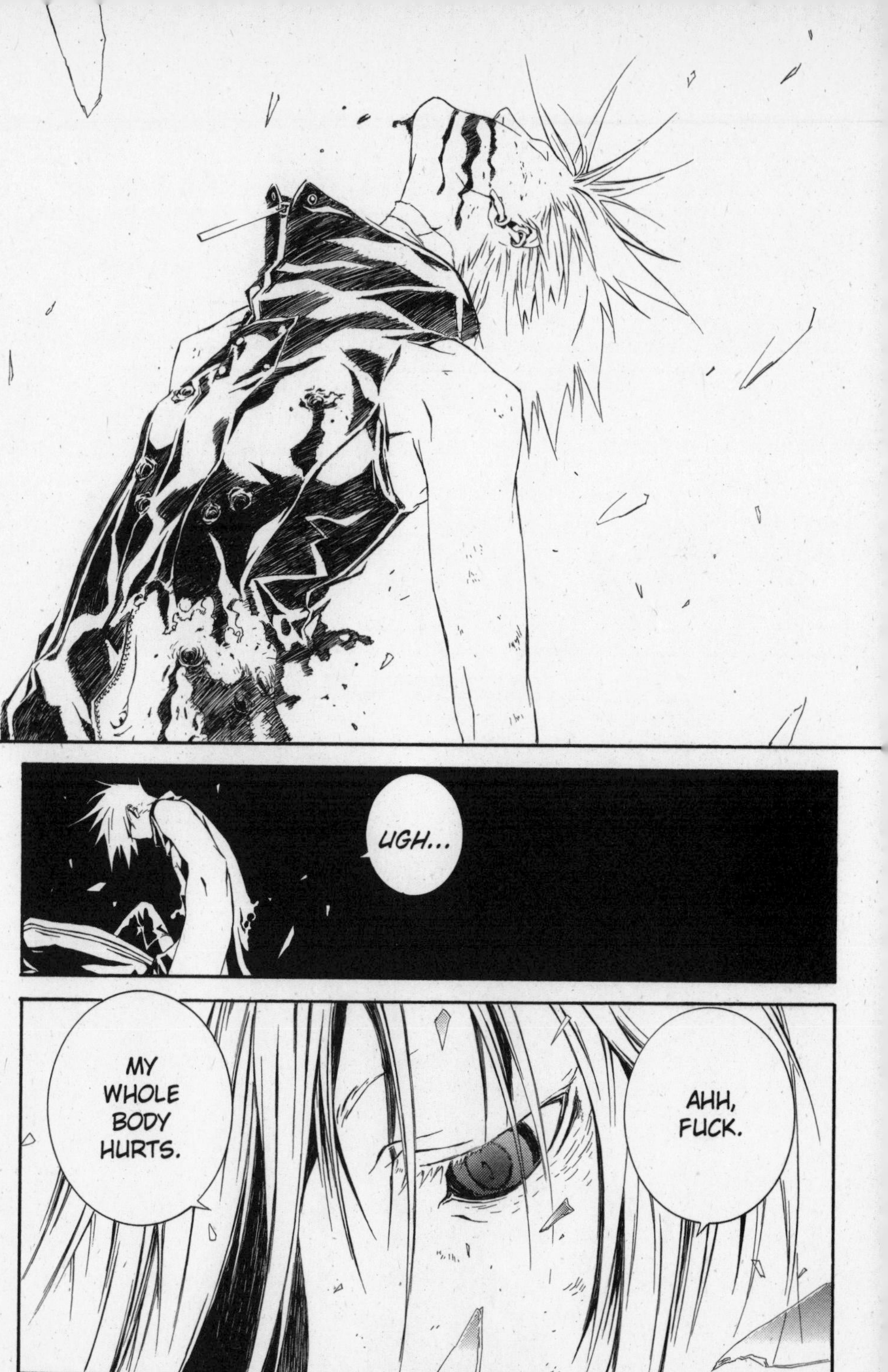
UGH...
AHH, FUCK.
MY WHOLE BODY HURTS.

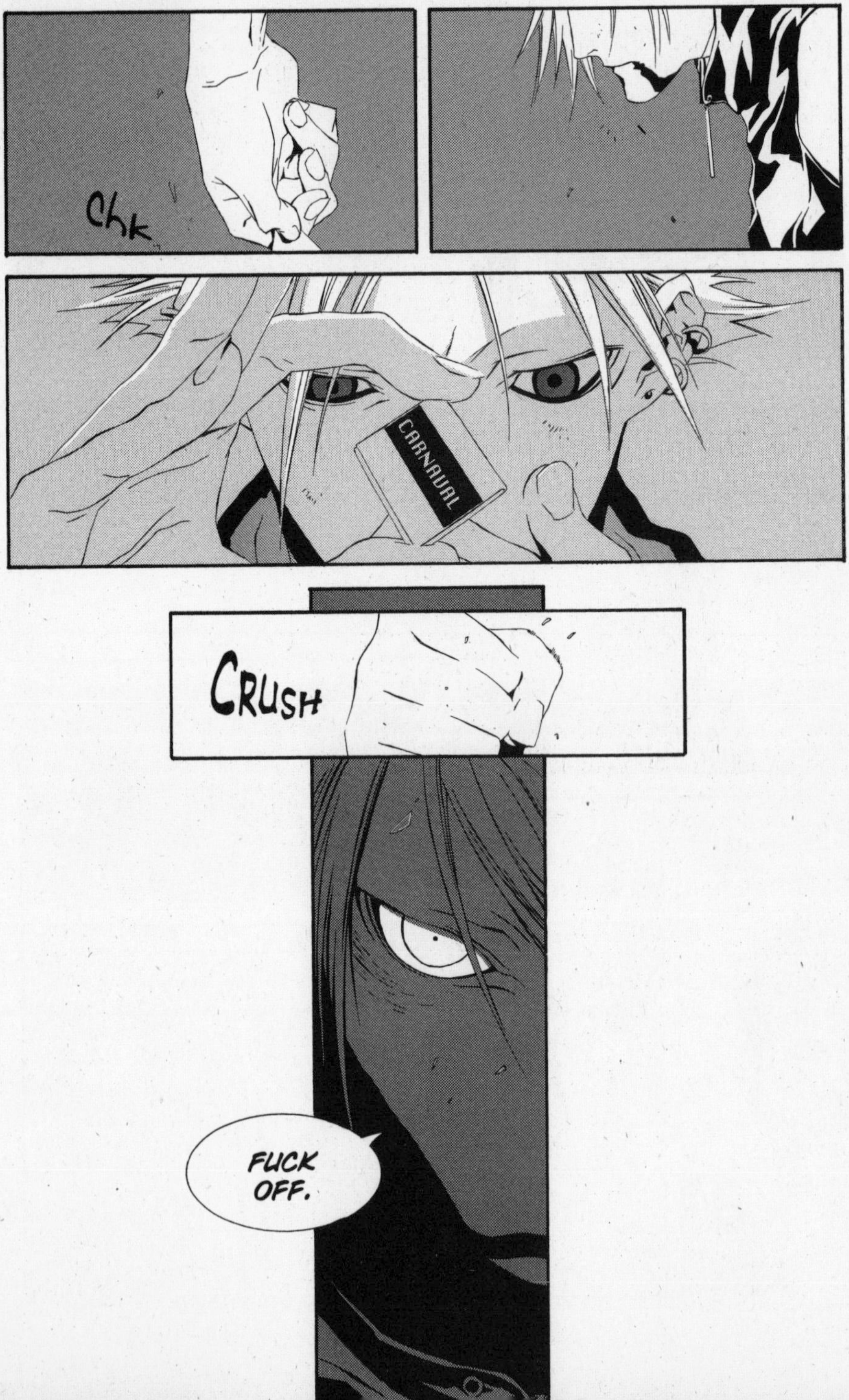
Chk
CARNAVAL
CRUSH
FUCK OFF.

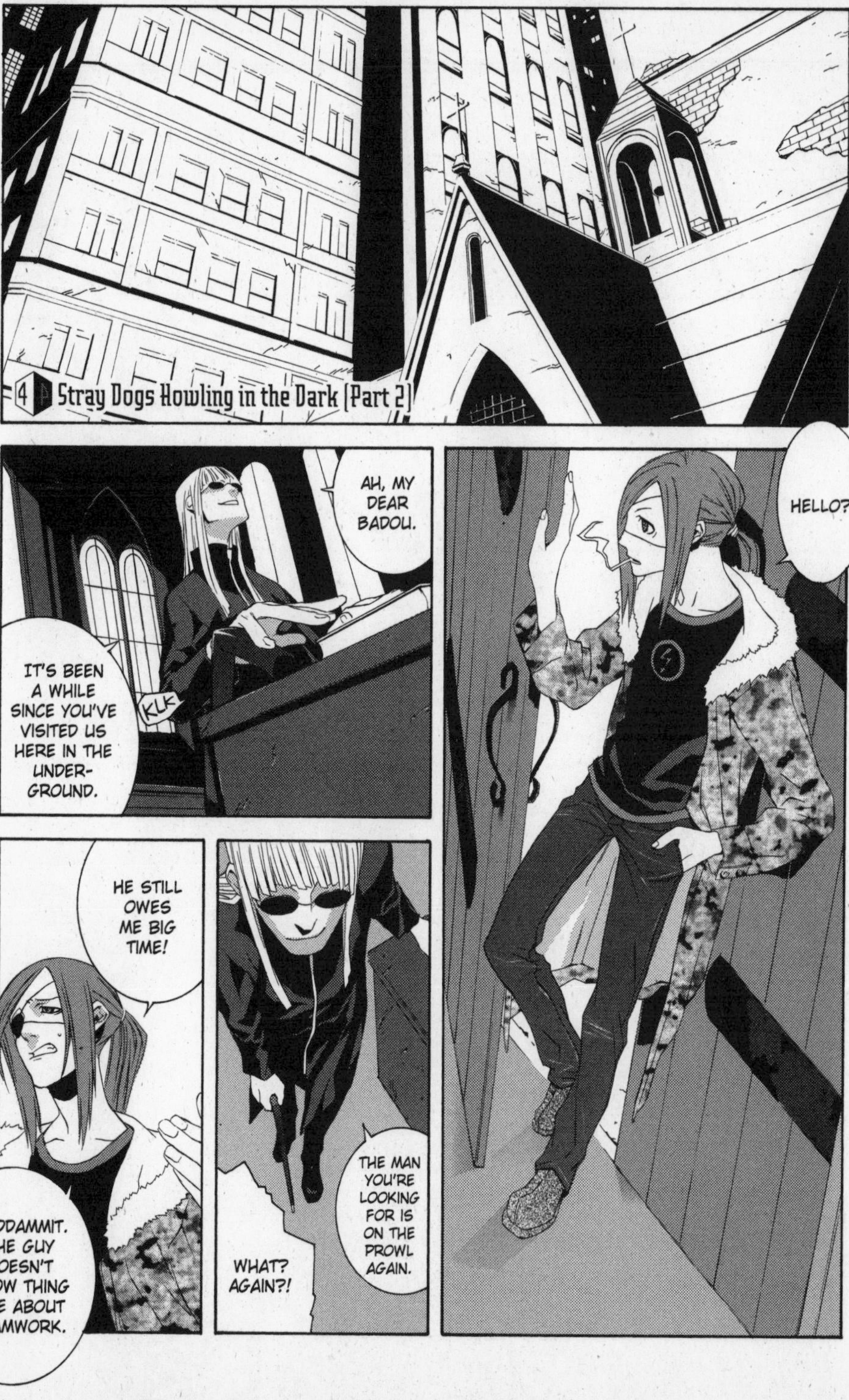
4 Stray Dogs Howling in the Dark [Part 2]
HELLO?
AH, MY DEAR BADOU.
IT'S BEEN A WHILE SINCE YOU'VE VISITED US HERE IN THE UNDER-GROUND.
KLK
THE MAN YOU'RE LOOKING FOR IS ON THE PROWL AGAIN.
WHAT? AGAIN?!
HE STILL OWES ME BIG TIME!
GODDAMMIT. THE GUY DOESN'T KNOW THING ONE ABOUT TEAMWORK.

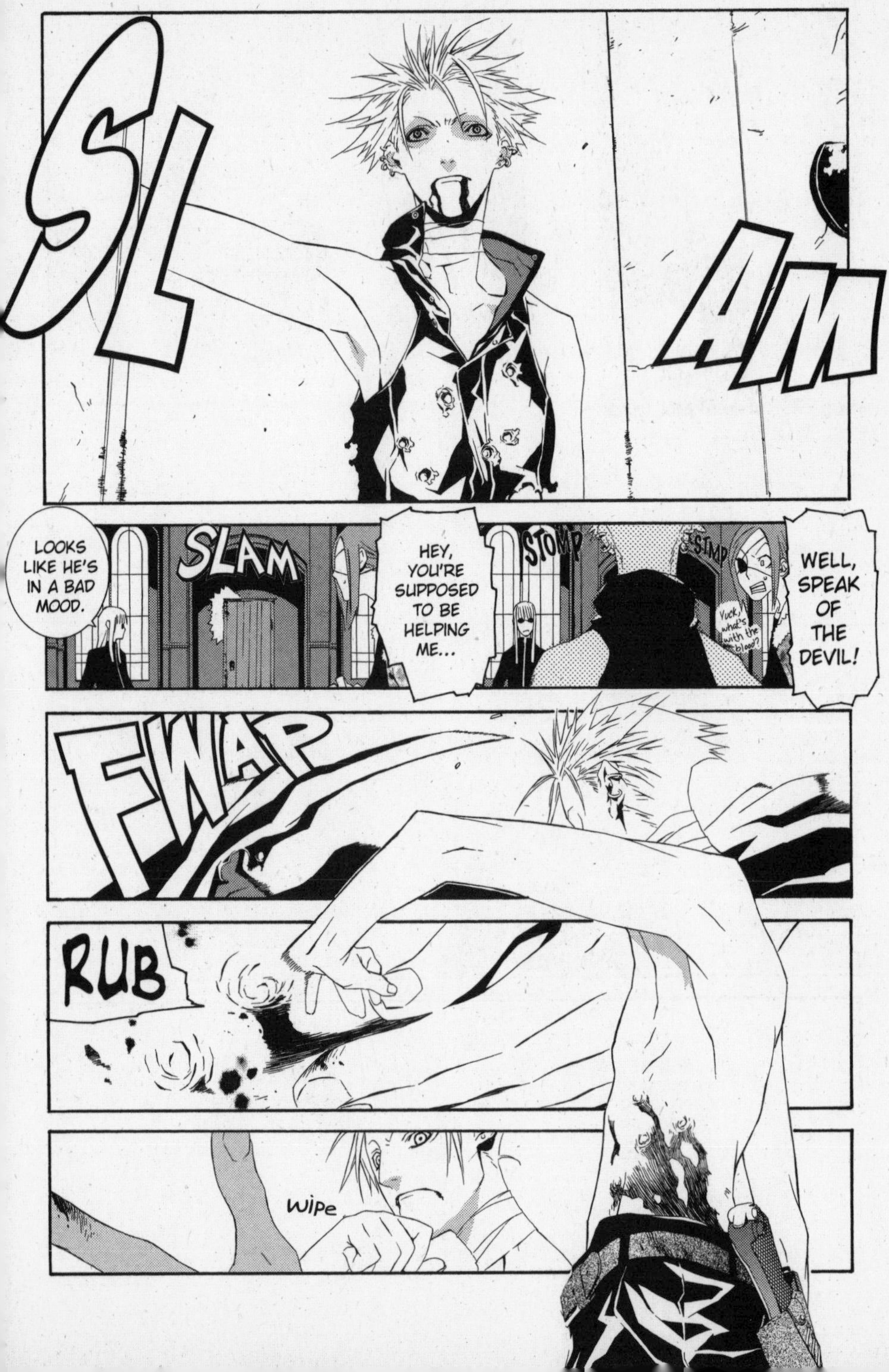
SL
AM
WELL, SPEAK OF THE DEVIL!
Yuck, what's with the blood?
STMP
STOMP
HEY, YOU'RE SUPPOSED TO BE HELPING ME...
SLAM
LOOKS LIKE HE'S IN A BAD MOOD.
FWAP
RUB
wipe

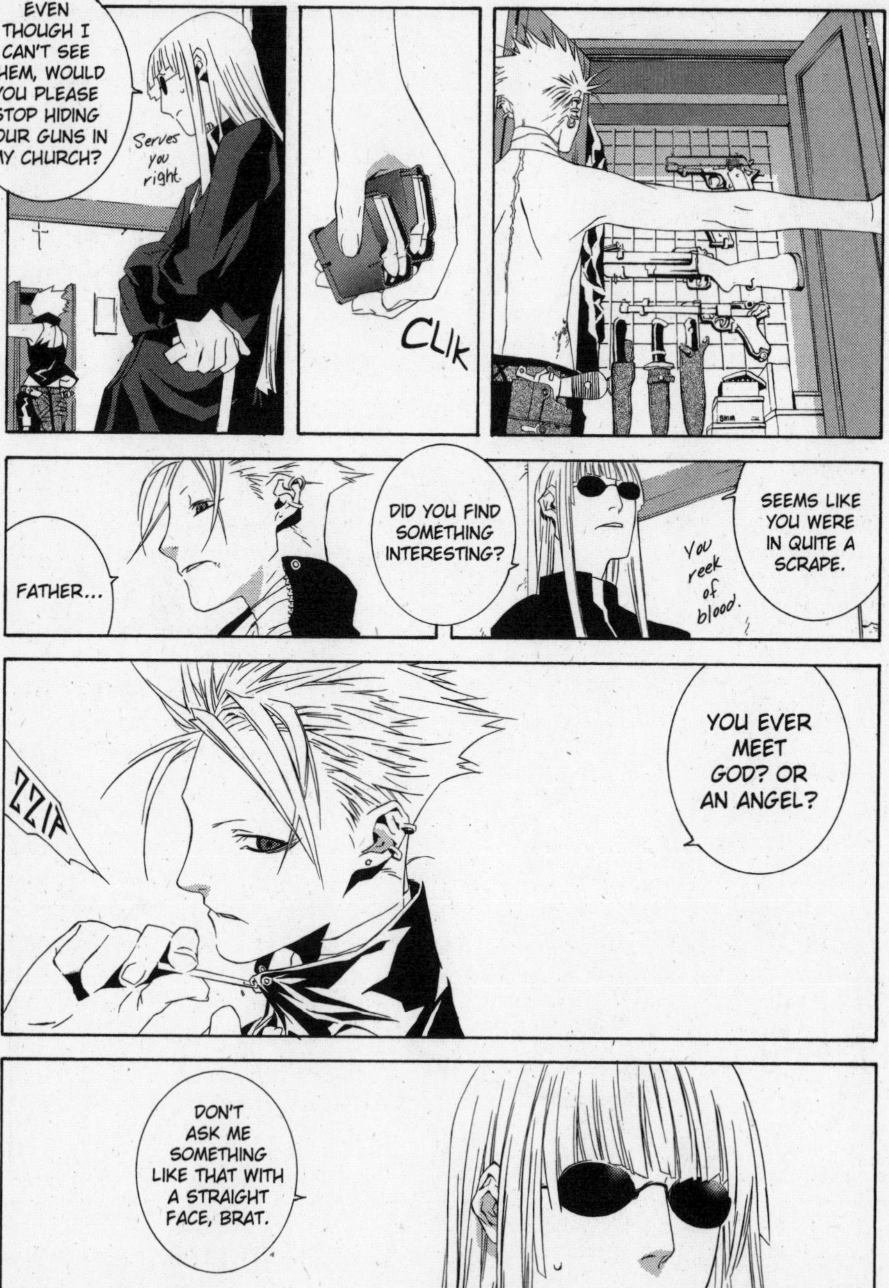
CLIK
EVEN THOUGH I CAN'T SEE THEM, WOULD YOU PLEASE STOP HIDING YOUR GUNS IN MY CHURCH?
Serves you right.
SEEMS LIKE YOU WERE IN QUITE A SCRAPE.
You reek of blood.
DID YOU FIND SOMETHING INTERESTING?
FATHER...
YOU EVER MEET GOD? OR AN ANGEL?
ZZIP
DON'T ASK ME SOMETHING LIKE THAT WITH A STRAIGHT FACE, BRAT.

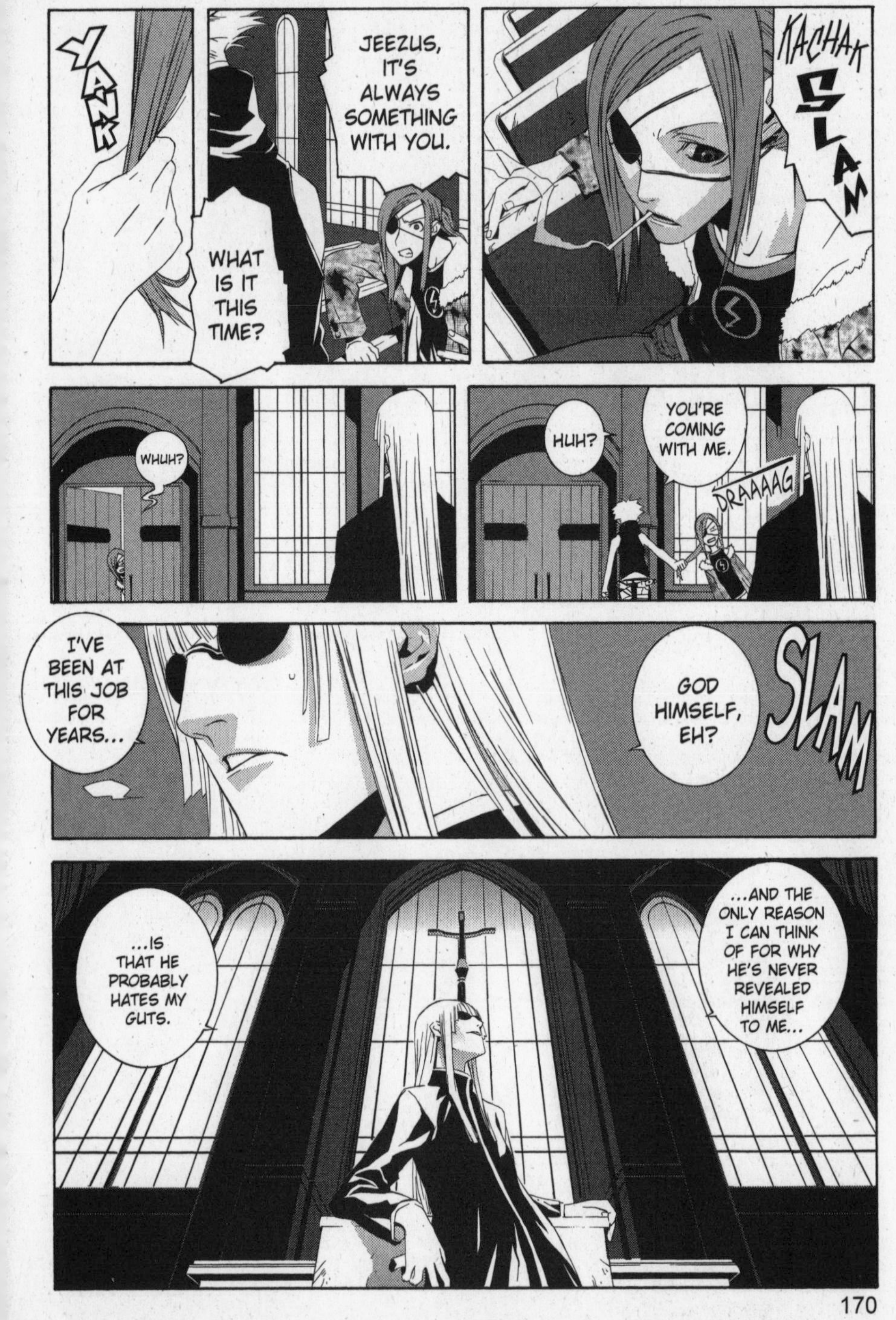
KACHAK
SLAM
JEEZUS, IT'S ALWAYS SOMETHING WITH YOU.
WHAT IS IT THIS TIME?
YANK
YOU'RE COMING WITH ME.
HUH?
DRAAAAG
WHUH?
SLAM
GOD HIMSELF, EH?
I'VE BEEN AT THIS JOB FOR YEARS...
...AND THE ONLY REASON I CAN THINK OF FOR WHY HE'S NEVER REVEALED HIMSELF TO ME...
...IS THAT HE PROBABLY HATES MY GUTS.

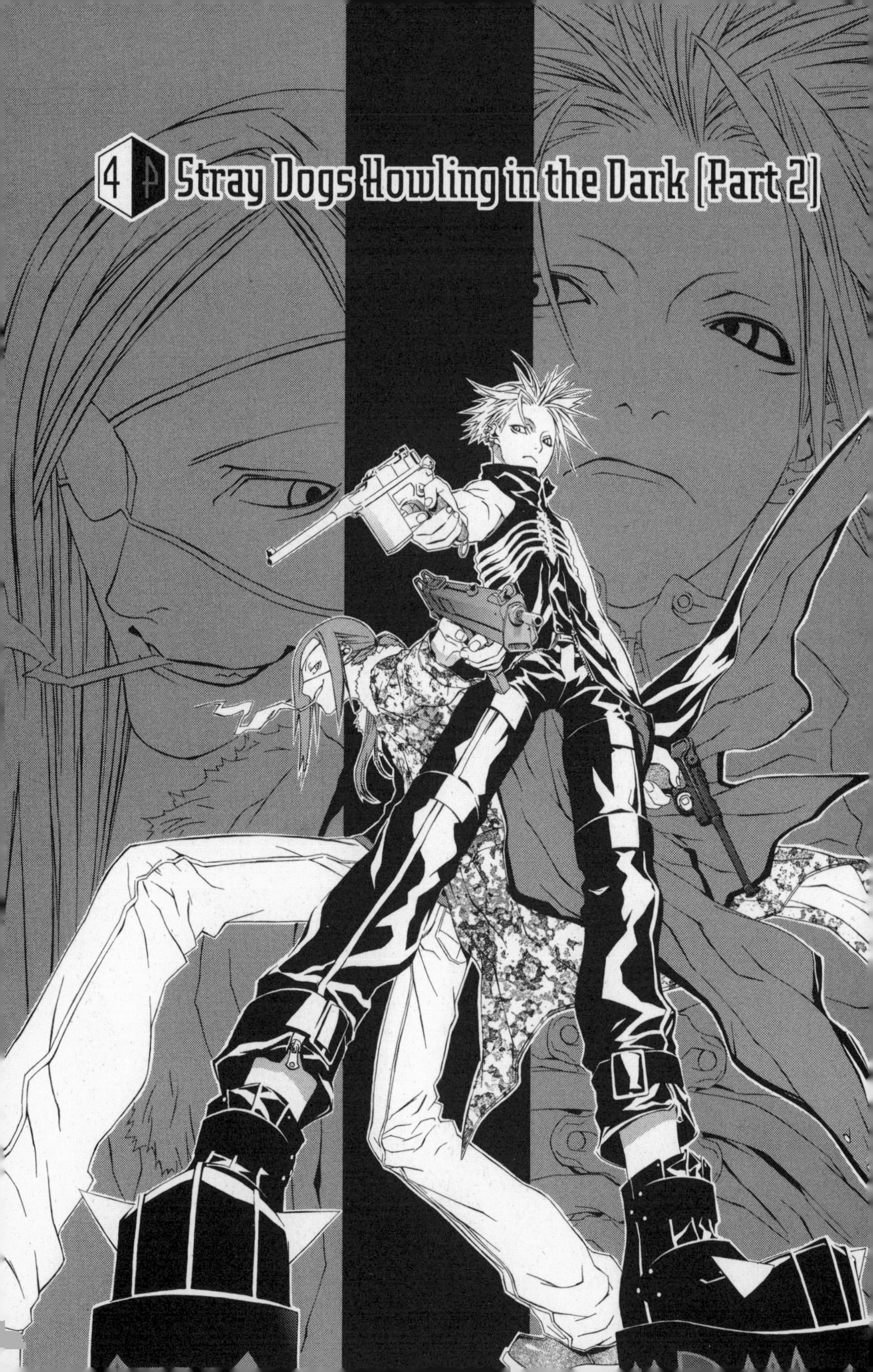
4 P Stray Dogs Howling in the Dark [Part 2]

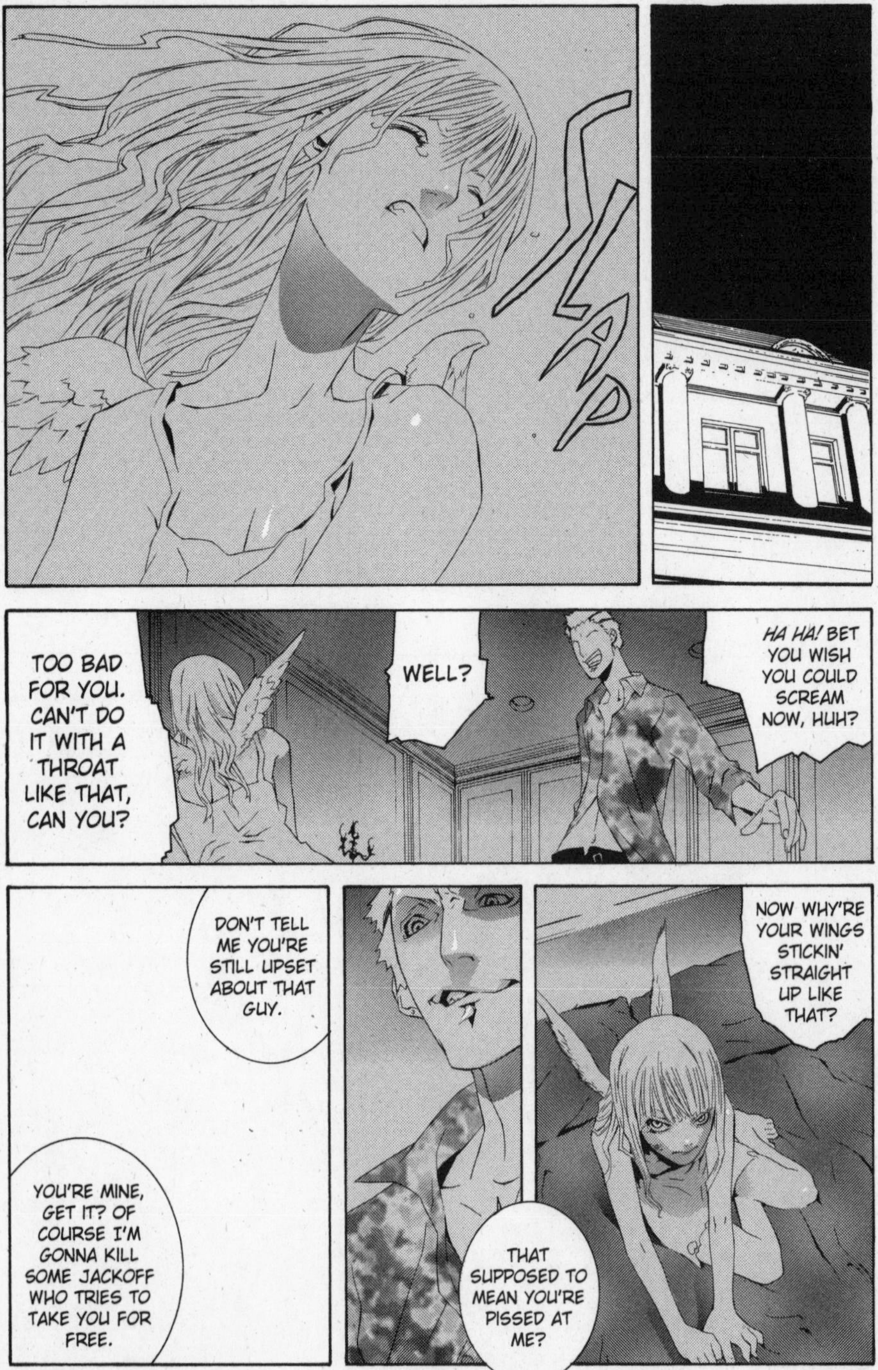
SLAP
HA HA! BET YOU WISH YOU COULD SCREAM NOW, HUH?
WELL?
TOO BAD FOR YOU. CAN'T DO IT WITH A THROAT LIKE THAT, CAN YOU?
NOW WHY'RE YOUR WINGS STICKIN' STRAIGHT UP LIKE THAT?
THAT SUPPOSED TO MEAN YOU'RE PISSED AT ME?
DON'T TELL ME YOU'RE STILL UPSET ABOUT THAT GUY.
YOU'RE MINE, GET IT? OF COURSE I'M GONNA KILL SOME JACKOFF WHO TRIES TO TAKE YOU FOR FREE.

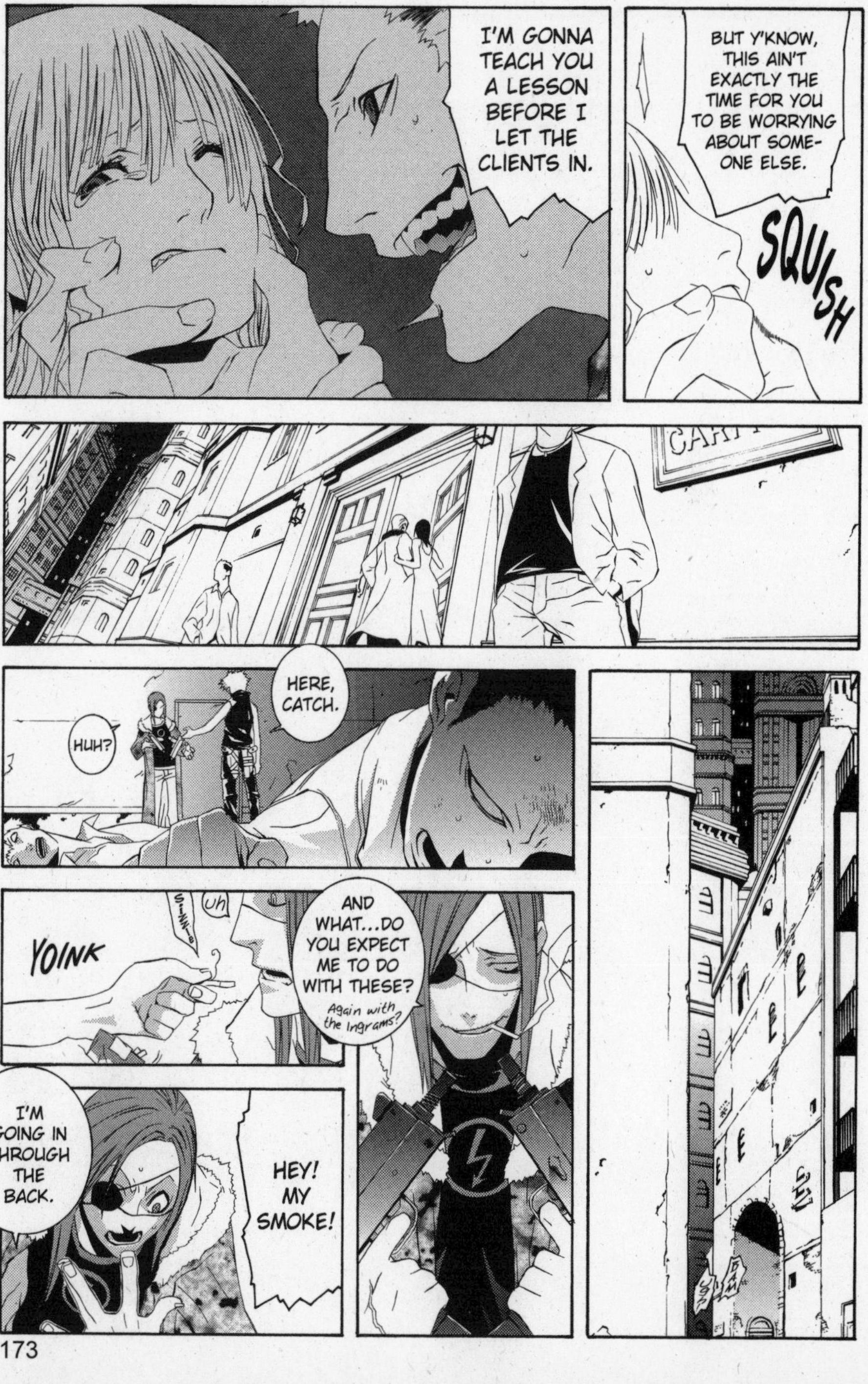
BUT Y'KNOW, THIS AIN'T EXACTLY THE TIME FOR YOU TO BE WORRYING ABOUT SOME-ONE ELSE.
SQUISH
I'M GONNA TEACH YOU A LESSON BEFORE I LET THE CLIENTS IN.
HERE, CATCH.
HUH?
AND WHAT...DO YOU EXPECT ME TO DO WITH THESE?
Again with the Ingrams?
uh
YOINK
HEY! MY SMOKE!
I'M GOING IN THROUGH THE BACK.

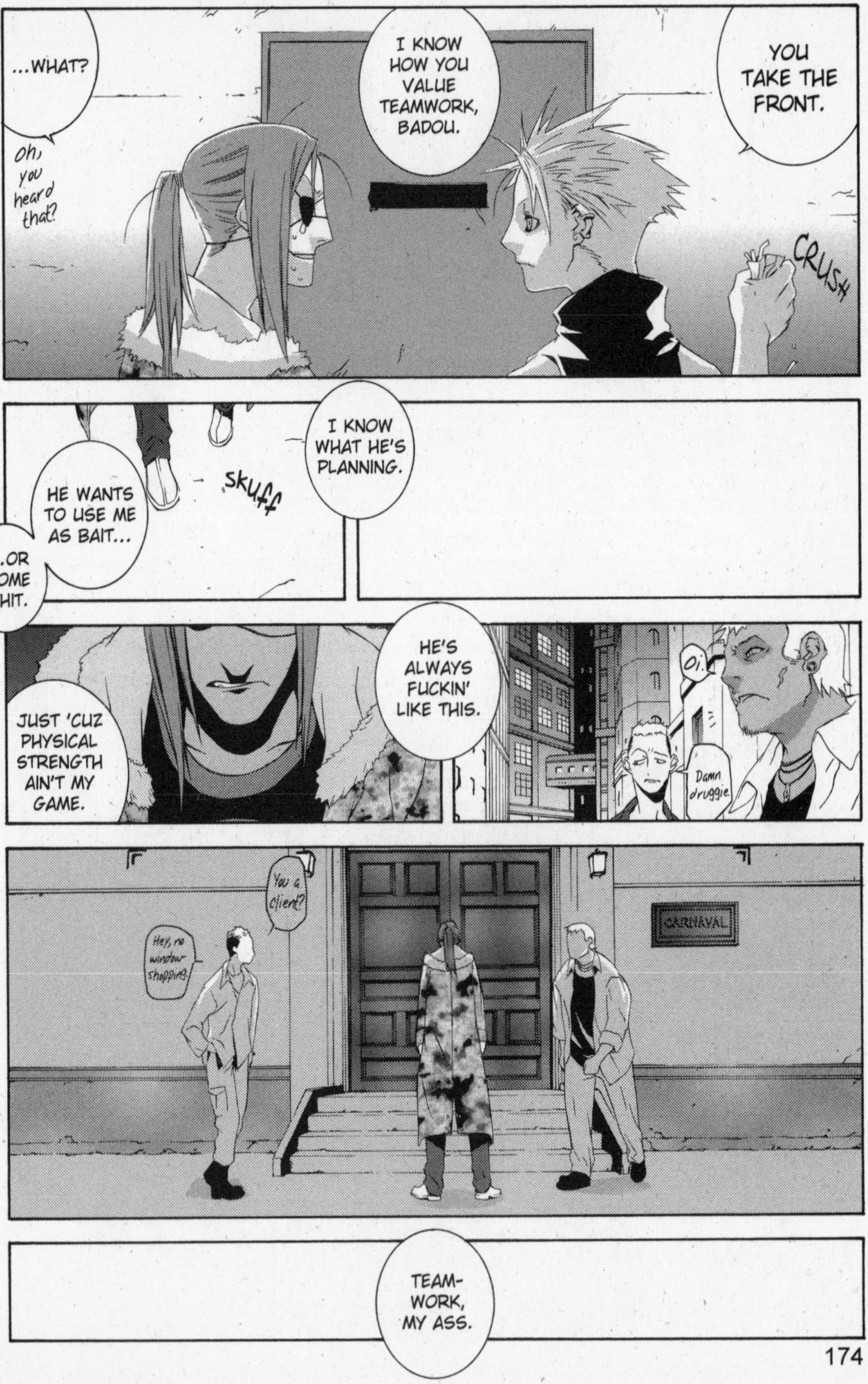
YOU TAKE THE FRONT.
I KNOW HOW YOU VALUE TEAMWORK, BADOU.
...WHAT?
Oh, you heard that?
CRUSH
I KNOW WHAT HE'S PLANNING.
HE WANTS TO USE ME AS BAIT...
...OR SOME SHIT.
skuff
Oi.
Damn druggie.
HE'S ALWAYS FUCKIN' LIKE THIS.
JUST 'CUZ PHYSICAL STRENGTH AIN'T MY GAME.
You a client?
Hey, no window shopping!
CARNAVAL
TEAM-WORK, MY ASS.

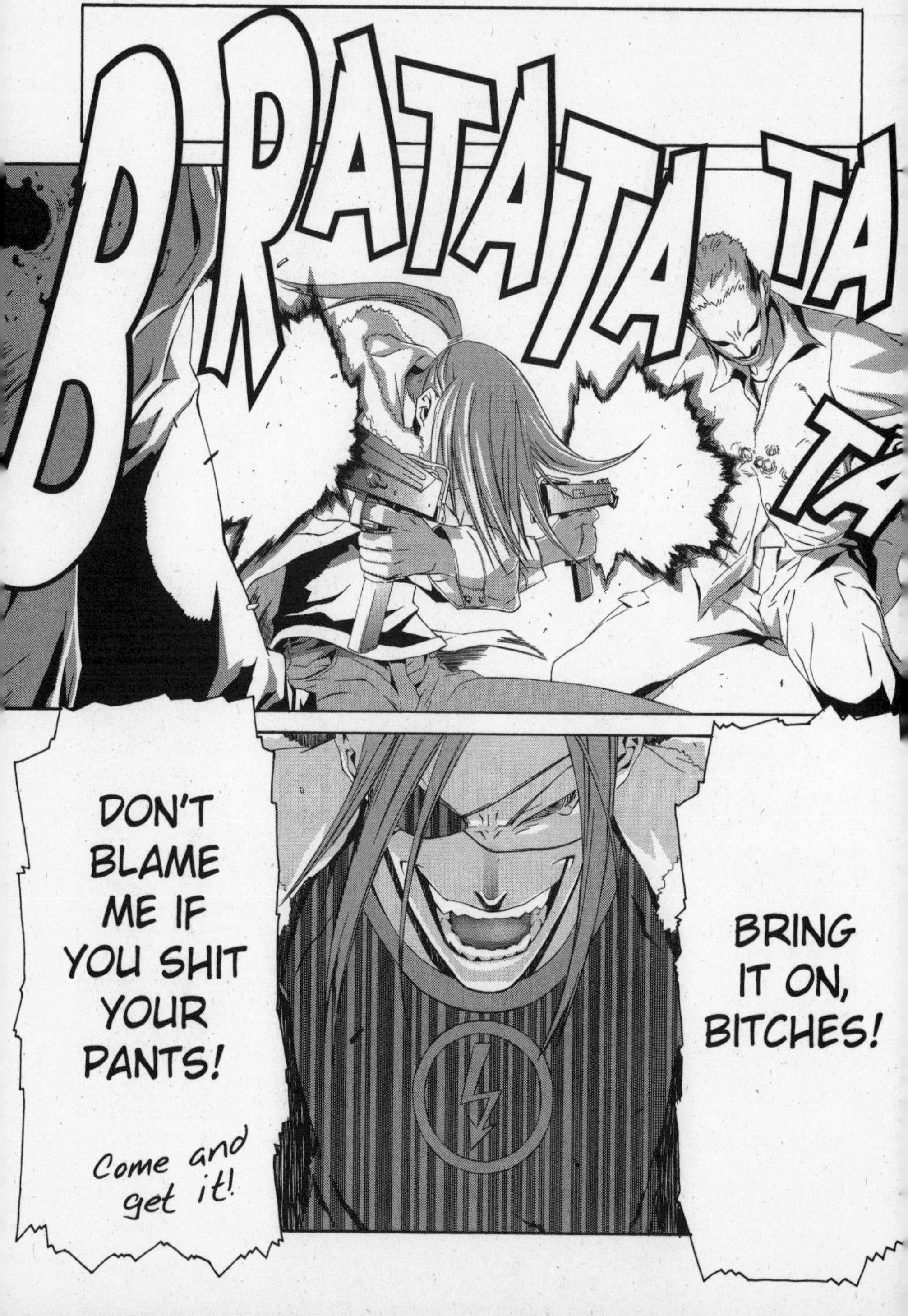
BRATATA
TA
TA
BRING IT ON, BITCHES!
DON'T BLAME ME IF YOU SHIT YOUR PANTS!
Come and get it!

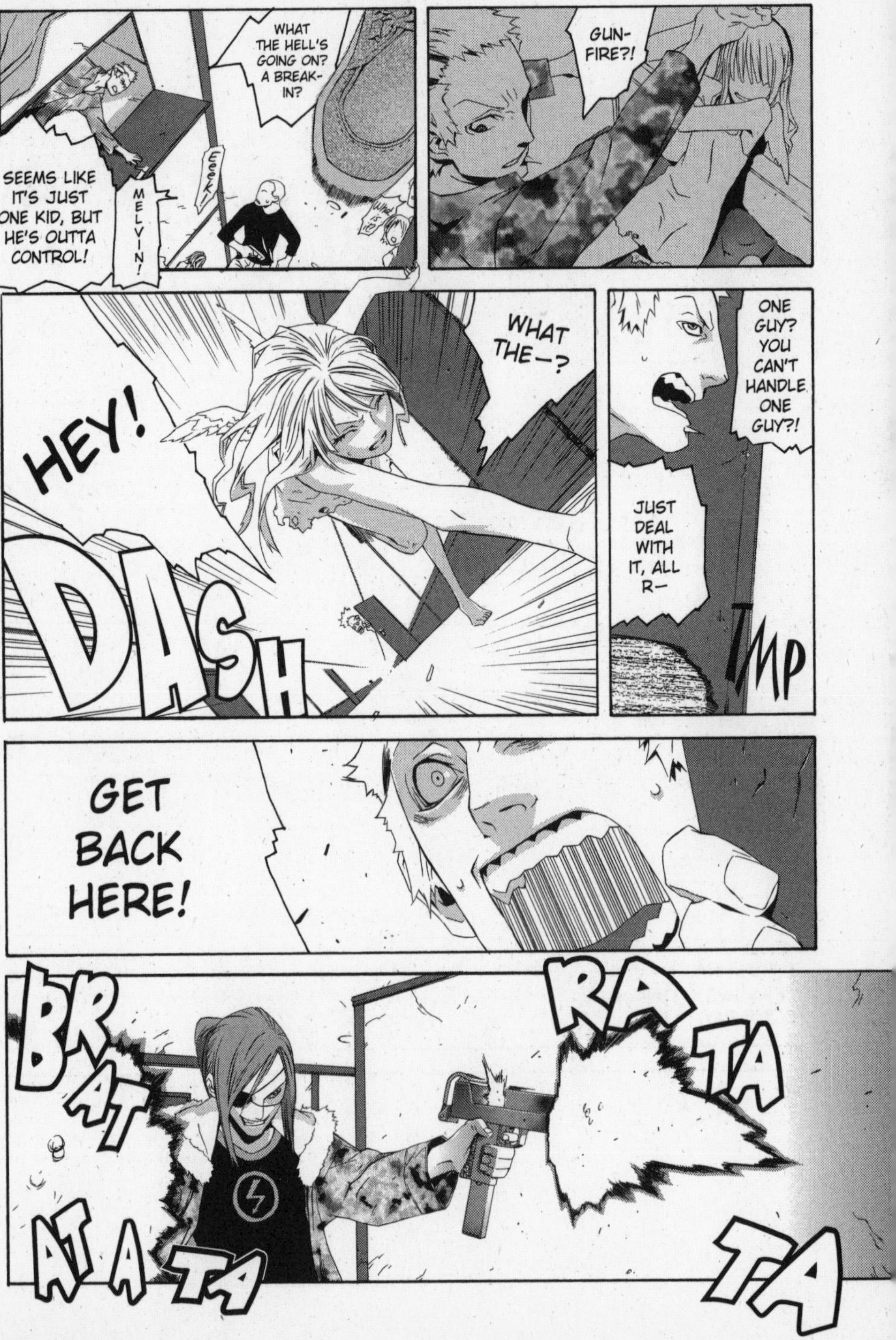
GUN-FIRE?!
WHAT THE HELL'S GOING ON? A BREAK-IN?
Eeek!
What is it?
MELVIN!
SEEMS LIKE IT'S JUST ONE KID, BUT HE'S OUTTA CONTROL!
ONE GUY? YOU CAN'T HANDLE ONE GUY?!
JUST DEAL WITH IT, ALL R—
TMP
WHAT THE—?
HEY!
DASH
GET BACK HERE!
RATATA
TA
BRAT
ATATA

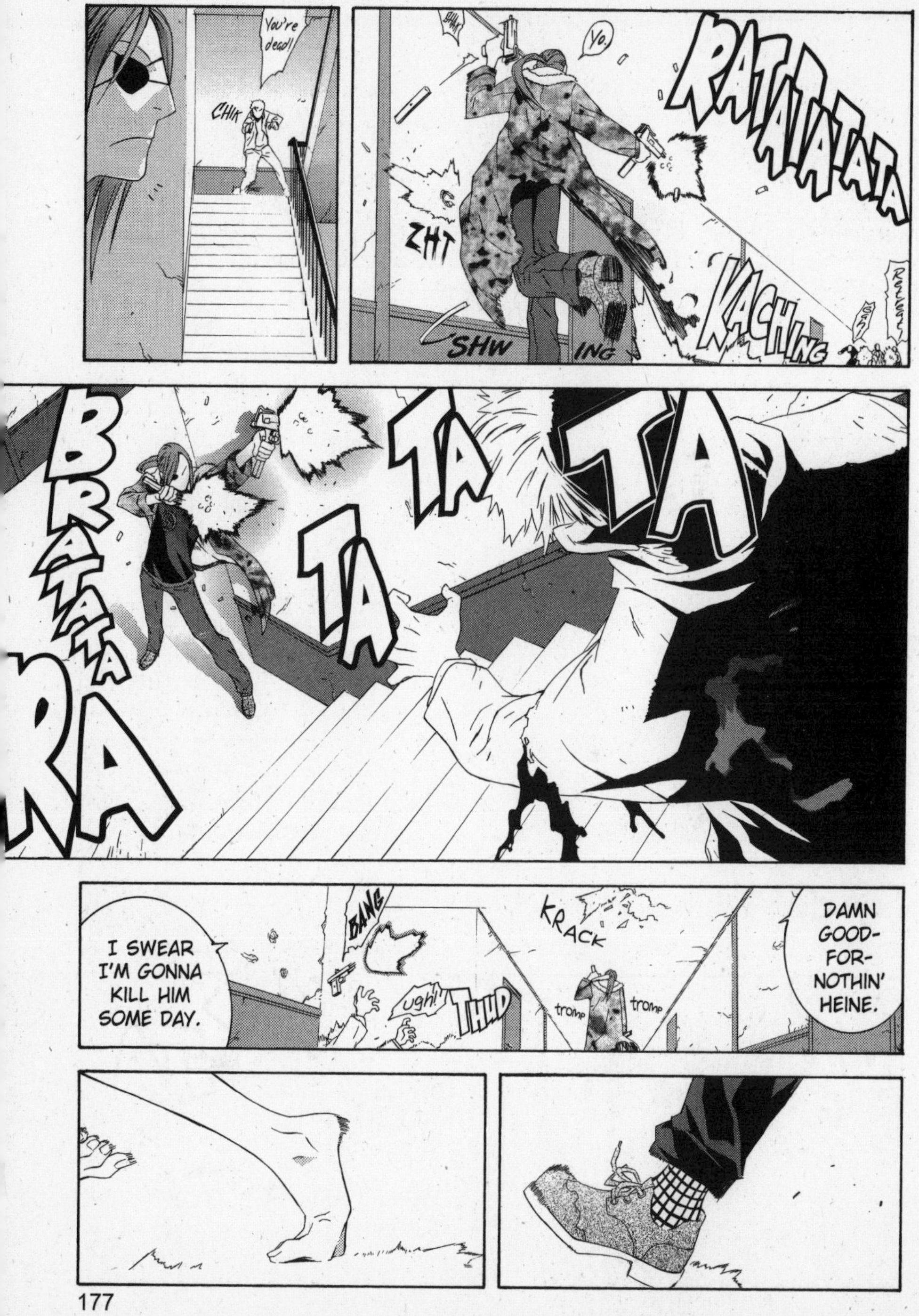
RATATATATATA
Yo.
KACHING
ZHT
SHW ING
You're dead!
CHIK
TA
TA
TA
BRATATATA
RA
DAMN GOOD-FOR-NOTHIN' HEINE.
KRACK
tromp
tromp
THUD
ugh!
BANG
I SWEAR I'M GONNA KILL HIM SOME DAY.

HAH

HAH

FUCK!

I FORGET HOW FAST THIS CHICK IS...

STOP, DAMN IT!

HOLD IT RIGHT THERE, YOU LITTLE BITCH!

TRMP

TRMP

TROMP

tat tat tat

I'M GONNA BEAT YOU IF YOU DON'T STOP!

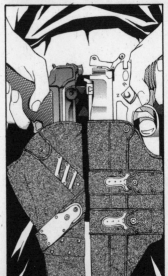

?!!

178

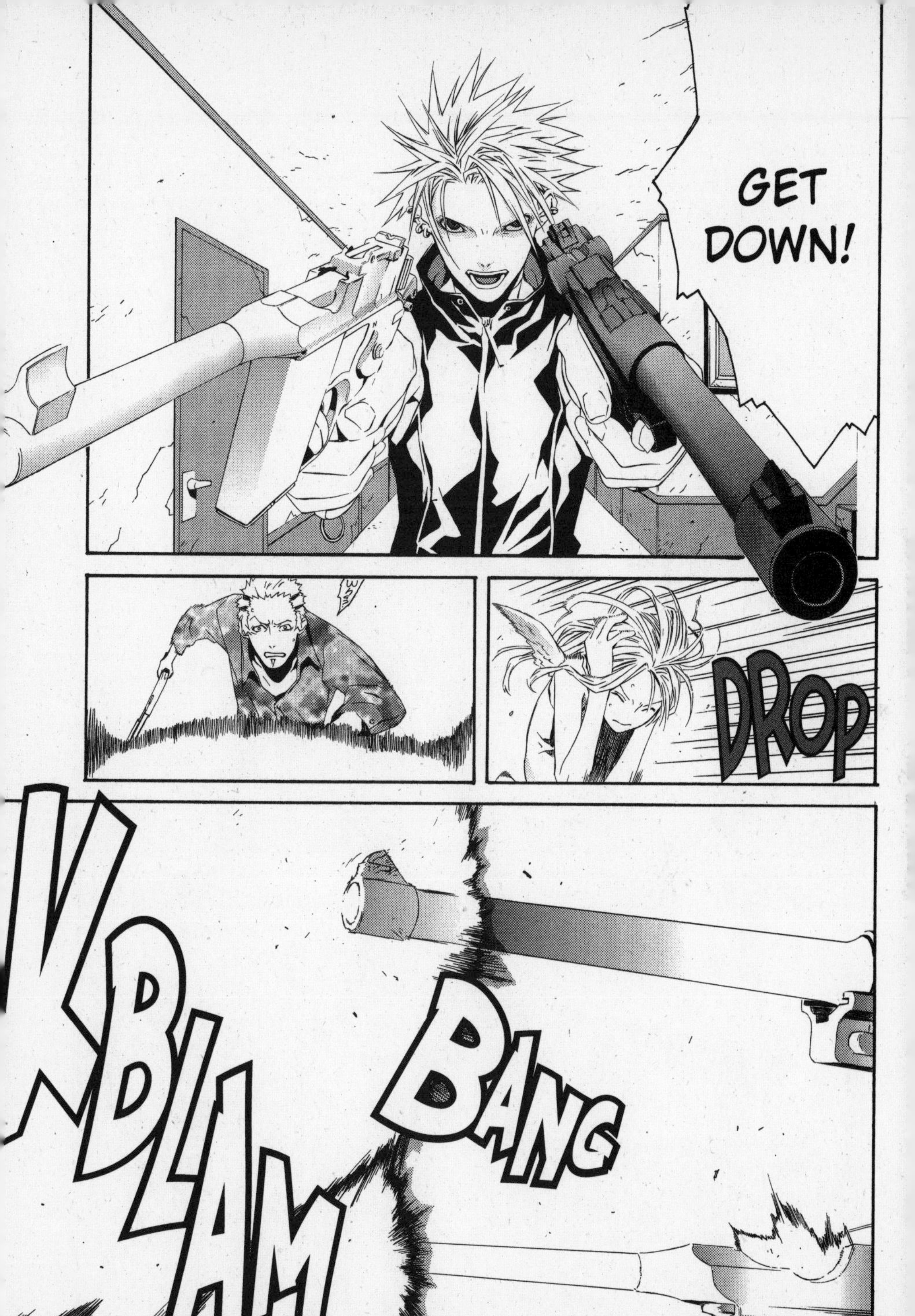
GET DOWN!
DROP
BANG
KBLAM

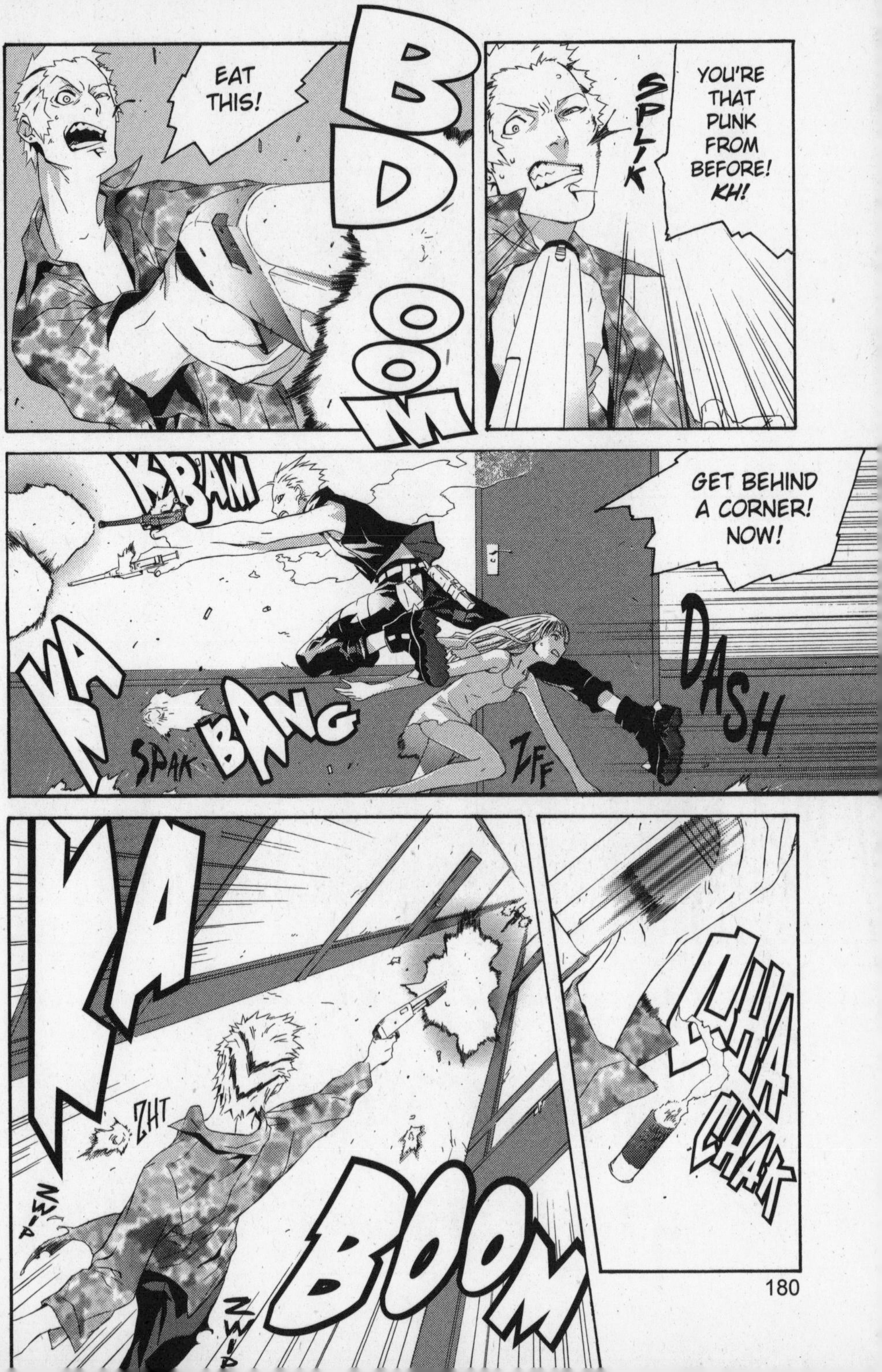
SPLIK
YOU'RE THAT PUNK FROM BEFORE! KH!
EAT THIS!
BDOOOM
GET BEHIND A CORNER! NOW!
DASH
ZFF
KBAM
BANG
SPAK
KA
CHA CHAK
ZHT
ZWIP
ZWIP
BOOM

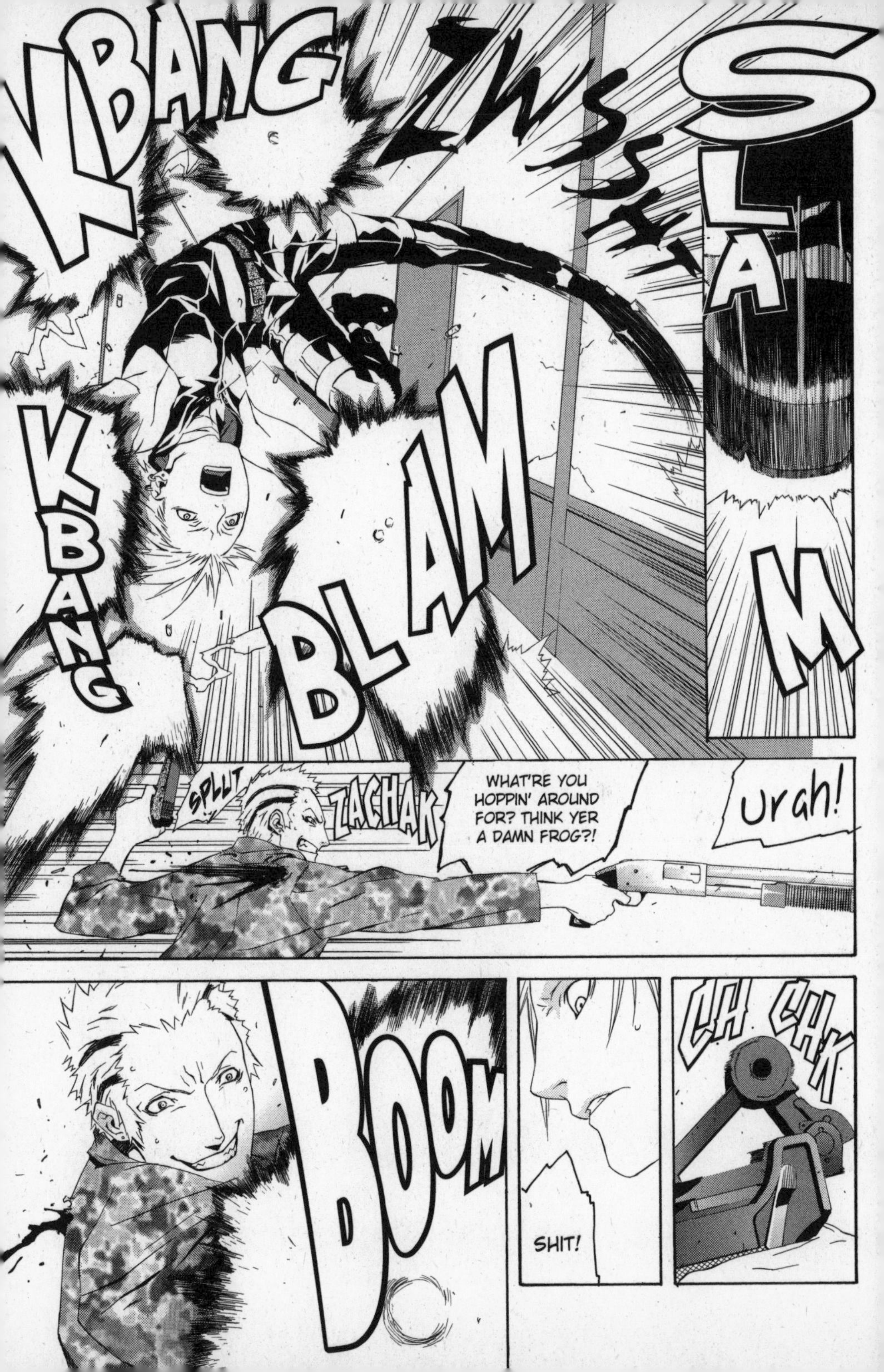
SLAM
ZWSSH
KBANG
KBANG
BLAM
Urah!
WHAT'RE YOU HOPPIN' AROUND FOR? THINK YER A DAMN FROG?!
ZACHAK
SPLUT
CH CHK
SHIT!
BOOM

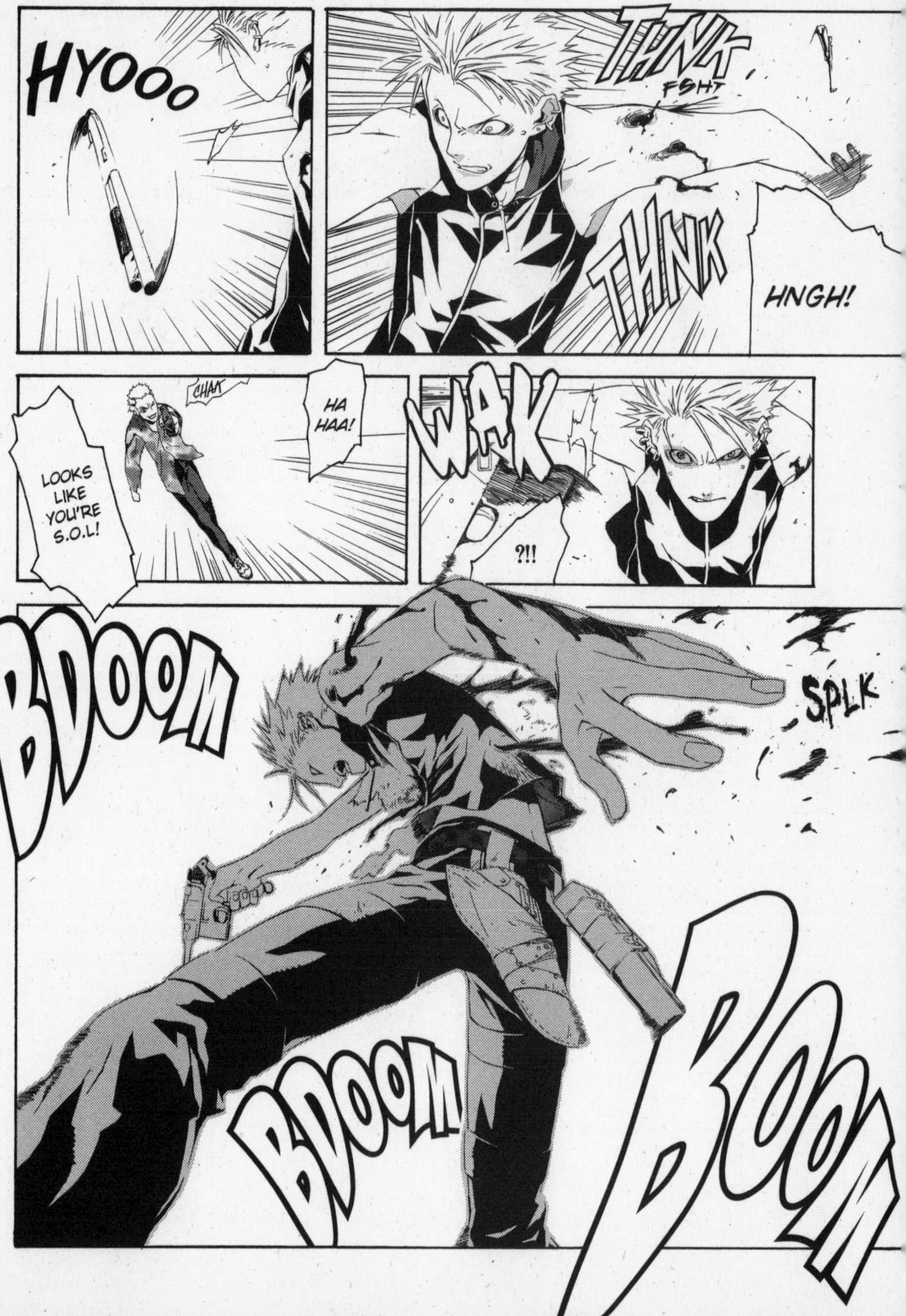
THNK
FSHT
THNK
HNGH!
HYOOO
WAK
?!!
HA HAA!
CHAK
LOOKS LIKE YOU'RE S.O.L!
SPLK
BDOOM
BDOOM
BDOOM

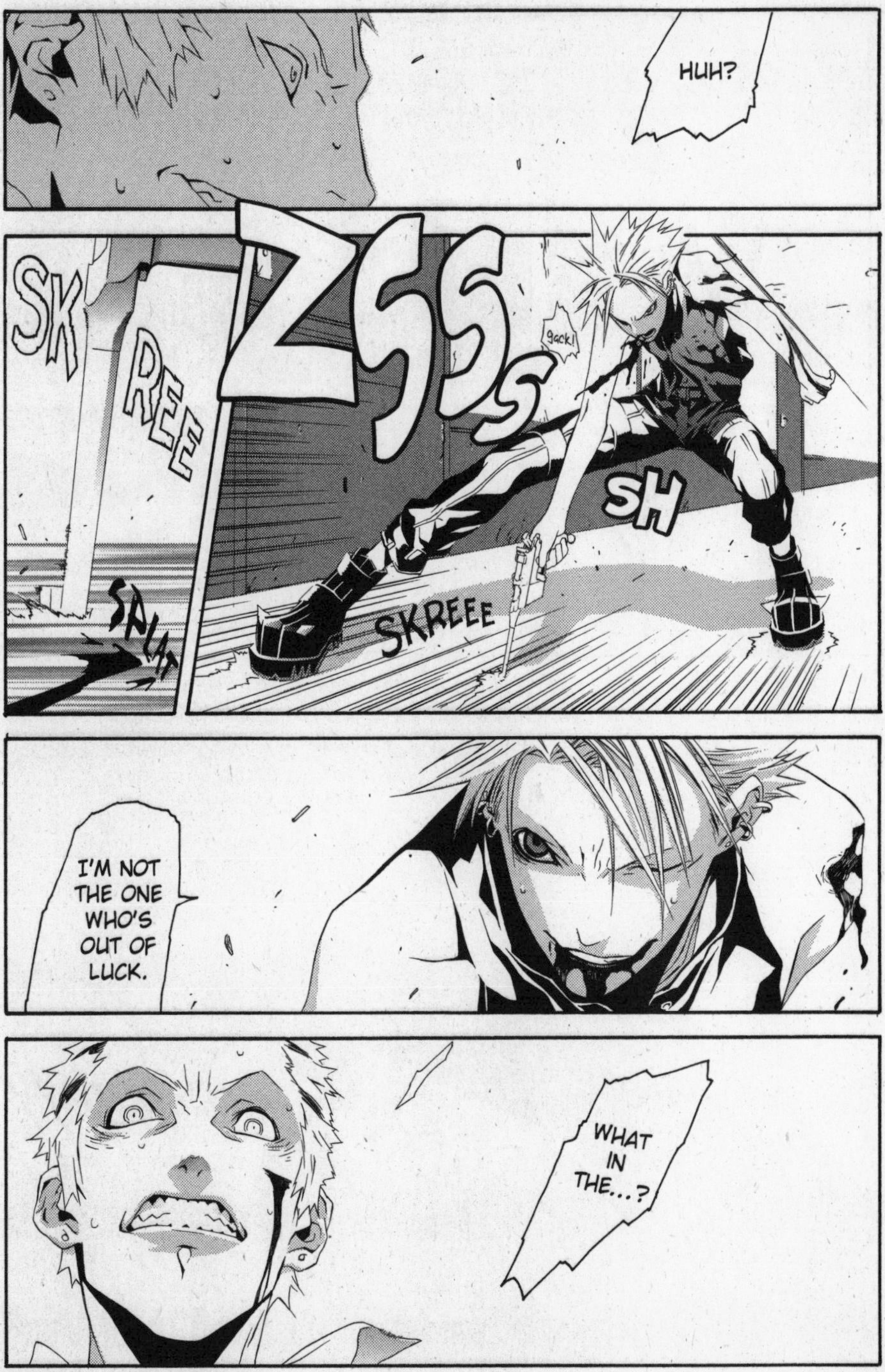
HUH?
ZSSS
gack!
SH
SKREEE
SKREE
SPLAT
I'M NOT THE ONE WHO'S OUT OF LUCK.
WHAT IN THE...?

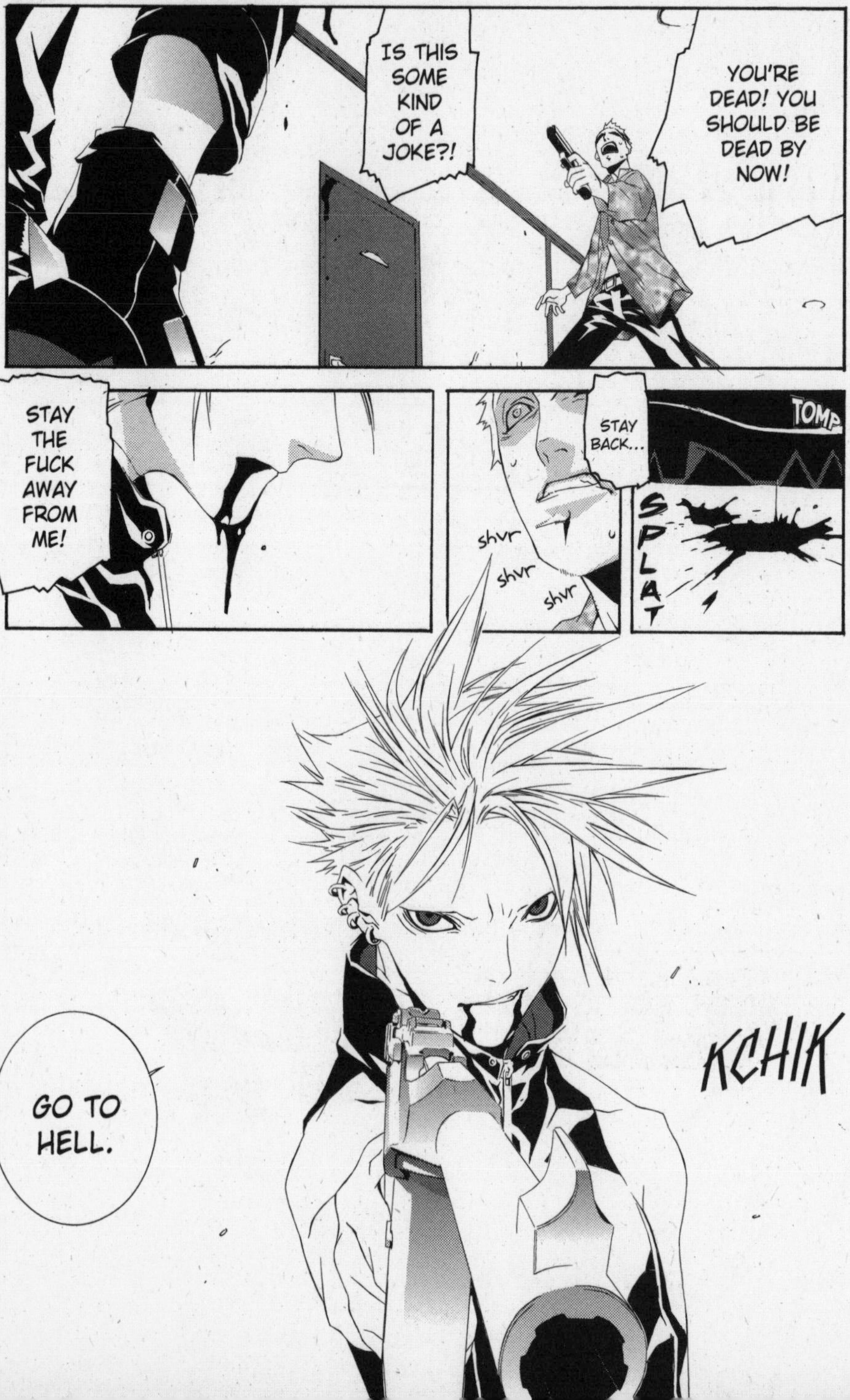
YOU'RE DEAD! YOU SHOULD BE DEAD BY NOW!
IS THIS SOME KIND OF A JOKE?!
TOMP
SPLAT
STAY BACK...
shvr
shvr
shvr
STAY THE FUCK AWAY FROM ME!
KCHIK
GO TO HELL.

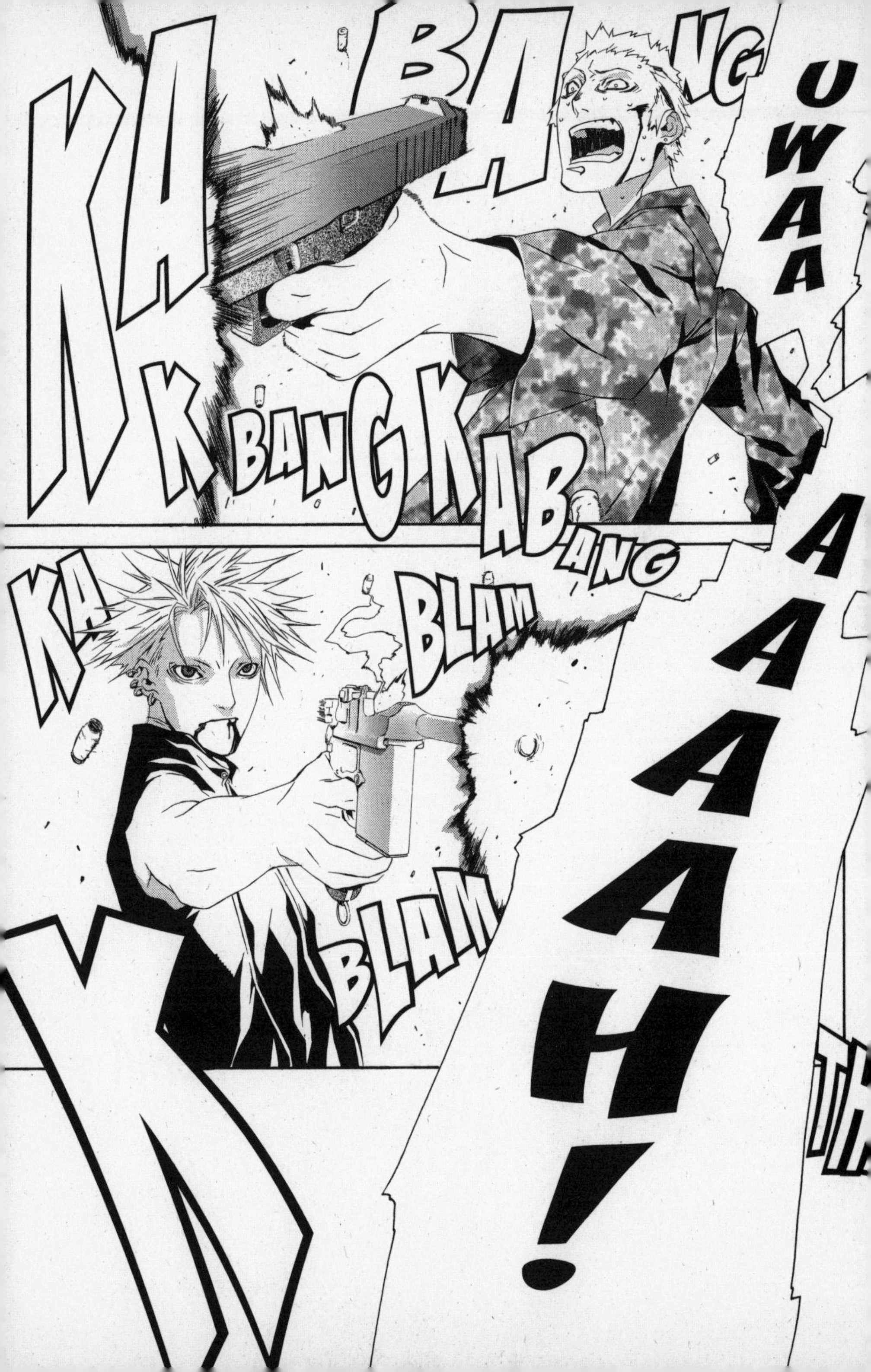
UWAAAAAAAH!
KABANG
KABANG
KABANG
KABANG
BLAM
BLAM
KA
KA

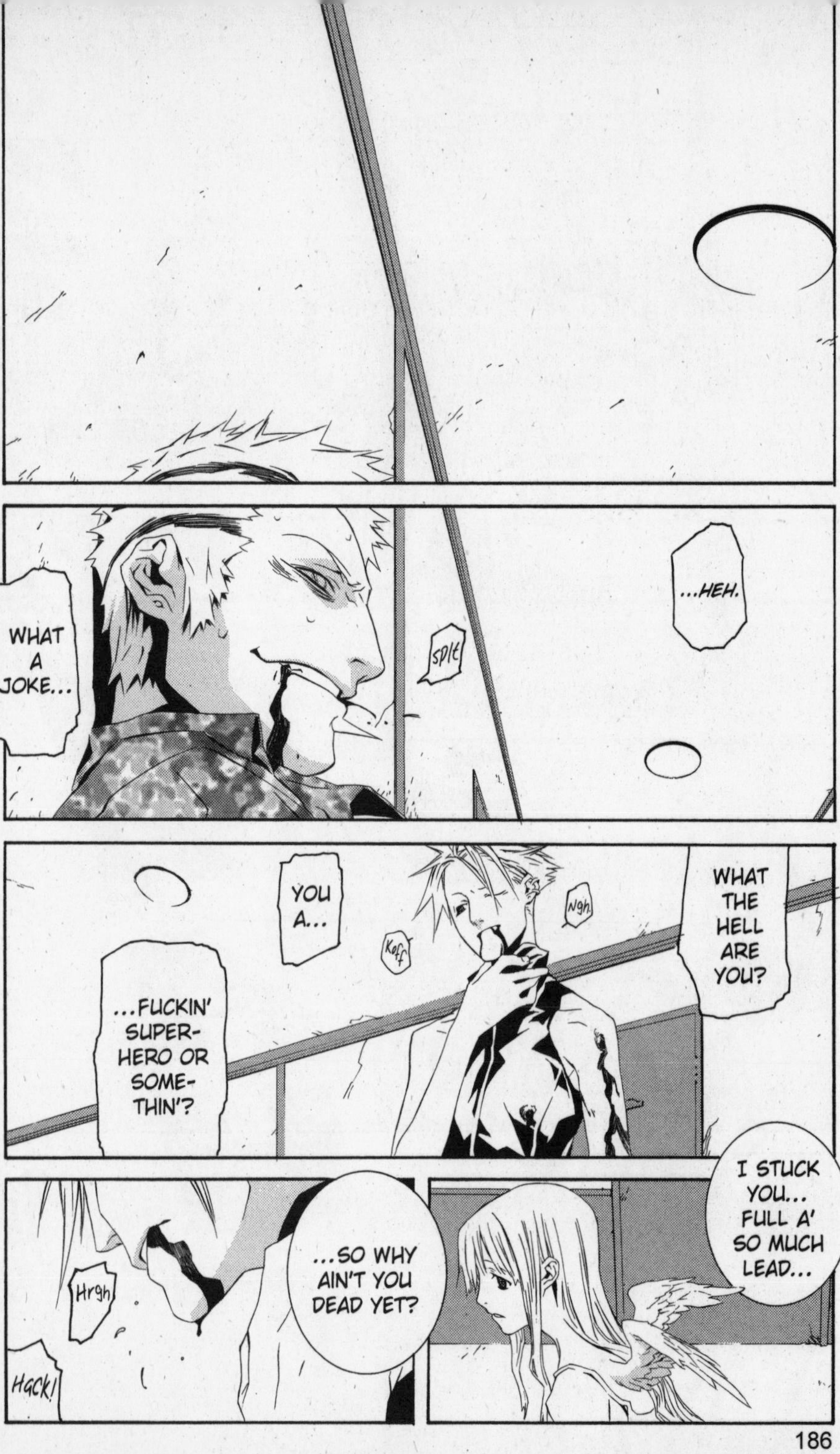
...HEH.
spit
WHAT A JOKE...
WHAT THE HELL ARE YOU?
Ngh
Koff
YOU A...
...FUCKIN' SUPER-HERO OR SOME-THIN'?
I STUCK YOU... FULL A' SO MUCH LEAD...
...SO WHY AIN'T YOU DEAD YET?
Hrgh
Hack!

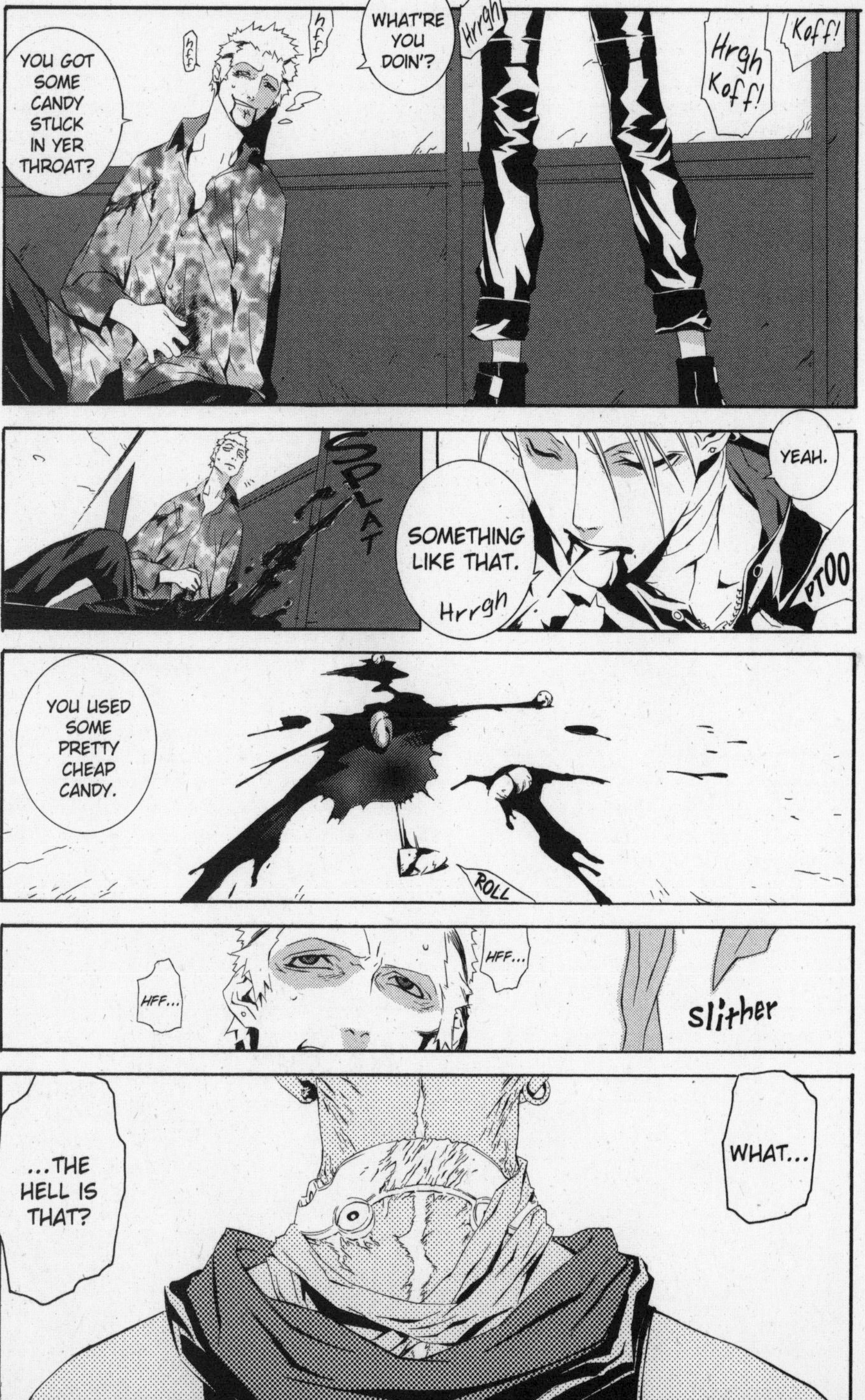
Koff!
Hrgh Koff!
Hrrgh
WHAT'RE YOU DOIN'?
hff
hff
YOU GOT SOME CANDY STUCK IN YER THROAT?
YEAH.
PTOO
SOMETHING LIKE THAT.
Hrrgh
SPLAT
YOU USED SOME PRETTY CHEAP CANDY.
ROLL
slither
HFF...
HFF...
WHAT...
...THE HELL IS THAT?

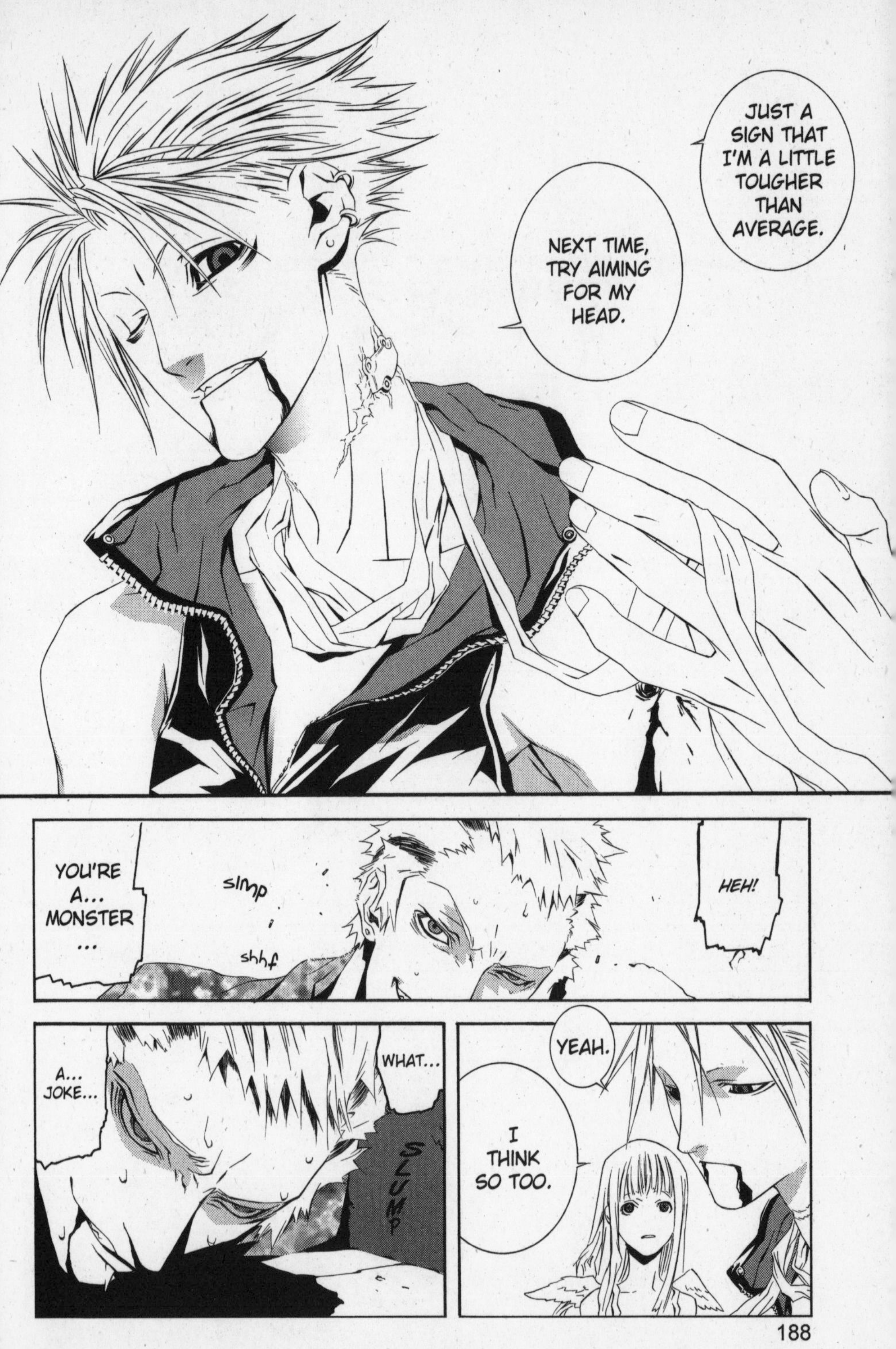
JUST A SIGN THAT I'M A LITTLE TOUGHER THAN AVERAGE.
NEXT TIME, TRY AIMING FOR MY HEAD.
HEH!
slmp
shhf
YOU'RE A... MONSTER...
YEAH.
I THINK SO TOO.
WHAT...
SLUMP
A... JOKE...

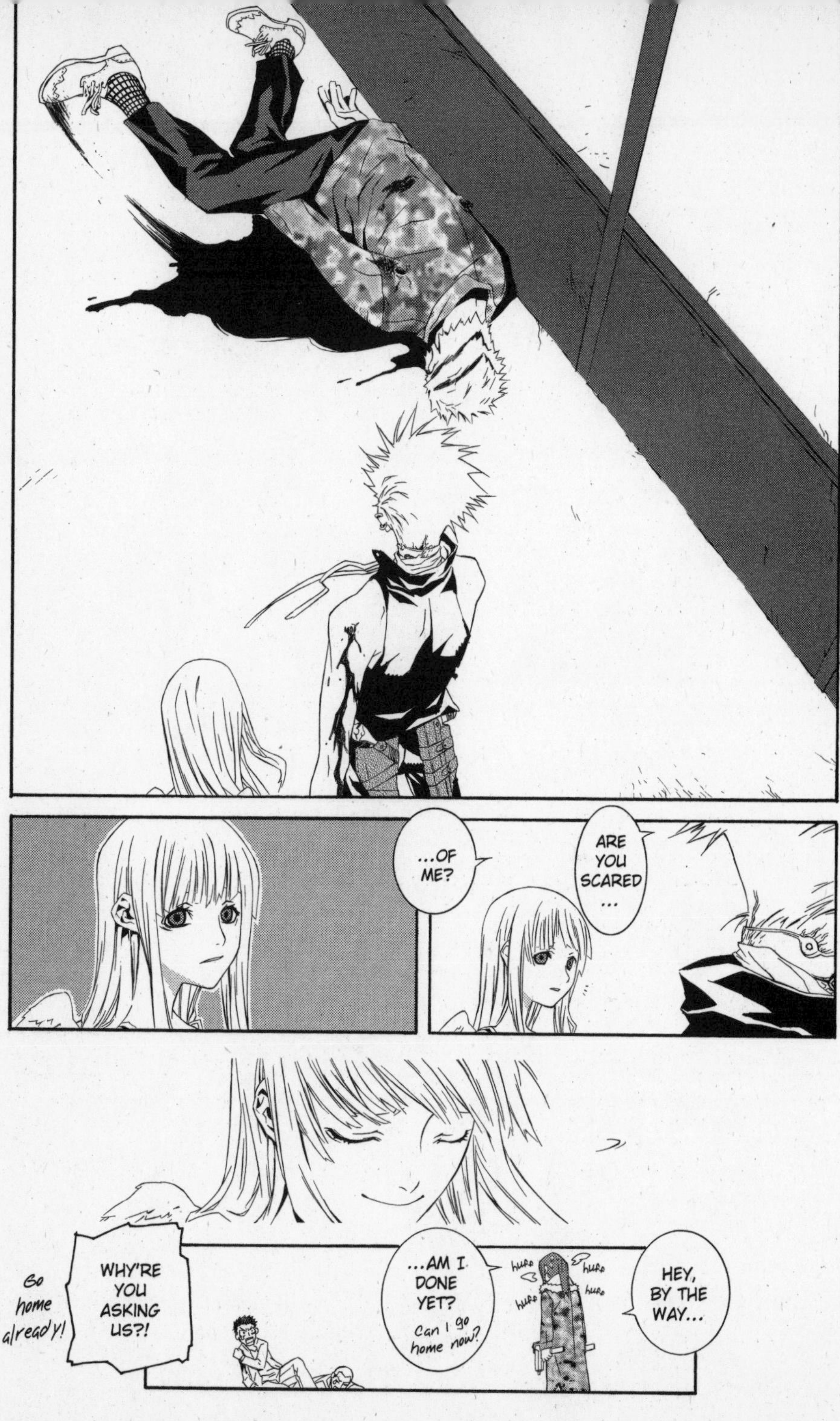
ARE YOU SCARED ...
...OF ME?
HEY, BY THE WAY...
huff huff huff huff
...AM I DONE YET?
Can I go home now?
WHY'RE YOU ASKING US?!
Go home already!

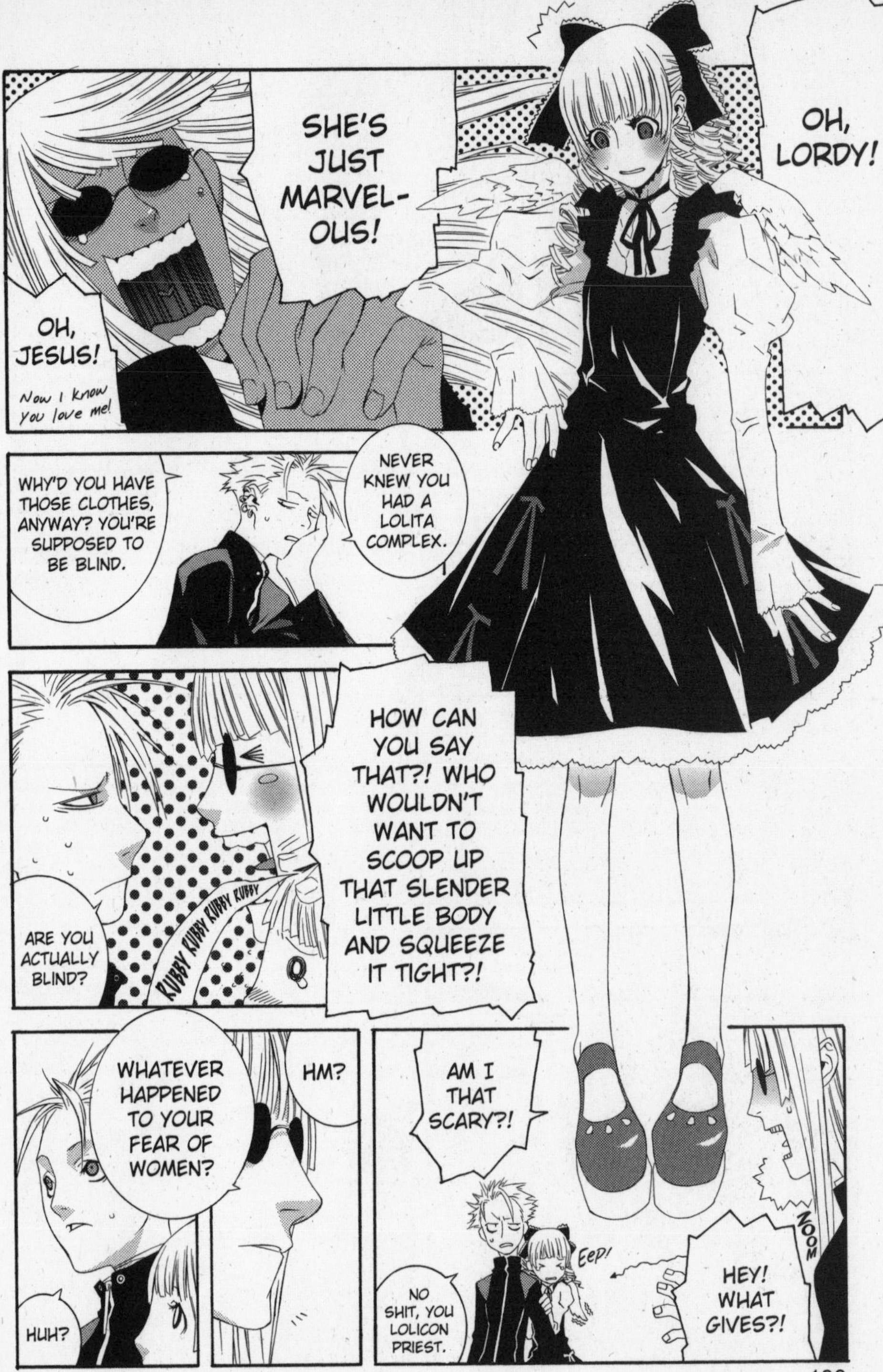
OH, LORDY!
SHE'S JUST MARVEL-OUS!
OH, JESUS!
Now I know you love me!
NEVER KNEW YOU HAD A LOLITA COMPLEX.
WHY'D YOU HAVE THOSE CLOTHES, ANYWAY? YOU'RE SUPPOSED TO BE BLIND.
HOW CAN YOU SAY THAT?! WHO WOULDN'T WANT TO SCOOP UP THAT SLENDER LITTLE BODY AND SQUEEZE IT TIGHT?!
RUBBY RUBBY RUBBY RUBBY
ARE YOU ACTUALLY BLIND?
ZOOM
HEY! WHAT GIVES?!
AM I THAT SCARY?!
Eep!
NO SHIT, YOU LOLICON PRIEST.
HM?
WHATEVER HAPPENED TO YOUR FEAR OF WOMEN?
HUH?

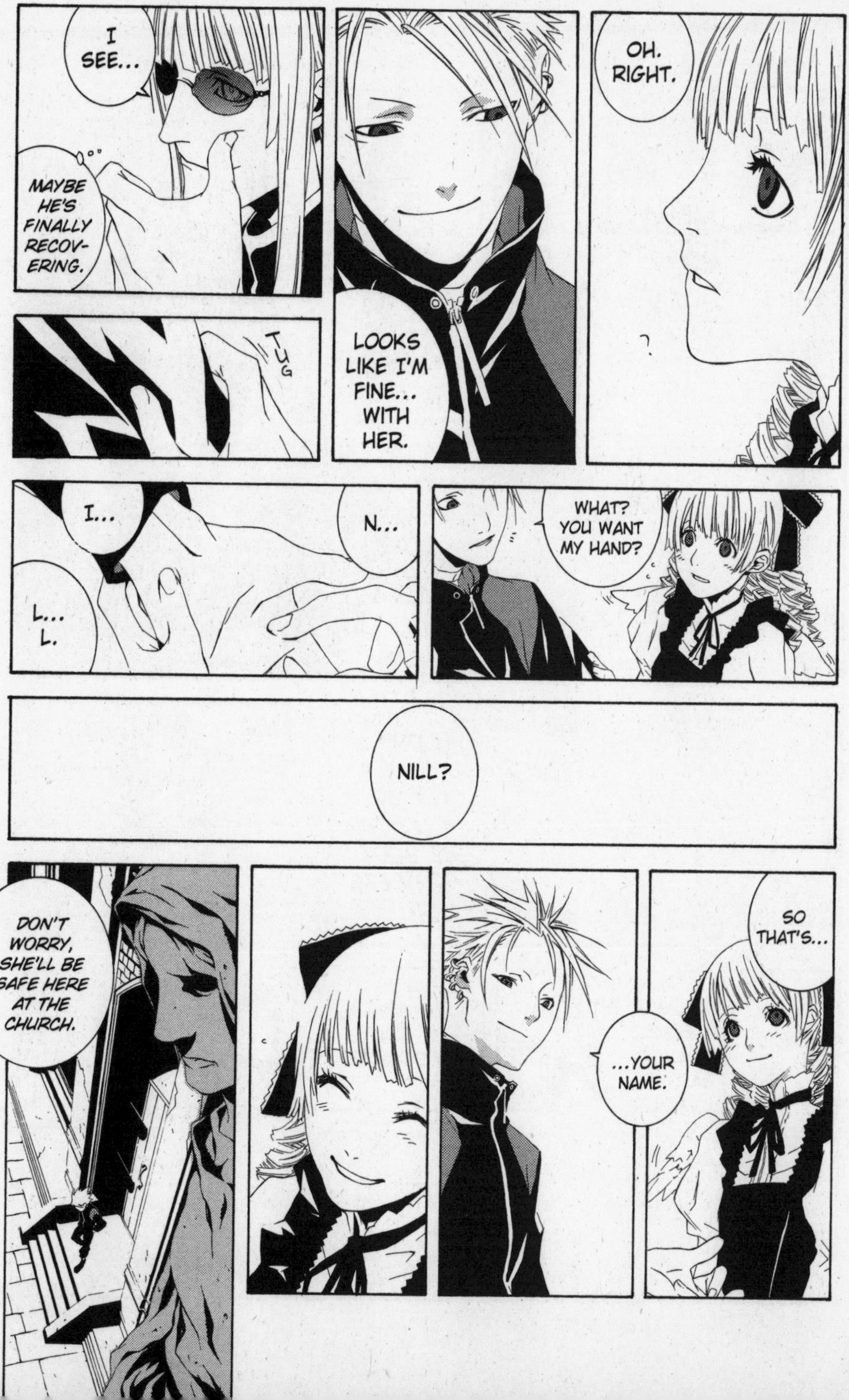
OH. RIGHT.
LOOKS LIKE I'M FINE... WITH HER.
I SEE...
MAYBE HE'S FINALLY RECOV-ERING.
TUG
WHAT? YOU WANT MY HAND?
N...
I...
L... L.
NILL?
SO THAT'S...
...YOUR NAME.
DON'T WORRY, SHE'LL BE SAFE HERE AT THE CHURCH.

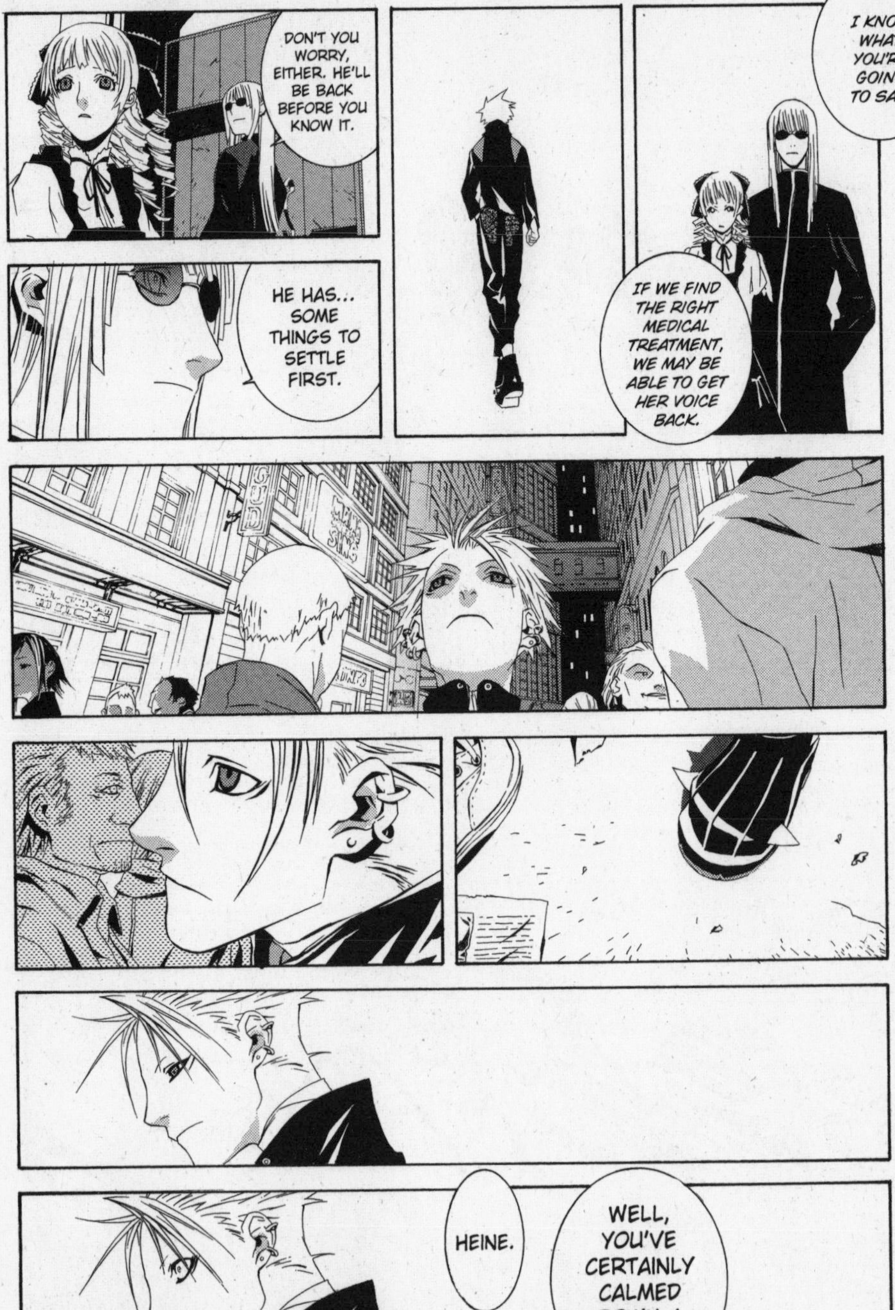
I KNOW WHAT YOU'RE GOING TO SAY.
IF WE FIND THE RIGHT MEDICAL TREATMENT, WE MAY BE ABLE TO GET HER VOICE BACK.
DON'T YOU WORRY, EITHER. HE'LL BE BACK BEFORE YOU KNOW IT.
HE HAS... SOME THINGS TO SETTLE FIRST.
WELL, YOU'VE CERTAINLY CALMED DOWN A BIT.
HEINE.

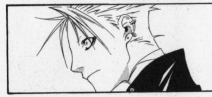

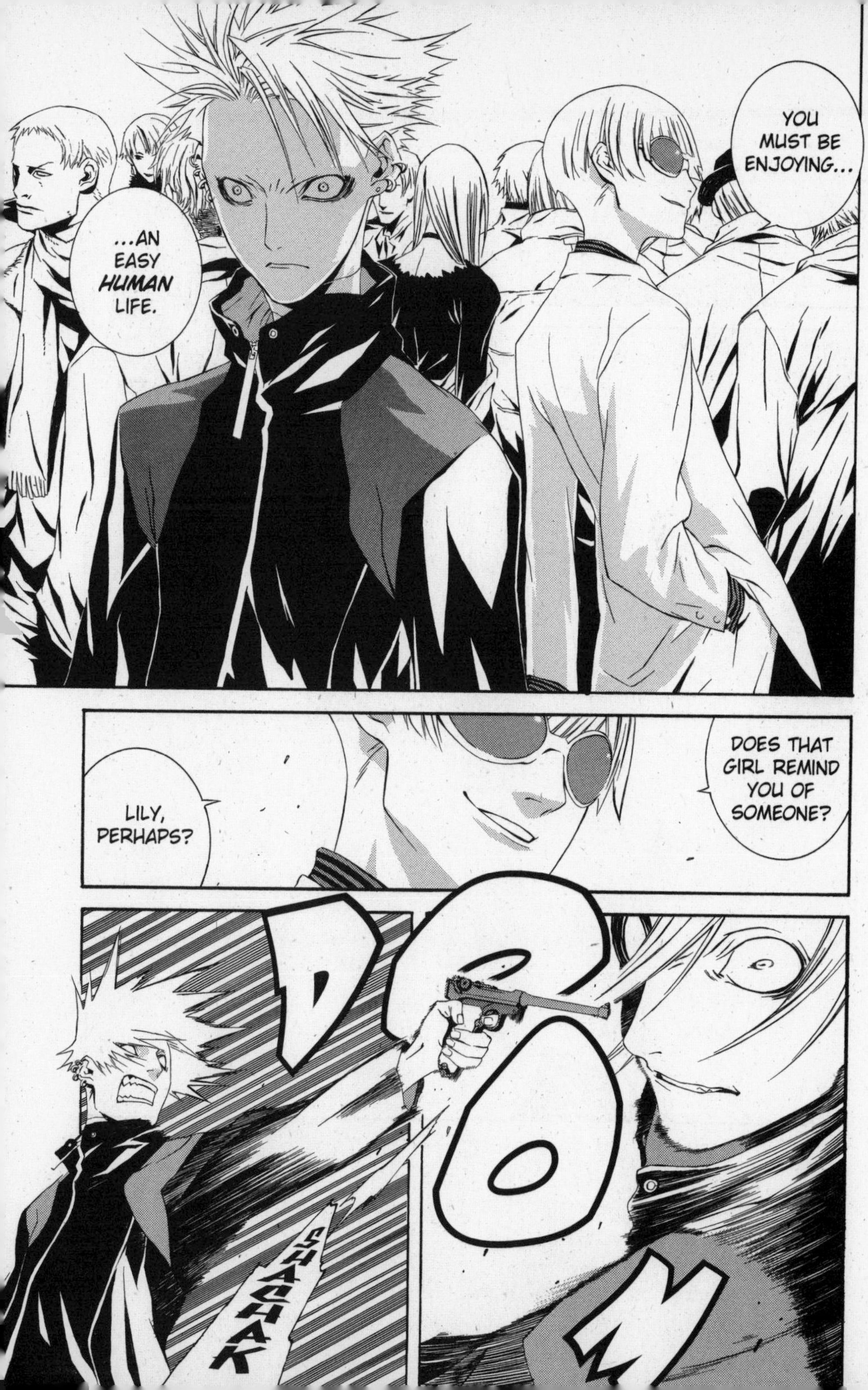
YOU MUST BE ENJOYING...
...AN EASY *HUMAN* LIFE.
DOES THAT GIRL REMIND YOU OF SOMEONE?
LILY, PERHAPS?
DOOM
SHACHAK

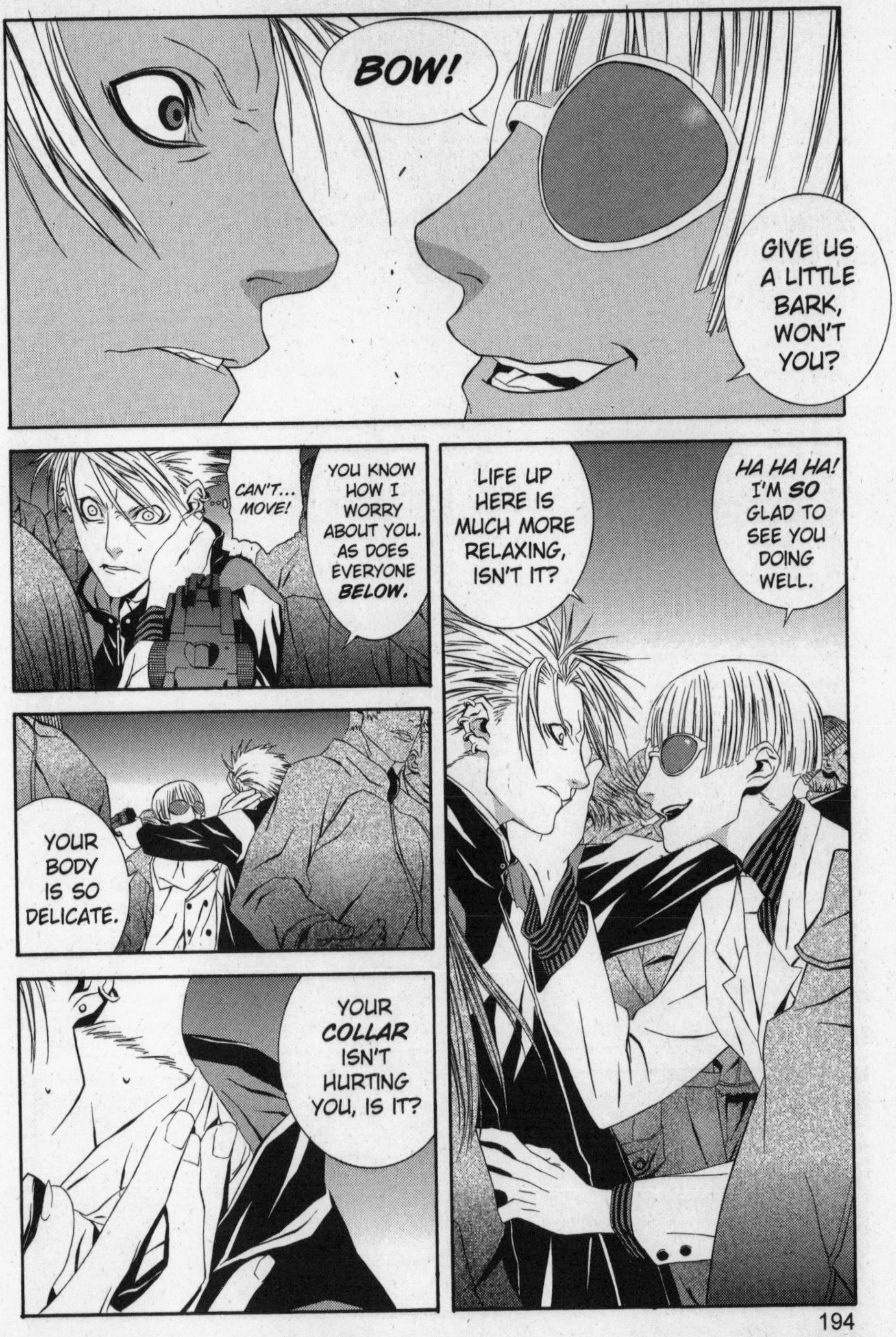
GIVE US A LITTLE BARK, WON'T YOU?
BOW!
HA HA HA! I'M SO GLAD TO SEE YOU DOING WELL.
LIFE UP HERE IS MUCH MORE RELAXING, ISN'T IT?
YOU KNOW HOW I WORRY ABOUT YOU. AS DOES EVERYONE BELOW.
CAN'T... MOVE!
YOUR BODY IS SO DELICATE.
YOUR COLLAR ISN'T HURTING YOU, IS IT?

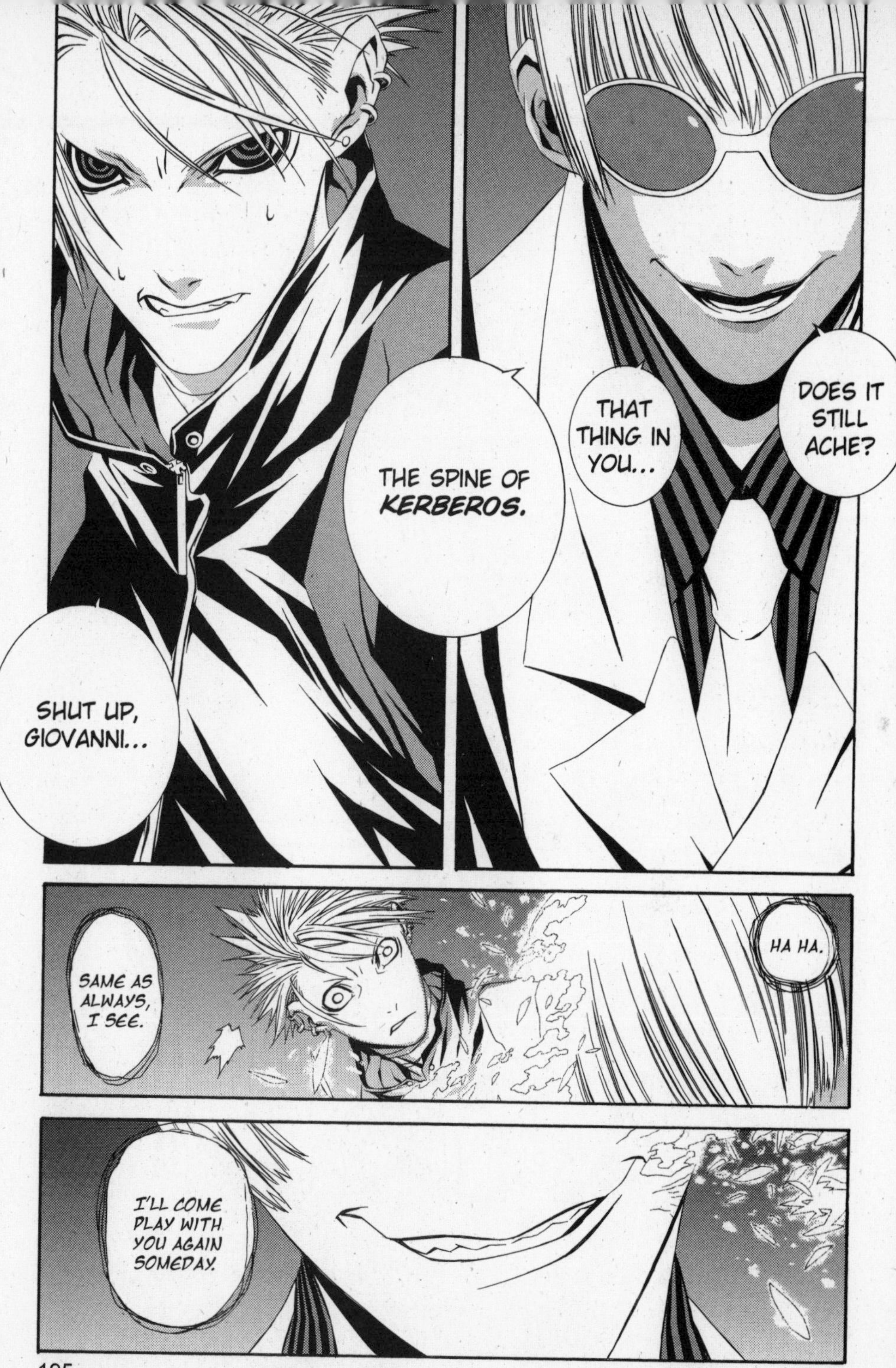
DOES IT STILL ACHE?
THAT THING IN YOU...
THE SPINE OF KERBEROS.
SHUT UP, GIOVANNI...
HA HA.
SAME AS ALWAYS, I SEE.
I'LL COME PLAY WITH YOU AGAIN SOMEDAY.

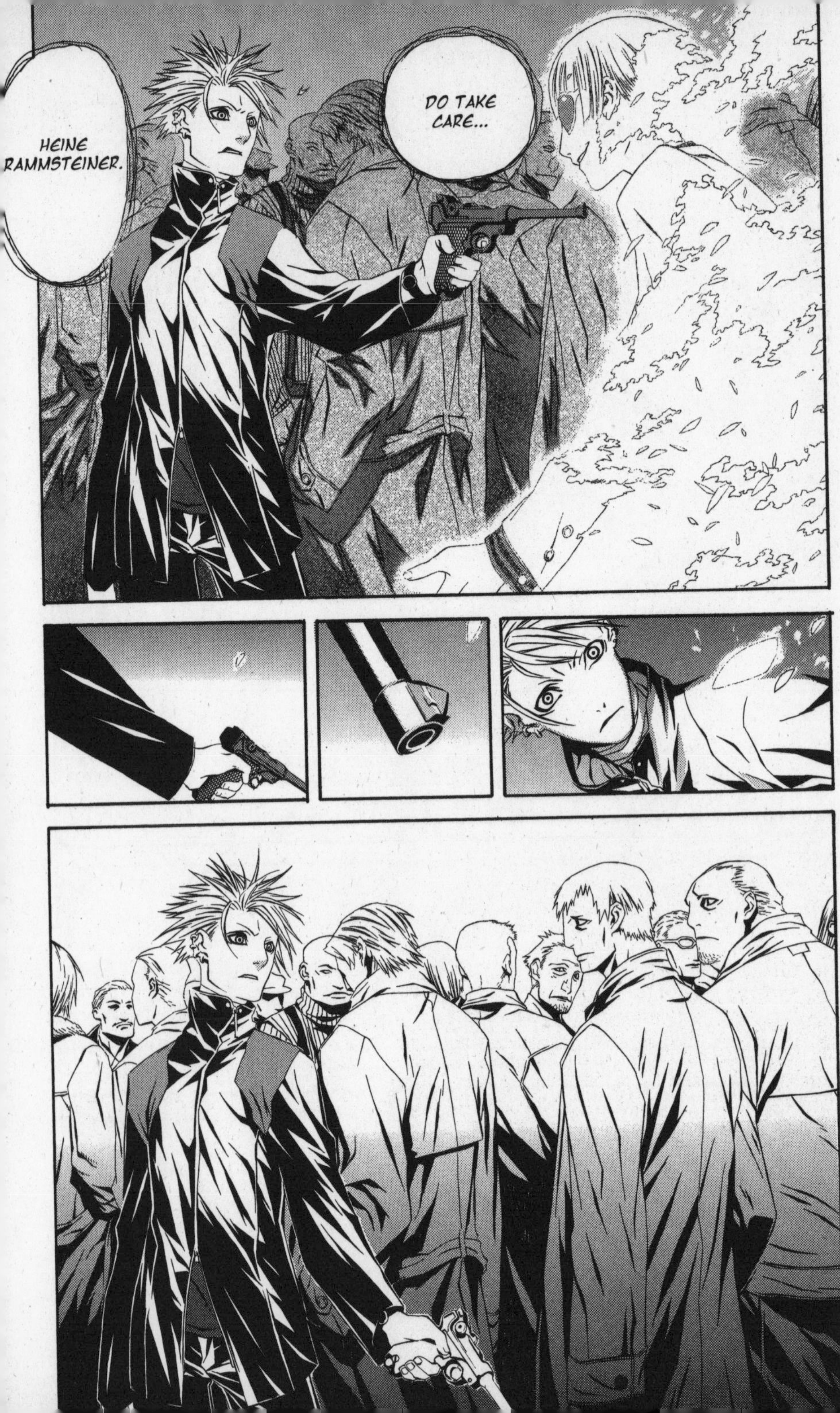
DO TAKE CARE...
HEINE RAMMSTEINER.

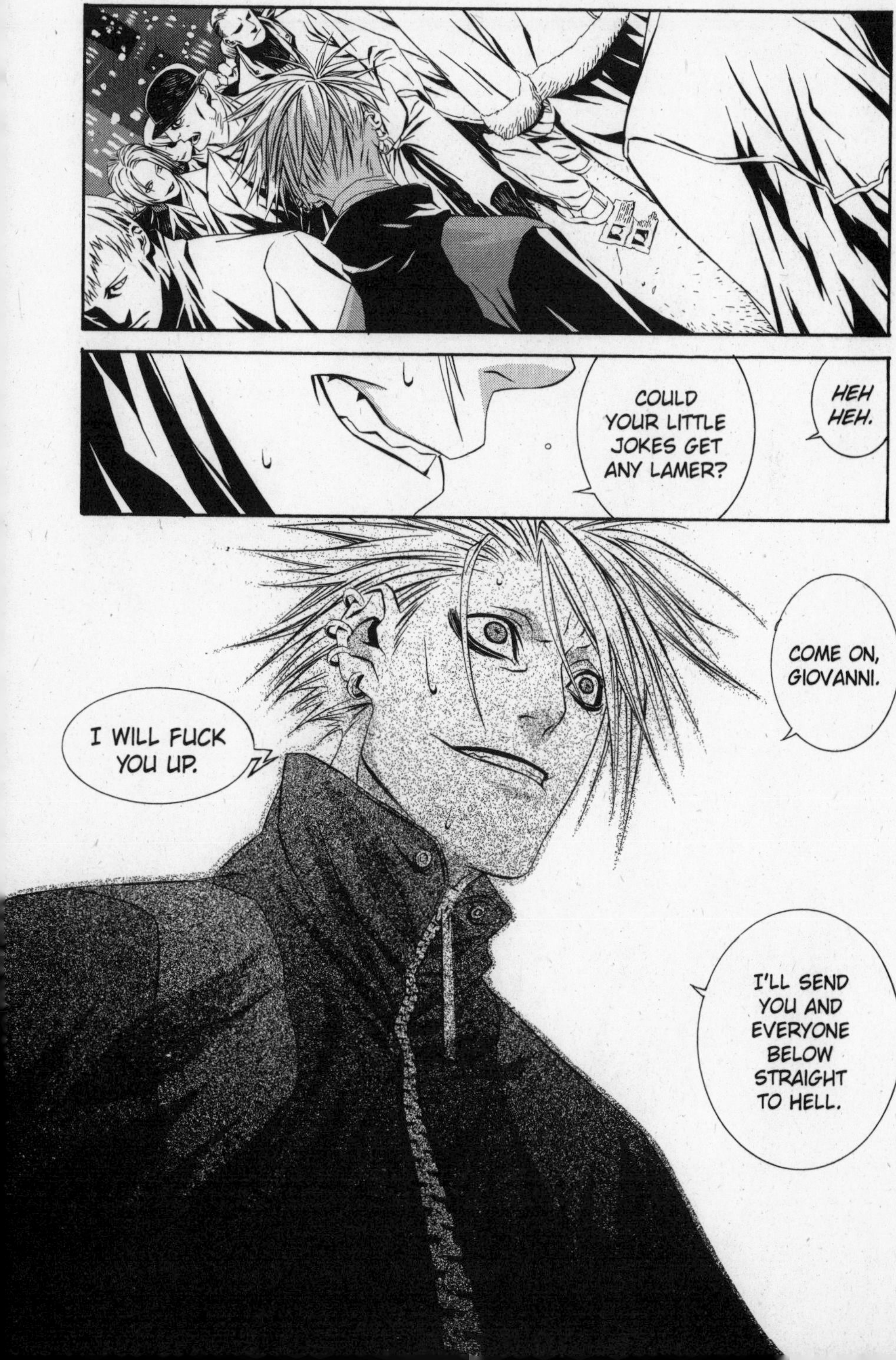
HEH HEH.
COULD YOUR LITTLE JOKES GET ANY LAMER?
COME ON, GIOVANNI.
I WILL FUCK YOU UP.
I'LL SEND YOU AND EVERYONE BELOW STRAIGHT TO HELL.

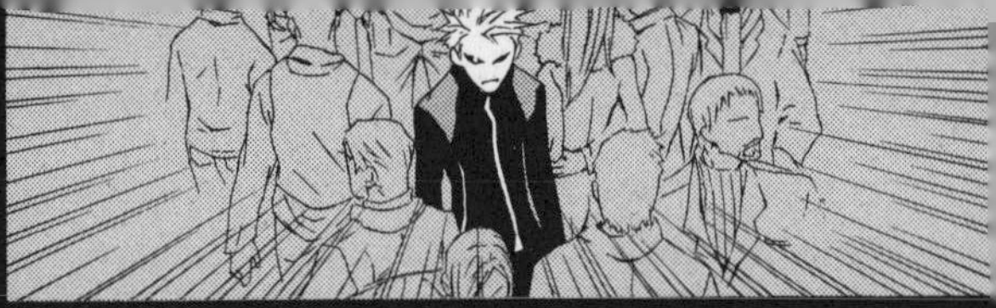

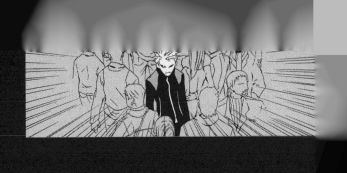

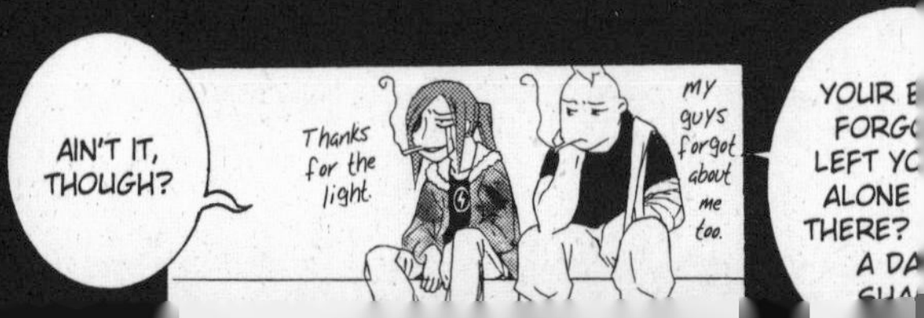
YOUR
ALONE
THERE?
My guys forgot about me too.
Thanks for the light.
AIN'T IT, THOUGH?

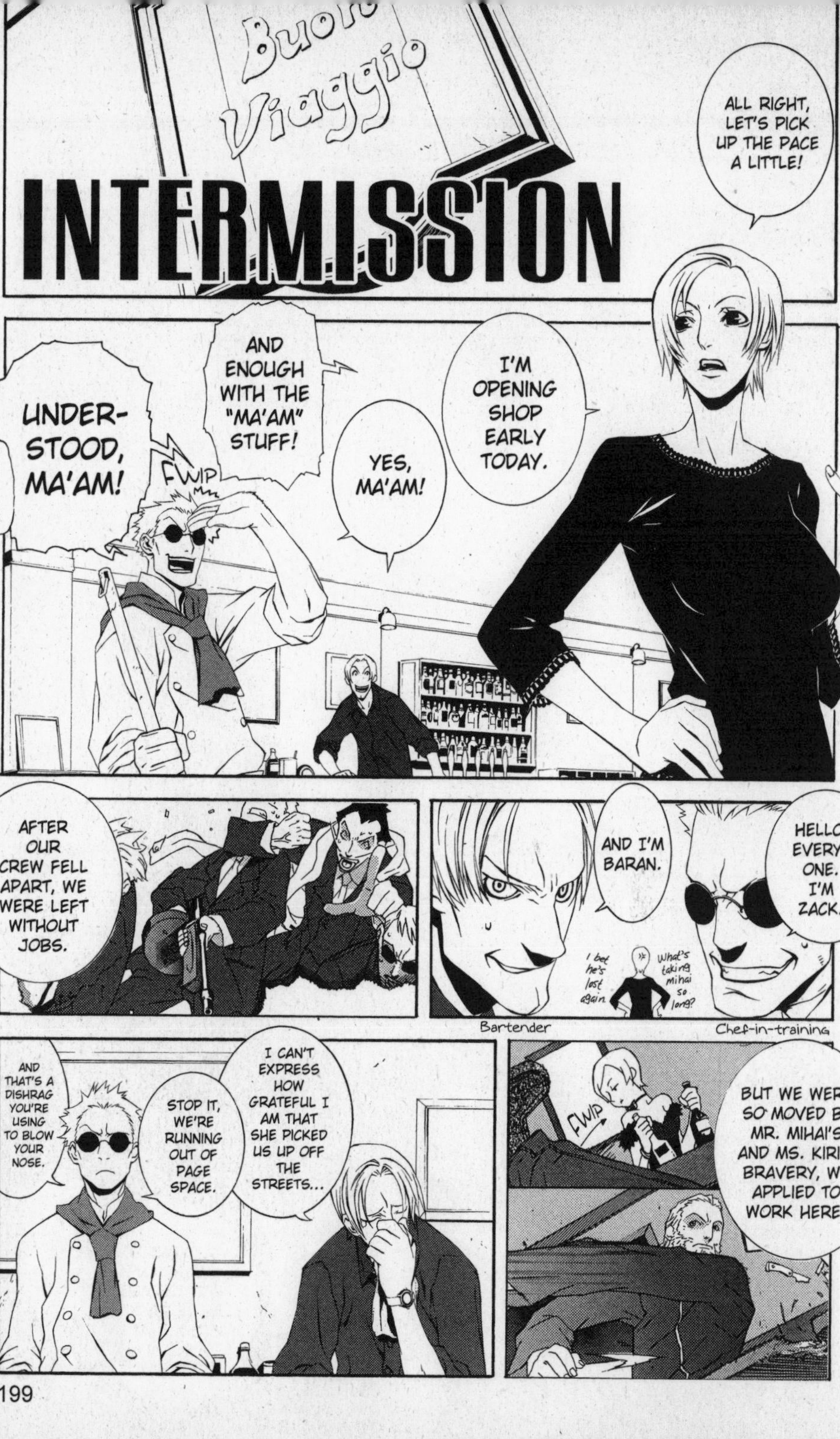
Buon Viaggio
INTERMISSION
ALL RIGHT, LET'S PICK UP THE PACE A LITTLE!
I'M OPENING SHOP EARLY TODAY.
YES, MA'AM!
AND ENOUGH WITH THE "MA'AM" STUFF!
FWIP
UNDER-STOOD, MA'AM!
......
HELLO, EVERY-ONE. I'M ZACK.
AND I'M BARAN.
What's taking mihai so long?
I bet he's lost again.
Chef-in-training
Bartender
AFTER OUR CREW FELL APART, WE WERE LEFT WITHOUT JOBS.
BUT WE WERE SO MOVED BY MR. MIHAI'S AND MS. KIRI'S BRAVERY, WE APPLIED TO WORK HERE!
FWIP
I CAN'T EXPRESS HOW GRATEFUL I AM THAT SHE PICKED US UP OFF THE STREETS...
STOP IT, WE'RE RUNNING OUT OF PAGE SPACE.
AND THAT'S A DISHRAG YOU'RE USING TO BLOW YOUR NOSE.

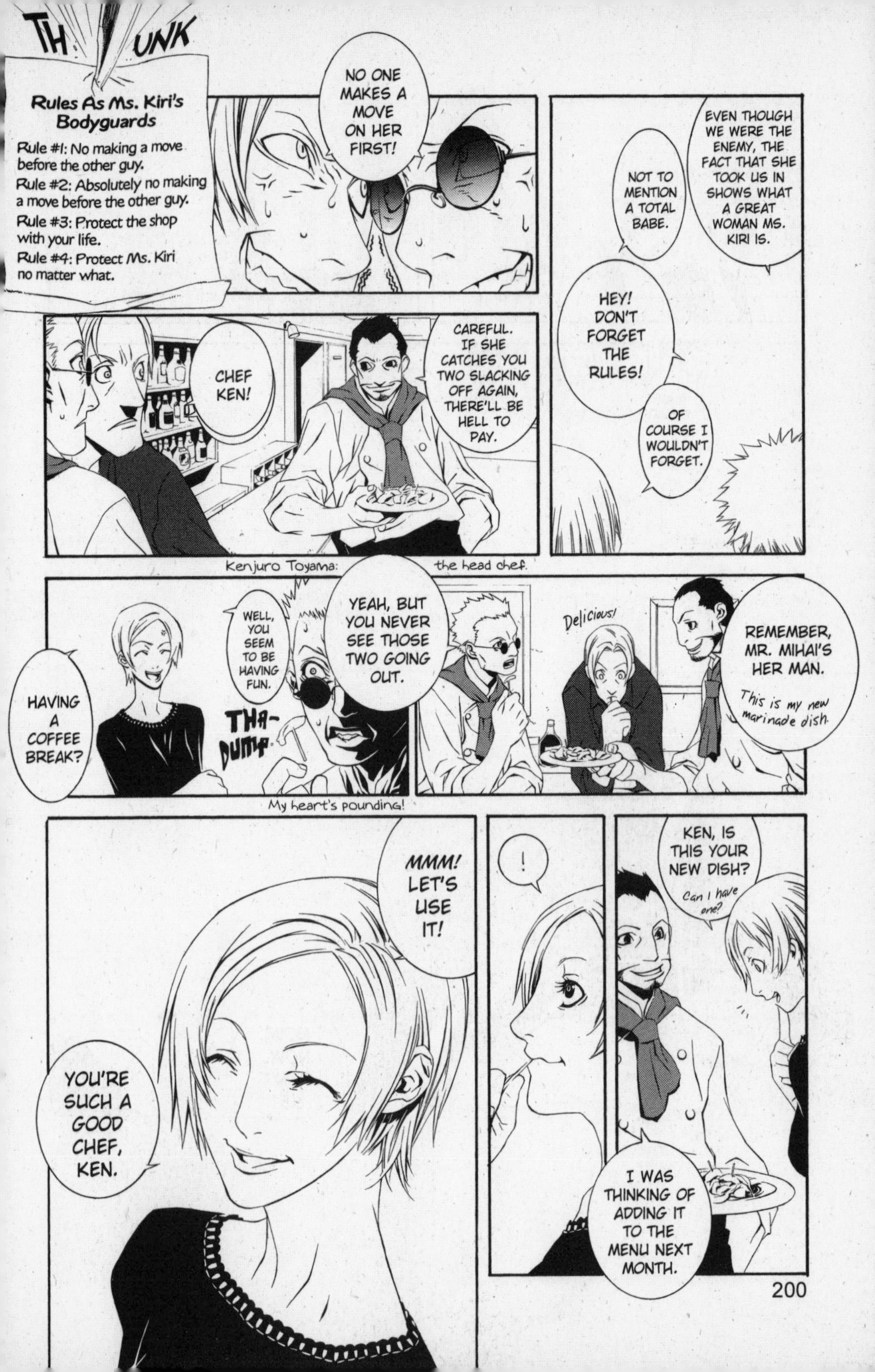
EVEN THOUGH WE WERE THE ENEMY, THE FACT THAT SHE TOOK US IN SHOWS WHAT A GREAT WOMAN MS. KIRI IS.
NOT TO MENTION A TOTAL BABE.
HEY! DON'T FORGET THE RULES!
OF COURSE I WOULDN'T FORGET.
NO ONE MAKES A MOVE ON HER FIRST!
THUNK
Rules As Ms. Kiri's Bodyguards
Rule #1: No making a move before the other guy.
Rule #2: Absolutely no making a move before the other guy.
Rule #3: Protect the shop with your life.
Rule #4: Protect Ms. Kiri no matter what.
CAREFUL. IF SHE CATCHES YOU TWO SLACKING OFF AGAIN, THERE'LL BE HELL TO PAY.
CHEF KEN!
Kenjuro Toyama: the head chef.
REMEMBER, MR. MIHAI'S HER MAN.
This is my new marinade dish.
Delicious!
YEAH, BUT YOU NEVER SEE THOSE TWO GOING OUT.
WELL, YOU SEEM TO BE HAVING FUN.
THA-DUMP
HAVING A COFFEE BREAK?
My heart's pounding!
KEN, IS THIS YOUR NEW DISH?
Can I have one?
I WAS THINKING OF ADDING IT TO THE MENU NEXT MONTH.
!
MMM! LET'S USE IT!
YOU'RE SUCH A GOOD CHEF, KEN.

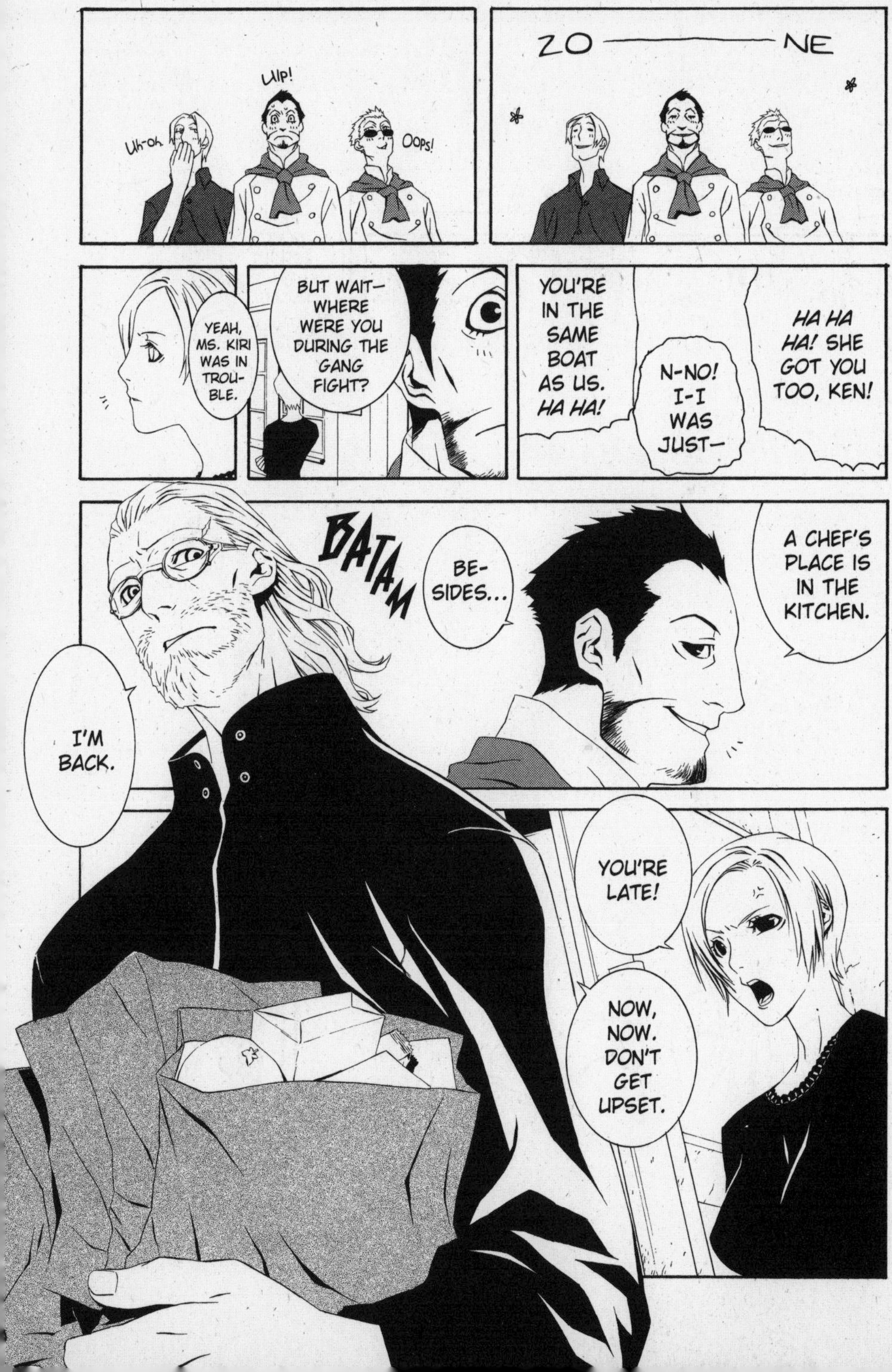
ZO——NE
Ulp!
Oops!
Uh-oh.
HA HA HA! SHE GOT YOU TOO, KEN!
YOU'RE IN THE SAME BOAT AS US. HA HA!
N-NO! I-I WAS JUST—
BUT WAIT—WHERE WERE YOU DURING THE GANG FIGHT?
YEAH, MS. KIRI WAS IN TROU-BLE.
A CHEF'S PLACE IS IN THE KITCHEN.
BE-SIDES...
BATAM
I'M BACK.
YOU'RE LATE!
NOW, NOW. DON'T GET UPSET.

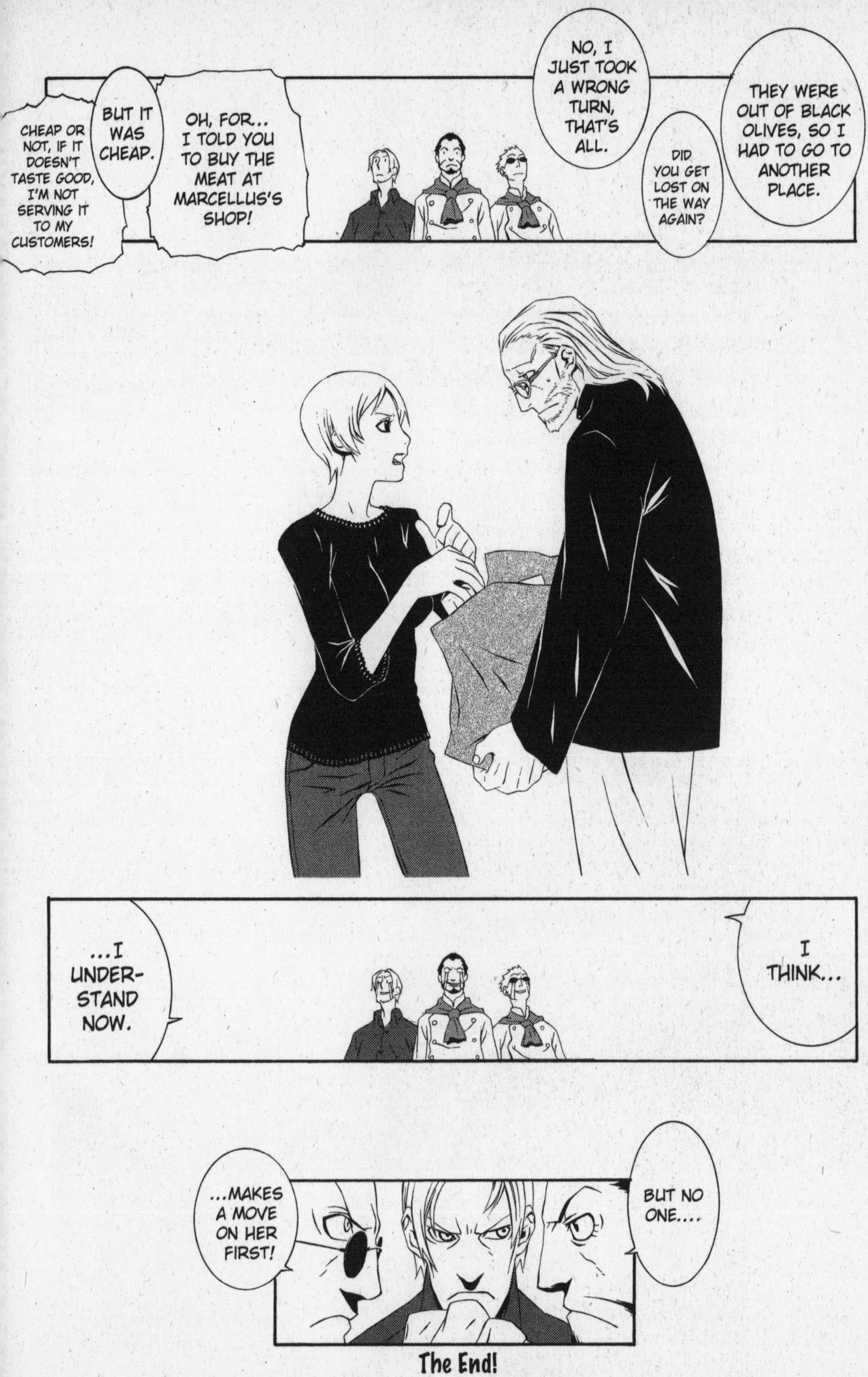
THEY WERE OUT OF BLACK OLIVES, SO I HAD TO GO TO ANOTHER PLACE.
DID YOU GET LOST ON THE WAY AGAIN?
NO, I JUST TOOK A WRONG TURN, THAT'S ALL.
OH, FOR... I TOLD YOU TO BUY THE MEAT AT MARCELLUS'S SHOP!
BUT IT WAS CHEAP.
CHEAP OR NOT, IF IT DOESN'T TASTE GOOD, I'M NOT SERVING IT TO MY CUSTOMERS!
I THINK...
...I UNDER-STAND NOW.
BUT NO ONE....
...MAKES A MOVE ON HER FIRST!

The End!

AFTERWORD

Pleased to meet you, everyone. This is Shirow Miwa, and this is my first-ever completed book. It took me nearly two years to write *Dogs*, and while half of me is relieved to see the whole thing bundled into a solid book, the other half of me cringes to see all my shortcomings... There's still so much I lack. I did manage to rework and rewrite some parts here and there, revise some backgrounds, and so on... Sorry for the incredibly long wait. Next time, I'm going to cut back a bit on the screentones. Using them is a lot of fun, but I really should restrain myself in order to maintain a better balance on every page.

As for what will become of *Dogs* from now on, I've been thinking about taking the protagonists from each of these four short stories and starting over in a steady series. I mean, may I, Tonda-san? I know I have many faults, but I hope you'll stick with me in the long run.

Thank you, and may we meet again.

STAFF
Hatchet Shindo
Honda the Blade

EDITOR
Brick Top Tonda-san
Bullet Tooth Hasegawa-san

SPECIAL THANKS
Yuu-san
Brother Henreki
Nanase-san
Ito Yuu sensei
Who-san

And all of my readers out there!

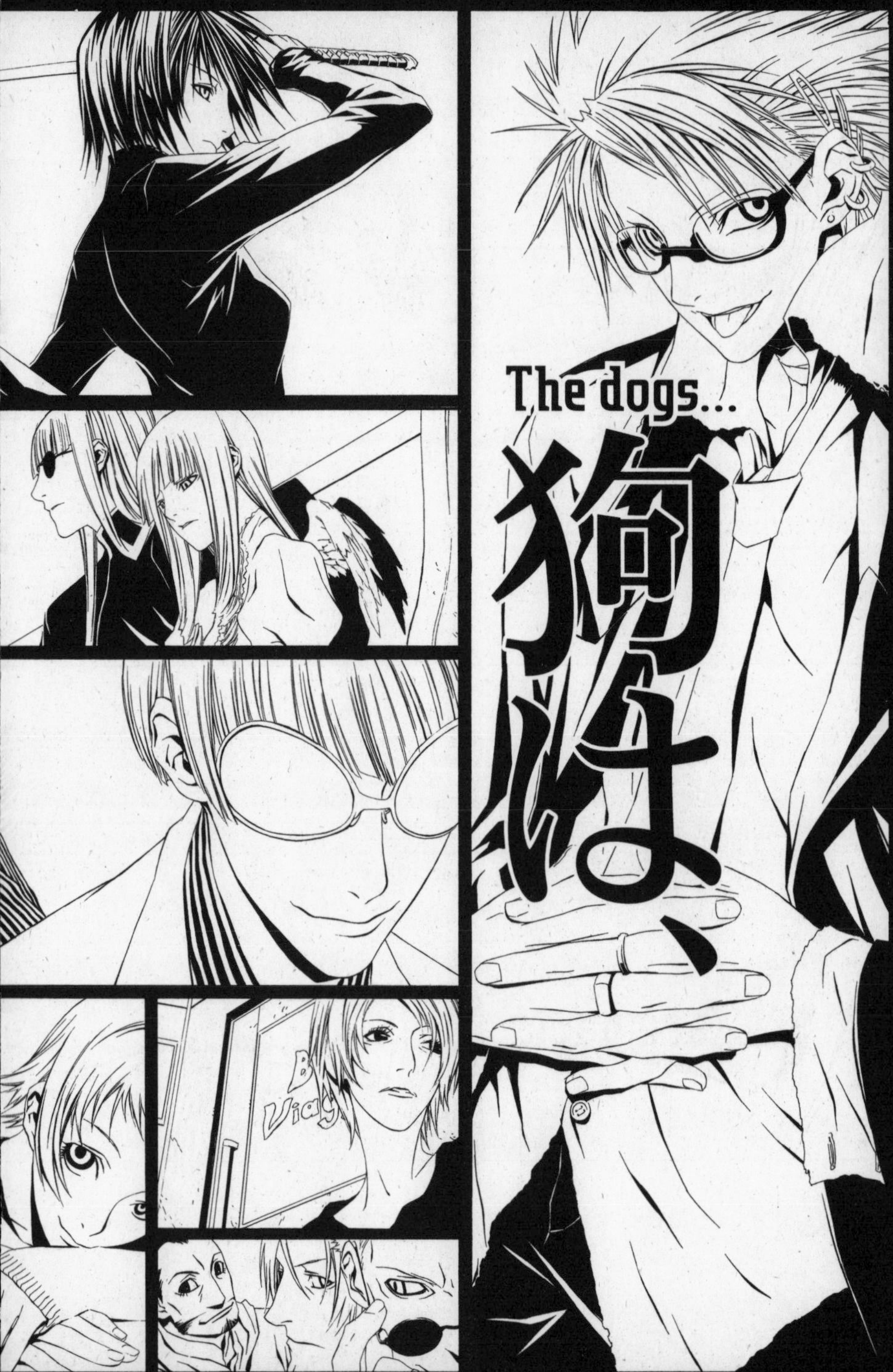
The dogs...
狗は、
B
Viag

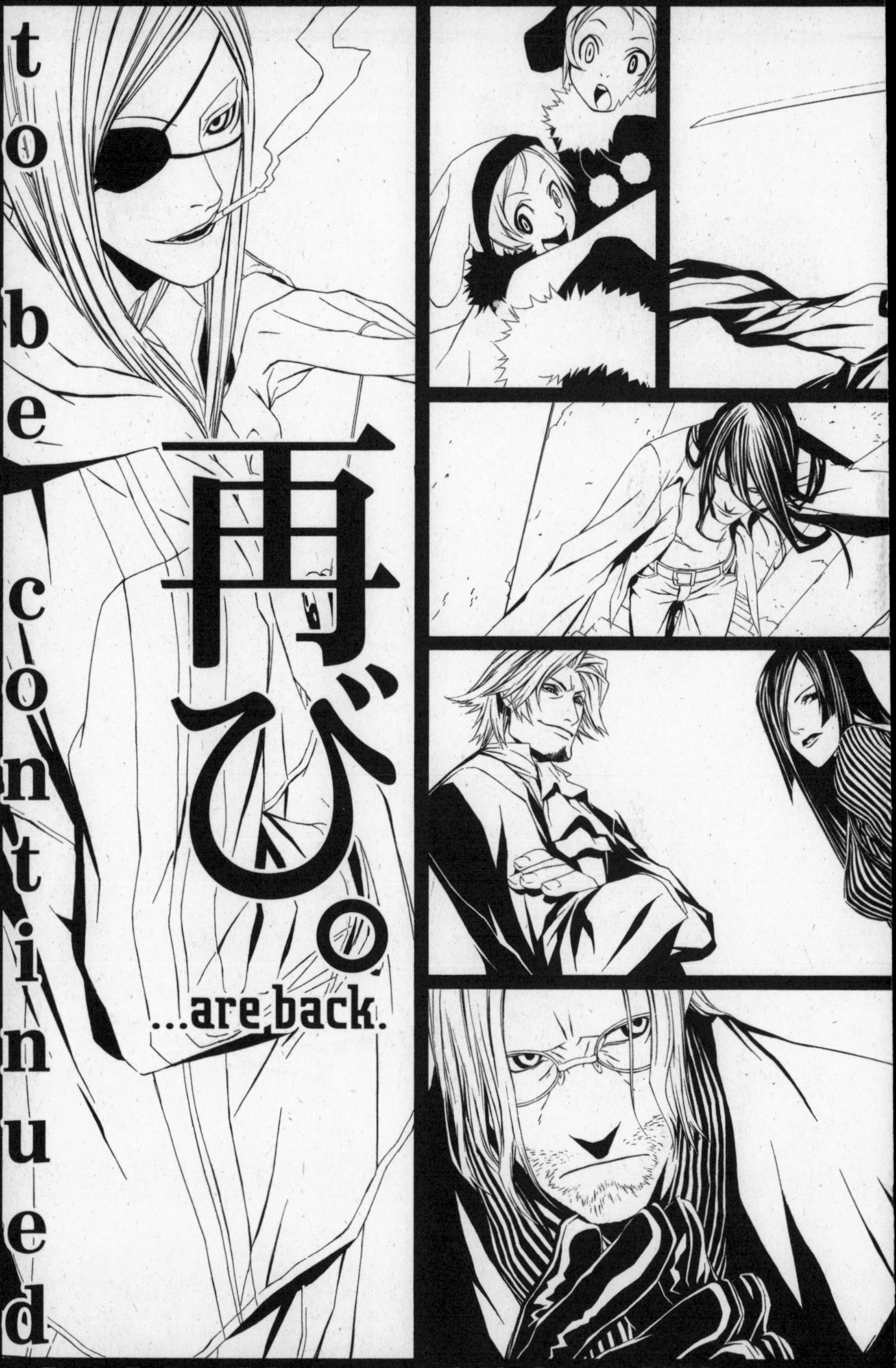
再び。
...are back.
to be continued

in *Dogs: Bullets & Carnage*, available August 2009

A NOTE ON NAMES AND GUNS

Naoto's name means "straight blade," "straight" having the additional sense of "pure" or "just."

Conversely, Magato's name means "curved blade," "curved" in the sense of "bent," as in warped or evil.

As you may have noticed, guns play a prominent role in this series. The main characters each have their own preferred models, which Miwa sensei has created based on the designs of some classic firearms.

Heine Rammsteiner carries a Mauser C-96 (the white gun) and a Luger P08 (the black one). His last name is in homage to the industrial band Rammstein.

Badou Nails somehow seems to always end up with a pair of Ingram MAC Model 10s. His last name is a nod to Trent Reznor's Nine Inch Nails.

Ian wields the M1911A1 given to him by Mihai.

And Melvin had a sawed-off 12 gauge shotgun, the proverbial "pistol grip pump." (Although it didn't help him much in the end.)

ABOUT THE AUTHOR

Shirow Miwa debuted in *UltraJump* magazine in 1999 with the short series *Black Mind*. His next series, *Dogs*, published in the magazine from 2000 to 2001, instantly became a popular success. He returned in 2005 with *Dogs: Bullets & Carnage*, which is currently running in *UltraJump*. Miwa also creates illustrations for books, music videos and magazines, and produces doujinshi [independent comics] under the circle name m.m.m.WORKS. His website is http://mmm-gee.net.

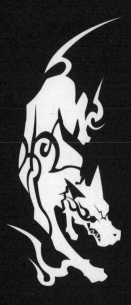

DOGS: PRELUDE

VIZ Media Edition

Story & Art by
SHIROW MIWA

Translation & Adaptation/Alexis Kirsch
Touch-up Art & Lettering/Eric Erbes
Cover & Graphic Design/Sam Elzway
Editor/Leyla Aker

Editor in Chief, Books/Alvin Lu
Editor in Chief, Magazines/Marc Weidenbaum
VP, Publishing Licensing/Rika Inouye
VP, Sales & Product Marketing/Gonzalo Ferreyra
VP, Creative/Linda Espinosa
Publisher/Hyoe Narita

Printed in the U.S.A.

Published by VIZ Media, LLC
P.O. Box 77064
San Francisco, CA 94107

10 9 8 7 6 5 4 3 2 1
First printing, April 2009

RATED M FOR MATURE

PARENTAL ADVISORY
DOGS is rated M for Mature and is recommended for mature readers. This volume contains graphic violence and mature themes.

ratings.viz.com

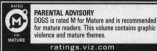

www.viz.com

store.viz.com

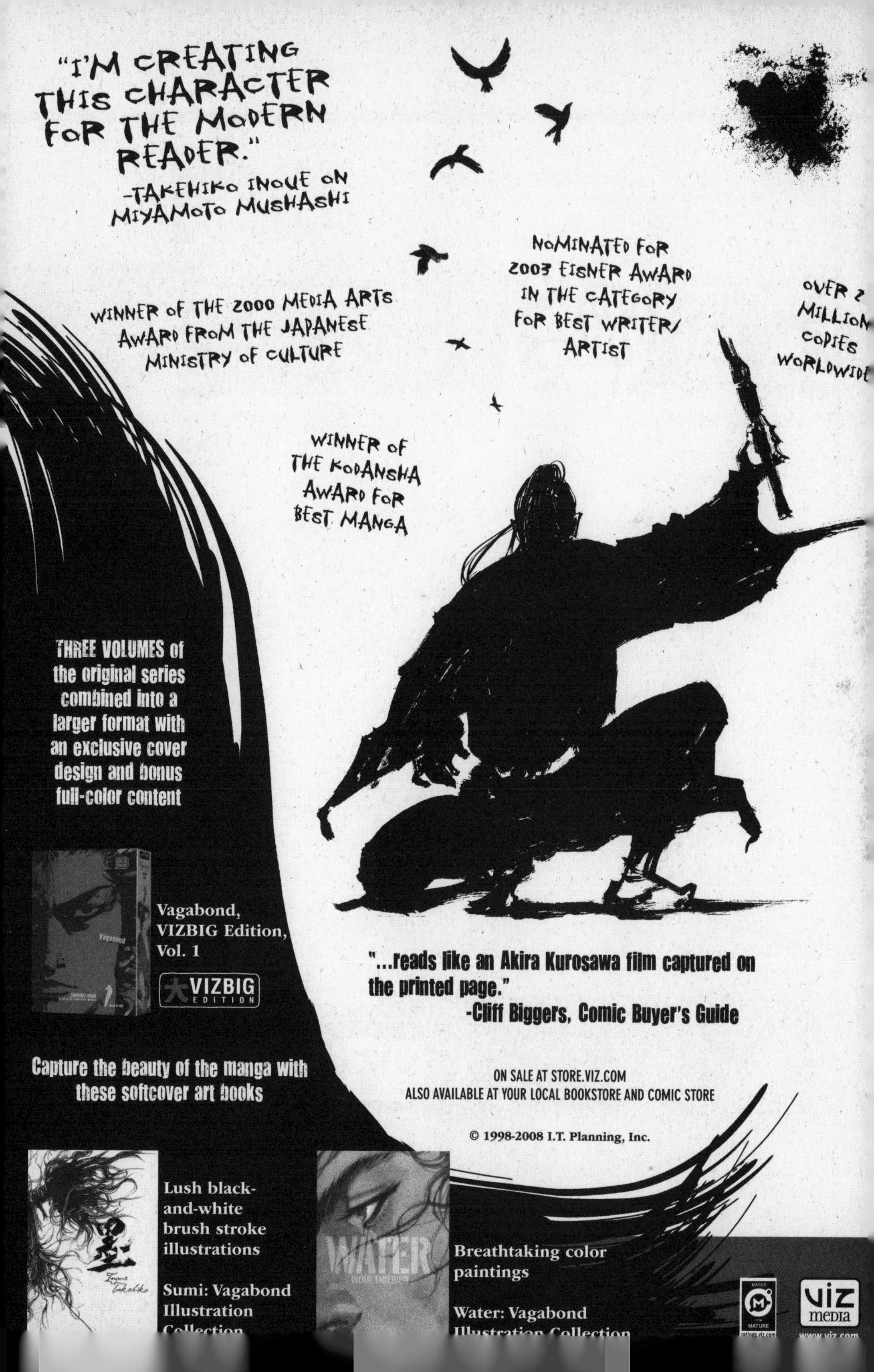
"I'M CREATING THIS CHARACTER FOR THE MODERN READER."
-TAKEHIKO INOUE ON MIYAMOTO MUSHASHI
NOMINATED FOR 2003 EISNER AWARD IN THE CATEGORY FOR BEST WRITER/ARTIST
OVER 2 MILLION COPIES WORLDWIDE
WINNER OF THE 2000 MEDIA ARTS AWARD FROM THE JAPANESE MINISTRY OF CULTURE
WINNER OF THE KODANSHA AWARD FOR BEST MANGA
THREE VOLUMES of the original series combined into a larger format with an exclusive cover design and bonus full-color content
Vagabond, VIZBIG Edition, Vol. 1
VIZBIG EDITION
"...reads like an Akira Kurosawa film captured on the printed page."
-Cliff Biggers, Comic Buyer's Guide
Capture the beauty of the manga with these softcover art books
ON SALE AT STORE.VIZ.COM
ALSO AVAILABLE AT YOUR LOCAL BOOKSTORE AND COMIC STORE
© 1998-2008 I.T. Planning, Inc.
Lush black-and-white brush stroke illustrations
Sumi: Vagabond Illustration Collection
WATER
Breathtaking color paintings
Water: Vagabond Illustration Collection
RATED M MATURE
viz media
www.viz.com

LOVE MANGA?
LET US KNOW WHAT YOU THINK!

OUR MANGA SURVEY IS NOW
AVAILABLE ONLINE. PLEASE VISIT:
VIZ.COM/MANGASURVEY

HELP US MAKE THE MANGA
YOU LOVE BETTER!